"*Saigon Guns* . . . [is] not only the best book I have read on helicopter operations during the '72 Easter Offensive in Vietnam— by far the most intense battles Army helicopter crews have ever experienced[—] . . . but [is also] . . . the best book on how we veterans were abandoned by our government. All Vietnam veterans should read, and more importantly, their children."

—Randall Larsen, Colonel, USAF, Retired; Cobra Pilot, A Bat 4/77 ARA, 101st Airborne Division, Author of *Our Own Worst Enemy*; Producer/Director *Black Hawk Down: The Untold Story*

"John's book on his experience in Vietnam is monumental. The level of detail and emotion brought me right back to the right seat of an OH-6a. I can even remember how to do self-defense flying (in case your pilot, usually a nineteen-year-old warrant officer, is hit). Perhaps the most important part of this memoir is the striving for justice for the men of the units then and later as unrecognized veterans. I am certain that any reader will be filled with outrage. I am also confident that John has created a true history and documented a legacy that deserves attention."

—Captain Casmir Garczynski, Artillery Officer, RVN 1971–1972

"It's a bit of a cliché to declare a new book one that readers will not be able to put down. Nonetheless, John Hoffman's *Saigon Guns: A True Story of Aerial Combat in the Fall of 1972* is without question that kind of book. With unflinching, eyewitness precision, Hoffman has written an unforgettable, utterly crucial book that collars readers from its very first chiseled sentence to its last. *Saigon Guns*—at once an autobiography, history, and a treatise on military strategy and unimaginable valor in service to America—is written in prose every bit as imagistic, nuanced, and textured as the most riveting fiction. Indeed, much of it is so mind-blowingly harrowing—so sweepingly adventurous, death defying, and overflowing with bigger-than-life characters—that readers must remind themselves that Hoffman's account all really occurred. It's an extraordinary, breathtaking book."

—Joseph Bathanti, North Carolina Poet Laureate (2012– 2014); Co-founder of the Charles George VA Medical Center Creative Writing Program (Asheville, NC)

The Saigon Guns:
A True Story of Aerial Combat in the Fall of 1972

by John Thomas Hoffman

ISBN 978-1-64663-946-5

Published by

◄ köehlerbooks™

3705 Shore Drive
Virginia Beach, VA 23455
800-435-4811
www.koehlerbooks.com

THE
SAIGON
GUNS

A TRUE STORY OF AERIAL COMBAT
IN THE FALL OF 1972

JOHN THOMAS HOFFMAN

VIRGINIA BEACH
CAPE CHARLES

For my dad,
Colonel George E. Hoffman Jr., USAF
1922–2010

For my son,
Colonel Brian T. Hoffman, US Army

And for Dusty, my stick buddy.
Captain Arnold Edward (Dusty) Holm Jr.,
Killed in Action, Republic of Vietnam
June 1972

CONTENTS

FOREWORD

I REALLY HATE when someone refers to *old people*—even though I am probably being very hypocritical as a septuagenarian myself. I must admit that I have used that reference in the past. Being older now myself, I look at the world through very different lenses than in my youth. I first met John Hoffman in 1972 while serving as a nineteen-year-old AH-1G Cobra pilot for F Troop 8th Air Cavalry. Though we had very different backgrounds, we both ended up in the same place and same time in a war almost nine thousand miles from the United States. As we flew missions together and drank beer together, I developed a close friendship with John and realized we did share one thing very important to both of us: a never-ending love of God, of family, and of country.

John had deployed to South Vietnam several months before my arrival and had been assigned to the 203rd Assault Support Helicopter Company (Wildcats) as a Chinook pilot. As a newly minted Warrant Officer assigned to F Troop, I mostly tried to keep my mouth shut and my ears and eyes open. As I came to know the other pilots of F Troop, I developed a friendship with Captain Arnold Edward ("Dusty") Holm Jr. Let me state first off that at that point as a new pilot I did not refer to Captain Holm as "Dusty." It would have been like saying "Hey babe" to the queen of England. Others called him Dusty, but I didn't feel I had been in the unit long enough to gain that honor.

With the Easter Offensive by North Vietnamese and Russian forces into South Vietnam, things began to get challenging very quickly. This was complicated by the stand down of several key US Army units in our AO or area of operations in northern South Vietnam. One result was the stand down for our supporting CH-47 company, the 203rd AHC. John Hoffman was then transferred to the 48th Assault Helicopter Company, a unit adjacent to F/8 Cavalry on Marble Mountain Army Airfield. The 48th and F/8 Cavalry often participated on operations together.

During the month of May and into early June 1972, I began to get my feet on the ground and flew many missions with Captain Holm and one of his close friends, Lieutenant James McQuade. They both flew the OH-6 (Loach) while at that time I was a copilot in a Cobra. I developed a deep respect for Captain Holm's flying ability but at that time still never called him "Dusty." I had heard Captain Holm refer to his friend John Hoffman often while watching him and others play post-mission poker in the hootch. At that time, I never joined in the games. On the evening of June 10, 1972, I was once again watching the pilots play poker in one of the hootches. Capt. Holm was playing along with Lt. McQuade and others. During a lull in the game Capt. Holm looked up at me and asked if I wanted to join the game. I was familiar with the game, as I had played it in college before being expelled for not showing up to classes. I said, "Sure Captain Holm. I would love to play," to which he replied, "Call me Dusty!" I asked what the game was and Dusty said it was seven card suicide. When I told them I was not familiar with the game, they quickly said that they would teach me. That was the understatement of the year! A hundred and eighty bucks later I still didn't know how to play!

The next day, June 11, 1972, both Capt. Holm, Lt. McQuade and their crews were shot down and killed by enemy fire. Capt. Holm was shot down first and then Lt. McQuade had flown to the crash site to look for survivors. He also was shot down. While this mission was occurring, I was on standby, along with other pilots, at Camp Eagle. To a man everyone wanted to mount another rescue mission to the two crash sites. Our commanding officer, Major Jack Kennedy, advised that no further missions were to deploy. At that time there were some really hard feelings about Major Kennedy's decision, but with days, weeks, and months of thinking about it, I realize it was the right one. We had lost two aircraft and crews in the span of one hour. We had no backup for further rescue attempts. F Troop was on its own, so we flew back to our base at Marble Mountain and began to grieve and prepare for the next day's missions.

With the later deactivation of the 48th Assault Helicopter Company, Captain John Hoffman was reassigned to F Troop flying the UH-1 Huey as the Blues platoon leader and as air mission commander. John and I became very good friends and have remained so for the past forty-eight years. John remained in the military to retire as a full colonel. Following my return from South Vietnam, I was assigned to Ft. Lewis as a newly promoted W-2, but the Army no longer needed so many helicopter pilots. I soon left the Army and headed back to Houston, Texas. I joined the Houston Police Department where I served thirty-two years, twenty-six of them as a homicide detective.

In 2012 John and I along with our wives made a trip to France for the sixty-eighth anniversary of the D Day landings on Normandy beach. On June 6, 2012, as John and I stood atop the cliffs of Pointe du Hoc and looked over the edge, we envisioned the 1944 assault by the 2nd Ranger Battalion under the command of Colonel James Rudder. The Rangers had to climb these cliffs under intense fire with a full combat load. John and I both agreed that neither of us could have climbed that cliff when we were eighteen years of age wearing nothing but gym shorts, T-shirt and tennis shoes, even if Raquel Welch was at the top with two cold beers!

Any man who has a military background progresses through his lifetime with multiple opportunities to meet people who are great leaders of men. But they are few and far between. I have had the great honor to have met four during my lifetime. First was my high school football coach, Vernon Ramn, a Marine who served in Vietnam. He taught me a little about football and a lot about life. Another was Major Jack Kennedy; commanding officer of F Troop

8th Air Cavalry Regiment, Republic of South Vietnam, 1972–1973. Pilots under his command would land their aircraft on the patio of Hell if he asked that it be done. Additionally, Captain Bobby Adams, captain of the Houston Police Homicide Division, covered my ass on many occasions during my career in that division. And finally, Colonel John Hoffman, US Army (Ret.), the author of this book. I flew with him, lived with him, laughed with him, and cried with him. John is probably the most interesting person I have ever met in my life. Enjoy the read.

Dwane D. Shirley
Warrant Officer II F Troop 8th Air Cavalry Regiment 1972–1973, Republic of South Vietnam
Houston Police Department 1973–2006

DEDICATION

THE FOLLOWING IS offered as an introduction to US Army helicopter pilots in South Vietnam written in such prose that I could never emulate. It is offered not as praise of myself but as praise for all of those fine, talented, and truly heroic pilots and crewmembers of what was then a new age in the Army of which I was so privileged to become a small part. Particularly these early pioneers of air mobile warfare who blazed the way for those of us who followed with their blood and experience. It is all of them to whom I and others owe our survival in those days that followed.

They proved in Vietnam to be ones who were the new warriors that brought "the others back."

Steinbeck on Helicopter Pilots

Prior to his death, novelist John Steinbeck traveled to Vietnam to report on the war. He reported via letters to his friend Alicia Patterson, *Newsday's* first editor and publisher. Those letters were published in a book by Thomas E. Barden, Vietnam veteran and professor of English at the University of Toledo. The book is entitled, *Steinbeck on Vietnam: Dispatches From The War*. Steinbeck was in Pleiku in January 1967, South Vietnam, and flying with 10th Cavalry when he wrote the following about helicopter pilots:

> Alicia,
>
> I wish I could tell you about these pilots. They make me sick with envy. They ride their vehicles the way a man controls a fine, well-trained quarter horse. They weave along stream beds, rise like swallows to clear trees; they turn and twist and dip like swifts in the evening. I watch their hands and feet on the controls, the delicacy of the coordination

9

reminds me of the sure and seeming slow hands of (Pablo) Casals on the cello. They are truly musician's hands and they play their controls like music and they dance them like ballerinas and they make me jealous because I want so much to do it. Remember your child night dream of perfect flight free and wonderful? It's like that, and sadly I know I never can. My hands are too old and forgetful to take orders from the command center, which speaks of updrafts and side winds, of drift and shift, or ground fire indicated by a tiny puff or flash, or a hit and all these commands must be obeyed by the musician's hands instantly and automatically. I must take my longing out in admiration and the joy of seeing it. Sorry about that leak of ecstasy, Alicia, but I had to get it out or burst."

PREFACE

I HAVE LIVED much of my life as a warrior. Not in the tradition of the ancient warrior who's entire being and sole function in life was as a destroyer but in the tradition of the Washingtonian citizen soldier. I have spent most of my adult life according to a credo long written and observed as an almost holy dedication by many Americans. It is a family tradition going back to the American Revolution, and of my father, my uncles, my cousins, myself, and now my son, borne of the necessity to resist that which might threaten what is held sacred, often above the value of home, family, and even life. That credo carried me through a thirty-one-year military career, with service in the United States, Southeast Asia, and Europe and then numerous long and arduous days in various civil-military operations helping the nation recover from disasters of one sort or another, and, recently, a stint with the new US Department of Homeland Security helping to protect this nation from another terrorist attack. No, you need not ask. I indeed do find it hard to say no, a vice that my wife often points out to me. I guess that was how I was made, as the son of a veteran of World War II, Korea, and Vietnam.

During my time as a civilian in government following the attacks on September 11, 2001, I was asked by a colleague whether my service in South Vietnam still haunts me. I was surprised at his question. He was much younger than I and he admitted that his understanding of the war in Vietnam came from movies and TV. I was not surprised. Few younger than my generation have direct knowledge of that war or its context. The result is that the current prevailing view of that war is actually a political fiction, fostered by the media. He also asked what most often reminded me of my time in Vietnam. I instantly, as always, knew the answer to that question. The smell.

I grew up with smells. Our military family lived all over the US, from Hawaii and Alaska to Florida, New York, and Virginia and even in postwar Europe. All had unique smells—some pleasant, some not—but at least most of the time anyway, you got used to them. I recall the strange smells on the WWII battlefields of Europe as a teenager. I remember the WWII veterans on the Normandy beaches talking about the *smell* of battle. Later, as I worked my way through college as a full-time fireman in Fairfax County, Virginia, I experienced new but unpleasant smells. These smells came from chemical accidents, trash, forest and structure fires, and human bodily fluids and functions and the dead. But the worst by far, at least up until that period of my life, was the smell of burned human flesh. It is a terrible, persistent, and penetrating smell. It does not quickly leave you as most smells do. It stays on your clothes and equipment, even after washing. And it hangs in the air, and it gets on you and stays there . . . and nothing smells worse.

Then I got to Vietnam. Yep, it can be worse. The smell that hit me the day I arrived at Bien Hoa Airbase, near Saigon, was sudden, overwhelming and almost like a physical blow to my body. *Oh God, I thought, is this place covered in dead animals, feces, trash fires and burning human flesh?* My mind raced through the potential sources of the smells filling that noxious air. My dad had warned me, after his two previous tours in South Vietnam. But a spoken warning is not sufficient, I now knew, to prepare you for the shock of that initial exposure. How could anyone live here, why would they want to live here, and what is worth fighting over in this odorous place?

No, I did not get used to that smell. It permeated everything. It was in my underclothes, my jungle fatigues, my flight suits and flight jacket, my survival vest, even, it seemed to me, in the metal of my sidearm. Of course, the insides of our aircraft over there were the same—they all smelled rotten, all of the time.

Even years later, after my final return from South Vietnam, that smell would unexpectedly assault my nose. This happened when I would climb into a helicopter or airplane that had spent any time in Vietnam. My dad and I would discuss that smell often over the years after our service in Vietnam. He and I served there at the same time in 1971 and 1972. We both would smell something that triggered the recall of that Vietnam wartime stench, or we would simply recall some event or experience *in country* and the smell would rush back into our minds unbidden. We both hated the smell and its return to our nose or mind in the years afterwards. But it was there, in an unpleasant life experience that we shared, along with so many other memories of that time.

This book will, I hope, convey the reality of service as a US Army combat helicopter pilot in Vietnam and also dispel some of the myths and falsehoods about the experience of serving in the United States Army in the early 1970s and as a combat helicopter pilot in Vietnam. While my experiences are truly only mine and I do not pretend to suggest that mine are the same as all others, perhaps my reflections here will help, in some small way, to correct what I have seen incorrectly portrayed across the press and in Hollywood, and to give you a taste of what it was really like to have been there, when I was there. I most importantly want to try and give you a sense of how many of us, from a Vietnam warrior's viewpoint, see that experience today. The facts and events narrated here are to the best of my recollection. Any omission and errors here are mine alone and the opinions I express in the book are mine and are the result of many years of thoughtful consideration.

This book contains the content of contemporaneous notes from my time in the Republic of Vietnam (RVN), letters I wrote and chapter drafts that I began in the early 1980s. It has taken me, working on and off between life events and the health challenges from having served in South Vietnam, decades to complete this book of my experiences as a young military officer and my service in the Republic of South Vietnam.

John T. Hoffman
Colonel, US Army, Retired

CHAPTER ONE
MY DAD WAS A FIGHTER PILOT

AS I WATCHED TV news during my junior year in college, I saw the reports of carnage and death in the war in South Vietnam. The quickly evolving "helicopter war" was becoming a very dangerous place for American soldiers, particularly so for helicopter crews. In 1968 US troop strength peaked at 540,000 in country and losses totaled 16,899 US soldiers that year alone. The news reporting was detailed, and images of combat appeared on television nearly every evening. The war was clearly not going in the direction that some in our government were suggesting. Aircraft losses in Vietnam were staggering, with helicopter crews seemingly getting the worst of it.[1] The news reports, I noticed, were focused on two things: first, how many Americans had died and, second, how many helicopters had been shot down the day before. Being a helicopter crewman was seen as one of the most dangerous jobs in the war. But not as dangerous as an infantry soldier, or *grunt*, on the ground, slogging through the jungle and rice paddies. I did not want to be a grunt.

I watched as friends and acquaintances were drafted. Even firemen in Fairfax were being drafted. There were very few protected jobs that could keep a young man from being drafted. Those of us in college knew that when we graduated, we likely were going to Vietnam, if the war had not ended by then. I had no intention of being an infantry soldier, particularly an enlisted soldier. I wanted a commission as an officer and by 1968, I realized I would be better off as a pilot. I hoped to be sent, after graduation and commissioning, to the year-long fixed-wing flight school. Staying in college and in Army ROTC earning that officer's commission was one way to dodge the draft for four years. Then another year in flight school and, hopefully, it would be all over before I could be sent to Vietnam. It did not work out quite like that.

I grew up in the military. As a child I never lived anywhere more than four years before my father was transferred. We lived in Hawaii, Colorado, New York, Alabama, Alaska, Virginia, and France, all before I reached high school. Starting in 1961, I attended the Paris American High school, in Garches, France. At the time I was one of six children of an Air Force officer assigned to EUCOM, the US Military Command for Europe in the 1960s, located near Paris, France. I grew up around the military and knew many of my father's military friends and associates. I grew up around fighter and bomber pilots, many of whom, like my father, flew in World War II and Korea. My father, a West Point Graduate and an Army Air Corps pilot during World War II, shared stories of some of his experiences in that war but most were stories of humor or unusual experiences flying or, on a very rare occasion, he related a specific mission or event. I also knew he had some involvement in the Korean War, but he always said it was very "peripheral." Growing up on or near military bases gave me some knowledge about the military, its organization, and the basic history of World War II. My father had flown in the Pacific Theater and but had not been involved in military operations in the European Theater of Operations (ETO). I did have a distant British uncle, Ifor Davis, who was a Battle of Britain pilot and I had heard some stories from his perspective but nothing about operations over Normandy and D-Day itself. Living in postwar Europe so soon after the end of World War II, where the destruction of that war was still all around where we lived, quickly brought me an understanding of the impact of war on the people who suffered through it and those who fought it.

Early in my freshman year at Paris American High School word passed quickly through the US military and dependent community in Paris that a new movie about D-Day was to be filmed in

Normandy. A few weeks later all students were asked to come to the auditorium after class. A Mr. Zanuck was introduced. He informed us that he was going to film a movie in Normandy, just an hour's drive north of our location, and he needed extras for scenes to be filmed on the weekends. There would be no pay, but we would learn a lot about movies, about D-Day itself, and we just might meet a few movie stars. Then he explained that they only needed boys for these scenes.

What followed on weekend trips to Normandy scattered over the next few months was an amazing introduction into film and documentary making. But most important to me was the grim, often horrific first-person history I learned from those who had landed on those beaches and drop zones on that incredible and bloody June 5-6, 1944, on the Normandy coast of France. We met and listened to the stories of paratroopers, infantry soldiers, and the airmen who had actually participated in the June 6, 1944, Allied invasion of France. The stories were both fascinating and horrifying to a fourteen-year-old. We watched scenes being filmed and on two occasions stood in as soldiers on the beach as some of the "long shots" were filmed as background scenes for the movie. It was fascinating to be present for filming, even if at some distance, when John Wayne was in the scene or on the beach when Sean Connery did one of his comic scenes in the movie as a British soldier. Of particular interest was at the filming of the action at Pegasus Bridge. Here we listened to actor and D-Day veteran Richard Todd, who in the movie played his commander, Major John Howard, relate the facts of the actual battle and his own personal experiences that day at Pegasus Bridge.

All the Hollywood actors, the current British and American soldiers playing the previous generation in the movie, and we young onlookers, stood in awe listening to his recounting of the actual operation that terrifying day. Even Sean Connery stood listening intently during one session. Of course, true to his British television character at the time, however, it was not long before he was telling humorous one liners to those around him, British, American, and German.

I, like many others present, came away with a new respect for what a hero is and what the price of courage is on a battlefield. I hoped I would never, ever be called upon to fight in a war.

During the filming of another small part in the movie, I witnessed the recreation of an event from the German Army perspective. While I did not see the full recreation of the event until the movie was released, I did overhear the translated, firsthand account of a former German officer who had been in the bunker. He recounted the experience and described his fear upon seeing the massive extent and scale of the Allied fleet coming over the horizon directly toward his position and the ensuing bombardment of his portion of the German defense line. It was clearly a very frightening experience for him, and his retelling of the experience left a strong impression upon me. What it must have been like for soldiers on either side of the battle that day! What a frightening, nerve shattering, and debilitating thing to find yourself amid such chaos and violence. How did any of the soldiers that day focus on their duty or function, whether attacker or defender? How does one overcome such paralyzing fear?

During this period my father decided that my brother and I should see some of the horrors left over from World War I and World War II firsthand. We visited WWI battlefields and graveyards. We saw the bones at Chateau Thierry, we saw the trench of bayonets at Verdun and the church where hundreds and hundreds of skeletons of WWI soldiers are interred behind glass. We visited WWII battlefields and the American Cemeteries in Northern France, including the one above Omaha Beach where Dad took us to the graves of members of his West Point Class of 1944 who died in the ETO after D-Day. It was very moving for Dad, my brother Kip, and me. We went up to the top of the cliffs at Pont Du Hoc and stood in fear and awe as we looked down and saw the extent of the obstacles that the Rangers had faced when they assaulted the dug-in Germans at the top. I recall that my palms began to sweat as I looked down. It made the war and its impact even more real to my brother and me.

Some weeks later our father took us to the concentration camp at Dachau just north of Munich, West Germany. He took us through the dormitory buildings and walked us along the fences, under the guard towers, and through the killing fields below them. He took us into a crematorium where skulls and bones were still laying where they were partially burned in the open ovens. This was 1961 and the stench of burned flesh was still overwhelming, as little had yet been cleaned up in this part of the camp. Even at my young age, the inhumanity I saw was mind-numbing. I was stunned and my brother and I both ran out and got sick. There were buckets outside the doors expressly placed there for this reason. I asked a camp guide outside why things were still left in there as they were when the camp was liberated. He said in accented English that "it is so, because we must never forget." My father then told us that the US Military Occupation Command still required that such camps were maintained as they were by the local German government and that local Germans were "encouraged" to tour the camps.

When *The Longest Day* movie premiered in Paris in 1962, we attended one of several premier showings at Paris theaters. During that showing there was little noise in the theater from the audience. All sat in complete but intent silence. No one spoke. No comments were heard. The audience had moved into some sort of numbed state. Everyone, including us young American students, were completely engaged. We young extras had only seen brief glimpses of portions of scenes during filming and had no idea as to what the final film would look like. The firsthand accounts of those who were there on June 6, 1944, were knotted in the movie into an irresistible, engaging, and moving whole.

For the many in the audience, our dad explained after the showing, they were reliving their own war experience and the promise of liberation that the horrors of D-Day portended. We had all just witnessed an amazing documentary production so complex and expensive that it nearly financially broke Daryl Zanuck. When the movie ended and the credits rolled, most sat in silence as first. Then slowly the applause began and grew. Then this mainly French audience stood up and clapped and clapped. This incredible, comprehensive, yet still incomplete retelling of the events of that very long June day could not possibly communicate the whole of the story. No such cinematic retelling can relate the whole or the scale of such conflict and its destruction, pain, and death. But I felt that the experience gave me an understanding of that day that I could never get from a history book.

Zanuck had taken the story first published by Cornelius Ryan in his1959 book and captured the essential parts of the story of D-Day for those who were there and those who had lived through it—soldiers and citizens of Europe. The film had captured the sense of the time and fears, foreboding of what still lay ahead in WWII and the horrible price paid that day. For those of us who were not there or even alive in June 1944, we had begun to have some understanding of the reality of what those soldiers were asked to do and the sacrifices that were made—on both sides of the conflict.

All of this has stayed with me all my life. I think my time as a teenager in Normandy, and on those battlefields, graveyards, and concentration camps gave me a view into the realities of life and military conflict that few ever get until they, themselves, experience "seeing the elephant"[2]. Little did I know what lay ahead for both my father and me.

My father was one of those men who had been there and done that. He had served all over the world, often for extended periods, but he was always still present in our lives. To me he was the perfect example of a father and mentor. He was a graduate of West Point's class of 1944, known as the *D-Day Class*, on June 6, 1944. He had gone through primary flight training concurrent with his studies at West Point, from which he graduated with an engineering degree in just three years. He transitioned to current frontline fighters immediately upon graduation. Within a few months, after marrying my mother, Anne P. Kelly from Albany, NY, he was sent to the Pacific Theater to fly P-51 fighters and then P-47s, primarily ground attack aircraft.

My father, George Earl Hoffman Jr. in 1945 in the Pacific Theater training in ground attack in his P-47 Thunderbolt. This photo became the subject of a US Air Force Heritage print in the late 1990s.

Dad flew combat missions over the Pacific until the war ended in August of 1945. At the time it ended, as the result of the atomic bomb strikes on Japan, his unit was preparing for an invasion of Japan. My father wrote his father that summer to tell him that the invasion was coming soon, and he did not think his prospects for surviving the invasion were very good. My dad, as were most of the men in the Pacific Theater who were preparing for the invasion of Japan, was confident that, unless the war was ended by some miracle beforehand, there would be an invasion and it would cost many, many more lives than D-Day had. Indeed, estimates prepared by the invasion planners assumed that there would be one million US casualties in the invasion to come. Dad was also escorting B-29 missions to and from Japan that summer, between training exercises in preparation for the coming invasion. Those were long lonely flights over vast stretches of open, inhospitable water. Long flights were where, as Dad put it, one had time to contemplate the future and do the math. And the math did not look good.

Then a miracle did happen, and the war ended before any invasion was launched. It was a near thing, as much of the Second World War was. After the war, Dad kept flying but he also stretched into other areas of the Air Force's mission, such as logistics and operations. These experiences resulted in his gaining expertise, which would be valuable when he was no longer a line pilot, a day sure to come to all older pilots. This led to him becoming an Air Force expert both as a pilot and an international logistics officer. This expertise kept him at the Pentagon for my first and third years at Georgetown University. It was also these areas of expertise that took dad away from home for duty in Southeast Asia while I was a senior at Georgetown

My dad, an Air Force lieutenant colonel when I entered Georgetown University as a freshman in August of 1965, epitomized, to me anyway, the fearless, confident, and competent aviation character found in the Steve Canyon comic strip. He always encouraged me to stretch myself and try new things. I doubt, though, that he saw me in a career as a military officer. He always thought I would end up in a government or legal career. But he never said anything to me except practical advice and encouraging words. Dad always tried to give all his children new experiences and in the 1950s and 60s he and Mom took their six children traveling to see the United States and Europe. Growing up on military bases, we explored Civil War battlefields in the US and the battlefields of the First and Second World Wars in Europe. We camped and hiked the Rockies, the Appalachians, and the Alps. We swam in the Gulf of Mexico, the Atlantic—on both the American and the European shores—and the Pacific. And we flew in planes. We flew in big ones and small ones as kids. Aviation was always part of our lives.

I started my own working career almost four years earlier at the outset of my college years as a fireman in Fairfax County, Virginia. It was a good way to pay for a college education and Georgetown was not an education that my father could fund. I had to work my way through college. So, I went to class during the day and worked a fourteen-hour night shift, four days a week. The pay was great, the hours were convenient (for me, not the married guys), and the work was exciting. I always liked to do things that were a challenge, mentally and physically. I also liked exciting activities. I liked to ski, to fly, and to climb things. Being a fireman was, of course, something every kid at least thinks about doing at some point. For me, my older brother, George, led the way when he became a Fairfax County fireman. During my senior year in high school, listening to my brother's fire department *tone set* going off in the night to rally available fireman to report to the station hooked me. As soon as I graduated from high school, I applied for basic fireman training.

Becoming a fireman was no great challenge for me, physically or mentally. Those long days in rookie school humping rolls of hose, climbing ladders in full turn-out gear in eighty-five-degree weather, learning to climb up and down the outside of a building and feeling my way through the smoke house were more fun than difficult. I will never forget one of the instructors telling me "Boy, you ain't here to have fun, wipe that smile off your face." Shades of things to come. I was assigned to Station One in Mclean, Virginia for my probationary months. Then I got an assignment at Station Eighteen in the West Jefferson area of Falls Church Virginia. The station captain was Charlie Waters. An experienced, gruff but very capable commander who, when not driving us hard during training exercises, kept us on our toes inspecting the bottoms of the fire engines for a speck of dirt or keeping us safe and out of trouble as we fought fires of all types.

I worked nights during the week. As a junior fireman in the station, I did all the dirty work and then some. But Charlie also made a point of making everything I did a teaching experience for me. He called me "College Boy" and always told me that I "did not know shit." But he taught me a lot and he seemed, to me anyway, to push me faster than most. The one thing that he pushed the hardest was helping all the men on his team gain self-confidence and competence in our jobs. He wanted us confident in our selves in everything we did. He had simple but effective formulas for life. He would tell me that there is no room for doubt. If you doubt, you get scared. If you get scared, you freeze up. If you freeze up, you die. And he would say that you better know your job and know it well. His philosophy of life was based on a single concept: know what you are doing and do what you know. And he had a very valuable talent I wanted to gain. He was a leader.

Station 18 was different than most other stations at that time. This was a much more active station than Station 1. It was in an older suburban area of Fairfax County and averaged multiple fires each week. During my time there many calls were very serious, multi-alarms fires. Many had casualties, both civilian and firefighters, and many were fires where the structures were fully involved long before we would arrive on the scene. Charlie Waters knew fire and knew how to attack it and beat it. Charlie also knew that it was not the trucks or the equipment or the water that beat down a fire, it was the guys on the hose lines, the guys wearing the Scott Air Tanks and the guys with the picks and axes. If they were aggressive, confident, and competent, they could prevail against the fire. Charlie was also a realist, and he knew when a fire was winning, when the fight was not winnable, and when he could and could not save a structure. I do not think he ever put any of us in danger to save a structure. But he would do it to save lives and he did. He taught me a lot about life and myself.

Incidents of one type or another occurred nearly every day. Most were, of course, minor and passed as just more time pulling hose, rolling hose, working in a smoky, wet environment, and cleaning up after we got back to the station house. Cleaning up was not just about getting the soot and grime, often a very foul-smelling grime, off our bodies and out of our clothes; it was more about the gear and the trucks. We depended upon our gear as we depended upon ourselves. Every call for service, every response and, in fact, every time the trucks rolled out the door of the station, no matter how brief or inconsequential the event, resulted in a full cleaning, top and bottom, inside and out of the truck and every single piece of equipment we used. This near worship of hardware and systems was vital to us. A failure of any piece of our gear, any pump, hose line, or any item of rescue hardware could mean a life, either of a victim or our own. I quickly learned a lesson: you are only as good and reliable as your gear is serviceable.

This equipment proved itself to me on many occasions, such as the day a pool supply facility caught fire. By the time we arrived on the scene, the building was fully involved in fire. The smoke was thick all around the building. It was a very hot and humid summer afternoon. As we neared the structure, Charlie yelled to us to don our respirator packs. He pointed to the sign on the building and yelled the words *chlorine gas* several times until he was certain that we all heard him. Then he advised dispatch of the nature of the facility and the potential for chlorine gas to have been released.

Sure enough, as we laid out hose, pressurized the lines and put water onto the flaming roof of the structure, the HAZMAT team confirmed a gas release. We knocked down the fire amidst a cloud of chlorine released from the pool treatment cartridges that had burned in the fire. Not a single fireman was injured, though several company employees were exposed and transported to the hospital.

Lesson: The gear works. Use the gear!

My only real conflict between Georgetown and my duties as a fireman came at the end of my first semester of my freshman year at school. A major snowstorm hit the DC area. We got several feet of snow, and the entire area was shut down for a week. All emergency service personnel were called to duty and all leaves and time off were canceled for the duration of the emergency. I too responded to the call and spent days rescuing stranded motorists, delivering babies, and distributing hot food and supplies to isolated homes. All schools, businesses, and government offices were ordered shut throughout the area. I assumed I would not miss my semester exams, scheduled for that same week. I figured wrong.

Georgetown University was the only school to not follow the public declaration to close down and Georgetown held its fall semester exams as scheduled. Most students lived on campus and most of the faculty lived on or near the university proper. At that time there was an academic requirement that all students must sit for exams to pass the course, no matter one's grade average prior to that point in the semester. I missed all my exams and was promptly notified that I had failed all my courses and would be expelled from the university. I was in shock. I had good grades up to that point and had done the right thing, in my mind, by answering the call to duty. I probably could have gotten to the school, as many others did, but I had other duties.

My station captain wrote a letter to the school. My dad went to see the school's president. My friends wrote letters and even one of my professors refused to cooperate with the school rules. But the academic department would not be moved. I had failed my courses and I was out. I went to see the dean of freshman, Father Royden Davis, to plead my case one last time. After we talked a few moments, he told me that he was way ahead of me on this. He had exercised his authority to formally request the university academic board to review the situation. He did not agree with the rule or the position of the college. He told me that he felt that the school could not defend its position in this case and would, ultimately, suffer more harm than good from such a stance. The Georgetown academic review board at that time was composed of faculty and a few students but no administrators. This was all great, but I also knew this was an *old school* campus with long traditions and rigid character. I knew that when I applied and was admitted. I knew this would be a crapshoot, but I had nothing to lose.

The review board heard my explanation; they listened to faculty from both sides of the issue and read the various letters of support. In the end they decided that I could stay in the school but the grades stood because they had no way around that exam rule because so many other students did make it onto the campus. It was also clear to me that the Georgetown University administration and faculty were not keen on having a common fireman as a student at such a prestigious university. They did not see that the actual case at hand was that of a student who was worked as a fireman to pay his tuition to this very expensive institution. The outcome was that I could stay in school on probation. My end of semester quality point index or QPI would be .6 on a 4.0 system. The .6 was the result of the one professor who refused to go along with the rule, while all the others I had did. I was still in school and would stay in school. I spent the rest of my time as an undergraduate on probation until the day my last semester of senior year grades came out and I achieved a QPI of 2.001! To do this I had carried an overall 3.2 average the remainder of my time at Georgetown, and it was good enough to graduate on time. Many years later Father Davis told me that no one had ever done that before or since.

Lessons: sometimes logic can prevail, even if the context is strange, and, as always, persistence pays.

At Station 18 we fought many types of fire, large and small, several times a week. Anyone who approaches a fire and is not scared or apprehensive is a fool. Fear keeps you alert and responsive to your surroundings. But natural gas leaks and tanker fires truly, deeply frightened me. The potential for massive detonations with huge destructive concussions and rapidly expanding fireballs was a constant threat until the leak was sealed, the gas cut off or the tanker cooled and capped. Leaking gas can quickly reach a fuel-air mix that, if ignited, can exceed the power and destructive killing force far beyond any conventional explosive bomb dropped by a bomber. After I saw the first such detonation, from more than a mile's safe distance, I was shocked and awed in a way that remained unequaled in my mind until years later when I experienced my first B-52 strike in Vietnam.

Tanker fires are exceptionally dangerous to the community and the responders. If the tank ruptures, the liquids or gases inside can spill out and rapidly spread over a large area. If it has ignited, it can engulf those nearby within milliseconds in a sea of searing and deadly fire. In one case an eight-thousand-gallon gasoline tanker had a brake fire on the southern side of the Beltway, I-495, just south of Falls Church. The driver pulled the truck up on a steep exit ramp, stopped, and ran from the truck. He left it there on fire and ran to call for help.

When we arrived, the tires on the rear of the tanker were burning fiercely and molten rubber and smoking and burning gasoline was already running back down the ramp toward the highway traffic lanes below. I saw this and thought, *Oh crap, this sucker is going to go up in a large ball of fire.* As we approached from the highway below, Charlie ordered us to stop the truck on the uphill side of the slightly banked roadway, about a quarter of a mile from the truck. We put out our markers and helped stop the traffic approaching the scene. We pulled out a heavy hose line and our large water nozzle, called a water monitor, set it up, and began to drop a heavy stream of water on the top of the tank to cool it. At the same time, we used a two-and-a-half-inch line to place water on the wheel set at the rear of the tanker. But we needed more water—a lot more water. Charlie called for water tankers and observed the burning tanker very nervously.

We seemed to be knocking the fire down, but Charlie was very anxious and moved back and forth between nozzle crews, intently watching the fire. As another truck arrived next to ours on the median, Charlie called for foam to be made ready in case we had a larger leak of the gasoline, and it caught fire. Another engine had approached from up on the roadway that passed over the Beltway and was soon putting more water on the truck from about seventy-five yards away. It looked like we had saved the day when a safety valve on top of the tank let go with a roar of vapor shooting straight up that quickly became a monstrous jet of fire. Charlie yelled at us to pull back and physically grabbed several of the guys by the collars of their turnout coats to drag them back from the monitor, which was setup on a tripod on the edge of the asphalt.

No sooner had we run to the far side of our own engine, parked in the highway median, when the back wall of the tanker blew out, spilling burning gasoline down the exit ramp in a huge whoosh of flame and smoke. In this case the tank did not explode with the force of a bomb; it was more of an exploding jet of fire out the back of the tanker. The effect on all of us was stunning. The heat was intense, even under our full turnout gear and helmets. We were all wet and the heat quickly turned the moisture on our clothing to steam. I remember my leather gloves suddenly causing a burning sensation on my hands and I shook them off and put my hands inside my coat. Hot hands, even burns from heated moisture in the gloves, were common. The heat of the burning gasoline that day even made my leather gloves too hot to touch and singed the hair on our eyebrows and even the hair under our helmets. All of us had minor burns on our faces.

The fire ran down the ramp into the roadway and then drained off to the side of the road into the drainage ditch. The flash of exploding fire was brief, though it seemed much longer than it was. Once the initial flash of fire died down, we could return to directing the water on the truck and foam onto the fire. We then were able to knock down the gasoline fire quickly and extinguish the fire under the truck's smoldering hulk of a tank. It was a close call for all of us. No one spoke much for the next few hours. We made sure the fire was out. We put down absorbent to soak up the remaining gasoline and we washed down the exit ramp and highway surfaces that had not burned. A large area of the roadway and the surface of the ramp had burned, and the repairs were going to be extensive. That evening back at the station, we cleaned our equipment for hours and it was late into the night before we had our crew meeting and our fire after-action review. It was a sobering discussion about what went right and what went wrong. Just how close we all came to disaster was not directly mentioned, but it was clearly understood by all of us.

Lesson: What can go wrong will go wrong. It is the prepared and alert that survives to fight another fire.

And so, the next three years went by for me as a part-time paid firefighter. College classes during the day, all year long, and fire duty four nights a week at Station 18. I fought fires, saved lives, and lost a few. I became a trained paramedic, though I completed my training a year before I was legally old enough to practice on my own. I fought big fires and small. I fell through a burning apartment building floor and walked out with only minor injuries because the department-issued personal turnout or running gear I wore actually protected me. I delivered babies in cars, homes, taxi cabs, on the floor of a grocery store, and once in the snow beside a wrecked car during a blizzard out on I-495.

Then there were the suicides. I hated those calls. They were miserable experiences for all of us. Dealing with the dead bodies until the coroner showed up. Dealing with the distraught families and friends. And then the inevitable statements to the police and often the court hearings. It was ugly and I saw too much death from accidents and crimes already to process and accept these self-inflicted condemnations of life.

But I learned a lot. I gained a lot of experience at working under stress. I became more self-confident, and I slowly evolved into a leader in my own right. I fought many bad, dangerous fires. Fires in homes, offices, and warehouses full of all kinds of stuff that burns. I fought car and truck fires. And I had to search for victims within fires and most often found them dead. In one case two of us entered a house that had been fully involved in fire, but we had knocked most of it down. Family members were screaming at us to find their father. We crawled along the floor in heavy smoke and intense heat. My small flashlight was useless. We approached a room that was completely charged with hot smoke and was already badly charred, from a flashover of some kind. As I crawled into what we thought was a bedroom, I felt around for the bed and called out. There was no response. I could not feel the structure of a bed, just debris all around me. I was using my hands to feel the debris and ascertain what was in the room and where the bed might be when my right hand came down upon and into something soft and spongy. As I instinctively pulled my hand away my glove caught on something jagged. As I worked my hand loose, I yelled for a battle lantern, the kind we got surplus from the Navy. These were very powerful and could provide an intense beam of light on a small area through smoke. As soon as one was retrieved, another fireman crawled in next to me and handled the lantern. He turned it on, and I was presented with a sight I will never forget. The poor soul before me was lying on his back on the floor amid the debris that had been his bed. His entire front side was burned away and there was a gory hole in the center of his chest where I had inadvertently leaned on my hand, as I had crawled and searched. Sticking out along the edges of the hole were his ribs.

I never saw fire the same away again the rest of my life. Fire is ruthless. Fire is unforgiving and all consuming. Fire is evil.

Lesson: those who play with or intentionally neglect the risks of fire are evil as well. I could write a book about it. But I have two younger brothers, Tim and Phil, who are still fireman today and their books would be much, much better. They are everyday heroes!

My nights at Station 18 taught me things that college could not. And my days in class sometimes seemed irrelevant to day-to-day life, so maintaining focus on my studies was often a struggle. Attending college full time while working full time is not easy for anyone and it was not easy for me. I typically maintained a reduced semester class schedule, as I would spread out my required courses through the fall, winter, and summer semesters. It was hard work and I had little time for the things most college students did. I did have some downtime on weekends. But I needed to pay for school, so I also worked at a local restaurant on weekends.

My time as a fireman ended earlier than I had anticipated. I had expected to continue working well into my senior year. But the push for long overdue social justice and racial equality, not just in the south but across the nation, gave rise in the summers of the late 1960s, to dramatic demonstrations of public will and the desire for change. What had been pioneered in the military, certainly with fits and starts, returned many young black veterans to a society that was not yet so equal-opportunity minded. Inevitably, this led in some cases to confrontations that turned violent.

What I did not expect in Washington, DC were the long hot summers of race riots that were sweeping the country in the late 1960s. With the start of these terrible events people began to burn things in the streets, then they began to burn houses, and soon buildings in many major cities were torched during the summers of 1966 and 1967. By 1968 racial confrontations had resulted in whole city blocks in Washington, DC and other cities being put to the torch. Being a fireman went from being exciting and challenging to being damned dangerous. Standing on a hose line, trying to put out a fire while people on rooftops dropped cinder blocks on you and shot at you was not fun. I couldn't shoot back, and I couldn't run. It was even harder to duck the stones and bricks. Then Martin Luther King was shot, and the riots became uncontrollable. I was missing classes I could not afford to miss. I was not even sure I would survive to graduate. I looked at my priorities and decided that getting my diploma and being commissioned a second lieutenant were what mattered most. If I left Georgetown University before I graduated, I would not be commissioned as an officer in the US Army—but I would be immediately drafted.

I resigned my position with the fire department. Since freshman year I had also had my weekend job working as a waiter, bartender, and cook at the 1789 restaurant in Georgetown. The tips were great, and I got free meals. When you're in college, free meals of any kind are a gift from the gods. A free meal from a restaurant like the 1789 was almost heaven. I figured that I had enough, combined with what money I had saved, my ROTC pay (wow! Fifty bucks a month!), and my income from the '89 to get through to graduation.

I spent the last part of the summer of 1968 at Indian Town Gap Pennsylvania attending ROTC summer training. I must have done well. Not only did I bring home about $250 in pay, but I returned to Georgetown to find out that I had been selected as the cadet colonel of the entire ARMY ROTC Cadet Corps at Georgetown University. Then, about the time school started, I was contacted by the local Metropolitan Police precinct. They needed a few good men for some part-time work. Congress had decided that the Washington DC Police Department was not big enough to handle the "hot" summers in DC. In fact, it was not big enough to handle a third of DC at any time of the year.

They needed part-time people who had the right background

to fill non-enforcement type duties to free trained police officers for the streets—and they needed them in a hurry. The pay was good, the hours were flexible, a promise of a police career was offered, and in a crunch, I would be far safer than being a fireman out on the streets. That was a welcome change! It sounded good to me, so I soon found myself assisting in gathering, sorting, and trying to understand information about just exactly who in the hell the groups like the SDS and others really were and where groups like the Weathermen fit into the picture and how they were financed.

The Students for a Democratic Society, or just the SDS, was an amusing name for a violent group who espoused a belief that all things democratic were evil and only a communist system was acceptable as a government. Most of the radicals, activists, and many students who joined this group had fallen under the attractive glow of various so-called peace organizations of the sixties, usually funded and promoted by groups like the World Peace Council, a Soviet government organ.

These groups used the word *democratic* and phrases like *people's government* or *power to the people* the same way Honecker had to rule East Germany in the 1970s and 1980s with such a blood-drenched hand. Few have ever misused the words *democracy* and *democratic* as did the Soviet and Eastern European rulers in the fifties, sixties, and seventies. The SDS was heavily influenced and funded by these Soviet actors. These various "peace groups" were assisted from the basements of several Eastern European embassies in Washington. Their goal was to cause as much trouble as possible and attempt to influence the outcome of various third-world conflicts in the streets and in the press across the United States. This was clearly an effort coordinated with the "wars of national liberation" policy of the Soviet leadership. This has been documented fully now, but at the time many of these connections were unclear and well obscured.

The effort was directed at using an American's idealistic views of how things *should* be in the best of all possible worlds. It twisted these views to support both outright military and clandestine subversive efforts from across the various communist countries and their allied or susceptible third world countries. It aimed at preserving a failing communist system by bringing under Soviet influence new sources of raw materials and wealth. The Soviets, and all the Eastern European countries, were already broke. Countries like Vietnam offered new populations to employ in support of the communist system. They offered new sources of raw materials and energy to shore up the failing communist economic system. This was a well-orchestrated, very successful operation.

Many Americans, both well-meaning and others, who had clearly selfish political or other suspect motivations, were caught up in this misdirection act and were willing participants in the confrontation and controversy for years to follow.

The greatest influence seems to have been on the liberal end of our political system and has spawned a left-leaning view of the way our society "ought" to be and has confused what America has always tried to be, sometimes with success, sometimes not. But always with an approach to governing based upon compromise and accommodation. In this view the consensus of the will of the majority, care for the less fortunate, and consideration of the needs and wishes of the minority have been corrupted into a need or even a privilege of the minority to dictate to the majority, and removal of the concept of compromise from our political system. This was leveraged by the Soviets to build and grow the anti-war movement across the United States. What few of the American activists realized was that it was the Soviet Union who was financing the North Vietnamese war effort. The Soviets wanted to force the United States to withdraw from supporting the South Vietnamese government in its defense against the onslaught from North Vietnam. It would not be until the last year of US direct involvement in the war in Vietnam that the extent of the direct participation in the way would become evident.

The result in 1968 and 1969, on campus and in the streets during the late sixties, was the origins of a new campus liberal community with greater acceptance of the communist philosophy than that of American Democratic philosophy. This also led to the mindset about the "proper" way to see things in the university communities, where the American Way is questioned and how, idealistically and ideologically, things ought to be. Today we call this view being *politically correct.*

These emerging issues led members of the United States House of Representatives to call for hearings by the House Internal Security Committee. It led the Washington Metropolitan Police Department to increase its efforts to counter violent demonstrations and to attempt to infiltrate radical organizations whose actions became progressively more violent, such as a shadowy group called the Weathermen. Campus unrest and the numerous confrontations across the city were getting serious, even dangerous. The potential damage caused by this political orchestration by so-called peace groups combined with the dark side of the free-love and drug culture was only just beginning to emerge.

The Metropolitan Police intelligence effort was also beginning to show a fuzzy connection between the abundant availability of drugs at certain times and places and scheduled demonstrations against the Vietnam war around Washington. I never really got very deeply into this area, as I was mostly concerned with what was called *order of battle* or *who is running all of this.* But I was deeply concerned about what it portended for our country and for our allies. What the future held was worse than anything I could have imagined!

For me, once again it was interesting, exciting, challenging, and it paid well. Now it's not like I was so mercenary, but college was expensive, and jobs were tough to get. My job at the 1789 did not hurt my connections around the area either. It gave me an ear to what was happening on campus and around the Georgetown area that I would otherwise not have, particularly as an ROTC cadet.

ROTC was not particularly popular on campus at this time. Its on-campus visibility, its connection with the "establishment" and the fact that the war in Vietnam had been caused by ROTC students, according to various "student" activists hanging around Georgetown those days, made ROTC an easy target for abuse. If you were in ROTC or had any outward sign about your person that might indicate that you supported your country, you were immediately identified as a fascist and criminal. These would-be radicals threw accusations of fascism around without any real understanding of the term, its context, and the cost paid by so many Americans to defeat and irradicate it from Europe. It was simply an easy term of art for these would-be communists, taught to them by others with even less understanding of the words true meaning in history. As the Army ROTC cadet colonel on campus my senior year, I was the chief criminal in town!

But I lived with myself just fine. I made enough money to pay my expenses and I was getting pretty good grades (no mean trick for me). Neither job demanded too much of my time. In fact, I had enough spare to time take advantage of an ROTC flight training program that enabled me to get my civilian pilot's license while a senior at Georgetown on the US Army's nickel. What a deal! All I had to do was agree to go to flight school after I went on active duty at some point in the future.

This was great fun for me. I had been around airplanes most of my life. You cannot grow up as the son of a US Air Force fighter pilot and not have an interest in aviation. While I could not pass a flight physical for the Air Force due to leg injuries when I was young, I was fit enough to be drafted, to be an officer, and to fly for the Army. I took lessons at PG Airpark in suburban Maryland. Larry DeAngeles, a senior captain for Eastern Airlines, was my instructor. He was a great teacher and further inspired my interest in flying. I got my ticket in the spring of 1969. As we neared the month of May, I looked forward to graduation and a summer of carefree living before active duty.

Then came that day at Arlington Cemetery and my first

experience at a military funeral for a friend. I stood near a hole in the earth as the Honor Guard of the 3rd Infantry put my friend and mentor at Georgetown for two years into the ground. Major Lawrence Malone had been an ROTC instructor at Georgetown, and he had further cultivated in me that sense of duty, honor, and country that had been originally put there by my father. As the son of a military officer, I had traveled with my six brothers and sisters all over the United States and Europe. I never, as a kid, felt any strong desire to serve in the military. But I knew I would because that was what the sons of the Hoffman family would do, and besides, there was the military draft. It would not be a career, but I knew I would serve in some capacity. When I had first gone to registration at Georgetown University that hot August day in 1965, I had stopped at the US Army ROTC desk and just signed up. I guess I figured that if I did not go the ROTC route, then I would most likely get drafted anyway. I knew enough to seek a commission over boot camp and serving as an enlisted soldier.

When I first joined the Georgetown University ROTC program, compulsory at that time for all freshmen in the college, I met Major Lawrence Malone. Here was the consummate career military officer. He was a West Point graduate, Airborne, Ranger, and a combat veteran. He was smart, resourceful, a talented leader, and one of the best teachers I ever had. Major Malone was both a mentor and friend. I know that if the North Vietnamese had not captured and tortured him to death, he would have risen to the rank of general officer.

As I turned away from his grave that day I felt the loss of a close friend, a feeling I would often have in later years from service in the Republic of Vietnam. But I was also very, very angry. While I knew that the students at Georgetown did not understand what was happening either at home or in Vietnam, I knew that politicians on both sides of the issue did. And so did those who were stirring the pot of campus unrest and who were eagerly trying to sacrifice young American men to satisfy their own political and ideological ends. I also knew that being an officer in the United States Army was going to be very different than it had been for my father. I already felt that sense of isolation and disrespect that would fall so heavy upon me in 1970, 1971 and 1973.

While my ROTC duties were not involved in my civilian activities, I worked with a new dedication and desire to make some difference, however small. I worked hard, held two jobs, took my flying lessons, spent long hours studying so that I would be sure to graduate on time, and served as the senior ROTC cadet, which also required a great deal of my time. The result was that my senior year went by very fast. I did not really enjoy it much, except perhaps when I was flying. I did not have the time to do so. As April turned warm in the spring of 1969, I decided to slow down and cut my hours for both jobs before May, so that I could join my friends and have some fun during my last weeks at Georgetown.

But on the twenty-seventh of May 1969, while pulling a shift in the bar in the basement of the 1789 called the Tombs, a large man in a three-piece suit came up to me and asked my name. We talked for a minute or so about the school and the '89. Then he took an envelope out of his pocket and handed it to me. He said that Congress had subpoenaed me. He told me that his name was Sanders and that he worked for the House Internal Security Committee. I was pretty sure that this would not go over well with the military. I decided to check with the professor of Military Science, head of the ROTC Department at Georgetown, to see if it could be stopped. I felt that my appearance before this committee would not be good for ROTC, for Georgetown, or for me. He and I chatted about the situation, and he became distressed as I explained what had occurred and showed him the subpoena. He told me to come back the next morning and not to talk to anyone about the situation or the subpoena.

Original
UNITED STATES OF AMERICA
Congress of the United States

13

To _____ John Hoffman _____

_____, GREETING:

PURSUANT to lawful authority, YOU ARE HEREBY COMMANDED to be and appear before the

Committee on Internal Security of the House of Representatives of the United States, on

a duly appointed subcommittee thereof, on ___Wednesday, May 4, 1969_____ at _____,

at __10__ o'clock, _a.m._, at their Committee Room, __309 Cannon House Office Building,__

__Washington, D.C 20515_____,

then and there to testify touching matters of inquiry committed to said committee, and not to

depart without leave of said committee. A copy of the Committee Rules of Procedure, and one
copy each of two Committee resolutions authorizing this particular investigation
and hearing, adopted 3/6/69 and 5/14/69, are attached.
YOU ARE HEREBY COMMANDED to bring with you and produce before said committee, or

a duly authorized subcommittee thereof, the following:

_____

_____

_____

HEREOF FAIL NOT, as you will answer your default under the pains and penalties in such

cases made and provided.

To __B.Ray McConnon_____, to serve and return.

GIVEN under my hand this ___26__ day of _____May_____, in the

year of our Lord, 19 _69_.

Chairman—Chairman of Subcommittee—Member Designate
of the Committee on Internal Security of the House of
Representatives.

If you desire a conference with a representative of the Committee prior to the date of the hearing, please call or
write to: Counsel, Committee on Internal Security, Washington, D.C. 20515, Telephone: 225-3051.

This is the actual subpoena that I was presented by Mr. Sanders

The next day I went back up to the ROTC offices in the Old
North Building to see the professor of Military Science or PMS,
Colonel Ralph Kuzzell, the head of the Army ROTC program at
Georgetown. I viewed him as my military commander and felt

his authority over me could influence my post-commission initial assignment. I wanted to do everything I could both to avoid being put before this committee and to avoid potentially embarrassing the Army. When I got to his office there were several senior officers there whom I had never seen before. I went with them into the colonel's office to talk about the subpoena. They asked me several general questions about my civilian background, and then got very specific about my civilian jobs and activities on campus. The questioning was not hostile, but I was not very comfortable with their attitude toward me. It turned out that these were JAG officers, Army lawyers who regularly dealt with senior officers who were scheduled to testify on official matters before congress. I was clearly a new wrinkle in their routine, but more importantly, I was suddenly a threat to the US Army, at least as far as its public image went.

After several hours, they told me that they were going to attempt to kill the subpoena and I was not to talk with the committee investigator under any circumstances until they got back with me. After a day or so went by, and I heard nothing. Then the investigator "found" me on campus between classes. He obviously had my class schedule. I told him that I was not to talk to him and that he should contact the Army if he wanted to talk with me. He laughed and said he did not need anybody's authority to talk with me, but I should relax, and he would get things squared away with the ROTC colonel and the Army. Sure enough, the next day I was told by the PMS that I could talk with the investigator and that the Army had not been able to kill the subpoena. He told me that I was to answer their questions but not to volunteer any information that would relate my activities outside of ROTC or to the ROTC program on campus. He then warned me to be very careful about what I said and did over the next week, as I had not yet been commissioned. I still do not think he meant that as any kind of threat, but instead he was genuinely concerned about me.

I met Mr. Sanders once again the next day at the bar in the

Tombs, under the 1789. We had a beer and he introduced me to another investigator. We talked about SDS activities on campus and around DC, about various personalities involved in the SDS, and campus anti-war activity. He never led me or put any ideas forward that I should pick up on. Instead, he seemed simply interested in what I knew and what light I could shed on what was happening on campus, around the Georgetown area, and on other nearby campuses. He only wanted to hear what I knew, not what I had heard from others. He told me that they would formally interview me first on all my on-and-off campus activities and work.

Then I would be put before the actual committee and would testify in public about what I knew of activities specifically on and around the Georgetown University campus. He was quite professional and put me at ease about what was going to occur.

The hearings of the Committee on Internal Security, United States House of Representatives, 91st Congress began on the 3rd of June 1969, five days before my graduation from college. The chairman of the committee was Richard H. Icord. There were eight other members; notable among them was Rep. Claude Pepper, Edwin Edwards, and Richardson Preyer. I did not testify on the third but was interviewed privately by several investigators of the committee. I waited all day to testify but was told at the end of the day to come back on the fourth. All my friends were enjoying their last week at Georgetown, and I was sitting in Congressional hearing rooms. Believe me, the novelty wore off quickly. The next day I waited through the morning to be called. Then in midafternoon I was finally asked to step forward to answer the committee's questions. I was sworn in, and the questions began. It seemed like hours, but the session lasted less than an hour. The questions were aimed at what I knew about the SDS and anti-ROTC activities on campus and around DC. They asked about various individuals who were leaders and major players in the anti-war movement on campus and their actual conduct. The committee members seemed particularly interested about the impact these activities had on the members of the ROTC program and the ability of the ROTC program to function amidst the virulent anti-war activities in and around the Georgetown campus.

They were very cordial toward me and expressed considerable pride in my fortitude and dedication in the face of what they believed to be a very adverse environment for an ROTC student, to say nothing of an ROTC cadet leader. I certainly felt that the conditions were adverse, but it was not terribly difficult to ignore the troublemakers and other assorted idiots who generally gravitated around the SDS. Obviously, some were sincere in their efforts to sway public sentiment on the war in Southeast Asia, but they were not the problem. I always felt that very few of the individuals who gravitated to the SDS, and related groups, had the brains or character to look clearly at what the issues were and who the real winners and losers would be in Vietnam, if and when we should pull out. The fact was that the vast majority of those who involved themselves in these activities on the college campuses in DC were in it for two very simple reasons. The first was youthful rebellion and the second was drugs. I always found it interesting that during this period, the people who complained and protested the loudest about our involvement in Vietnam to save the poor suffering North Vietnamese, were the same ones who demanded the right to cook their brains into mush with drugs.

I doubt that I had ever actually soaked a suit like that since I was in baby clothes. Sitting in front of some of the most powerful men in our country, in public view, in an imposing hearing room in the Capitol of the United States is a very intimidating experience for a twenty-year-old. As my testimony concluded, the committee members expressed their thanks and I rose to leave the room. Boy did I need a shower!

I was still sweating profusely when I walked out of the Congressional Hearing Room on Capitol Hill in Washington, DC. I never knew that the ends of your fingers could sweat, but the pools of water on the highly polished table at which I had been sitting were evidence that this was so. Why I was there in the first place was its own reflection of the time and the complex issues facing America. As I walked out of the hearing room and through the large, imposing entry doors, I was looking for a restroom sign but almost ran over an Army major who stepped directly into my path. Surprised, I tried to step around him, but he took my arm and put a sheet of paper in my hands. I looked down at it, then at him. He hesitated for a second or so and then asked if I was John Thomas Hoffman. I said I was, and he looked around me as people brushed past us. Just then a gentleman with a notepad, who I assumed to be a reporter, came up to me and called my name. Before I could answer, the major turned me away from the reporter and simply said "Lieutenant, you are to be at Ft. Benning on nine June. Those are your orders," and he walked away. I never saw him again.

Immediately three reporters pushed me in several directions at once, trying to get my attention while they fired questions at me. Suddenly I thought "Five days? Wait a minute . . . I've got a delayed entry on active duty!" I pushed away from the reporters, both because the House investigator told me that was what I was to do and because I felt confused and frustrated. I wanted some answers and some help. This whole testimony thing had been a severe strain and had completely ruined what should have been a carefree and joyous week before my college graduation from Georgetown University.

It had started out bad and got worse with each day leading up to my testimony. I wasn't even supposed to be doing any testimony for anybody on anything! I was about to graduate from college after spending four years working full time, often two jobs at a time while going to college full time, twelve months a year! My college life had been anything but carefree and easy going. It had been a demanding, work-intensive period. But it was the only way I was going to get a degree from a school Like Georgetown University and the only way I wanted it. But I did want some time off. I needed some time off and I deserved some time off. I had some money in the bank, not a lot, but enough to have some fun and I knew that once I was on active duty in the Army, any real vacation was a long way down the road and, probably, after a combat tour. Dad was, once again, in South Vietnam at that very time and not available to provide his usual very valuable counsel. Yet, I knew what he would say: "Suck it up son and do what you have to do. You can handle it." That was Dad all the way. "Do the right thing" he would say, "and you will be all right."

Dad had been traveling to and from South Vietnam, on and off since 1967. His repeated, extended travels on military duty were a strain on my mother and our family. Now Dad was in South Vietnam for a year-long tour. This was particularly tough for my mother, with five children still at home, ranging in age from three to eighteen. The demands of working my way through Georgetown University and my studies meant I could not be there for my mother to the degree she wanted, perhaps needed. So, I was always between issues at home for Mom, work, and my studies. The one piece of advice that my dad communicated to me regularly was, "Your primary job is to graduate."

As I headed back to Georgetown that afternoon, I considered the fact that I was to graduate in four days and had to be on the way to Fort Benning the day after. I would get no break before going on active duty. I had to get this changed. I wanted and felt like I deserved a free summer after four straight years as a student with two jobs. When I got back to school the next day, I went up to the campus ROTC office in Old North to see what could be done. I was devastated when I found out that I could do nothing. I was being sent to Fort Benning, Georgia as soon as possible and I was to talk to no one from the press and to stay out of sight.

There was only one thing to do: find my friend and classmate, Hank Pramov, down at the '89, and see how much party time we could get in during what remained of my abbreviated graduation week. The next three days are still a blur to me. A lot happened so fast that, like most college graduating seniors, the parties, ceremonies, and celebrations went by too quickly to distinguish one from the other. This was true for all but two events. These have stuck with me over the years with incredible clarity.

The first was my commissioning ceremony. This took place on the steps of the Healy building at the front of the campus. It struck me as I stood there in the June heat, that many of my Georgetown predecessors must have stood or been seated in the same spot as they were about to be inducted in the Army of the United States and sent off to war. This was true for the War of 1812, the Civil War, the Spanish American War, both World Wars, Korea, and now Vietnam. Established by an Act of Congress in 1789 for the express purpose of educating young men for military and government service, Georgetown, despite being a private university, has sent her graduates to defend this country for as long as we have been a country. Indeed, this military tradition was the source of many great officers and leaders in the US military.

And yet, as I gazed back at the anti-war protestors, who by now were de rigueur for any military function on campus, I wondered how many of those who had gone before me did so under such burdensome adversity and antagonism. My mother was there along with my girlfriend, Karen Schultze, to offer support and congratulations. My dad was still in South Vietnam. As I stood there and raised my hand to swear my allegiance to the Constitution of the United States of America, I knew that as surely as the tomorrow would come, I was going to find out if I had what it took to meet the obligations I was so easily swearing to and which I had touted as so honorable to all who would listen, even in the halls of Congress.

But as those sons of Georgetown before me had done, I knew that if I was ordered to fight in Vietnam, I would go. I only hoped I could measure up to the task and do so with honor. Maybe this was a rather corny, passé attitude for a college student of the 1960s, but the impact of my father, my family, and, yes, my education was stronger than the effect of the demonstrators and their compatriots out in the streets of Washington. I only wish that my dad had been there to pin on my gold bars. My mother did an admirable job, and I very much appreciated it, but it was not quite the same. The fact that at that time Dad was serving his second tour of duty in the Republic of Vietnam was somehow even more poignant for me.

My graduating on time had only just been assured when final grades and course credits were posted. Father Davis, who was by now the dean of the college, had considerable faith in me. Without that faith I never would have made it past that first semester of freshman year. Because of the decision of that academic review board, I had been on academic probation all four years! Graduating on time in only four years was quite a feat while on probation and had never been successfully accomplished by any student of Georgetown. Father Davis informed me, about three days before graduation that I would indeed graduate on time. I had told him not to worry, those Jesuits had taught me math well, so I knew my numbers.

But more importantly, all my Georgetown professors and instructors had made a major impression on my life and my values. My perseverance, my sense of duty, and my broadened view of the world and our place in it were due to their influence. And so, on graduation day I took my place in the long line of graduates and roasted under the hot DC sun while several speeches were made and charges about our duties to the future were expounded upon. Then someone called my name, and I went forward, in shock, and collected a blank piece of paper, which symbolized the real sheepskin artwork, a long Georgetown University tradition, which I would be sent later. I stood there and realized that it was time to go. It was time to transition my lifestyle and that the stakes had just gone up considerably. It was not that I now had to go to work, hell, I had been working my ass off for four solid years. It was not that I might have to risk my life for someone else, I'd been doing that for four years also. No, now it was about standing up for something, now it was being counted and counted on. Now it was about being sent into harm's way, trying to survive, and still make a difference.

The next day I had to pack to leave for Ft. Benning. I had twenty-four hours to get there. I had to clear my stuff out of our apartment and get in all the goodbyes I could.

CHAPTER TWO
RANGER SCHOOL

I GRADUATED FROM Georgetown University in early June 1969 having worked full time as a Fairfax County fireman for three years, working part time at a famous Georgetown restaurant and college watering hole, the 1789 and, during my senior year, doing part time work for the Metropolitan Police Department in Washington, DC. Working full time was the only way I could afford such an expensive education. It meant that I had little time for sports, extracurricular activities, or for the many social activities that most enjoy while in college. But I still managed to graduate in four years, and I obtained my pilot's license on the Army's nickel. This was because I also participated in ROTC program at Georgetown University and graduated with a regular Army commission and had agreed to become an Army aviator. I was given forty-eight hours after graduation to report to active duty. My family and my girlfriend and future wife, Karen Schultze, were not happy. Nor was I.

I arrived at Ft. Benning two days after graduation and checked in at the office marked *New Arrivals* just inside the main gate to the post. There, an overweight and very irritated NCO told me to report to 3rd Ranger Company to start Ranger school. While now it is more common to do this, back in 1969 you were not qualified for Ranger training unless you had completed Infantry Officer's Basic

Course (basic Army training for newly commissioned officers) and Airborne training. I had been told that they had specific orders about this for me and to get there ASAP. I drove out to the Ranger camp and checked in with a very large and very fit, highly decorated master sergeant. I gave him my orders and asked him to whom I should report. He laughed, looked me up and down, and said "obviously there was a mistake." He told me to have a seat and he left the office. A few moments later a captain came in and I stood up and saluted him (my first salute on active duty!). He asked me, not very politely, what the hell I was doing there. I related my instructions once again to him. He said, "That's bullshit. Someone just fucked up, that's all." He left me standing there as he left the room again. My first impressions of the "real" army were somewhat confused. They didn't seem to know who was supposed to be where, they were all in a bad mood, and they had worse language than I did. I stood there looking out the window of the converted World War II wooden barracks building and thought that at least this was a pleasant, if old, barracks area, like you might see in a John Wayne war movie.

About five minutes later the captain returned and looked me over rather pointedly. He asked, "How long have you been in the Army?" I looked at my watch and then replied, "Well sir, about twenty-four hours." He shook his head from side to side. He next question was "Lieutenant, how old are you?" I told him "twenty-one, sir." Then he said, "Boy, you sure must have pissed someone off really bad! You are to stay here and start Ranger training with the next class and if you fuck it up, you are to stay here and start it over until you graduate. And by the way you are not to leave the post." He told me to start running five miles a day. He then told me I had no duties other than to prepare to start the next class in two weeks. What I did not know until much later was that "someone" had felt that I needed to be out of circulation for several months, most certainly because of my testimony before Congress. Ranger school is absolutely the best place to completely hide someone while they undergo training. The nine weeks of Ranger training are complete isolation for the Ranger student. You are totally cut off from the outside world, except for mail about three times during the entire period.

What I did know about Ranger school was that I was completely unprepared for such intense, high-level tactical training. It wasn't the physical aspect that worried me, I was in reasonably good shape; it was my lack of basic small-unit tactical knowledge and personal military skills. In the late 1960s, Ranger school was intended for those who had already completed their initial entry training at an officer basic school and who had some level of experience in the Army. That first level of post-commissioning, initial entry military schooling is supposed to provide basic, branch specific individual qualification training such as infantry, artillery, or engineer. For enlisted personnel, the rank of sergeant (E-5) was the minimum qualification, meaning that they generally had at least two years of in-service experience. I had been in the Army for less than two days! I had only rudimentary skills at being a field infantry officer. It wasn't that ROTC didn't give me some good officer-to-be training; it just wasn't field-craft oriented. Ranger school was intended as very advanced leadership, small unit patrol operations, insurgent and counterinsurgent, and small-unit, high-intensity operations training[3]. It was assumed that you had a reasonable base of experience prior to beginning this training. Finally, Ranger training was most often the last stop for infantry branch company grade officers and NCOs prior to departure for Vietnam.

I knew from the introductory Ranger training I had received during ROTC what the training would be like. It was going to be rough! I had almost no time to prepare. The level of my military skills incompetence was clear when you consider that during ROTC we had trained with the M-1 Garand rifle from WW-II. In Ranger school the issue rifle was the M-16 Colt assault rifle. I had never even held one in my hands. It functioned very differently and was constructed very differently from an M-1. Hell, I didn't even know how to close the bolt on an M-16. In fact, I didn't even know if it had one!

Each day before the class started, I reported into the 3rd Ranger Company headquarters to see if there had been a change in my orders. Each day I found that I had been given no reprieve. About three days before the class was to begin, an NCO in the orderly room gave me a piece of advice which proved to be very useful to my survival of Ranger school. He told me that during the first three weeks, when most students fail and are dropped from the school, I should just "turn my brain off and follow my Ranger Buddy." He told me to just do what I was told, question nothing, and don't expect explanations or reasons for anything I was told to "just do it." I wonder if he later went into advertising.

I very much wanted to talk with my dad about what was happening to me. But he was in Vietnam, in those days another place where you are often incommunicado, as it were, because in this time before the Internet, cell phones and instant communications, there was no commonly accessible phone service between the United States and South Vietnam. He was out of reach. I was on my own and about to mature into an Army officer very fast. I ran and ran and ran. I did everything I could think of to get ready for the next two and half months of hard, intense training. One of the Ranger school NCOs told me to eat as much as I could in the week before the school started, as lack of food was a major part of the hardening training during the course. I did very much enjoy that part of the wait to start Ranger school.

The morning of the first day of the course arrived all too quickly. I, and more than three hundred other prospective Rangers, officially reported in to Third Ranger Company and processed into the program. There was paperwork to be completed, equipment to be issued, and an orientation on the course we had to listen to. We were formed into platoons and each member of the class was assigned a Ranger buddy. We were told to remove all rank insignia from our uniforms. For the remainder of the course, we were just

"Rangers"! As a brand-new second lieutenant that did not mean much to me, but for some of the senior NCOs and captains in the course, this was a blow. We were all to be equal as students in the course, with no one having any advantage over anyone else as we started out. It gave everyone an equal chance to develop as a leader and to surface any latent leadership or initiative skills, which might otherwise not be demonstrated. For some reason it made perfect sense to me, but I was in a distinct minority.

On the first day, we were herded into bleachers for a final briefing before the actual training began. The chief of the Ranger Department at Fort Benning spoke to us about the challenges that lay ahead and how he hoped that each of us got as much as we possibly could from the course. He told us that this one course would not only keep us alive in Vietnam but would enable us to save the lives of our soldiers and ensure that we could get our assigned missions completed. Then he told each of us to look at the Ranger student on each side of us. We did while he paused. Then he very slowly stated that those on each side of us were probably not going to finish the course. Indeed, he said, many would wash out from lack of ability, lack of stamina, or lack of personal drive. Many, he said, would be injured, cut from the program, or possibly even killed. Most just chuckled as if this were the usual Army dribble about how tough this or any other course is supposed to be. Frankly, he scared the crap out of me. Major Malone at Georgetown University had told me on many occasions just how tough this course was and how few graduated from the course with the award of the coveted Ranger Tab, an insignia one would wear on his uniform for the remainder of his Army career. He had told me about the injuries and deaths during the course and that no one who ever attended this school was ever quite the same afterward. His opinion was that the only thing tougher he had ever done was to have survived combat in Vietnam. You can bet I was scared!

On that first day of the Ranger course, we were issued our field gear, called TA-50, bunk assignments in the barracks (didn't get to use that bunk very damn much), and our Ranger hats. These hats were similar to the old, brimmed Army field hat of the 1950s (like Castro always wore) but without the stiff sides. They were soft, floppy hats with two pieces of plastic tape that glowed in the dark, sewn on the back. These *Ranger eyes* enable the person behind you to see you when patrolling in total darkness in the field. These hats were a symbol of the Ranger student. It meant that you were in what is probably the toughest, most demanding training course the Army has.

We then lined up at the arms room to draw our weapons. I saw those ahead being issued M-16 rifles. I had never had any training on this rifle. What I knew about it was from news accounts and stories around ROTC about how unreliable it was. I did not want to be embarrassed in front of all these more experienced soldiers. When I got to the door of the arms room, I saw that there were also M-14 E2 automatic rifles being issued. I asked for one of those and immediately volunteered to be the *automatic rifleman* in my squad. Everyone looked at me like I was crazy. The M-14 was an older rifle. It was bigger and weighed twice as much as an M-16 and took considerably more TLC to maintain. But it worked basically like an M-1 Garand and I both understood it and knew how to shoot it. Many of the other students had never actually used this heavier caliber assault rifle.

This was both a triumph and a reprieve for me personally. Sure, it was heavy and older, but at least I could do something with confidence. However, I had broken a cardinal rule—I had volunteered for something. Volunteering, I was told by several other students, was not a good idea. It was a way to catch a lot of trouble and extra work. This was an old "saw" of the Army I had heard all through ROTC. My own brief experience did not agree with this adage. Ranger School was to prove to be a true experiment for me on how to both survive and use the system to one's advantage. The trick, I found out, was to know for what and when to volunteer.

I was more than just a little awed with my fellow students. I was unique indeed as a novice soldier in this group. There were numerous recent West Point graduates, many senior NCOs, many company grade officers (lieutenants and captains) from most of the combat arms branches of the Army, and even some majors, one of whom was a medical doctor. Not only was he a doctor, he was a qualified Special Forces officer! Even more impressive to me was the fact that almost half of the other students had completed at least one tour of duty in Vietnam before reporting into this class. We even had several Navy SEALs in the class. Navy SEAL training is reputed to be the absolute toughest training in the entire US military. I was hardly qualified to be a Ranger buddy to any of these guys.

We were awakened the second morning of Ranger school at 0400. We had only gone to bed, after numerous classes, meetings, and formations, at midnight. We were shoved out of the barracks into formation for roll call and physical training or PT. I was miserable, tired, and about half lost as I followed my new Ranger buddy, an engineer captain with two tours of duty in Vietnam, down a sandy road on our first PT run of Ranger school. As I fumbled through my thoughts on how to stay up with everyone else, I remembered what the Ranger sergeant had said to me: "Just turn your brain off and do it." I did that, right then and there!

The next few days were a fog of exhaustion and pain. The first three weeks of Ranger school, conducted at Camps Rogers and Darby, are a period of physical hardening and basic soldier- and leader-skills development. There was little food, even less sleep, and constant pressure to both master skills and to keep going under mounting resistance by your body and your mind. But the instructors were constant in their forcing each of us to drive on, to push us to our limits and beyond. They also focused on team building during each training task. During this course of training the average Ranger student will get somewhere around two thousand calories per day—if he is lucky. Losing weight and constant minor injuries plague every student throughout the course. I dropped from 205 pounds on my six-foot, one inch frame to 161 pounds by the end of the course.

During this phase of the training, referred to as the *Darby Phase*, students will be mentally and physically stressed and stretched while undergoing all manner of physical and technical training. We were introduced to such pleasant experiences as the *Darby Queen*, perhaps the most difficult and complex obstacle course in the entire United States Army. We swam, we ran, we conducted long forced marches on roads and through the woods, we underwent weapons and demolition training, and we learned advanced hand-to-hand combat. All of this was under the constant watchful eyes and guidance of our lane graders or Ranger instructors, referred to as *RIs*. These RIs graded each student every day on their individual progress and performance.

This team building, developing self-confidence and a willingness, even a drive, to overcome your own shortcomings through teamwork and to overcome the odds with cunning, skill, and daring while always striving to succeed, are critical objectives for this phase of the training. It starts with the two-man team, the Ranger buddies. It then builds on the squad as a team and then the platoon. All training seemed intended to push you to your limits. This training presents you with nearly impossible goals and forces you to face your internal fears and overcome them.

Ranger school is not an environment where the individual can excel in a vacuum. All the tasks to be trained, all of the missions to be accomplished, and even your survival depend upon a team working together. A soldier alone in the woods is just a soldier alone in the woods. While a soldier can shoot, move, and hide, he only wins wars alone in the movies. A Ranger team in the woods, whether a squad or platoon, is both lethal and capable. It can protect itself, accomplish its mission and, usually, survive. This code of self-reliance and this tradition of being driven to always succeed have placed Rangers at the forefront of every modern war in US history.

This is so ubiquitous as a role for Rangers in the US Army that it has led to a motto known by nearly every soldier: *Rangers lead the way!* You will find the letters *RLTW* are common in documents, letters, and memos across the Army.

While the school's orientation is only on small unit operations, its impact is felt throughout the Army, in every size unit. The leadership skills, the organizational talents, the resource management abilities, and most importantly, the decision-making skills that are developed in this school produce what are arguably the best company- and field-grade leaders in any army, in any country. This is, indeed, some of the toughest training in the US military. In my class we had many, many experienced soldiers, sailors, and marines. In addition to the special forces officers and NCOs and several Navy SEALs, there was also a US Air Force commando with a tour in RVN running pilot rescue operations already under his belt. These soldiers were truly tough as nails, while I, at the beginning at least, was just Private "Snuffy," with little to contribute to my squad and platoon.

The skills training we received during the *Benning Phase*, as the first three weeks are also sometimes called, was extensive and thorough. It is designed to give each student a broad base of technical and leadership skills. It is also intended to bring out the unique talents in each Ranger student. Some excel as marksmen, some as medics, some as navigators, some as demolitions experts, and others as uniquely qualified small-unit leaders. This talent identification and development is a key part of learning how to form and build a Ranger team. In time, I found that I excelled in four areas.

First, I was already a good marksman, thanks to my father. I learned I could hit the target with just about any firearm I was handed. Second, my experience as a fireman and paramedic suited me well in combat lifesaver training, rappelling and climbing (skills I learned in fire rookie school and used often on the job in Fairfax County). As a result of my background, I quickly became the platoon medic. Third, I could navigate. For some reason I had a well-developed sense of direction, location, and map reading—no doubt, again, thanks to Dad. Finally, I not only did well as a patrol leader, but I also preferred to be the leader. Most of the students hated it when they were called upon to assume the rotating role as patrol leader. They did not want to be responsible for the success or failure of the patrol; rather, they preferred to follow and let some other guy screw up, get lost, or be responsible for any shortcomings on the assigned patrol. I disagreed, along with a few others. I did not see this training as a career maker or breaker. My motivation was quite different, as I had no previous military experience to shape my attitude on risk taking. I knew that I could get the leader jobs done faster and with less effort than most in my squad and platoon. The one thing that I hated about being on these training patrols was marching aimlessly along tough terrain following a lost student patrol leader! I sought out the opportunities to plan and lead the patrols. I quickly became the patrol planner for my squad and then for my platoon.

As a fireman back at Station 18, Captain Charlie Waters had drilled into the rookies that you learned by doing. Further, he taught us that each fireman had to learn to assume team leadership at any time. He always said that you never know in what circumstances you might find yourself having to take responsibility for everyone on your team. Firefighter training and thousands of emergency response calls had taught me self-confidence and initiative—two skills that served me well in Ranger training and later in combat.

One of the most challenging parts of this portion of Ranger training is land navigation. The school invests an enormous amount of time, energy, and resources into land navigation training. While the reasons may seem obvious, the importance of knowing where you are, that is, where *exactly* you are on the ground anywhere in the world, is a matter of life and death. Not only must a small-unit leader be able to get where he is going, he must be able to get to a specific location on time and with his resources intact. Further, he must always know precisely where he and his unit are at all times.

This was all long before GPS was available to even the military. If the leader needs artillery fires to defend his unit, or if he needs air support against any threatening enemy force, he better know where he is and where the enemy is. The alternative is casualties caused by what we often called fratricide, or friendly fire. And, if a soldier needs to be medevac'd, you must know exactly where you are because the helicopter pilot does not.

Land navigation training is tough to master, even for those with a good sense of direction. Ranger school starts this training with a daylight compass course through the woods of Ft. Benning. On these courses, one navigates by using a compass and a map over a set course of routes. These routes all begin and end with a numbered post in the ground in a large, forested area. A student starts at his assigned starting post. From there you must walk a set distance in a precise direction to find the next post. When you do find the next post, you navigate from there, over a set distance and direction, to the next post, and so on, until the end of the course. If you miss a post, you can get very lost. If you hit a wrong post, you will likely end up at the wrong ending post, if you even find one, and you fail that course. That can mean doing it over again, or being "washed out" of the course, if it happens too often.

These daylight compass courses progressed to more and more difficult terrain and then into night compass course missions over long distances and swampy terrain. They varied in length from two to fifteen kilometers. On these land navigation courses you initially worked as a two-man team with your Ranger buddy. As you're patrolling and field skills were built, the cross-country navigation exercises became a component of every squad- and platoon-sized training event. One Ranger kept a pace count while another used the compass to guide the team in the correct direction, or at least he tried to do so. Finding yourself on a map, in the middle of the night, in the pouring rain, using a red-lensed flashlight, under a poncho to hide the light while you study the map is a true test of your skills, determination, self-confidence, and your ability to cooperate with your team. Consensus was sometimes an ingredient to the decision process but most often it was a patrol leader decision. These courses were physically demanding, psychologically tough, and great confidence builders, for those who mastered them. Never again will you feel lost and alone in a strange place, as long as you had a map and a compass. I did well on these compass courses and enjoyed being out in the woods and away from the constant harassment and push-ups around the base camps.

Yes, we did lots of pushups. Rangers do not walk anywhere. Rangers do not talk except when required. Rangers run and Rangers do pushups, unless they are on patrol, in a class, in the mess hall, or in the sack. The instructors required no cause to make you do pushups. They made you do them when they felt bored, when they thought *you* were bored, or when they thought someone else might think you were bored. But if they did find a cause for you to do pushups, such as a sense that you might be losing motivation, or that you did not follow their instructions very precisely, or worse yet, if you disobeyed an instruction, you were about to become very sore. Fifty pushups at a time were the norm. That's not a particularly difficult, albeit uncomfortable, number. But when it was seventy-five or one hundred at a time, it got really old. The command "Drop and give me fifty!" was as routine as the heat and humidity of southern Georgia in the summertime. Usually, if one Ranger student was given pushups to do, every member of his squad or platoon present at that time was expected to do the same pushups. While this, too, contributed to a sense of team, a dud or constant screw-up would quickly earn the wrath of the rest of the platoon.

The demands of the daily training in hundreds of subjects, the physical toughening, and the constant evaluations of every aspect of your performance quickly began to take its toll on the class. Before the first week was out, we had lost several students. Some just quit, others were washed out by instructors as not acceptable, and some were injured. The instructors always reminded us that we could quit at any time with no repercussions to our military career, as this was a strictly voluntary program. All one had to do, they told us, was take off your Ranger hat and give it to an instructor and you would be out of the school before the day was over. The events that had led to me being there in the first place belied the notion that one could just quit that easily. And for the officers, if you did just quit, the likelihood of rank above major in an Army career was low.

You can get kicked out for being stupid, endangering yourself or others, or for flunking too many patrols. Often, Ranger students will be recycled through the program if the instructors feel a student has the aptitude but needs more training to advance in the school. No one is kicked out of Ranger school for pain. You could be washed out of the program, break something, or be unconscious and carried off . . . or you quit. I was not going to quit because I knew that I would simply be put back into the school and told to start over. No chance I wanted to go through all of this again! So, no matter how hard, how painful, or how tired and hungry I was, I was staying with the program to the end, period. If I graduated, they could not send me back through, or so I hoped at the time, anyway.

During the second week of Ranger school the physical demands, much to my disbelief, got tougher. We ran longer and more often. We ran the obstacle course over and over. We trained in hand-to-hand combat until we literally dropped from exhaustion. We averaged about four and half hours of sleep each night. The food was plentiful during the Ft. Benning phase when you were given the opportunity to eat in the Ranger mess hall, but we never had time to eat much of it. Often one had less than three minutes to eat an entire meal in the mess hall. The C rations, or combat rations, proved to be the only opportunity one had to eat a full meal, such as it was. At least in the field during tactical training you could eat the whole meal over a longer period of time as you walked or waited to move out on patrol or whenever the opportunity presented itself for you to stuff some food in your mouth. The problem was that you often only received one C ration meal per day while in the field.

Mess hall food was good—when you could get it. The C rations were edible. The C ration, a combat ration developed at the end of WWII and used extensively as the basic field ration for the US military until the mid-1980s, was a canned food ration in a small cardboard box. It was composed of several small cans, one containing a "main" course. These varied by box from cans of spaghetti with meat balls to chili to beef slices to ham and eggs. You never knew what menu you would get until you were given your small box of rations. There was also a small can of crackers with an even smaller can of peanut butter or jam at the bottom or, in some cases, a crumpled-up packet of instant drink of some kind. If it was cocoa, it was great for making hot chocolate . . . if you had hot water. If it was a fruit drink, it was terrible. This instant fruit drink powder was intended for use in water purified with Army issue water purification tablets to make it drinkable. They missed the mark on that one. Sometimes, you won the lottery and instead of crackers you got a small tin of bread or pound cake (loved that). As the can might have been made in 1950, it was amazing that these relatively tasteless wonders of the Army bakery system were even edible! Then there would be another small can of pears or peaches or, most desired, applesauce. Lastly there was the all-important accessory pack. The little cellophane package contained those comfort items that made daily life possible: toilet paper, chewing gum, instant coffee, sugar, a small portion of some kind of candy (like a small Tootsie Roll or Life Savers), waterproof matches (well almost waterproof—missed on that one as well) and a small green pack of five Lucky Strike cigarettes (usually unfiltered and useless to me except as trading material for someone's pound cake or apple sauce!) Seriously, I always asked myself, what are they trying to do, give us all lung cancer? They did make good fire starter, if you did have the opportunity to build a fire to heat water for your cocoa mix . . . of course that never happened in Ranger school! C rations plagued me as a frequently supplied meal by the Army for years to come!

Everything else was strictly off limits. No candy or junk food was allowed, period. This rule was so strict that, throughout the entire school, the instructors would suddenly stop the training or the patrol, declare an administrative halt, and make each ranger empty his pockets and dump his rucksack as the instructors searched for *pogey bait*, as junk food was called. This usually happened at the beginning of a training event, but not always! Anything found was confiscated on the spot, and we were told that a large black mark was put in a ledger somewhere to record the incident. I ate nothing but allowed food for the first three weeks until the first of our eight-hours leave periods between the Darby phase and the Camp Merrill mountain training phase. When I did eat that first chocolate candy bar after three weeks of little food, I found out what the "Ho Chi Minh Two Step" really was!

During the second and third weeks of Ranger training, the emphasis was on small-unit tactical operations and the preparation of and execution of a five-paragraph field operational order. One of the tenants of Ranger training is that every leader must be able to assess a situation, prepare a workable plan, issue that plan as an order to his unit, and then execute that plan—all in a minimum amount of time. Those who mastered this skill succeeded. Those who did not failed and left the school or were recycled to start the training all over again from the beginning.

As with most such tactical field operations activities, the Army has a standard form or plan for such processes. This is the five-paragraph field order. It is designed so that each aspect of the normally required tasks to be accomplished in preparing, issuing, and executing a plan are covered. Again, as with most fundamental Army technical procedures, but surely not all, it makes absolute sense. The five-paragraph field order covers the who, what, where, and how of most small-unit military operations.

1. **Situation:** (what is going on out there right now?)

    A. **Enemy** (who and where are the bad guys)

    B. **Friendly** (who and where are the good guys)

2. **Mission** (what are we supposed to actually do)

3. **Execution:** (How do we do it?)

    A. **Concept of the Operation** (What is the basic idea of the plan)

    B. **Tasks to each subordinate** element (what each element is to do)

    C. **Coordinating Instructions** (how do we avoid killing each other)

4. **Service and Supply** (logistics for the mission: who provides the beans and bullets)

5. **Command and Signal** (who is in charge)

    (Where will he be?)

    (How do we talk to each other)

    (What radio frequencies do we use?)

    (What signals will we use?)

    (What do we do if it all turns to crap?)

This is the format for all patrol operations orders that we used for all our planning and briefing of the other Ranger students when we served in leadership roles during our training. This the same basic format for US Army operations orders used up through Division level for decades.

Everything we did from the second week on we did using the five-paragraph field order or "the plan" as we began to call it. Every assigned task or mission was to be analyzed, and an order prepared, issued, and executed.

Another basic principle of Ranger training was to give each student the maximum opportunity to screw up. As we were often reminded, we learned best from our mistakes. The school wanted each of us to develop our full potential as leaders. This means that each of us had to be given frequent opportunities to be in leadership positions. Being a student patrol leader gave us opportunities to exercise leadership skills under pressure, whether squad or platoon sized, and this duty was constantly changed or rotated from one student to another in no discernible order and with no logical timing. The result was that we all had many such opportunities, often on very short notice, to plan, brief, and lead the patrol on a mission. Hence, we were each frequently evaluated as a leader in every aspect of small-unit leadership and management. But this did not mean that when someone else was in the "bucket" you could just cruise. A given student might plan a mission and prepare an order, and he might even get to brief that order, but more than likely he would then be declared a casualty and another student was suddenly appointed as the new patrol leader. He, then, had to carry out the order and lead the patrol on the mission. He might complete the mission, or he might, in turn, be declared a casualty and a new leader assigned. This meant that each of us had to pay full attention to the complete planning and orders preparation process. Each of us had to know and understand the current plan.

As the days went by, the time allowed for planning a mission and the complexity of the assigned tasks changed in inverse proportion to each other. We had to quickly size up a task, our status, and our capabilities and then prepare and issue an order. No allowance was given for shortcuts or missing a required task in the process. We were pushed to do it better and better and faster and faster. By the end of the third week, I knew how to prepare and issue a five-paragraph field order in my sleep. I had learned more in those three weeks than I had learned in four years of ROTC and six weeks of ROTC summer training at Indian Town Gap, Pennsylvania. I now felt some degree of self-confidence in this new environment and knew I had mastered what had seemed to be unattainable skills.

What amazed me even more, after three weeks, was how many combat veterans had dropped out of this training. My engineer Ranger buddy suddenly just quit during the third week, and this left me for several days with no Ranger buddy. A new one was assigned for the mountain phase. He was gone so quickly that I do not remember much about him. What bothered me at this point, after just three weeks of training in the "real Army," was the apparent failure of so many experienced officers and NCOs. Surely combat in Vietnam is tougher than this. How could all these experienced officers, in particular, just not be able to do this? I was certainly no athlete, I was not an experienced soldier, and I had virtually no tactical skills prior to the start of this training.

I began to realize that there were two reasons for these guys not making the "grade" as it was called. First, attitude was everything. You had to be able to see the big picture and be oriented on the mission. Everything else was irrelevant. As the sergeant had said, "Just do it!" Too many of the officers and NCOs were not used to this type of intense training and the way we were treated by the instructors. And the resultant psychological and physiological pressures were simply too much for some. Second, I realized that these guys were, indeed, not very well trained before coming to Ranger school. The majority of those who dropped out were officers and NCOs with a considerable amount of prior service. But the poor skills and performance spoke volumes about their past training and experiences. Most of the officers had only attended their officer basic branch school. Then they had served in a unit or overseas. They probably never had intense small-unit tactical training. They had become comfortable with their stations in life and their specific assigned duties, which they probably did very well. They had never had to handle such pressure to perform and never had to master field tactical and leadership skills to such a degree. And, I realized, that just because they had a tour in South Vietnam before attending this course, it may well have been a rear echelon, non-combat, and low pressure, low risk duty assignment.

The majority of those still in the class were new lieutenants, just out of officer basic schools, experienced combat arms NCOs, the Navy SEALs, and the Army Special Forces guys (thus far, this training was a cakewalk for them), and three recent West Point graduates. Like me they had not been to their officer basic course yet. While it was rare for West Pointers to attend Ranger School first, in those days, a new ROTC type *never* attended Ranger school first. He was not considered qualified or experienced enough to successfully complete Ranger training and the training was very expensive to conduct. Today that has changed, and I think that providing this training immediately to new combat-arms-branch commissioned officers is an excellent idea. It avoids many of the problems that I later saw and the resulting waste of precious resources and often lives.

At the end of the Ft. Benning phase, we were given an eight-hour pass to wash clothes, repair uniforms, call loved ones, eat a full meal, and get some sleep. It takes more than eight hours to really do that, but we tried. I had dreamed of another candy bar during those long days of little chow. I bought one in the PX and sat down after lunch to eat it. It was not with me very long. Unlike my classmates, I was told I was still restricted to the immediate area around the Ranger school, so I slept for a good four hours. What a luxury!

Our passes ended at 1800 hours on a Sunday evening and we stood in platoon formations while information was briefed on our next phase of training at Camp Merrill in the north Georgia Mountains. It was also announced that a captain in the class had been seen wearing his rank on his uniform during the eight-hour pass period. This was a violation of the school rules that were well known by each of us. He was called out of the formation. We never saw him again.

Late on that Sunday evening we were issued additional field gear and given additional briefings on our movement north. We were told that the mountain phase would be the most physically difficult phase of our Ranger training. We were going to be transported to Camp Merrill by *deuce and a half* trucks (a two-and-a-half-ton military truck). The trip would be about six hours and we would leave the next morning. We packed our gear and hit the sack. Early the next morning we loaded the trucks and our convoy got under way. The class now had fewer than 250 students. We had begun with 360.

The trip up to the mountain Ranger training facility, near the town of Dahlonega in the north Georgia end of the Appalachian Mountains, was very pleasant. I rolled out my sleeping bag on the floor of the truck and went to sleep. I had learned that there are three things you must always do whenever the chance presents itself. First, you sleep whenever you have the opportunity. Second, you eat whenever you have the time and the food. And third, you relieve yourself whenever the opportunity exists. I slept almost the whole way to the mountains.

When we arrived at what is now known as Camp Frank D. Merrill[4] for the mountain phase of our Ranger training, the weather was clear and warm. The beauty of the camp was astonishing. It sat on 290 acres of Georgia mountains and is home to the 5th Ranger Training Battalion. It was very near to the Southern end of the Appalachian Trail and close to the small town of Dahlonega, Georgia. Here was a mountain retreat with several nice log-cabin style buildings, beautifully kept grounds, and a very relaxed air about the place. Well, my first impressions were pretty accurate— except for the last one. We were greeted by a swarthy looking full colonel who spoke with a strong Eastern European accent. He welcomed us and then gave us the same speech we had heard at Fort Benning about the Darby Phase: this was the toughest part of our Ranger training, and many would not complete this phase of the school. He introduced us to the staff and outlined the extensive mountaineering training and the continued tactical operations training that lay ahead. He sure seemed to know his stuff! Here I learned another quote from history that had been adopted by Rangers, this one from Heraclitus:

Out of every one hundred men, ten shouldn't even be there, eighty are just targets, and nine are the real fighters—and we are lucky to have them, for they make the battle. Ah, but the one; one is a warrior, and he will bring the others back.

This was the reason for Ranger training of officers and NCOs across the Army. The objective was to try and put a qualified Ranger in every company and platoon-level combat unit who is the real *warrior* who can lead and train the others with greater skill and ability than most in the unit.

I had long since forgotten to worry about the physical pain of this training. I wanted to learn. I wanted these skills and I wanted to master them. I did not want to go into combat poorly trained, as I now suspected many were doing in Vietnam. There is an old saying about this phase of Ranger training that I still recall. It says that the mountain phase of Ranger training puts the fine edge on the rough knife that was forged during the Darby phase. I know that I left the mountain phase with a high degree of self-confidence, my body hardened and my field craft highly refined.

After our welcome, we moved into our "new" barracks at Camp Merrill. They were much smaller (they called them "Hutments") but, to me, much nicer than those at Ft. Benning Ranger Camp. Our first instructor, however, told us not to get comfortable. He said we would not be here much. He was right.

Training classes on mountaineering skills began that afternoon and ran late into the night. The food was better, and we had more time to eat it . . . at least at the base camp. There was even a small PX, but we were not allowed in there yet. The new jargon of mountain training and the astonishing array of new equipment were very intimidating at first. I fell asleep that night wondering if I could absorb all of this in just three weeks. The next morning, we continued training on equipment, ropes, knots, the hardware of mountain climbing, and on mountain lore. We learned about the terrain, the creeks and rivers, the slopes and cliffs, and the vegetation. The training always presented each new skill in the context of a tactical or operational application. We also learned that the training area used for the Mountain Phase extended far into civilian-owned land and the nearby National Forest lands. We were obliged to leave no trace of our presence as we conducted field training operations.

Once again, we trained on land navigation. Now we had to think three dimensionally. Not only is there north and south, east and west, but there is also up and down. What appears flat on a map, even with contour lines, is far different when standing on the steep side of a mountain. Just walking across the slope or face of a mountain is a challenge when you are carrying sixty-plus pounds of equipment. Navigation, maintaining a correct azimuth or direction, and keeping a correct pace count to measure distance is very hard to do accurately. It takes lots of practice. And we got lots of practice.

After the first few days of skills training, safety briefings, and classroom lectures, we began, once again, the small unit tactical patrolling. Now, however, instead of the limited terrain, many roads, and restricted-maneuver corridors of Ft. Benning, we had whole mountains on which to get lost. Instead of the occasional opposing enemy force or OPFOR (other soldiers operating as a simulated enemy force) we encountered at Ft. Benning, here there was always an OPFOR force out there looking for us. It was normally bigger, better trained, had vehicles, and knew the country well. To get where you wanted to go, to get there on time, and to prevail in each engagement was progressively more difficult with each new mission or patrol we were sent out to accomplish. The rotation of leadership positions continued, the searches for pogey bait continued, the pressure to perform and succeed increased. The danger level of what we were doing had also gone up considerably.

Our first serious injury occurred on the first mountain patrol. A Ranger fell on the steep terrain and broke a leg. He was out of the program. Any injury that took you out of the current training for more than one day required the student to be dropped from the class. If the injury was such that complete recovery could be achieved within a few weeks, the student could be recycled to the next class. If it was serious, he was normally just dropped from the school. If you had only a minor injury, you were expected to get medical aid and then *drive on*. Sprains and twists were examined, wrapped, and the student given Darvon as a painkiller. The phase "drive on with Darvon" became the customary answer to minor injuries.

Unknown to us was how closely we were being monitored for health, fitness, stamina, and performance. On every patrol or training event, a Ranger instructor or RI was sent with each squad or platoon-sized element. Some of the cadre were referred to as lane instructors or LIs. They were training-task-specific instructors, usually a senior Ranger NCO. For longer duration missions, such as longer than eighteen hours, there were two sent with each element, one RI and one LI. These instructors carefully noted the performance and condition of each student. Upon their return to the base camp, after being relieved by a new set of instructors, they prepared detailed reports on each student. On several occasions, medics showed up and examined one or more of us for any problems or complaints. If a medic decided you were not fit to continue, he could jerk you off the patrol. Generally, however, it was up to you to decide whether to continue or not. Some quit, some did not, and some should have.

Patrolling, or moving tactically in a small unit, across mountainous terrain is difficult, physically demanding work. Navigating across unfamiliar, undulating, and steep, rocky terrain, where the map only shows the most significant changes in terrain elevation is extremely challenging. Add to that thick woods, deep ravines, frequent uncharted streams and the constant *wait-a-minute vines* that grabbed your gear and clothing at every step (which continuously inflicted small scratches and cuts on your arms and legs). We found that moving through all of that in the pitch black of a moonless night became not only difficult but also dangerous.

As you moved on patrol in the pitch dark you watched the

Ranger eyes on the hat of the man in front of you. Often that is all you can see as you move silently through the forest. You cannot see the hole in front of you; you cannot see the eye-level branch you are about to walk into; and you cannot see the steep cliff, a pace or two to the left or right, from which a fall will certainly be injurious, probably fatal. And if you lose sight of those Ranger eyes to your front, you will suddenly find yourself leading the remainder of the patrol element, all those behind you, and be completely lost!

If you were the leader of the patrol, these conditions required careful map study, frequent stops for map checks under a closed poncho to hide your red light, and, as always, careful counting of paces walked.

An all-night march across mountainous terrain may get you where you need to be, or it may just get you lost. We accomplished both during those first nights in the vast mountainous training area used by the 5th Ranger Training Battalion. About the third night of mountain patrolling, I was moving as the fourth man in our squad across the face of a thickly wooded, steep mountainside. I, for once, had no task during the move to a platoon assembly point. Our mission was to link up with the rest of our platoon and conduct a raid on a small "enemy" outpost along a mountain road some fifteen kilometers away. I'd had little sleep in the past twenty-four hours and was very tired. I was having real trouble just concentrating on moving quietly and carefully through the thick forest while at the same time trying not to lose the Ranger eyes on the guy in front of me. I had listened to the detailed brief on the patrol's mission and the plan for the raid. I knew what, where, when, and how. But I had no idea where we were along the planned route of march. As we walked along, my fatigue grew worse, and my concentration slipped rapidly. We had been moving for several hours and the time was around midnight.

The temperature began to fall, as it does in the higher elevations. We had just stopped and taken up security positions while the patrol leader consulted the map. I huddled to conserve warmth and to rest as much as I could. I suddenly became aware that I could not see or sense the guy who was ahead of me. I strained to see in the dark around me and then moved up to try to regain contact with him. I quickly realized, he and the forward portion of the squad had moved out. The patrol had resumed moving without my being aware of it. Clearly the guy to my front had failed to relay back the order to move out. I recontacted the man behind me, and we led those behind us forward. I may have dozed and not realized it. I could see almost nothing ahead of me. We had not changed our direction of walk in some time, so I assumed that the patrol was still moving in the same general direction. I moved forward as quickly but as quietly as I could. I had gone maybe fifty meters when I stepped on something soft and heard a brief moan. I stopped and knelt to feel what was at my feet and a hand grabbed and jerked me down. The Ranger who had been in front of me pulled my head to his and sternly said "can't you tell when I stop and get down?" "Yeah, yeah," I said, "it's dark out here."

How in the hell I managed to go straight to him through the thick woods and pitch black I will never know. It was like some sixth sense of when and where to move. At any rate, I was saved from certain embarrassment and a probable poor evaluation by the RI or LI. The experience had my adrenaline flowing and I was now wide awake for the first time in several hours. It was a good thing. About two hundred meters farther ahead the RI stopped the patrol. He came down the line of Rangers and walked up to me. He asked if I was aware of where we were and where we were going. I answered that I knew where we were going but lacking any opportunity to check the map in the last few hours and with no pace count, I did not know where we were along the route of march. Generally, at night the only way you checked your map in the dark was, as always, under a poncho, during a halt, with a red lens flashlight. This process was cumbersome but a necessary security measure and required the other patrol members to provide vigilant guard while the patrol leader and pace counter huddled under the poncho. As a result, the other members of the patrol often have no idea where the patrol actually is.

The RI led me forward to the head of the line of Ranger students. Then he called the outgoing patrol leader to join us under a poncho. The other Ranger pointed out where we were on the map and the RI concurred that he was correct. The RI then told me that I was now the patrol leader and that we were an hour behind schedule. He said we had to make up the time or we would miss the rendezvous and cause the mission to fail. If we failed to link up and the rest of the platoon conducted the raid and moved on without us, we would miss our daily resupply and therefore miss getting any food that day. It had already been more than twenty-four hours since we had been supplied with C rations and water.

I studied the map for a few minutes and told the Ranger who was keeping our pace count that we would be moving quickly and to have the Ranger behind him keep a pace count along with him. I figured that if we moved fast over this terrain, it was likely that an accurate pace count would be difficult. But with two Rangers keeping the count, an average of the two counts would be more accurate. I pulled out from under the poncho and moved up to the point man leading the patrol through the woods. I told him to pick up his pace but be very careful of noise and to watch for enemy observations posts, or OPs. I then told the Rangers behind me to pass the word back down the line that we were picking up our pace to insure we linked up with the platoon. I also directed that a count be sent up. This would verify for me that I had the entire patrol. My own experience that night warned me that it was too easy to leave part of your force lost in these *boonies* (Army slang for boondocks). With the count confirmed, we moved out at a quick pace.

With each significant change in elevation or crossing each identifiable terrain feature like a ridge or deep ravine, I stopped to get the pace count and check the map. I did not want to get lost and miss the link up. I was hungry, very hungry. I had no pogey bait and the entire patrol had been thoroughly searched by the LI before we left on the patrol. All the C rations I had been given the day before were long gone. About four hours later we reached the deep ravine on the map that was to be the linkup point. I found no sign of any other Rangers from our platoon. I put the patrol in a defensive position and sent a two-man patrol to the far side of the ravine to look for the rest of the platoon. They returned almost immediately with news that they had walked up on the other element as they were descending into the ravine. I had one of them lead me to the where they had made contact. We were within fifty meters of the rest of the platoon. I figured that that was not bad for a seven kilometers (or *clicks*) move in the pitch black of the Georgia Mountains for a bunch of amateur Rangers. My predecessor had done well, and I had only to stay the course to affect the link up. As the new squad leader, I was briefed by the new platoon leader, who had also been selected on the march, that he would conduct a leader's recon of the objective in ten minutes. We were to put our squads in a platoon defense and establish security. We were some twelve hundred meters from the objective, and he wanted the platoon to get some sleep but to maintain good security, so he directed a fifty percent sleep/security posture.

I returned to my squad and moved them into position to tie in with the rest of the platoon. I positioned the squad in buddy positions, assigned sectors of fire within the overall platoon defensive position, and told them they had at least two hours before we had to prepare for our predawn attack. I returned to the platoon's CP and moved forward with the platoon leader to recon the objective. We moved about five hundred meters until we hit the paved road on which the "enemy" checkpoint was located. We paralleled the road by about fifty meters and moved another five hundred meters toward the checkpoint. As we neared the checkpoint, we halted and the platoon leader began checking for trip wires. Almost immediately he found one. He marked it and we moved up until we could overlook the objective. We could see a truck and at least two soldiers smoking with their cigarettes unshielded. The glow of these cigarettes seemed to illuminate the faces and the immediate area around the smokers in the near total darkness of the night. The objective seemed little more than a truck and several soldiers. We had been told that there were at least ten enemy soldiers manning and overwatching the position. We could not yet see the enemy overwatch position. The platoon leader sent one squad leader up the hillside to look for them and he sent me down toward the road to look. As I moved carefully down toward the road, I found three OPFOR soldiers below me with a machine gun pointed down the road. These soldiers were in a position to protect the checkpoint, but not themselves. There had to be another position farther up the hill. I returned to the platoon leader and advised him where these enemy soldiers were located but that they were exposed unless their position was covered by another position. A few minutes later the other squad leader returned and said he found a position just above us that could cover the checkpoint as well. It was quickly apparent that this position covered both of the others, while at the same time it was well protected by the terrain.

We withdrew back to our defensive position and huddled under a poncho to plan. The platoon leader studied the map and asked a few questions of each of us about what we saw. He then briefed us on his plan. We then rehearsed the plan on the map and on a crude model we scratched into the dirt at our knees. Satisfied with our understanding of his plan and our mutual coordination, he directed us to move out in thirty minutes and cross our line of departure (LD), the imaginary line on the ground the crossing of which signifies the start for the operation. The attack was to be conducted by two squads with the third squad providing both a base of fire support and a reserve if needed. My squad was to take out the enemy position along the road and then move up and take the check point itself. The other squad was to take out the enemy position up the hill and then move to a position just above the checkpoint and support our move to seize the checkpoint and to overwatch the road against any reinforcements while the third squad moved up. The attack began just as we planned it. We took out the two positions guarding the checkpoint and the OPFOR soldiers surrendered. But as we moved to take the checkpoint, we ran into about six more OPFOR soldiers and a machine gun instead of just the two or three OPFOR soldiers we were told to expect. As with most military plans, it become *obsolete by events*, or OBE, at the first shot! We fired at each other with hundreds of rounds of blank ammunition until the other squad from up the hill joined the fight. Then the RIs stepped in and stopped the fight and ordered the opposing force soldiers to withdraw in their truck.

I had been so caught up in the mission and the conduct of the operation that it had all seemed very real until that point. With the sudden stopping of the firefight, the sense of danger and total focus evaporated. I was suddenly dead tired. But no sooner had we occupied the checkpoint, processed our prisoners, and consolidated and reorganized the platoon when the LI reported that a company-sized enemy force was coming to counterattack. The platoon leader ordered the platoon to withdraw as squads to our predetermined rally point, from which we were to move to our resupply point.

As we withdrew up the hill that ran parallel to the road, we ran smack into about five people in civilian clothes. At first, I thought they were hunters. But they all carried large cloth bags and were picking up the brass from our firefight. These *brass pickers* became a common element in our operations. They knew where each "fight" normally occurred and were always ready to profit from our expenditure of blank ammunition. It was my first exposure to organized and illegal recycling of military ammunition residue. It would not be my last.

We had a long six-click march to our resupply point. I was replaced as the patrol leader about halfway to the resupply point. I was exhausted and I do not remember much more of that move. I discovered for a fact that you could walk while you are asleep! We were resupplied with water and one C ration per student along with live chickens, and raw vegetables: onions, potatoes, and carrots. We were told this would be the last resupply for thirty-six hours. We were to go into a defensive position, prepare and eat a hot meal, clean weapons and equipment, and prepare for the next operation. It was clear that we had to eat the chickens and vegetables and save the C rations. But we had no pots, no utensils, not even a recipe! One of the RIs was a survival expert and he was quite amused at our lack of field expedient culinary talent. He proceeded to explain that every part of the chicken was useful and what each meant to us. The blood provided salt and vitamins. The meat, of course, provided protein. The skin could be fried in the fat into hard, chewy jerky-like pieces that could be saved.

The meal, while a bit of a struggle at first, proved to be a feast. Well satisfied with our results, we took turns cleaning our gear and ourselves and getting some much-needed rest. The next day we were given classes and hands-on training with various pieces of mountaineering gear and our introduction to actual mountain climbing and rappelling. From my fire training I already had extensive experience with climbing and rappelling, and this proved a real asset. But I was the exception in the entire platoon. While I certainly did not know the finer points of military climbing operations, the principals I knew, and I had long ago overcome any fear of working at heights. As a result, I quickly became the platoon's demonstrator for the Ranger instructors. I found the tasks not only easy to do but such fun that one instructor stopped me at one point to ask me to at least look scared for the other Ranger students. He said while it is okay for the instructors to make it look easy, that if I, as a Ranger student, made this look too easy, the other students would not start with a healthy respect for the inherent dangers in this training. His point was well taken, so I began to use a serious frown on my face as I did each task. As I had a somewhat youthful countenance, my trying to look serious may have been seen as much more humorous than serious. However, later one of the other students came up to me and said "Hoffman, you are so full of shit. You loved that shit and you scared and embarrassed the crap out of the rest of us."

The instructors, however, got even with me later in that training with the Australian rappel. This I had, of course, never heard of but I was volunteered to demonstrate this technique without any warning of what I was about to do. When the instructor explained it to us, I was put in my place. The Australian rappel differs from standard rappelling in that you face forward, down the cliff, as you rappel down. Further, you control your descent with only one hand so that you have a free hand with which to aim and fire your assault rifle as you go down. This technique allows vertical attacks down a cliff. It works well but is quite intimidating to master as a rappelling technique. This mountaineering training cost us several Ranger students to serious injuries from falls. Our first student fatality was during this training event. It was tough to deal with the loss of a fellow student and it was not the last that we would experience.

One other climbing skill that was a personal challenge for me was the inverted horizontal climb. This technique enables you to move up, under, out and over most large overhanging rock outcroppings. With full combat gear this was very difficult for me as a large individual because the cumulative weight of my own body and the equipment we carried severely tested my upper body strength. This was exhausting, mentally difficult training where you had to put pain aside and focus on succeeding—a skill tough to master and tough to retain. But these were skills that would serve me well in the years ahead. Further, they are the skills that this school was designed to foster in the Army's best small-unit leaders. This series of training events and simulated combat patrols continued for several more days. The learning curve was steep, and our increased proficiency was rewarded with more demanding tasks.

Rather unexpectedly we were given a break from patrolling and loaded onto trucks for our next move. Much to our surprise we were driven back to the base camp and then herded into a large classroom with all our gear still on our backs. As soon as we were in the room the lights went out and we expected a new mission brief or a new training event to start. Out came our notebooks and maps as we awaited the instructor to begin. Instead, a TV came on and voice said, "This is Houston Control, the Eagle has begun its descent to the lunar surface." Someone spoke out, "What in the hell is this? We get to see a space movie?"

Then it dawned on me, the lunar landing was to take place in July, this was July, and maybe this was it! Sure enough, the camp commander had arranged for all of us to see this historic event live on TV. Not everyone on the room appreciated the significance of what was happening high above us that summer afternoon. Snoring was heard from several very tired Ranger students who only saw this as an opportunity to catch up on much needed sleep. But for most of us this was an amazing event to witness, and it captured our fullest attention. We watched that TV for about two hours and saw Neil Armstrong step onto the lunar surface and heard his famous words about "one small step." As tired as I was, I still vividly remember watching that event.

Then it was back onto the trucks later that afternoon and back to the woods for more training, more hunger, and more pain. We did get a day and a half break at the base camp after about ten days of training. We washed and repaired clothing, got hot showers, and had a full meal with plenty of time to eat and enjoy it. We then had a day of classroom training on mountain survival, mountain tactics, and new equipment. Then it was back to the mountain forests once again. This time we had more skill and less apprehension about what lay ahead. We also had more arrogance and tried to act with greater creativity and initiative. It did not take long for the instructors and the OPFOR to put us in our place. That, combined with hunger, fatigue, and more pain from climbing, crawling, falling, sliding, and the ever-present *wait-a-minute vines* left us aware once again of just how tough a combat environment can be, even without a real enemy taking you under fire. But we survived and we prevailed often in each successive training engagement and our pride and confidence in our team grew stronger. But once again I found myself without an assigned Ranger buddy, as mine had suddenly quit after a grueling patrol. I carried on alone for two additional days. The value of this training became abundantly clear to all of us as we progressed through it. Our self-confidence and personal motivation reached new heights and we thought we were becoming iron men with iron wills—maybe not bulletproof but close.

After three weeks the training at Camp Merrill ended as abruptly as it had started, and we headed back to the Ranger Camp at Fort Benning for another eight-hour training break. This time, nearly everyone ate and slept, as we knew we would soon head south to the Florida panhandle and Eglin Air Force Base for the last phase of Ranger training. After another long ride in the back of some deuce-and-a-half trucks, we found ourselves at Field Seven at Eglin Air Force Base for three more weeks of the jungle-training portion of the school at Camp Rudder, home of the 6th Ranger Training Battalion.

Now the terrain was flat as a skillet, for the most part wet or covered with water, and densely covered in trees, cypress knees or swamp stumps, and thick vines. The trees provide multiple overhead canopies, so the sky and the sun were only occasionally visible. Navigation is difficult when you only have limited visibility in any direction and no obvious land mass references. Further, the flora and fauna in this environment can not only be deadly, but some of the creatures are quite capable of eating you! Suddenly all our confidence and arrogance were once again dashed. It was like starting over, as we had a whole new set of skills to master. Further, this was training which was closer to what we could expect in actual combat in South Vietnam. If we expected any easing of the rules here, we were quickly disappointed. Limited food, frequent inspections, infrequent sleep periods, and demanding training patrols through very tough, mainly wet terrain all but sapped us of our drive and stamina.

I was not overly intimated with the swamps and jungle, as were most in the class. While I had never been to Vietnam, I had been through these same swamps and jungles with my cousin George Dewey, who was a Marine flying helicopters in Vietnam at that time. He and I had explored this area by boat and canoe during my visits to the family home in Pensacola, Florida. The large body of water to the east of the city of Pensacola is referred to as the East Bay. This bay leads directly into the vast swampy region that is the Ranger training area. The rivers and the major creeks, while not well known to me, were at least familiar and did not give me the foreboding that the other Ranger students were experiencing.

I understood the general lay of the terrain and the orientation of the various bodies of water. Once again, I found myself helping the patrol leaders navigate and acting as point man on patrols when I was not the assigned patrol leader. Walking in near absolute darkness, in waist deep black water, with snakes and small alligators swimming around you can be quite an experience. Doing this while you try to maintain a sense of where you are, where you are going, and avoiding an "enemy" force is hard, stressful work. This training continued to separate "the men from the boys." My latest assigned Ranger buddy lasted five days and he was gone. I never had another assigned Ranger buddy during the remainder of the course. Perhaps I was bad luck for Ranger buddies, but all had been far more experienced than I.

During this phase, physical prowess and size were less important than courage, stamina, and personal drive. Mental attitude and mission focus were everything. Unlike the mountain phase, the problem here was not physical pain. The challenge here was mental stress. I saw more students break mentally here than I saw break physically in the woods and mountains around Dahlonega, Georgia.

The night patrols in this Florida jungle were very hard, exhausting training events. But once again we learned to survive, to prevail at whatever it was that we were assigned to do and to accept risk and use it as an advantage. After only a week of this training our confidence returned and our feeling of personal power and even a degree of invincibility grew. We continued to mature into confident, trained Rangers who would be, I thought, more than ready for the rigors of small-unit combat in Vietnam. But we had two more weeks of training to go and soon we realized that our performance now would decide who got the coveted Ranger Tab at the end of the course. Unlike most Army training, simply graduating did not get you the Ranger Tab. You had to excel in the eyes of the instructors. Indeed, if you won the Tab, it meant that you were awarded a unique Army Additional Skill Identifier or ASI that meant you could be assigned to a Ranger unit or occupy an infantry position that required this ASI, as I would later in Vietnam. It also meant that you were qualified to return to the school in the future as an instructor yourself. There was a great deal of pride associated with this award, a pride that remains throughout the Army even today.

Unknown to the Army and our instructors, the greatest test of our skill and mental focus was brewing out in the Gulf of Mexico. We had received no warning of Hurricane Camille because we never had any contact from the outside world during the course, except for the moon landing. Such isolation was a key factor in the overall training plan. During all training we adhered to strict radio security procedures for all communications. Such radio security measures were drilled into us repeatedly so that we learned to minimize the risks associated with enemy interception of our electronic communications, as was often the case in Vietnam.

One day I was carrying the platoon radio, along with my medic bag and other gear and I received a radio call in plain English. I was reluctant to acknowledge the radio call without the usual coded security signals. But when the caller demanded that I put the lane instructor on the radio, I sensed an urgency that bordered on fear in the caller's voice, and I hastened to the LI. He took the radio handset with a disapproving stare that changed quickly to a look of astonishment and then deep concern.

After he completed his conversation, which I could not overhear, he called an administrative halt and asked us to gather around him without any security measures or the usual tactical postures. We knew something serious was up. The RI with our squad was a captain with a tour in Vietnam behind him. He spoke with the LI for a few moments and then he instructed me to call the rest of the platoon on the radio and have them rendezvous with us at a small hilltop about five kilometers away. While I began the radio calls, he explained that a major hurricane was approaching, and we may be in danger if we do not get out of the swamps within a few hours.

A check of the map and knowing the terrain between our current location and the small hill he wanted to move to, told me that this extraction was not going to happen if we only had a few hours. I completed the notifications to the other two squads, and we set out toward the hilltop. Almost immediately, we noticed that the water levels were dropping somewhat, and currents had increased in the creeks and the Yellow River. We were heading through the dark jungle environment to a crossing point in the river where we could affect a safe crossing of this swift, deep river. On the way we linked up with other two squads, so we now had twenty-six Ranger students in our column. As we reached the crossing site, I received another radio message for the LI. The message was that we had two hours to reach the hilltop landing zone (LZ) for helicopter extraction. After that it would be too late because the storm was coming in fast.

With renewed urgency we sent a swimmer team across with a rope to secure it to the other side so we could use it as a safety line for everyone else and our equipment. No sooner was the line secured to both banks than a small, motorized assault boat of the type used by the special forces units who also trained in the area came gliding up the river. Normally, we operated against these units as part of our training. Obviously, these guys had not gotten the word about the approaching storm, but they seemed quite surprised that we did not react to their arrival, but simply stood and watched them approach. As they neared the line across the river one of the SF guys in the boat suddenly reached up with a knife and cut our line. They laughed and sped up the river; unaware of the misfortune they had set up for us. The RI and LI with us were furious at them and let them know it, but they just ignored us and left the area.

Now we had a real problem. We knew we could no longer make the LZ in time for the pickup, but now that we had the team split between the two banks and we were in very low ground and faced a serious threat from rising water from what I knew was the likely initial tidal surge as the storm approached. At this point, two of the Ranger students who were also Navy SEALs told the RI captain that they could retrieve both ends of the rope and splice it in mid-stream to restore the crossing safety line so we could all get across. I looked at the current in the river and the width of the crossing site and figured there was no way these guys could accomplish that. Perhaps they could swim out and retrieve the sections of the line, return to the shore and then splice them together. But then we would have to restring the line, and all of this would take time. But to all our surprise, they got both ends of the line and joined them in a smooth splice, all while treading water in midstream against a good ten-knot current! It was an amazing feat.

With the line restored, we continued our slow crossing with all our equipment. Once we were on the other side, we quickly moved toward the LZ site. We arrived there about two hours later, but too late for an extraction. I called the Ranger headquarters in the clear on the radio, ignoring our customary coded tactical radio procedures, to let them know our location. They did not have good news for us. We were the only Ranger element left in the field; all the others had been extracted back to Ft. Rucker, Alabama. They told me that landfall for the main impact of hurricane was expected in a matter of hours, but that very high winds and rough sea had already reached the area. They told me that the eye of the storm would make landfall west of Pensacola and that we would see significant storm effects. They expected a major tidal surge and were evacuating the field headquarters and they would try to contact us as soon as the storm passed. The officer on the radio told me to tell the RI to dig in and try to ride out the storm on the highest ground we could find. Then he wished us good luck and was off the air. I was stunned! How could they leave us out here, on our own, with no way out? We did not know how quickly the track of the storm had changed from the earlier forecast and that we faced a tough night, but nothing like the folks who lived west of Pensacola were going to have.

I knew about hurricanes and their effects on coastal areas. Being on the east side of the storm meant we were on the worst side of the storm, due to the way hurricanes rotate. I had no idea how large the storm was but I expected we were way too close to the center of the storm. The RI captain was extremely worried and he made it clear that he felt we were in serious trouble. We wasted no time in getting ourselves organized for the storm. We buried most of our equipment in deep holes on the top of the small hill. The hill was probably all of twenty feet above sea level, but we were a good three kilometers from the waters of the bay and there was Santa Rosa Island between us and the Gulf of Mexico. I explained what I knew and the message from the field headquarters to the RI, LI, and the other Ranger students. The captain decided that we all needed to dig ourselves into chest deep holes with canteens of water and our rucksacks. He then told us to clean our weapons and wrap them in ponchos to keep them clean and functional. We dug furiously and prepared to hide in our holes from flying debris and trees, if it came to that. About sundown the wind started to pickup and the water in the swamps around us became agitated and started to rise up the hill. I knew stories from my family about hurricanes that had hit the Pensacola area in the past, but I had never been in a hurricane myself and I was getting very worried. The sky became dark and ugly, the wind grew much stronger and the rain became very heavy as the sun set.

Well into the night the storm reached a furious peak in our area. It was clear that the main part of the storm was elsewhere, but the wind and rain we were getting was very violent. The flashes of lightning showed the trees around us bent over double and a lot of debris was flying through the air. Moving around on the hilltop was nearly impossible and quite dangerous. The lightning also showed us that the population on the hill was growing rapidly! I heard screams and cries from other positions and knew that they had received visitors in their hide holes. Soon the NCO LI came crawling around to tell us to fire our weapons down the hill to scare off the snakes and alligators that were coming up out of the water. All we had were blanks but they are loud and spit out fire and heavy vibrations, which did the trick. At one point I saw two very large snakes directly in front of me at about two meters. They were coming up the hill in the heavy rain and wind. I fired about six rounds toward them, and they disappeared. This sporadic firing continued for several hours. It may or may not have been useful, but it made us feel better, anyway.

The storm subsided some during the night and I fell asleep buried up to my chest in wet sand. When I awoke the sun was just breaking on the horizon. The sight around me was astonishing. There were the heads and shoulders of the rangers sticking up out of the sand, surrounded by lots of debris and just about every kind of living thing that the swamp held. There were lots of snakes, lizards, turtles, what looked like wet beavers, skunks, and squirrels and even three small alligators! I just about crapped in my shorts. I just held my breath and said nothing. I then realized that our firing probably deterred the snakes and such from joining us in our little sandy holes, but little else. This was their hill and they had occupied it all night for the same reason we did. I saw other heads beginning to move just as the various animals began a hasty exit from the hilltop and back to the swamp and the trees. It was an amazing sight.

As soon as full daylight returned, we began to inventory our gear and get a head count. Everyone was safe and, amazingly, we did not lose a single piece of gear. I began calling on the radio to see if anyone answered. After about an hour I got a response from a helicopter pilot. He told me he was on the way to find us and that, once he did, additional aircraft would come in and get us out. Two hours later we were back at the field headquarters at Field Seven for hot chow and a shower. We had survived. Then we learned just how bad Hurricane Camille had hit the Alabama, Louisiana, and Texas coastal areas. We had been very lucky. If the main part of the storm had come near or actually hit the Eglin area, the tidal surge alone might have drowned us all. As it was, fortune smiled upon us, and we escaped with no damage.

The remainder of the training at Eglin was somewhat anticlimactic for us. We had been tested and survived. The only other sobering event of that last week of training was that one Ranger student was hit with a live round during one of the very demanding live-fire courses. His wound was serious but not life threatening. He was medevac'd out and I doubt he ever recycled. We were graduated out on Field Seven. At this short graduation ceremony, we learned that 108 of 205 finishing the course had qualified for the Tab. This was followed by a trailer full of beer and burgers. One beer and I was toasted.

I had survived the training and completed the course. That was no small thing itself. I was one who had qualified for the Ranger Tab and I felt, no matter what other training I would undergo before going to Vietnam, I could surely handle it after this. At the end of the Florida phase of Ranger School I discovered that Georgetown classmate Gary Garczynski was a student in a later Ranger class. Gary and I had been in the US Army ROTC program together at Georgetown and had been part of the Student Ranger Company. That had been merely an introduction to small-unit tactical and leadership training. I would serve again with Gary at Fort Hood and later in Vietnam.

We returned to Ft. Benning for out-processing from the Ranger school. I was given new orders to attend Infantry Officer's Basic Course (IOBC) and then to proceed to Fort Hood, Texas for my first duty assignment. Strangely, no unit of assignment was designated at Fort Hood. I also ran into the same NCO I had encountered upon my initial arrival at 3rd Ranger Company. He told me he was really surprised I had not only finished the course but that I had earned the Ranger Tab without a recycle. I told him that his advice and my utter ignorance of what I was getting into served me well. With no expectations and no prior military experience of consequence to influence, I was literally a clean slate when I started. That made it easier for me absorb information and to adapt to the program. My only real challenge, I told him, during the entire program was learning the needed technical and tactical skills fast enough to stay ahead of the grade curve. The physical demands, while tough, were never overwhelming to me and the mental stress, while great, never exceeded those I had experienced as a firefighter or in the riots of 1967–68 on the streets of Washington, DC.

CHAPTER THREE
MILITARY POLICE AT FORT HOOD, TX

AFTER RANGER SCHOOL I had two weeks *snowbird* time before the start of Infantry Officer Basic Course (IOBC). I was told I was no longer restricted to the post but that I was restricted from talking to anyone in the press or discussing my testimony before Congress back in May. So, I took it easy, rested, and ate small but frequent meals to regain some of the forty pounds I had lost during the training. I soon found out that there was a daily US Air Force plane that flew around the country to various bases that stopped at Lawton Field (the Air Force Base for Fort Benning) and then went to Washington, DC. I also discovered that I could stand by for free trips on a space available basis if I showed up two hours before the flight and was in class B uniform, which was a more formal look than our fatigues. This was a transportation system that I used with great regularity for the next few years.

I got a three-day pass from the student company commander and did not have to be back at Ft. Benning until Wednesday of the next week. So, I caught a ride on the Air Force's "Capitol Flyer" to Washington, DC to visit my girlfriend, Karen Schultze. I wasn't much company as I recall because I either slept or ate and little else. Karen was appalled when she saw me in my uniform. It was now several sizes too large. My deep tan did not hide all the bruises and cuts on my arms and legs. That was probably the least I had weighed since very early in high school. We went to the Delaware beach for the weekend, and I enjoyed the relaxed change of pace and the seafood feasts! Then it was back to Fort Benning on Monday.

When I in-processed to the IOBC course they told me that I could live off post because housing was critically short on base, but I was now restricted to the area of the post area. I was to talk with no one from the media. This was all somewhat absurd at this point because I had just been on a three-day pass to DC. It turned out that there had been press types trying the track me down all over DC and at Fort Benning the whole time I was in Ranger school. I had managed to avoid ever being interviewed or even photographed after the testimony in Congress and the Army wanted to keep it that way.

A week later, after getting settled in a short-term rental apartment, I reported to building four, Infantry Hall, to begin my IOBC training. The TAC officer for our class asked to speak with me after I formally signed into the school. He asked if I was prior service, and I said no. He then asked if I had attended another officer basic course already but was now transferring into the Infantry. I said no. He asked if I had graduated from a military college such as Norwich or VMI. I replied no, and I asked why the questions. He then said that when he saw my Ranger Tab, he assumed that my records were not complete because he had never known of a case where a newly commissioned ROTC officer, just out of a civilian college, attended and *tabbed* out of Ranger school before any other training in the Army. He then said that completing Ranger school and then going through IOBC was like attending college before going to high school. I was a bit taken aback because I thought IOBC was a rigorous program where I would learn about new technology, more about how the Army worked and how to become an infantry leader. He told me that I probably already had learned 75 percent of what the IOBC program would teach me.

He then pulled out a master schedule for the entire IOBC program. He took a pen and began marking through classes and training events. When he finished he handed it to me and said, "Son, look I hate wasting anyone's time in this man's army." That was a new but refreshing attitude for sure. He continued. "You make sure you are at all of the events and classes not crossed out and be sure to hit every exam on the schedule. I will take care of the daily morning report so there is no problem if you don't show up for days when there are no classes that you need to attend." He then looked at my records and said, "I don't know what this other crap is all about but stay out of trouble and out of sight. I don't care where you go or what else you do as long as you're here when you are supposed to be, and you sit for all of the exams." IOBC was a breeze.

During this otherwise pleasant time in the fall of 1969 a message was delivered to me in class one day from the Post Red Cross office. When I first looked at the envelope and the markings, I felt a cold chill go down my back and I was apprehensive about opening the envelope. I suddenly realized that the instructors were silent, and the entire class was watching me. They had a pretty good idea that this was not good news. In the Army the Red Cross serves many valuable purposes in aiding and assisting the nation's warriors, and their families, in time of war and peace. While most of these functions were to make life just a little bit better than it might have been, another of those functions was the notification of bad news, often really bad news, to a service member and his family.

I left the room and walked outside to read the short letter. It was a message from my father to inform me that my cousin, George Dewey Hutcheson, had been killed when his CH-46 Marine helicopter was shot down over the Hi Van Pass near Da Nang, RVN. George Dewey had been based at the Marine Corps airfield called Marble Mountain, just outside Da Nang. Dad told me that he was designated an official escort officer to return George Dewey's remains home. He then informed me that I had also been designated an escort officer at the specific, written request of George Dewey on his next of kin notification card, and I was to proceed immediately to NAS Pensacola to meet the arrival of Dewey's casket. I was dumbstruck! I had been fishing with George Dewey not more than four months before, during my last spring break from college, while he was on leave prior to his third tour in RVN. He loved helicopters and he loved the Marines.

This was a sad day for me and my entire family. Military service has always been a part of our family. Our family has made its share of sacrifices for our country, but sometimes the sacrifice is truly cruel. George Dewey's father was a naval aviator who was lost in the Pacific during World War II. George Dewey was buried with full military honors in Pensacola. His mother, my father's sister, June, would not let go of me for most of the time I was home. She made me promise that I would not die in Vietnam. I told her that I thought the war would be long over before I had any chance to be sent there.

I finished IOBC on the Commandant's List for academic excellence after several very restful months during which I split my time between IOBC at Fort Benning, the beaches in Pensacola, and the 1789 in DC. The Capitol Flyer had become a regular bus ride for me.

After IOBC was complete the personnel folks told us that they had openings in the next jump class. They asked if any of us who were not already scheduled to attend would like to go to jump school. I immediately said yes. I had made the water jump at Eglin after a day of abbreviated training and I figured that I should make the bookends complete—Airborne Ranger—so I volunteered. This gave me another welcome week's break before starting Jump School.

The in-processing for airborne training included a short physical examination during which I was asked if I knew of any injury or medical condition that would prevent me from completing the course. I knew of no problems, so I said no, and the doctor signed me off for starting the class. The first week was challenging but not tough. Lots of running, pushups, PT tests, yelling, running, sitting in bleachers, yelling, running, classes on falling, running, yelling, more falling, and more running. I was already in pretty good shape and there was no hazing these *Black Hat* Airborne instructors could give me that could even bring about a reaction after Ranger school. I did catch some grief over the fact that I was already a tabbed Ranger but had not been through Jump School. Occasionally, a Black Hat would ask if I got my Ranger Tab from a Cracker Jack box, "but only after falling off a chair," I would reply. This was an old joke for Airborne Troops who were not Ranger qualified. I just smiled and reveled in the fact that I was, indeed, a Ranger and had been there and done that. This was easy duty, really, with evenings off. Imagine that—evenings off to myself in a school that the other guys thought was demanding. But I must admit that I did not enjoy the hot weather or the damned uncomfortable straps of the parachute harnesses we had to wear. This jump harness design must have been found in a medieval torture text or something. They certainly were not intended for the comfort of males. Ouch! Tower Week was fun but a bit on the painful side. I had serious concerns about certain of my bodily functions or my ability to be a father after that week.

On Friday of the second week of Airborne School, I was called to the Jump School student company offices. The student company commander had my medical records in front of him. He said he appreciated my enthusiasm and commitment, but he wanted to know why I had lied about my being physically fit to attend airborne training. This tone and the intimation set me back a bit. Somewhat with an irritated tone I responded back that as far as I knew I was and that I had had no problems with the course so far. He then showed me that in my medical records I had a "profile" from Ranger school that prohibited me from "running, jumping, or extended marching" for a period of ninety days from the time it was issued. Imagine that! Not being allowed to run, jump, or do extended marching in Ranger school? What kind of crap was this, some kind of joke? He pointed out that profile was put in my records at the end of Ranger school because I had bruised my right heel bone during the mountain phase. The pad I had been given had worked like a charm and by the time we got to Florida, it was healed to the point that I forgot about it. I had no idea that they would put something in my records, particularly a profile against running, jumping, and marching . . . while I was in Ranger school! Talk about a stupid waste of ink.

Lesson: never, but *never* underestimate the idiocy of the bureaucrats in the Army and their unending drive to cover their asses at all costs.

I asked about a training class recycle for one week because the profile expired in less than a week. The student company commander replied, "No can do. You are required to be at Fort Hood, in fact you are already supposed to be there. Someone screwed up sending you here in the first place! You are supposed to go to flight school at some point and you are not supposed to attend Jump School anyway. The Army already paid for your initial flight training during college, and they do not want you injured before you can become a helicopter pilot."

I corrected him "A fixed-wing pilot."

"Whatever," he said. "Get your shit and get out of here. You have three days to get yourself and all your meager belongings to Fort Hood, Texas!"

"Why the rush?" I asked.

He just shrugged his shoulders and told me to get out of his office and gone from Ft. Benning. Yep, someone must have really screwed up because he really, really wanted me gone yesterday. If I had gotten hurt in jump training, he must have worried that it would have been his career on the line.

After being summarily ejected from Jump school just before Jump Week, I departed Fort Benning for Fort Hood. As I out-processed at the student personnel office, no one seemed to know why a shiny new *butter bar* second lieutenant was in such demand at such a huge post, but it was not my place to reason why.

I hit the road early the next morning and proceeded to Fort Hood via Pensacola, Florida so that I could at least say hi to my grandparents and others in my family before I headed west. It was not out of the way because I planned to take I-10, which was mostly finished and the nearest interstate that went west. I did not know when I might see them again. The drive to Fort Hood would only take two days, so this would not delay me. I also wanted to drive along the coast to see the damage I had heard so much about from Hurricane Camille.

After a brief visit with my family, I headed west on Interstate 10 out of Pensacola. I did not see much damage until I got into southern Alabama. Then it just got worse and worse. The effects of Hurricane Camille on the Gulf Coast were horrific. Roads were gone. Buildings were gone. Large tracks of homes were gone, with only front stoops and the foundations for fireplaces left to show where they had once stood. I even passed a big ship on my right as I drove west toward New Orleans! It must have washed at least a half-mile inland before it came to rest, sitting almost straight up on its keel! The devastation was complete for mile after mile. People were living in tents, in cars, in the backs of trucks and out in the open. What also struck me was how communities seemed to be working together. Stores were not open and most of the ones I saw for long stretches were partially or completely destroyed. Yet I saw people, who I could only assume were the owners or operators of these stores, operating from makeshift tables to give away to their neighbors what they could salvage from the wreckage of their stocks. I stopped to try and buy some sodas in western Mississippi. The storeowner looked at me, saw the uniform and smiled. I will never forget what he said: "No, we don't take no money now. Take what you need, and you be careful now! God bless you and stay safe." That was one of the few times in the 1970s that I ever had anyone not also in uniform treat me with such respect and care. Here I was trying to do something to help him, and he would have none of it.

When I got to Ft. Hood, I proceeded in via the main gate where there was a military police office and a sign for new arrivals to check in before proceeding onto the post. I parked my 1969 Mustang convertible and walked into the small MP office. The MP NCO at the door looked out and said, "nice car." I nodded and went into the office. There, a large, powerfully built NCO looked up from his desk and asked who I was and where I was headed. I told him that I was a newly assigned infantry lieutenant and headed for the Post G-1 (personnel) office. He asked for my name. When he heard it, he sat up a bit and told me that the post provost marshal had left word that I was to be told to proceed to billeting and get a room and then report to him at 0730 the next morning.

I thought *Oh shit! What have I gotten into now?* I knew I had no traffic tickets or accidents on the way, and I was not late. So, I again asked where the Post G-1 shop was and the NCO looked at me like I was deaf or impaired in some fashion. Then said "as I told you before, sir, there is no need to go to G-1. You are to report to the PM in the morning." Very strange. What would the post provost marshal, certainly a full bird colonel of the military police, want with me?

I went to the billeting office for a room, with the potential reasons for my required meeting with the military police in the morning rolling over and over in my head. The billeting clerk gave me a key and a map to an old WWII wooden "temporary" barracks building in the old training section of the Ft. Hood's cantonment area. The building was quite worn and lacked any level of reasonable upkeep, as far as I could tell. Inside there were bunks with wall lockers separated by short partitions. The paint was peeling, the rafters were covered in dirt, the floor tile was broken and peeling up, and the barracks bed, the lower half of what was normally a troop issue bunk bed, had a mattress that was clearly worn out by the time WWII troops had used it. There were clean sheets and a blanket at the foot of the bed. When I sat on it, several springs let go and I found myself sinking into a hole in the side of the bed. After about an hour of repair with tools from my car, the bed was usable. I had heard that Ft. Hood, like many other posts, had a badly neglected infrastructure, but if this was what officers were billeted in, then the enlisted ranks must live in really crappy facilities. The post had a reputation, I had already learned at Ft. Benning, for being unruly, fraught with racial tension, drugs, and the highest crime and AWOL rate in the Army. So far, my impressions of the post suggested that this must have a thread of truth.

I slept well until several other junior officers came in about midnight. They were noisy and loud and had no idea that anyone else was in the building. I asked them to keep it down. They were clearly surprised I was in the building, and they came into my bed area and introduced themselves. Both were also new lieutenants and were assigned to line mechanized infantry units, but neither had a platoon leader assignment as yet. They both saw my uniform hung in the open locker and asked when I had graduated from OCS. I asked why they would think I had come from OCS. They both laughed as if I was putting them on or something.

One said, "Well you can't be a ring knocker, you are here too early."

The other then said flatly, "You are a Ranger and a new L-T, so you must have been prior enlisted."

"No," I responded, "I am an ROTC officer and I have just come from IOBC. One of them looked at me and said, "you mean you just got out of Ranger School after IOBC en route here?"

"No," I explained. "I went to Ranger school right after I graduated from college and then I went to IOBC."

They both looked at me like I was a moron and one said, "Cut the shit. It doesn't work that way. I hope you really are a Ranger grad and not just wearing that because it looks cool."

I was stunned at such a suggestion, though I found out some time later that wearing awards and decorations that were not earned was more common than one might think. Some years later a Navy admiral retired early because it was revealed that he had worn decorations that he had not been awarded. Still, at this time in my career such a concept was beyond me. I jokingly offered to break both of their arms to demonstrate my training, if they needed concrete proof. Both backed out of my area, and we never spoke again.

The next morning, I was sitting outside the Fort Hood provost marshal's office at 0715 hours in my Class A uniform. I had polished everything on it and had spit shined my shoes. I figured that if I was in some kind of trouble, a good impression might work in my favor. About five minutes after I arrived, the provost marshal, or PM, at that time, Colonel Atherton, came into the office, known as the PMO (and yes, the US Army does run on acronyms). He was an impressive man, wearing a substantial crop of ribbons on his Class A uniform. This was no post dandy. This guy had been in the crap and, obviously, acquitted himself well. At his age, I suspected he was a veteran of several recent wars. Indeed, it turned out, he was. He stopped for a cup of coffee on the way into his office. Shortly thereafter the duty desk sergeant and the PM's sergeant major briefed him on the previous night's blotter contents, which I overheard and whose contents reaffirmed the somewhat unkind and unpleasant things I had heard about Fort Hood. Then the PM called for me to come into his office.

I reported with as much military bearing and crispness as I could muster. He told me to be at ease and have a seat. I sat down and he looked at me and said, "Relax, Lieutenant, we just need to chat for a few moments." He took a sip of coffee and looked at a file on his desk. It had a lot of pages in it, so I assumed he was still reviewing the information from the desk sergeant. He then held it up and said to me, "Your file is an interesting read."

My file, I thought, *Christ, I have only been in the Army for about five months, how could there be that much stuff in my personnel file?*

He asked about Ranger school, and I told him it was a challenge. He looked at me and simply said "I'll bet it was." He then asked me about Georgetown and life in college. I said only that it was a great school, and that I had gotten a great education. He looked at me sideways and said, "It looks like you got a lot more than that." I said nothing because I had no clue where he was going with these questions.

He opened his desk drawer and took something out. He held it in his hand for a moment, looked up at me and then handed it to me. I looked at what he had given me and saw that it was the crossed pistols insignia of the Military Police Branch. I looked up at him and he smiled and said "Welcome to the Military Police Corps." I was confused, to say the least. I said to him "Excuse me, sir, but are you sure you have the right Lt. Hoffman? I am sure there are many others with the very same name. I am, after all, an Infantry officer. I have not been to the MP Officer's Basic Course and, therefore, am not qualified to be an MP."

He looked stern for a moment and then said "Lieutenant, you graduated from Georgetown University in June with a regular commission, right?"

"Yes, sir," I replied.

"You used to be a firefighter in Fairfax County, VA, right?" he added.

"Yes, sir," I said.

"You testified before Congress in May, right," he said.

"Yes, sir," I replied again.

"I've got the right John T. Hoffman, recently from the Ranger course and IOBC. Son, you got more real experience with law enforcement and emergencies than most of the MP officers on this post. You will do just fine here" he stated with finality.

What the hell? I thought. "But, sir," I added, "I will only be here a short while, until my flight school orders come down from Infantry Branch."

"What?" he asked. "Are you nuts? You want to leave this nice safe job and fly helicopters?"

"Not actually, sir," I responded. "I am going to fly fixed wing."

"I doubt it," he said with a certainty that suggested some inside knowledge of something or other.

He then asked where I was billeted. I told him about the old barracks building across post. He said that it would not do. It was too far from the PMO and did not have a phone. He told me to see the sergeant major on my way out and he would fix up a more appropriate billet. He then simply said, "I have enjoyed meeting you. I have looked forward to your arrival. Welcome to Fort Hood. Now I have a lot to do, so if you will excuse me, I will get on with my day." I stood up and saluted. He returned the salute and I walked out of his office in a bit of a daze.

The sergeant major informed me that he had already anticipated the colonel's wishes and I was to move into the brand-new high-rise bachelor officer's quarters (BOQ) right away, get settled, and then report back to get briefed into my new duties. He then cautioned me that I was going to be the first second lieutenant to be billeted in the new high rise, so I might get some crap from some of the field grade officers that had already moved in. It seems that as big as it was, it only actually met the needs of billeting captains and above. They made an exception for me because it was close to the PMO and each room had a phone, which I would need.

I went over to the high rise to check in and found a less than enthusiastic reception. First, I was told there was a mistake, and I was not authorized to be in that building. Calls were made to somewhere and I heard a long stream of "but . . . but . . . but . . . but." Then I heard: "I understand. Okay, if you say so." Then I was handed keys to a room on the second floor, a floor, I came to learn, that was dedicated to field grade and above. The second floor had larger rooms, with kitchenettes and a small dining table. The outer hall area that greeted me when I stepped out of the elevator had a very nice, well-appointed common area with a TV, couches, and large windows that looked out toward the highway that ran past the main gate. Company grade officers, captains and promotable first lieutenants, if any, were supposed to live only on the top floors, where the rooms were smaller and, in many cases, where the more junior officers were billeted two to a room. I went into to my room and found it to be large, well-furnished, and it even had a refrigerator. I put my gear away and changed into fatigues. This was certainly better than that old WWII–era barracks building! It had a wonderful officer's mess on the first floor, laundry facilities, and even a small PX.

When I came out of my room, I ran into a major who looked at me with distain. I said, "Excuse me, sir," and tried to go around him, but he stepped in my path. "Son," he said, "hasn't anyone told you that this floor is for field grade only!"

"Yes," I replied, "I was assigned this room and this floor."

"We will see about that," he countered.

I said, "Yes sir, of course," and then went into the elevator. I drove back to the PMO.

When I got there, a captain named Castleberry met me and proceeded to fill me in on what it was I was going to be doing there. He was an assistant operations officer for the PMO. First, he told me that I was the new post traffic officer, and my principal office was in the building at the main gate. Then he told me that I would also be the 7th MP Group Headquarters and Headquarters Company commanding officer. "This," he told me, "will not take a lot of your time, as you have a great first sergeant and a good clerk staff who will keep things in line for you." Then he proceeded to list my various extra duties: post game warden, supervisor of the range patrols, supervisor of the PM's AWOL detachments in Fort Worth, Dallas, Killeen, Austin, and the surrounding areas, post payroll escort officer and PM liaison to CID and, most important, another assistant operation's officer of the PMO. Talk about a minor detail: assistant operations officer?

"With all due respect, sir, how the heck," I asked him, "am I going to do all of these jobs?" I told him, "I haven't even been to MP school, for Christ's sake!" He simply told me to relax, I had good NCOs who knew their jobs and I just needed to let them do them, stay informed, and step in where I was needed. "Just how many MPs are on this post and how many other company grade MP officers are assigned here?" I asked him. He said there were "a lot." In fact, he said that each division had at least two MP companies, there was a post Gate Company, the Confinement Company, the Corps MP Company, the other units in 7th Group, etc. I then asked him what all these branch qualified MPs in those units were going to think of an outsider coming into the PM shop? He said, "Do not worry about that. They are combat MPs, and they have plenty to do. Duty in the PMO is not where most of them want to be anyway."

Lesson: Never assume that there are people more qualified, experienced, and willing than you who will fill the key duty positions. Just when you figure that you have been trained for the work before you, the Army will step in, with seemingly no malice or forethought and give you something to do that you were not trained to do.

As the first week went by, I got settled into my two new duty offices. The Post Traffic office was at the main gate and my Traffic NCO was none other than the same NCO who had greeted me upon my arrival with the instructions to report to the provost marshal in the first place, Master Sergeant Blankenship. He turned out to be a great NCO who taught me a lot, very quickly. This was a huge Army post. The population of Ft. Hood was equal to a small city and everyone on post seemed to have a car. Accidents, speeding, property damage, auto theft, and parking were typical community problems that plagued Fort Hood. The post had an extensive network of paved and unpaved roadways that covered hundreds of miles. The main range roads were all paved and most who used them thought the speed limit was 75 mph! Unfortunately, much of the post was also a designated open range and was heavily populated with longhorn steers. As there were few fences on this range, the steers went where they wanted, and this included crossing roads to get to new grass. The resultant collisions between cars and steers were sobering to see. Neither fared well in such meetings.

Also of concern was drinking and driving. This accounted for about half of all accidents on post. And this was a remote, isolated post, located then within a so-called dry area of Texas. There was little to do for most soldiers, except go to the on-post clubs and drink inexpensive, if good quality, spirits. Reducing traffic accidents across the post, including the range areas, was a constant point of commanding general officer interest. Therefore, it was made a clear priority by the PM. This made it a major priority for the Post Traffic Section and me.

Making an impact on the accident numbers was tough. Cars were fast, gas was cheap, drink was cheap and ubiquitous, soldiers were bored and restless, and we had lots of long, straight open roads, sometimes shared by those very large steers. The math simply was not conducive to low accident rates. I aggressively tackled the problem with a mix of increased traffic patrols, radar and VASCAR speed traps, information for use during command briefs, and a publicity campaign about how speed, drunk driving, and yes, steers, can kill you or your family. Of course, this was a battle I could not win, though I would like to think that I made some small dent in the problem and saved at least one or two lives somewhere along the line.

As to my other duties, being post game warden had it perks. Being the payroll escort officer was a novel function for me. It was not until I had conducted my third or fourth major payroll movement that someone from the Federal Bureau of Investigation field office at Fort Hood bothered to share with me that several MPs, including the escort officer, had been killed in an ambush-style robbery on I-35 just a few years before. Funny, Captain Castleberry had failed to share that little tidbit with me when he assigned me this task. Of course, I could only imagine how a very lightly armored truck on an Interstate through open, unpopulated countryside, transporting around twenty million dollars in cash might be an attractive temptation for criminals. I took it very seriously from the start. That is a lot of money to move through a state where nearly every adult male had and carried a gun. We never had a problem, but if we had, the resulting gunfight would have been horrific. I had a plan for each movement that provided for two lead and follow cars, unmarked, with four MPs in each, all with fully automatic weapons, a transport truck equipped with an M-60 machine gun and an escorting OH-13 helicopter, also carrying an MP with a bungee-cord-suspended M-60 machine gun in the left door. Additionally, we always had at least one Texas Department of Public Safety patrol car somewhere within eyesight of the convoy riding *shadow* for us.

Lesson: in the Army, a little Ranger background never hurts and the basics on things that you do not know much about can be found somewhere in a field manual or textbook. Someone sometime has had to do that before, and they probably wrote something down about it.

Something else I noticed around Killeen Texas after I got settled into life at Fort Hood was that everyone seemed to carry a gun wherever they went. They were ubiquitous. Most wore them in western style belts and holsters. You saw them in stores, bars, even on people on the streets. It took a while for me to realize that almost everyone in this part of Texas worked in the outdoors. Texas was eaten up with snakes. Big, bad, ugly snakes. I hate snakes. The guns suddenly became quite appropriate, in my judgment. The fact that there were very, very few local bank or other armed robberies suggests that armed citizens can make a pretty good deterrent in such a circumstance.

Then there was AWOL Detachment duty. This was managing and supervising the various small teams of military police NCOs stationed across Central Texas who had the less-than-pleasant duty of seeking out, apprehending and returning to military control those unhappy soldiers who had elected to depart and achieve that unique military status of *Absent Without Leave* or AWOL. These soldiers went AWOL for a wide variety of reasons: homesick, lost, confused, sick of the Army, sick of taking orders, and, of course, even in some few cases, sick of being sent to "the two-way rifle range" in Southeast Asia. This duty was further endearing to me when I learned just how eager local law enforcement was to stop and detain otherwise law-abiding, valued soldiers simply because of the bounty paid by the US Army for all AWOL soldiers that they were returned to military control. This was a badly abused program, framed and established, like so many others, on the altar of good intentions.

At that time, when a soldier who had been declared AWOL by his unit was apprehended by local civilian law enforcement, the US Army would pay a fifty-dollar bounty directly to the apprehending officer. In 1969, fifty dollars was a lot of money. That was nearly a quarter of my monthly Army pay!

While most AWOL soldiers were certainly so designated quite appropriately, some were actually the victim of legal kidnapping and were literally held for ransom by some local municipal and county law enforcement officers. In one case, we discovered, after several "returned" soldiers were found to have the identical stories about their AWOL experience, that a certain Texas county was stopping soldiers on the Interstate and then holding them under trumped-up causes until they were declared AWOL, normally only twenty-four hours after they failed to return from leave, or their three-day passes. This was a very disturbing development for me, and I took it as a personal mission to make life miserable for those involved. While I cannot say more here about this case, suffice it to say that within a few weeks, no soldier had to face that local law enforcement agency's greed again.

Imagine the impact on these young soldiers and their families after such an event! How often this happened back during the days of the draft-based Army I can only speculate. I enjoyed Texas and I have great respect for the state, its traditions, and its people. However, this one aspect of rural Texan justice, while not widespread, occurred enough to give credence to the TV portrayal of Southern justice in that era.

And finally, but not least, was my role as the most junior assistant operations officer for the PMO. In this capacity I also liaised with the

Criminal Investigation Division team (CID) and the FBI field office on the post. This was the job that occupied the majority of my normal duty hour activities. But, as a junior officer, I also had to pull various types of night and weekend duty (this is, of course, to keep junior officers from being bored, limit their available free time, and to "widen their experience base and skills"). Sleep was often a major challenge for me, as was that ringing phone in my room. There were many days when I wanted to throw it out the window and get some sleep!

I caught a lot of the tedious management work for the PMO shop, but I also found myself directly engaged in numerous criminal investigations and III Corps policy actions as they related to law and justice issues on the post. At this time Fort Hood was viewed by many as the worst military base in the United States from the standpoint of crime, unrest, racial issues, fatalities, and drugs. At one point a major media outlet referred to the post as *Fort Pothead*. While a small percentage of soldiers on post were involved in crimes, given the huge military population of the post, the resultant criminal and legal problems were immense.

If these problems were not enough, we also had problems with the surrounding civilian population. Any military complex as large and infrastructure rich as Fort Hood, is an attractive target for theft and other crimes. Take for example, aluminum. Like brass, the military uses this metal in enormous quantities, particularly in a time of war. It is everywhere and used for so many applications that it would surprise you. The matting for temporary runways, originally made with steel and called perforated steel planking or PSP, was, by this time, made of high-grade aluminum because it was lighter and easier to transport and assemble. Power lines across the post were made of high-grade aluminum. Vehicle parts, even armor on light tanks and armored troop carriers, were made of aluminum alloys, as were the projectiles employed for tank gunnery practice, which were referred to as the tank projectile, training or TPT round. At that time, this round came in 90 mm and 105 mm and was fired in great quantity out on the tank firing ranges. The 105-mm TPT projectile was solid, very high-grade aluminum and weighed just over twenty-three pounds. As scrap it was very valuable. Because of this value of aluminum and the need for vast quantities of these rounds, the Army would mine the impact areas of the tank target ranges on an annual basis to recover the spent rounds so that they could be recycled into new TPT rounds and fired again in training.

This was not lost on some industrious criminals who lived in an area north of the post. These brave folks (they were either very brave or very stupid to go out onto a live fire impact area, where there were numerous dangerous, unexploded ordnance items) would sneak onto the post at night, go out into the impact areas, and pick up, by hand, expended TPT rounds and haul them off. They would also come onto the post at night and take up huge quantities of aluminum PSP and haul it away. And finally, with some regularity, the lights would go off in the middle of the night in areas of the north part of the post when entire stretches of overhead aluminum power line would disappear. This problem fell into my lap. I was told to find them, catch them, and put a stop to this theft of aluminum because it was impacting unit readiness and post operations. This became a daily briefing item for the Corps commander, which, I unfortunately was often called upon to provide, in person.

The scale of the operations and their consistency made it clear that this was a large scale, organized criminal enterprise. The FBI field office was on the case but had no clue as to who was behind this or why (beyond the obvious resale value of the stolen metal). Local law enforcement had been less than helpful. Any residual evidence of the crimes would be difficult to detect in the field environment. No one had ever had a sighting of anyone actually stealing anything and all the roads in and out of the range, and there were many, were open and ungated. This was open range and local ranchers placed their herds on these range-training areas for grazing. It was a tough nut to crack.

The PM told me to be creative. "Do not think like a cop, think like a crook," he told me on more than one occasion at the outset of this investigation. Well, I certainly wasn't much of a cop so thinking like a crook seemed a more useful approach anyway. I sat down one afternoon with one of my MP NCOs, a very competent sergeant, and we war gamed the issue. Here my Ranger training came into play. How would I do this if I were assigned the mission to get onto Fort Hood and steal such items as power lines and PSP for quick cash? We also had to consider how one might handle the metal in larger quantities where it would be heavy and bulky. And then, we had to consider how the crooks turned the stolen aluminum into cash. Such large quantities also suggested they had to be taking this stuff somewhere that could process large quantities of used aluminum. The Corps commander wanted these crooks in jail, along with everyone involved. The PM said to coordinate with the FBI, the US Attorney's office, with JAG in my back pocket, and get it done. So, I developed a basic Ranger five paragraph operations order. It was not a traditional law enforcement or CID investigative approach, but it was what I had and knew.

First, we needed to know what was actually happening out on the range. That meant surveillance and night operations. We initiated nightly patrols and surveillance outposts overwatching the tank target ranges and the power lines. In a matter of days we had direct evidence of thefts by armed intruders of TPT rounds and PSP planking. We were ready to track the thieves off post. For that we needed the FBI.

We could prove to the FBI that we were finding and tracking the thieves while on post and where they exited the post. We now had reasonable cause to bring in the FBI to conduct off-post operations. To do that, FBI field office SAC made it clear he would need our support for their operations off post because we had "toys" that they did not have. For that we needed a "finding" of imminent danger to the civilian community and that this was a national security issue. Those findings the III Corps Judge Advocates General team procured for us. That done, we were ready to assist the FBI with some off-post support. This initially involved using already planned aerial recon training missions to capture nighttime infrared (IR) images of the crooks, where they went and what they did. For that to be useful evidence, the JAG said I needed to be the expert interpreter of the images because the Intel types were not allowed to do that, and the FBI could not participate in the imagery capture, processing, or interpretation. That meant some schooling for me.

I soon underwent an intense, but informative, training course in aerial photo interpretation to include night IR imagery. As I would be expected to testify at any criminal proceeding that might result, I had to be competent and knowledgeable in the subjects surrounding our probable cause for arrest and evidence used in any trial. My experience in photography (extensive hobby and some aerial work during my flight training) gave me a leg up to start. We could not give the FBI or the US Attorney any actual imagery that might be captured. I would have to be able to testify to what was observed.

When I saw the extent of the US government commitment to this investigation, I realized that this was bigger than a few brass and scrap pickers making some extra money. We captured the goods on armed suspects entering Fort Hood's ranges, stealing literally tons of aluminum, from PSP to wire to TPT rounds and removing it from post to civilian property where it was heated, cut up, and loaded into fifty-five-gallon drums and then likely driven to a large aluminum processing plant. Oh yeah, this was a lot bigger. When the FBI moved and began arrests, it was a major, high visibility bust of a huge theft and fraud operation committed against the United States government that involved the operators of a defense plant in Rockdale, Texas. The PM was happy, the Corps commander was happy, and the FBI field office was very, very happy.

As the assistant operations officer, I also got involved in many other investigations, from drug interdiction operations to car thefts and robberies. We even had an attempted bank robbery one day on post. On this day a few less-than-bright young civilians decided to try to rob one of the banks on post. While this was technically an open post, meaning that non-military civilians could drive on and off most areas with a visitor's pass, we did have gates with MPs at almost all points of entry to the main cantonment areas. What the crooks did not expect was that we could stop all traffic in and out rather quickly. So, we did, they were caught and went to jail. The looks on their faces when they were stopped by a barricade at the East Gate manned by a dozen MPs in full combat gear with shotguns and M-16s was priceless.

On another night, my phone rang, as it always seemed to do whenever I fell asleep. I answered to the duty officer apologizing, again, for waking me up. He then asked me to come to the PMO because we had a murdered soldier in one of the division barracks. Where in the barracks, I asked him, and murdered how? He replied, "In his bed with a single gunshot to the head." *Damn*, I thought, *sounds like an execution style attack*. I dressed and went downstairs. Out front of the BOQ waited an MP patrol car with its red and white lights rotating on the vehicle's roof. I jumped in, assuming it was for me, and the night shift duty MP NCO drove us toward the division area.

"Good morning, sir," he said. "It's another great day to be in the military police."

"Right," I said. He drove me straight to one of the division barracks to see the body and the crime scene. CID arrived about the same time that we did and began their crime scene investigation. There were about eight soldiers standing to one side of the room under the watchful eye of two MP sergeants. I looked at the body and the name on the bunk and asked if anyone in the room knew who had done this. No one replied. It was another long night, supervising the detailing of the crime scene, collecting statements, interviewing the unit's leaders and the cleanup. Not fun and not very pretty to watch. This incident, along with several others followed me for some time as the crimes were investigated and proceeded through the courts and court-martial process. Indeed, this murder and a few others resulted in my returning to Fort Hood, in later months, even after I departed my duties there, so that I could testify during the court-martial proceedings. This one was, indeed, an execution carried out between two rival groups of soldiers who were into a rather extensive on-post drug distribution ring. The entire ring was brought down as the result, but that positive outcome would certainly not help the family of the young man murdered that night on that lonely, remote army post.

Duty with the MPs meant little sleep, frequent night duty shifts as post MP duty officer or weekend duty at the post confinement facility. Now *that* was a depressing place to work. The post confinement facility, or stockade as most referred to it, was a semi-isolated group of old wooden, two-story structures, divided by barbed wire fencing into what we referred to as cell blocks, that were fitted out with either long rooms of bunks and wall lockers or, in the case of two of the cell blocks, individual metal lined cells with large metal cell doors and substantial locks. Each cell block had lights all around to provide full exterior illumination at night, fenced in walking paths for the roving guard patrols, and two cell supervisors, or *turn keys*. That moniker indicated that they carried the keys to the cell blocks and cells themselves. Night duty within this facility required frequent walking inspections, head counts and interrupting the occasional fight among the prisoners or dealing with an unruly, rebellious type who refused to cooperate with the requirements of the facilities' mandatory daily routines. I hated confinement duty! Where were those damned flight school orders?

One of the main functions of the military police community on post was to keep or, when lost, restore order. Restoring order was one of the more common functions every night. There seemed to be a fight or brawl at one of the various enlisted or NCO clubs every night. There were fights in the barracks or, even more unpleasant, domestic issues in the post residential housing. *Domestics*, as we called them, involved everything from husbands beating wives to wives beating husbands to child abuse or child on child attacks. These were the worst to deal with and most demoralizing for the MPs who had to intervene and try to bring order to these sad homes and the consequential, often violent confrontations. Having to enter a home, with children present, with a drawn side arm was ugly duty for all of us. One never knew exactly what one was walking into, in such cases. With all the pressures of frequent reassignments to combat duty in Southeast Asia, the effort to try to maintain the appropriate level of military readiness by the units on post was a major challenge. With constant shortages of equipment, parts, personnel, and funding, caused by the demands of the ongoing fight in Vietnam and the frequent cutbacks of the military budget by Congress as they tried to influence the conduct of the war, the effects on training, morale, and the military families were more than just problematic. Combined with the distain that most in the media portrayed as the view of the American population toward soldiers, it was little wonder that this stress had dire effects on the post's soldiers and their families. It was sad to witness and even sadder to try to intervene and help. Most often we were not seen as helping, of course, but that was what we were doing when we were called for by family services, the chaplain, or a unit commander. Family intervention was thankless duty that always required the presence of the MP duty officer or me. With these events most common at night, sleep was almost always in short naps, with a very rare entire night of rest.

Unfortunately, some confrontations, whether in the housing area, the division area, or at an on-post club, were violent and involved weapons of some type being used or their use threatened. Also unfortunate was the fact that several of us in the military police community were forced to use lethal force during my tenue at Fort Hood. I thank the Almighty that, to my knowledge, I never actually caused anyone's death in the exchanges of fire that I experienced at Fort Hood. The shooting investigations that followed were just as onerous as the events themselves.

We had, however, some moments of fun and laughter. It was, in general, a professional, affable group of officers and soldiers that made up the military police officer and NCO corps on Fort Hood in those days. We participated in regular family gatherings and unit events, such as cookouts and evenings at the o' club. Most of the MP community stayed to itself and did not interact with the remainder of the post community on a social basis. I, on the other hand, observed no such social separation. I had several close friends on post, such as Gary and Linda Garczynski, who both were classmates from Georgetown University. As a result, I had a larger circle of friends and was a bit more engaged with the rest of the post's officer corps and activities. This presented no problems, most of the time. There were, however, a few occasions when my duty and assignment on post was realized by new acquaintances and conversation stopped abruptly. Not everyone saw the MPs in the same congenial light as most of my regular friends. Not too different from civilian society, I suppose, but still, not what I expected in the military community. But it was not a major burden for me either.

Second Lieutenant Gary Garczynski and I had also graduated from high school together and had known each other for a long time, with many shared experiences. Gary and Linda had a small home that they rented in Copperas Cove, just off post. Off-post housing was in very short supply. This house was small, old, and somewhat ramshackle and was located right next to the Atchison, Topeka, and Santa Fe Railroad tracks that ran by the west side of the post. But it was a nice little place to get away from post and have some down time with Gary and Linda. I had some good times there and rapidly learned the cure for railroad noise at night, when a passing train could quite literally bounce you out of bed . . . a good round of fine drinks before you tried to sleep. I found this solution often useful, later, in Vietnam. The little house had unique and entertaining aspects about it. For one thing, it was old and of a historic farm design from decades past. It had a comfortable living room, an old-style front porch that looked out to the RR tracks and a kitchen that produced wonderful smells. Gary was assigned to an artillery unit on post, so I only saw him off duty, as our paths never crossed on duty. We did try to escape the post on the few weekends when we were not on call at the same time.

One of my other, less frequent duties, turned out to be serving as a security team lead for very senior VIPs visiting our area of the country. Apparently, I did a pretty good job at this from the start. I simply looked at each task from the perspective of a bad guy. If I was one and I wanted to take out or take control of a VIP, how would I do it? How would a Ranger do it? Then I planned my security perimeter and overall defense plan accordingly. Nothing ever happened on my watch. One of the more notable tasks assigned was to provide supplementary security to Former President Johnson's Texas Ranch (to augment the Secret Service team there that looked after the retired president) because he was hosting a large, Texas-style barbeque for friends, DOD officials and some members of Congress. Another frequent task was to provide a security detail to the secretary of the Army, the Honorable Stanley Resor, whenever he was in the Southwest.

On the more serious side, in mid-April of 1970 I was called into the PM office one morning, along with others on his immediate staff, as was the custom whenever something major came up. He opened the meeting with a bit of a commentary on how the nation's media had turned on the military and how many of the "nuts out there" were taking full advantage of the situation. Without any direct explanation of a connection to the word "nuts" he asked if we were all familiar with the recent activities of Jane Fonda. I read the constant stream of police intelligence that came in every day, as this was one of my more minor duties, and therefore I was familiar with the reports of her trying to get onto military reservations around the country to create confrontations. I also had read and had been following background information about her. I expected that one

day Fort Hood would be on her itinerary. So, apparently, did the PM.
He then directed me to "get smart" on her activities, check with the
"G-men" for what they might have and check in with the PM shop
at 3rd Army (our next higher headquarters) and find out what they
knew and what they expected. This was, he explained, a purely police
matter and we were to keep this strictly in law enforcement channels.
We all clearly understood the rules, but we also knew that he did not
want to be blindsided, nor, apparently, did the III Corps commander.

I gathered current information about her military installation-
related activities and built a "read file" on her activities for the PM.
There was every indication that she planned to come to a post in
the southwest at some point. We tracked her activities from law
enforcement reports. She had a new movie coming out and had
lost a lot of weight and her appearance seemed strangely different,
from what I could tell, certainly different from what I had seen in
her other movies. She bore no real resemblance to that character in
the movie *Barbarella*. But then, little from Hollywood did resemble
reality. Hollywood actors, writers, directors, and producers live in
and portray a fantasy world. From my research, it seemed that Miss
Fonda not only portrayed a world of fantasy, but she also lived it and
believed it. Based upon what I learned of her recent activities and her
abrupt withdrawal from supporting the American Indian Movement,
her previous cause, she was clearly very self-centered, always seeking
an opportunity to gain personal media attention. It was a level of
self-adulation and self-promotion that must have made others in her
trade either incredibly jealous or disgusted with her.

In early May, the Post Public Information Office received a call
from her publicist that she planned to pay a visit to Fort Hood to meet
with the soldiers and share her political views about the war and what
she called *GI rights*, as if she had any idea what that might actually be.
Our PM was spooled up over this news and he got everyone focused
very quickly on developing a strategy to keep this event, if it occurred,
as low profile and non-confrontational as was possible. He wanted

Miss Fonda treated with kid gloves. He liked her father, Henry Fonda, and felt that, whatever the daughter's proclivities, we would try not to embarrass her father, if we could avoid it.

With that command guidance we began to plan and research options. The Operations officer called me into the PM's office about two days before the expected visit. Then the PM told me, "Son, we want to keep this both low profile and low precedent. We do not want Miss Fonda met by any field grade officer. This will be treated as the minor event it is. Therefore, you, Lt. Hoffman, will meet her at the arrival gate, once we know which one it is, and advise her of both the requirements of the UCMJ and that of the United States Code as they relate to political activity on a military reservation." Then he informed me that the Corps commander wanted to personally brief me prior to Miss Fonda's arrival. Per the plan we had developed, the PM told us that we would escort her to the post football stadium and allow her to speak to any soldiers who found their way there. We did post notices of her planned arrival and this opportunity for soldiers to listen to her, if they wished. However, the PM was very clear, as was the Corps commander the next day that she was not to be allowed to hand out or post any literature of a political nature anywhere on the military installation. Doing so would be a violation of the Hatch Act. If she did so, she was to be apprehended and brought to the PMO to be processed and put before a federal magistrate for adjudication. Then the PM looked at me and said, "Son, you are going to need to wear a strong scowl and try to look at least twenty-one!" He was dead serious.

The morning of her arrival, 11 May 1970, she came from a local café that catered to the anti-war crowd, called the Oleo Strut Café in Killeen. The local police kept us informed as to her movements and advised us that she was headed to the East Gate of the Post. With Sergeant Blankenship as my driver, we headed to the East Gate to meet her. She arrived a little after eleven in the morning dressed very casually in a faded blue-jean type shirt and blue jean trousers. I use the term *dressed* in a very liberal sense, at least as it related to her body above the waist. She had the shirt almost entirely unbuttoned and was wearing no bra. This was a custom for protest by many feminists of that time. But it was not suitable attire on a US military reservation or for exposure to the media gaggle that was accompanying her. She arrived in a rather beat up old station wagon and got out just outside the gate. She had a rather frumpy older woman with her who only addressed her in French. This woman, Elisabeth Vailland was a friend of Jane Fonda's from France. Vailland and her husband (who had died in the mid-sixties) were major players in the French Communist scene in the 60s and she was closely tied to various Russian-sponsored activities in the 70s, including the World Peace Council. She showed up in some interesting places during the 1970s. She appeared to be orchestrating the entire affair at Fort Hood for Jane Fonda.

We later learned that she was indeed representing the World Peace Council, then claiming to be based in France. At the time, this organization was an indirect instrumentality of the Soviet Union ... small world. I have always wondered how much Jane Fonda's father knew about the people managing the activities of his daughter. For my own part, had I known that in just two years she would be in North Vietnam pretending to shoot down American airplanes while I was in a bunker in Da Nang, trying to stay alive under North Vietnamese shelling, I might have been a bit harsher with her. Her posing in the seat of a North Vietnamese Army (NVA) anti-aircraft gun in May of 1972 wearing an NVA helmet was not only morally and legally wrong as an American citizen in a time of war, but it was irrational. I became convinced that her passion for publicity overwhelmed her capacity for good judgment.

Over the past few years, I have seen an effort by Jane to rewrite the history of all of this. At one point in an interview, she denied ever being on Fort Hood, saying she would have gone to the post if she had been invited but that she never was. She also represented in another, very contradicting interview that she simply was participating in a larger anti-American and anti-war demonstration when the "MP thugs" (presumably me) suddenly came up to her and grabbed her and hauled her away. Later she told David Letterman and others that she only went there *after* all American servicemen were gone from South Vietnam and she put no one's life at risk. That is revisionist bullshit! There were tens of thousands of us still in Vietnam and still in combat every day. Her actions emboldened the North Vietnamese and probably prolonged US direct involvement in day-to-day combat operations.

The bottom line is that Jane's conduct was costly to America and to American troops. It was dangerous for me in both 1970 and 1972. Worse, I submit that Jane Fonda extended the war by convincing the North Vietnamese and their Russian supporters that American resolve to prevent their takeover of South Vietnam by force of arms was failing. She encouraged them to resist overtures for a peaceful conclusion to the war. Her actions did, in fact, cost many soldiers their lives and she brought pain and suffering to countless American families. Finally, her actions significantly contributed to the ability of the North Vietnamese, supported by Russia, to rebuild its army in 1974 and 1975 so that it could conquer South Vietnam unopposed, after our military withdrawal, in direct violation of the Paris Peace Accords they had signed. But her actions and those of a few others forced America to turn its back on the South Vietnamese and the entire population of Southeast Asia. The result was the death of millions of Southeast Asians in South Vietnam, Cambodia, and Laos. It is no wonder that she is so sensitive to the frequent disrespect shown her by many Americans. She knows her own culpability and responsibility in the aftermath of the war in Vietnam.[5]

But in May of 1970, as far as I was concerned, she was simply a movie star with a political agenda that needed to be managed away from a confrontation with the military, if possible. It wasn't.

As we stood before each other at the east gate to Fort Hood, she first wanted to know who was in charge (I overheard Mrs. Vailland tell her in French to ask for someone more senior to deal with). I told her I was in charge at that time. She did not like that answer. She then asked if she could enter the base. I told her that she could and that we had arranged for her to speak to some soldiers at the post football stadium. I also told her that she needed to button up her shirt. Several media photographers, apparently too timid to make that point before, then piped in to echo the request so that they could take pictures that could be published. I do not understand what the point was in her mode of dress, but none of us were titillated in the least by her rather disappointing chest and the saggy adornments thereon.

She clearly did not like that answer about the opportunity to speak at the stadium. I told her I would show her the way and that there were soldiers already there awaiting her speech to them. She said, "That is not what I want." She turned to Mrs. Vailland and asked what she was to do. Mrs. Vailland responded to her and said, "Hand out something political and you will be arrested." Jane Fonda then walked through the gate and onto the post and Mrs. Vailland handed her some sheets of paper that were clearly political statements about the war, the draft, and GIs. I had seen them earlier. As she turned and handed several to one of the gate guards I told her to cease her distribution of political materials. This poor MP was so confused as to what to do that he just stood there with it in his hand like it might bite him. But he also seemed afraid to let go of it. I repeated my command to her to stop as she turned to hand another to one of the military photographers present. We had arranged for a photographer to record the events just in case there was a confrontation. We had several others on hand, including those from the media.

With that, I told her she was to be detained as she was in violation of Federal law prohibiting the distribution of political literature on a military base. I gently took her arm and I formally apprehended her and escorted her to my patrol car. I looked at Sergeant Blankenship and I thought he was about to have a heart attack. He was ashen faced and seemed unable, for a moment, to move. He exclaimed, "Holy shit," and then his training kicked in. He quickly helped put Miss Fonda and her French escort into the car. We rapidly drove off toward the PMO, per our prearranged confrontation plan, leaving the media standing at the gate snapping away with their cameras but unable to follow. I called the desk sergeant on the radio and requested that he let the PM know what was transpiring and requesting that the PMO operations officer meet us at the PMO. As we drove to the PMO, Mrs. Vailland told Jane Fonda that I was just a very young soldier who did not know what he was doing, all in French. I turned to them in English and told them that I most certainly did know what I was doing, and it was a pleasure to do so. They rode the rest of the way in silence.

Upon arrival at the PMO, we had two WACs (at this time, the only women in the US Army were nurses or those in the Women's Army Corps or WAC) standing by to escort the two detainees and to conduct a quick search to ensure that they were not armed or carrying anything dangerous into the PMO, a very strictly adhered-to standard operation procedure (SOP) for arriving detainees of any type.

That done, we escorted Miss Fonda alone to the magistrate's office and we read her the contents of a letter addressed to her that notified her that, due to her illegal conduct on the reservation, she was henceforth barred from reentry onto the Fort Hood Military Reservation and that violation of this order at any time in the future would result in her immediate arrest and prosecution. The letter was duly recorded by the magistrate and delivered to Miss Fonda. I then escorted her off the post via a different gate. We did, however, have the Killeen police waiting for her just off post. It seemed that one of our post drug dogs had alerted on their car and we advised the Killeen police of this fact. I gather she had a rather chilly reception in Killeen.

Actress Jane Fonda is taken into custody by Military Police Lt. John
T. Hoffman of Washington, D.C., after she handed out anti-war
leaflets at the Fort Hood Army base near Killeen, Texas, May 11,
1970. (AP Photo/Ted Powers)

Placing Ms. Fonda and Mrs. Vailland into my patrol car on
May 11, 1970 at Ft Hood, TX.

Of course, the affair was duly photographed and reported by the media. As a result, the next day my mug appeared with that of Miss Fonda in papers across the country and overseas in an AP wirephoto. The result was a deluge of mail, both supportive and hateful, from around the country. It also resulted in speculation as to exactly who I was, why I was at Fort Hood, and where I had been since my testimony before Congress the year before. The conspiracy theorists had a field day. The reality was much less intriguing. This event followed me for many years into the future. Sometimes it came up in conversation for simply amusement and other times for much less honorable and less pleasant reasons. I also received death threats via mail, via telephone calls to the base, and to newspapers in Texas and in DC.

Lesson: sometimes, no matter the truth, people will believe what they want to believe.

A few weeks after this confrontation with Miss Fonda, an FBI agent in the Fort Hood field office called and asked to see me in his office. "What about?" I asked, and he said that he needed to have a face-to-face discussion. In fact, he came to my office, sat down, looked me over and then said, "Boy, you look like you are about fifteen years old." We had met before but in a larger group meeting where I was somewhat pissed about poor FBI support to the PM. It was after that meeting that I was told that my demeanor when angry always changed my countenance to a more mature appearance. *Okay*, I thought, *what the hell is this about?* Then he said he had two things to discuss with me. First, my old adversaries from my days in Washington, DC and Georgetown, the Weathermen, had added me to their assassination list. But, he said not to worry. I was in good company, along with the secretary of the Army, several governors, members of Congress, and a few general officers. I was, however, the only lieutenant they knew of on that list and likely the easiest target. Therefore, they would keep an eye on me, and the post CID office would be responsible for looking after me. This issue followed me for the next year and created both amusement and misunderstanding on the part of others. It really angered me that these assholes, led at that time by a guy named William Ayers, under the guise of peace activism seemed to relish causing destruction and death with their bombings of federal facilities and college ROTC offices and in creating mayhem and personal risk for the nation's law enforcement and military communities. This is something for which only a few members of this group or their leader have ever been called to account.

"What is the other thing you wanted to discuss," I asked? He then stated that they had their eye on me and wanted to know if I would be interested in leaving the Army and joining the FBI. I laughed out loud. I told him the last thing I wanted to do was spend my adult life as a federal agent. Yes, my grandfather had been a somewhat legendary federal officer with the Justice Department and a famous US Attorney. Yet that was a family tradition that did not suit me. I was polite, if colorful and emphatic. "No fucking chance of that, my friend!"

Shortly after this affair, I was told by the deputy PM that I had come down on orders for Fort Stewart, Georgia and the US Army Fixed Wing Training School located there. "But," he said, "the Corps commander has nixed them. You are not going any time soon," he continued. It seemed that, according to him, the PM and the Corps commander felt that I was too valuable to the post and the MPs to be reassigned at that time. "Look," he then added, "this delays your entry to flight school and any potential assignment to Vietnam afterwards. The longer this is delayed, the less likely you will ever get sent over there," he concluded. In my mind, RVN was already winding down. Flight school was a yearlong endeavor. I felt that the chances of my getting there, even if I left for flight school that day, were slim. I was not a happy camper that day. Duty at Fort Hood sucked. The military police community had some wonderful members with whom I enjoyed working. Yet the work was onerous, it was seemingly unending, and it was dealing with the seamiest side of life. It was dangerous, it was tedious, it was frustrating, and it was twenty-four seven! I had been around army aviation enough to know that, while flying is, of course, somewhat dangerous, the duty was a lot better than this and the pay was a whole lot better. I had made first lieutenant by this time and the pay raise was less than half of what my flight pay would be! I wanted out of the military police corps. It had been interesting, challenging and, at times, even fun. But it was not what I wanted to be doing.

I called a close family friend and West Point classmate of my father, General Jack Hennessy. I had grown up with him and many other senior, even famous, officers around our household. He took my call (not customary for young lieutenants calling two-star generals). I explained that I thought I was being screwed. I had done everything I had been asked to do. I had put up with a lot since Georgetown and met the challenge every time. Why, I asked him, was I being denied flight school when I had an actual contract with the Army to fly? He told me to be patient. He told me that the orders would come down in the next few months and that I should not worry. He told me that my duty performance at Fort Hood was a matter of record all the way to the chief of staff of the Army. For most, this would be a major accolade. But for me, as I told him, any lt. with his face on the front page of the *Washington Post* was a little too visible. He laughed and allowed that I had a good point, but the truth was that my actions had brought very positive comments from his fellow senior staffers, and he was proud to know me. "Well fine," I said. "You might show me how proud." Strong words from a lieutenant to a general, but I had more than once sat upon his knee, and I was an infantry officer on his recommendation. He simply told me to keep up the good work and hang in there, flight school was coming. "Yes, sir," and "thanks" were all I could muster to end the conversation. I sure wished Dad was around and I could talk to him. So, I wrote him a letter and made the same case, for whatever good it would do. I figured he would have some opportunity to talk to General Jack somewhere along the line.

As I got more and more involved with the AWOL detachments and our fellow civilian law enforcement departments in Central Texas, I found myself on frequent joint patrol operations. Joint patrols in Dallas and Fort Worth by MP officers or senior NCOs were something that we were tasked to do at least once a month. This served to monitor our local AWOL detachment, it helped maintain a cordial relationship with these departments, and it established ties that could enable better cooperation and information sharing. These were all good ideas on paper. The application of this was more problematic. If I was to conduct a joint patrol in Dallas, I had to drive up there, participate in the joint patrol, usually a night operation, and then be back at Fort Hood the next morning. The pool of available and PM approved officers and NCOs for this duty was very small, about ten of us. Therefore, this duty had to be passed around and we each had this duty every few weeks. It wasn't bad, really, the food was good, the companionship was good, and I always learned a lot about municipal law enforcement operations, but the hours and the driving got old. Where, again, were those flight school orders?

Not too long after the confrontation with, and my subsequent apprehension of Miss Fonda, I traveled back to DC, driven most of the way by another Georgetown classmate assigned to Fort Hood, Jim Johnson, to get married to Karen M. Schultze. Karen and I had dated in college and became engaged just before I was transferred to Fort Hood. She was the daughter of a prominent economist and a former Cabinet officer in two administrations. Charles Schultze was less than enthusiastic about our impending marriage. But the wedding proceeded as planned. At the rehearsal dinner, Karen's father stood up during the toasts and proposed a toast to Karen along the lines of "Here is to the woman who beat out Jane Fonda." It got a huge laugh, however absurd.

After a fun honeymoon in Maine, Karen and I returned to Fort Hood to set up housekeeping in an off-post apartment. The Army was a bit of a shock to Karen. Fort Hood was a shock to Karen. Killeen, Texas, was a shock to Karen. Indeed, just about everything there, including my job and the phone that did not stop ringing was a shock to Karen. But she overcame and persevered like a real trooper. But she, as I, could not wait to get out of what, at the time, was a very remote, dry, dusty Texas town and head to a new post, preferably one with a flight school. Well, I was the one who wanted the flight school assigned. She was far less enthusiastic about that prospect.

I did actually get some flight time at Fort Hood. The Red River Army Depot flight detachment had both fixed-wing and rotary wing aircraft. And there was a flying club. So, I not only got in some time in Cessna 150s and 172s, but I was also able to get some right seat time in T-41s (actually a Cessna 172 in Army livery). I also got some introductory stick time in OH-13 helicopters with an experienced chief warrant officer who was an instructor. This brief introduction to rotary wing flight helped me later in flight school, no doubt. This all happened because I was the MP that brought the aviation community into law enforcement on post in a regular way and some of our investigations brought some real interesting flying to a group that otherwise simply flew training flights to maintain time and currency or to transport some VIP to and from a nearby commercial airport or the occasional flight to Fort Sam Houston or Fort Bliss. Cool, so when do I get to do this full time? Orders, all I needed were those damn orders!

One day, after a long night as the confinement facility duty officer, the desk sergeant called me to let me know that I had come down on a *levy* for Vietnam. Oh great, just what I want to hear! No orders for flight school. No such luck. After all I had put up with over the past fifteen months, I was going straight to Vietnam, do not pass go—no $200 and no flight school. I went directly from the post stockade over to the PMO to see what the orders said. When I got there, the SGM told me not to worry, that the boss would kill those again. Somehow, this did not seem likely. I picked up the orders and looked at them. Sure enough, these were orders to depart Fort Hood in January 1971 and, as I read the fine print, I was to proceed to Vietnam with Officer Rotary Wing Flight School en route. I did a double take. It said flight school en route. My initial reporting station was Fort Wolters, near Mineral Wells, Texas. This was a small aviation post where primary flight training was conducted. It was just up the road from two major cities, Dallas and Fort Worth. This was all okay by me. Flight school was a year in length. I figured there was little chance I would get assigned to Vietnam before things wound up there. After all, they were already holding peace talks in Paris! The deputy PM came up to me just about then and said that he was very sorry to tell me that he had just heard that these orders came out of the office of the chief of staff of the Army and the Corps commander could not do anything to change them. "Change them," I said, "I love them, and I do not want them changed!" Everybody in the PM shop thought I gone 'round the bend and was just tired and talking nonsense. No indeed, I was very happy. Finally, flight school orders that would stick!

When I told Karen, she was happy for me, but clearly concerned about the future. For her, I suppose, the question was which was worse, MP duty in this remote location or flight school and the potential for duty in Vietnam? There was no question in my military mind. Flight school and flying—finally! While this was not the fixed-wing school, which was what I really had hoped to get, it was flight school and it got me out of Fort Hood!

CHAPTER FOUR
FLIGHT SCHOOL

I OUT-PROCESSED FROM Fort Hood in late January of 1971. As my orders transferred me to duty in the Republic of Vietnam, with temporary duty (TDY) en route for Rotary Wing Flight training, this process included all the normal steps for an individual about to proceed directly into a combat theater, such as shots, weapons qualification, threat indoctrination, etc. This all took about two weeks, which gave Karen and me time to get packed and ready to move to Mineral Wells. We were able to locate a nice apartment on the edge of town, not far from the main gate to Fort Wolters. The move was done by the Army via a contractor who seemed to view our property as a source for completing their own inventory of personal effects. When we unpacked in Mineral Wells, for example, the small case in which I kept little keepsakes had been emptied of anything valuable.

As we did not actually have much to start with, the losses were not consequential, and my focus was on getting started in flight training. Karen set up our meager household and we began to process into the Army's Primary Flight Training School. First up was a welcome to the newly arriving Officer Class of 71-30 by the school commandant. Each flight school class wore a distinctively colored baseball hat. Ours was white. We wore our rank insignia on the hat, and once you had soloed, your student pilot wings. The only thing that stands out in my mind about that brief welcome was the admonition to the wives to feed a good breakfast every morning to their flight trainee husbands because it might save their lives. What, failing to eat breakfast was more dangerous than flying helicopters?

The first month was focused on the prerequisite introduction into the theory of flight and the basics of the helicopter systems, weather, and aerial navigation. This traditional entry path into the world of aviation is called ground school in the civilian world and preflight training in the military. As I already had my pilots license from the FAA and had been through ground school before, most of this was refresher training for me, at least until they began to teach us about how and why a TH-55 primary flight training helicopter was able to achieve flight over the ground and not summarily fall to earth.

The T stood for Training and the H stood for helicopter. The 55 was the actual model number of this series of helicopters. The TH-55 was a piston-powered machine that could carry, on a good day and in the right weather conditions, two pilots and enough fuel to run you into a state of yellowing eyeballs. Now this was not due to any extraordinary longevity of flight endowed in this small machine. No indeed, this was simply because the vibration profile of the machine set in motion, in most human bodies, an accelerated vascular and kidney function that resulted in rapidly rising bladder pressure, which in turn seemed to back up other systems, causing one's eyes to take on the color of jaundice. The machine was manufactured of steel, plastic, and aluminum. I hoped none of the aluminum was from Rockdale, TX. Any metals from that plant were probably contaminated with a wide variety of undesirable substances from the ranges at Fort Hood and the backyard of certain Texas criminals. It also seemed that most of this machine was actually plastic of some type or another. It was powered by what I knew to be an exceptionally reliable Lycoming horizontally opposed internal combustion engine that was used quite successfully in a wide range of fixed-wing airplanes. The aircraft's systems all seemed quite reasonable to my semi-experienced aviation mind until the instructor got to the part about the drive belts.

As with everyone else in the class that day, I am sure the look on my face was a mix of astonishment and trepidation upon hearing this explanation of the aircraft's power train. By this I mean the method for transferring the power of the engine to the main transmission which, in turn, drove the three small rotor blades. Belts? Belts, as in what kind of belts? Rubber belts? You mean this thing is driven by rubber bands? At this point in the class-wide epiphany on how this thing achieved actual flight, several of our officer student aviators were clearly ready to join the Navy or go back to the infantry, artillery or even the MPs. Rubber bands drive this thing?

The universal question at this point was "so what happens if the rubber bands break?"

"Well," responded the instructor, "you can auto-rotate to the ground." Then he added, "But of course it doesn't happen very often." Obviously suggesting that, indeed, at least occasionally it did happen!

Lesson: the ubiquitous rubber band drives everything and probably always will.

"By the way, what is auto-rotation anyway?" someone else in the class asked. At least here I was on familiar ground. Back at Fort Hood, while out on an aerial range patrol with an experienced chief warrant officer pilot in an OH-13, he said to me one day, "Here, watch this!" The bottom seemed to suddenly fall out from under us as we fell out of the sky. He quickly recovered the aircraft into level flight, but this was my introduction into the ability of helicopters to use the wind rising through the rotor blades, as the aircraft falls, to cause the blades to rotate and thereby generate some lift. This resultant windmilling or spinning of the rotor blades produced sufficient lift to slow the descent, not stop it, but slow it enough to permit a soft, gentle (in the hands of an experienced pilot) touchdown on Mother Earth.

My first ride in the cockpit of a helicopter at Fort Hood as a student pilot was exciting. When my Army training began at Ft. Benning and in Ranger school, I rode in helicopters several times. But occupying a seat in the cockpit as a student pilot was where the action was.

I already had my fixed-wing pilot's license. I had been flying fixed-wing planes for more than three years already. But the sensations and dynamics of rotary-wing flight are vastly different than that of a fixed-wing airplane—particularly in that period between departure from the ground and achieving level flight. The most significant change is the attitude of the aircraft and the visual perspective of the ground and horizon and the sensations you experience. In a fixed-wing airplane, one accelerates, employing the power and thrust of the engines and propellers (if it is so equipped), down the runway until sufficient speed is achieved whereby the air passing over the wings generates sufficient lift to enable the plane to lift off the ground. This is generally initiated by an applying upward pressure on the elevators (affixed to the aft of those small horizontal wings at the tail of the airplane) that will cause the nose of the airplane to rotate up. As the nose comes up, the plane lifts gently into the air and climbs up to its initial cruising altitude.

In a helicopter, as it was demonstrated to me that day at Fort Hood, you do the opposite. You lift the helicopter to a hover about three feet over the ground. Then you push the nose of the helicopter down by applying forward pressure on the stick or cyclic. This causes the helicopter's rotor disk plane to tilt forward. This forward tilt pulls the aircraft forward to gain airspeed. As speed increases, the helicopter rotor disk gains additional lift, and the helicopter rises. Sounds simple. Looks and feels, especially to an airplane pilot, real dangerous and is very disconcerting. And this was just the takeoff!

I was also introduced to the execution of an autorotation. Planes do not, at least not in any manner of controlled flight, suddenly fall nearly vertically from the sky like a streamlined brick. Helicopters not only do this, but they do it intentionally and can recover from this precipitous fall and set down upon the ground with the gentle touch of a graceful bird (well, a gooney bird anyway). Planes, on the other hand, rarely recover from such descents and, even if they recover in some fashion, will ultimately be rendered into a pile of broken airplane parts. As an airplane pilot taught not to enter into such a regime of uncontrolled flight, at least not anywhere near the ground, autorotation was counter intuitive, and a cultural, educational, and mental barrier that I was not confident I could overcome.

Once I had experienced the full, breathtaking initial drop and sense of impending doom and then gently gliding under the rotating blades, but without the sound of the engine generating the power normally required to overcome the pull of gravity, I began to appreciate the subtle advantages of rotary wing flight. Because, as with most helicopter landings, in autorotation one did not need a large, open strip of ground on which to land. You could still put the aircraft down safely on a relatively small open spot.

Lesson: I can land anywhere in this thing without the engine, as long as it is directly below my feet as I look out the chin bubble!

But to the rest of the class, this was still a subject of mystery and awe, something yet to be experienced and something almost dreaded but clearly unavoidable in our future training. The response of the instructor was simply, "Oh autorotations? That is when you are really having fun in flight school!" He said this as if he really meant it. Little did we know!

This rubber-band thing still bothered me. After all, I was supposed to be headed to fixed-wing flight school. Fixed-wing aircraft are just that. The wings stay in place. They are solid, sound, and big. These things had wings or rotors that were less than a foot wide! Fixed-wing aircraft had the propeller firmly and solidly attached directly to the engine, not driven by rubber bands. Fixed-wing aircraft had wheels and brakes and ailerons and rudders and tail planes and stabilizers and, and, and . . . this thing had rubber bands! Fixed-wing aircraft inherently want to fly. Helicopters most assuredly do not want to fly; you have to *make* them fly. Oh well, I figured a lot of fine folks had learned to fly helicopters and it was, after all, flight school, which is what I wanted. And it was better than night duty at the Fort Hood post stockade!

And then, of course, there was the money. In addition to my base pay, now about four hundred dollars per month, I got a housing allowance, I got flight pay, and I was getting TDY supplementary pay of almost twenty-five dollars per day! These were huge sums to me in those days, especially after living at Fort Hood on only my base pay for so long. This vast new monthly financial stream meant a lot of different things to different people. For some, particularly the bachelors, it meant a fast new car or a big and fast motorcycle. This car and motorcycle phenomenon was a major headache for the command at the US Army Aviation Center and School. Here were young officers with lots of ready cash, an already demonstrated propensity for excitement and speed, and lots of free time on weekends and evenings. What this translated into was one of the highest accident rates and, oh by the way, fatality rates for any population of officers in the entire Army! Selecting, screening, and training individuals to be combat pilots was expensive. Keeping student pilots safe on and off duty was a challenge all through the year-long flight-training process.

The pool of available "fodder" for this particularly casualty-intense combat force was limited to those with exceptional eyesight, coordination ability, aptitude, higher than average excitement threshold and, to a great degree, a certain level of fearlessness. This meant, of course, that the appeal of fast cars, fast motorcycles, and flying resided in this same pool of individuals. The command at

Fort Wolters, and later at Fort Rucker, placed enormous emphasis on safety on and off the flight line and a serious intolerance for those who got speeding or DWI tickets. Of course, not so serious that they could overlook the also serious shortage of combat helicopter pilots, so punishment was not dismissal, just an Article 15 under the Uniform Code of Military Justice. An Article 15 hit your wallet hard, as well as the rest of your military career, if you planned on one. Nearly every flight school class lost at least one member to a fatal car accident sometime during the year of flight training, though our class was an exception. We collected our share of tickets and had numerous near misses, but we lost no one to a traffic accident.

Lesson: Fast small cars are fun, dangerous, and expensive. Big cars are fast enough, comfortable, and inexpensive and are career enhancing.

Even with this emphasis on safety, there was no effort to dissuade any of us from seeking out, obtaining, and driving whatever fast car or motorcycle we wanted. Indeed, the local economy in the Mineral Wells, Texas area seemed to be firmly built upon car dealerships that sold high-dollar vehicles to Army pilots drawing flight pay. All other significant commercial activity around the base seemed to be there only to ensure that these pilots were available and postured to lay down that new wealth on shiny new cars and motorcycles. Take for example, Captain Arnold (Dusty) Holms, who was already a Vietnam veteran. Dusty was a stick buddy and became a great friend to me during the year-long training and the following year in Vietnam. Dusty owned a huge, bright-orange Dodge Superbird, complete with a large horizontal stabilizer wing on the back of the trunk and Superbird decals on the side fenders. This was one flashy car that looked like it was going100 miles per hour even when it was parked! It got Dusty a lot of tickets because the cops assumed it was always speeding. It was the source of great humor for the class, but Dusty loved it and drove it with great pride.

For some of the married couples this newfound wealth meant

paying off the wedding bills or buying new furniture or the ability to afford having a baby. For others it was their first opportunity to begin investing and saving for the future. And finally, there were those who simply wanted a higher standard of living. For Karen and me, it was a little bit of new furniture to expand our meager household asset base and a new car. But, as I had already been driving a fast car, I decided it was time for a more traditional family car with room, comfort, and capacity. I was tired of trying to cram the majority of our stuff into a small convertible that was fun to drive but cold in the winter and hot in the summer. So, we opted for a very nontraditional pilot's car—a four door Ford sedan. It had a big trunk, big seat, big glove compartment, big engine, big everything. It was like driving in a limo. You could put several army foot lockers in the truck and still have room for suitcases. Our entire closet of clothes could fit on a hanging bar across the back seat. And with gas going for about thirty-five cents a gallon (even twenty-five cents in some areas of Texas), mileage was not a major consideration, but tank size was. This Ford Custom Cruiser could hold twenty-five gallons of fuel and could go four hundred miles on a tank of gas. The Mustang could pass everything on the road except a gas station! This big new Ford sedan was for traveling in comfort.

Of course, most of the class did not quite have my perspective on transportation. I had grown up traveling the world and spending long hours in our family car driving across both the United States and Europe. I had been there and done that when it came to fast sports cars and motorcycles in high school in France and in college. As a former paramedic, fireman, and police traffic officer, I had seen enough to know that fast and sporty also meant deadly and messy. Car travel was, to me, transportation. It was not a statement of any kind. I, at the ripe old age of twenty-four, wanted comfort and space.

When I drove it to the flight line one day, Dusty asked me about the fate of the Mustang and why I was driving what looked like an unmarked police car. This suspicion of my actual duties was fostered by my somewhat dubious public notoriety and the fact that I knew most of the MP community on base. I was often contacted, sometimes during classes, to respond to inquiries about some case or the other that I had worked at Fort Hood. I also was called back to Fort Hood to testify in a couple of military trials. This was a great inconvenience to the school, and they tried repeatedly to kill the TDY orders that would show up at the 65th Student Officer Company orderly room that directed my immediate travel to here or there for a day or so. But the military judicial community had more juice than the commandant of the school because these orders had the force of subpoenas, and I went when and where I was directed.

To further create discomfort was the security issue. Being on that stupid hit list of the Weathermen meant that the CID detachment at Foot Hood was still checking on me with the officer student company and the post PMO. This led to, at the time, a hilarious circumstance where the student company commander, a young captain, came to think that I was some kind of problem officer that might reflect on his own career. He was not used to having the military police show up at odd times asking about where a student officer was. I never spent much time with him, as he was usually off somewhere doing the unit's business. It was the unit staff that dealt with us daily. One day he stopped me and asked what kind of trouble I was in and added that he had no tolerance for an officer who couldn't stay out of trouble. I thought he was kidding me. He wasn't, he was dead serious. He told me that he would not allow me to bring any discredit to his command or himself. I told him not to worry, that he and his command were not involved with my MP activities. I told him if he had issues, he should take them up with the provost marshal. I gather that his discussion with the PM did not go well. I saw little of him from that point until my departure from Fort Wolters.

None of this interfered with my learning curve or my progress through flight school. It was more an annoyance to me. But to some in the class, there was always that suspicion of who I was and what I really did for a living. This resulted in some hesitance, on occasion, on the part of some of the younger student officers to say things in front of me or share information about their weekend escapades. For my part, I could not have cared less what they thought or how they acted. I had already grown that thick skin of indifference that many in the law enforcement community must grow to deal with such attitudes on the part of the public and even, at times, among their friends.

Lesson: The military police and intelligence communities are like hot tar paper—once you touch it you have a very hard time totally disconnecting, it is very easy to get burned, and most people avoid contact with you.

Preflight training lasted about a month, and we learned all about how the T-55 operated, how it was constructed, how it was maintained, and how it was flown. Because the airframe was a combination of metal and plastic components, it was fragile. The landing skids (these helicopters did not have wheels) were horizontal hollow metal tubes that were attached to the underside of the helicopter's fuselage via four vertical compression struts and several cross braces. These struts incorporated oil-filled shock absorbers, called *oleo struts*, that both cushioned landing and reduced the effects of the vibration from the engine and transmission as they passed through the helicopter's airframe to the landing skids and the ground. Because the aircraft had significant vibration and because the rotor blades were not rigid, but flexible, it was possible for a vibration pattern to become established that would result in the vibration being reflected from the airframe to the ground and back into the aircraft. Unchecked by the dampening effect of these struts, the vibrations could build to a dangerous level and shake the aircraft apart. If you were sitting in the aircraft when this happened, your day would go to hell very fast. So, checking these struts was a critical component of your daily preflight of the helicopter. These struts did create some exciting, bouncy landings for students until we mastered the art of placing these small helicopters firmly on the ground as quickly and deftly as we could.

The aircraft's airframe always seemed more plastic than metal. The *data plate*, a small metal information plaque attached to the airframe, indicated that parts of the aircraft were made by the Mattel Toy Company. This gave rise to the nickname for the TH-55: "The Mattel Messerschmitt." The forward area of the helicopter was simply one large thin Plexiglas window. The engine was located below and aft of the cockpit floor. Immediately behind the cockpit were the fuel tank and the main transmission. Those rubber bands on the rear of the engine, or *V-belts* as they were called, transferred power from the helicopter's engine to the main transmission that drove the rotor blades. The belts rotated on two large drums and were a focus of every preflight inspection to ensure they had no defects and were not frayed (which they sometimes were, resulting in the grounding of that aircraft for belt replacement by maintenance). While the use of these large belts to drive the main transmission was a source of considerable concern to all of us at the outset of our flight training, they proved to be efficient and reliable.

The main transmission, mounted above the engine, turned a large mast that rose vertically out of the top of the transmission. The rotor blades were attached to the top of this mast by means of the rotor head. The rotor head was held on in place by means of the *Jesus Nut*. You did not want that nut to come loose! The blades were mounted so they could flex up and down and could partially rotate to change the angle of attack of each. The *pitch*, or angle of each rotor blade was controlled by a *link*, or small metal arm that came off the blade and down to a rotating, two-part disk mounted just below the rotor head. This disk is called a *swash plate*. The upper side rotates at the same speed as the rotor blades. The lower half does not rotate but is attached to small rods, tubes, and *bell cranks* to transfer control inputs from controls located in the cockpit, to the rotor head via this spinning, tilting assembly. Interestingly, the control inputs from the pilot via the pitch change links and swash plate, were always ninety degrees from the desired direction of change to the rotor disk. This is the result of a phenomenon known as gyroscopic precession. This causes all inputs to a spinning disk to occur ninety degrees from the input point on the disk. Are you lost yet? I was convinced, as I learned about how all of this worked, that the guys who invented all of this were probably smart and also probably pretty weird.

Inside the cockpit, in addition to the pilot's controls, there was an instrument panel with the necessary gauges and indicators one needed to safely operate the helicopter. These instruments were limited to the most basic necessities for monitoring the status of the engine, altitude, airspeed, a turn and bank needle, attitude gyro, rate of climb indicator, fuel gauge, engine and rotor rpm gauge, and a few caution lights. These small, segmented lights were intended to warn the pilot of any developing abnormality within selected aircraft systems.

We also studied weather (once again for me this training was not nearly as thorough as what Eastern Airlines Captain Larry DeAngelis had given me back at PG Airpark) and we learned about the military weather reporting and forecasting system. We learned about fight navigation, aeronautical charts, and aids to navigation maintained by the FAA and the Department of Defense. We learned about military aviation radios—how they worked, and how to properly use them, speak over them, and the military aeronautical communication procedures to use when doing so. This period was punctuated with exams and failure to meet the minimum standard meant either a recycle or dismissal from the program. We lost a few students before we ever took our first flight. That surprised me because the Army required a comprehensive flight aptitude test, before anyone was considered for flight training. I took it after I completed my civilian training and I found it to be thorough. It seemed to me that if you passed that test, you had the basic knowledge to become an Army aviator, but only if you also had the fortitude and coordination—something only actual flight training would reveal. Losing students at this point indicated to me that the guys really did not want to fly, not that they did not have the aptitude to do so. Me? I was not that afraid of rubber bands.

After completing the preflight training, our officer class linked up with our counterpart "white hat" warrant officer candidate training class. The Army had integrated helicopters in a big way into its combat doctrine. This meant that there was a great need for both pilots and officers, who were also pilots, who could command aviation elements from flight platoons up through aviation groups and brigades. That meant that there needed to be a large number of both warrant officer pilots, as the basic pilot force, and officer pilots, to be the leaders. So, the Army trained commissioned officers to fly, and the Army selected enlisted soldiers with an aptitude for flight training to go through Warrant Officer Candidate School, or WOC School, to become both pilots and warrant officers. For each officer flight school class there was a corresponding WOC class.

As officers and gentlemen, of course, we trained from 0700 to, normally, about 1700. Our evening and weekends were free, except where and when we needed to study to prepare for exams and the occasional night training events. The WOCs, on the other hand, lived, breathed, and thought aviation and warrant officer candidate training twenty-four hours a day, seven days a week. To be a warrant officer pilot and go through that year-long program took a special dedication and focus. Of course, the officers had been through their equivalent officer training prior to flight school. It too was demanding and long, but it was not concurrent with the mental and physical demands of flight training. I have always maintained a special level of respect and gratitude toward warrant officer pilots in the US Army that exceeds that which I hold for most other ranks in the service.

With preflight training over, we began our actual introduction into rotary-wing flight training. By this time, with all the safety training, safety admonitions, and awareness of recent fatal accidents, our apprehension about this next phase of training was heightened.

Obviously, this was intentional. Military aviation is an inherently dangerous activity. It is unforgiving of mistakes, complacency, and neglect. In this atmosphere, we were paired with stick buddies and introduced to our primary flight instructors. Stick buddies changed around over time, but our primary flight instructor remained the same until we moved into cross country, remote area, confined area, and pinnacle landing zone operations. My initial instructor was Mr. Lee, a civilian instructor. He was an experienced pilot with thousands of hours under his belt in a wide variety of rotary and fixed-wing aircraft. He was a decent guy with a pilot finesse and expertise that set a high standard for me. Having some flight experience served me well in the preflight training but it accounted for little here. In rotary wing flight, there is little to compare with fixed-wing aviation until one is airborne and in cruise flight mode. Taking off, hovering, climbing, descending, hovering again, and landing are totally different flight regimes and require entirely new skills.

Mr. Lee introduced me to the new flight environment of the helicopter and our training area. He was smooth and subtle. He did everything with a touch and smooth transition that belied the inherent instability of the TH-55 helicopter. The *cyclic*, or stick, was between your legs and controlled the attitude of the aircraft: nose up, nose down, tilt left, right, or back. The *collective*, on the left side and sticking forward out of the floor toward the front of the cockpit, controlled the pitch in the blades. This pitch controlled the vertical movement: more pitch into the blades or up collective, lifted the aircraft above the ground; less pitch in the blades, or lowering the collective, can initiate a descent. The pitch input into the blades also increased the speed in forward flight as the increased angle of attack of the blades, combined with tilting the rotor disk forward with the cyclic, increased the forward thrust while reducing it reduced the forward speed.

My first flight instructor at flight school, Mr. Lee, standing with me by a TH-55 helicopter.

One "slight" additional requirement when the pitch in the blades was increased or reduced was to control engine rpm and the power the engine developed. As the pitch was increased in the main rotor blades, the engine power output also needed to be increased while maintaining the proper engine and rotor rpm—have I lost you here yet?—via a throttle on the end of the collective. Did I say *slight*? The control component required a coordinated up and down movement of the collective while, simultaneously rolling in or out throttle to control the engine. So, not slight.

The next controls to master are the pedals. These control the yaw or sideways rotation of the aircraft, to the left or right. They are connected to the tail rotor, that other little rotor or propeller at the end of the aircraft's tail boom, out yonder behind you. You cannot see it, but you better have control of it. Are we lost yet? You will be, as I was at this point in the training at the very beginning of actual flight training in the US Army TH-55 helicopter.

In a helicopter when power is added to the engine, because the pitch in the main rotor blades has been increased, the aircraft wants to rapidly yaw to the right. To counter this natural yaw, caused by that basic law in physics: *for every action there is an equal and opposite reaction*, the left pedal needs added pressure, increasing counter thrust in the tail rotor, to keep the nose pointed in the correct direction. This was most difficult when at a hover (or "hoover," as I mispronounced it early in our flight training), when slight power or collective changes had the most dramatic effect on the aircraft's attitude and orientation. The effect also occurs in cruise flight, though less dramatically, where the pedals keep the aircraft fuselage in *trim*, or aligned in the correct direction. As one added power to the main rotors, which are spinning in one direction, the body of the aircraft wanted to spin in the opposite direction. I know I may have lost you at this point. For myself at this point in the training, I began to understand why so many prospective helicopter pilots washed out of the training. Learning to simultaneously coordinate the movement of the collective, the throttle, the cyclic, and the pedals of a helicopter is daunting.

So, let's review. To hover you controlled attitude with the cyclic to stay level with your right hand. You controlled your height above ground with the collective in your left hand. You control engine power, needed to maintain your height above the ground with the throttle by rotating your left wrist. You countered the natural desire of this inherently unstable, often uncooperative, spiteful, and infernal machine to rotate around its rotor mast by means of the pedals by using your feet. Of course, always remembering that any change to the collective, pedals, or cyclic if you drift in any direction, requires throttle control changes by you left wrist and subtle adjustments of all the other controls. Got it?

Now you might ask "how exactly does a helicopter fly?" Simple, the wings provide the lift needed to get off the ground and fly. "Wings, what wings?" you might ask. For all aircraft (not rockets, they simply use raw power to overcome gravity) the air passing over the wings creates that lift. The theory of winged flight, first practically demonstrated by the Wright brothers, or Augustus Whitehead, in either 1901 or 1903 depending upon whose history you are reading, is actually quite simple. As the air passes over and under a wing it creates lift. This is because the wing is, generally, almost flat on the bottom and curved on top. This means that the path of the air is shorter under the wing than over its top. This difference is why we can fly. The air on the shorter path remains denser and creates higher pressure than the air traveling the longer path over the top of the wing, which becomes less dense and has less pressure. The pressure difference between the top and bottom is why a wing has lift and why we can overcome gravity and fly. For airplanes the thrust of the engine or engines forces the plane into forward flight, thus causing the air to pass over and under the wings, creating the lift needed to rise off the ground and fly forward through the air.

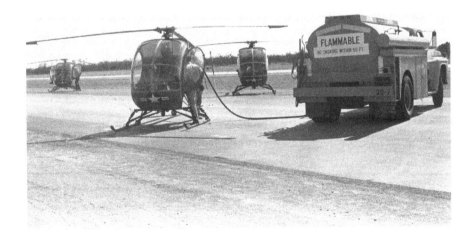

Refueling a TH-55 Helicopter.

For a helicopter, the engine, via a transmission, and, in the case of smaller helicopters such as the TH-55, a few very tough rubber bands, provides the power to spin a mast on which are attached two or more rotor blades. These rotor blades have the same type of cross section as an airplane wing, generally flat on the bottom and convex on top. As the rotor blade is spun through the air, it generates lift. That is the basic reason why a helicopter can fly. Lesson: With enough power and fast-moving parts, you can beat the air into submission and cooperation!

With our shift into actual flight training, we flew from one of the many stage fields built around the training areas of Fort Wolters. These consisted of a flight operations building and classroom, a large ramp that could hold ten to twelve aircraft, and long narrow strips of pavement that constituted short runways with helipads at each end. The day would start with a bus ride out to the stage field or a ride to one of the main heliports on the base where the aircraft were normally stored and maintained and then a short flight with the instructor out to the stage field to begin the day's flight-training operations. The first flight with Mr. Lee was simply an orientation on the aircraft, how to preflight the machine, how to strap in and prepare for flight, how to complete the preflight cockpit check list, how to start the engine, how to test the systems and controls before lift-off to a hover, and then how to air taxi, also at a hover, to the departure pad and the takeoff. This first flight took us out into the traffic pattern around the stage field, introduced the communications procedures, flight paths to follow, and the approach and landing sequence. It was great fun, and I was anxious to begin actual hands-on flying with this new, wondrous machine!

The flight soon ended, and I was introduced to the landing, shut down, postflight cockpit check list, and the postflight and tying down of the aircraft. We watched the aircraft be refueled and then returned to the operations building classroom for a post-mission debrief and training session. We were evaluated, both in a verbal debrief and in writing, by the instructors after that first flight, and then after every flight we made for the remainder of flight school, until the day we graduated. We soon learned that flight evaluations were a constant. They are part of the overall Army aviation safety and proficiency program and are a part of an aviator's flying career until the day he or she retired. Of course, at this time in the Army, there were no female pilots or crew—only pilot jocks with big watches, sunglasses, fast cars, and fat wallets.

Speaking of fashion, we were issued and wore the latest in US Army flight clothing. Due to the tremendous number of fatalities from post-crash fires, both in combat and stateside, the Army had moved away from the gray cotton one-piece flight suit that had been traditional since the Second World War to a two-piece suit made of the then new fire-retardant material called NOMEX. This came in an olive drab color with zippers instead of buttons. It had Velcro closures on the legs and sleeves. It also had a high collar around the neck with its own Velcro closure to make the collar stand up and protect the neck from fire. To this we added NOMEX gloves with leather palms and leather boots.

This outfit was completed by the SPH-4 flight helmet. It was made of very hard laminations of plastic fibers and Kevlar to make it resistant to impacts, such as one might experience if you ran into the ground instead of landing softly upon it. It also contained noise-suppressing ear cushions, a must in the very noisy environment of an Army helicopter, and an integrated microphone and headset. There was a cable connected to the helmet that enabled you to plug into the aircraft's intercom and radios. It also was equipped with two visors: one clear and one tinted, that you could slide down over the upper portion of your face to provide some additional protection from flying debris, or in the case of the tinted visor, relief from the glare of the sun.

When fully ensconced in this attire, one looked like one had just stepped out of an alien space vehicle, particularly with the darkly tinted helmet visor in the down position, providing a somewhat bug-eyed look to one's appearance. We thought we looked very cool indeed! However, it took some time to get used to wearing all this flight attire correctly. It also, to a degree that irritated some, hampered your freedom of movement in the cockpit. The result was that there was a consistent effort on the part of the instructors and the school to counsel every student pilot on the need to wear the full kit properly. This same issue would plague some of us later in combat and failures to wear the full outfit properly, along with the mandatory (in my mind) body armor, proved costly to many, including some in my flight school class.

Lesson: The Army had a lot of experience behind our flight clothing and protective equipment—use and trust your equipment!

The first time that my initial instructor, the very patient Mr. Lee, allowed me the unique privilege of holding, in my right hand, the control grip of the cyclic, and only the cyclic, we sustained a level, stable attitude while at a hover for the period of about .003 seconds. Shortly after this brief period of controlled hover, I was thrashing the cyclic around the inside of the cockpit, trying to recover to and sustain that stable hover. My thrashing around with this single control continued to the point that Mr. Lee became convinced that I was trying to punch out both side windows in the process. He very calmly said "I have the aircraft!" with such authority that there was no question in my mind that I was to immediately relinquish all thought of trying to control this beast. He recovered absolute, immediate control and returned the aircraft to a stable hover in just about .002 seconds, all with just the tip of the index finger of his right hand. I was awed on the one hand and disgusted with myself on the other. All of this while only trying to control *one* of the assorted controls I was intended to learn and master!

I am truly and surely screwed, I thought. *How will I ever master all of this in the required twenty hours of initial training?* That first day was sobering and not a little humiliating. I, of course, assumed everyone else had simply taken the controls, instantly figured it out, and were all hovering with great joy and efficiency all over the stage field. Upon returning to the flight operations building, the look on the faces of the others in the room told me that I was not alone in both my failures in the cockpit that day and my concern about my ability going forward in this program. The looks in the briefing room that afternoon ranged from *someone just killed my dog* to *I have been walking around all day with my fly open*. But we had begun our formal flight training in the aircraft. And we were, therefore, now entitled to wear an embroidered single bird wing symbol on our white hats, signifying that we were now flying. The symbolism here was clear: no bird can fly with just one wing, just as we could not yet fly alone.

I quickly understood the challenges of developing the eye-hand-foot coordination one needed for flying helicopters. I always felt, either you were coordinated, or you were not. Helicopters did, indeed, require a level of coordination far beyond what was needed for flying fixed wing aircraft. I later learned that research showed it was far easier and safer to teach a helicopter pilot to fly fixed wing than the reverse. In my own case, I had little problem with coordination, aside from the fact that I could not, initially, find the *hover button*. Our flight instructors often referred to the gaining of the needed eye-hand-foot-brain coordination to intuitively and easily maintain controlled flight at a hover as *finding the hover button*. What I needed was practice and experience, and a very patient flight instructor. I was afforded both.

Lesson: sometimes the Army gets it right, despite itself.

Mr. Lee shared with me that hovering was part coordination, part state of mind, and part intuition. The coordination piece was overcoming the challenge of making your brain, through your hands, arms, and feet, operate the helicopter's controls in a coordinated manner. The mental part was overcoming fear of the machine and developing both a conscious awareness of the machine, its systems, and its attitude with respect to the horizon. The intuition part was developing the unconscious awareness of the attitude and flight condition of the aircraft, as if it were a part of you and you of it. This is, he would say, like learning to balance and ride a bicycle. As with a bicycle, once your brain and body figure it out, you do it unconsciously. Once you and your brain figure it out, you will always be able to do it. Mr. Lee patiently taught us the fine art of hovering. He would start by placing the helicopter at a stable hover and hold it there with the tip of one finger. He would then have us take just the cyclic control, or the stick, and try to maintain a level hover without drifting one way or another, while he controlled the collective, throttle, and pedals. This single control familiarization method was tried and true, but still frustrating to us novice "rotor heads."

With repeated attempts, we finally would master each control, one at a time. Then we moved to the next, far more sophisticated arena of controlled flight where we had the opportunity to employ two, and only two, of the controls simultaneously. In my case, during the third day and fifth hour of accumulated flight time, I had reasonable control of the cyclic. So now I was tasked with maintaining level, stable flight at a hover and employing the collective to maintain a steady height of three feet above the ground. This proved much easier than my experience with the cyclic on that first day. Once I proved I could sustain level flight at a hover, Mr. Lee told me to put my feet on the pedals to keep the aircraft pointed in one direction as I maintained the stable hover at three feet. While I initially had some difficulty coordinating the foot pressures on the pedals with my adjustments to the collective, I mastered this pretty fast.

During each flight training session, Mr. Lee would also take us up into the stage field traffic pattern and let us use each control in various aspects of the flight around the pattern. We began to learn about the shift in the nature of flight by helicopter, called *translational lift*, as the aircraft moved out of hovering flight into forward flight and the return from forward flight into hovering flight. With this growing awareness of the characteristics of helicopter flight and the feel of the changes that occurred as we hovered, flew forward, and then came back to a hover, my confidence rose. Translational lift occurs when the forward speed of the helicopter increases to a rate of movement through the air where the entire rotor disk begins to act like a wing, but with varying degrees of lift across the rotor disk.

Soon I could sustain hovering flight and then push the cyclic forward and cause the aircraft to move forward and gain airspeed. I learned to initiate an ascent to a higher altitude, fly the traffic pattern, and then descend to a hover. But I had yet to lift off the ground and set the helicopter back on the ground myself. To do that, Mr. Lee explained, there was one more, somewhat minor skill that you needed. You had to learn to control the engine's throttle. Once you had mastered the throttle, you could safely maintain, by yourself, safe flight from takeoff to landing. The throttle, as I explained, was located on the end of the collective and was controlled by turning the wrist, while you are lifting up or pushing down on the collective to raise or lower your altitude.

The collective control enables the pilot to change the pitch in the rotating wings or blades, something most airplanes cannot do (there are some exotic planes and a few high-performance jet fighters that can change the angle of their wings to a small degree). This change in pitch increases the amount of lift these rotating wings or blades can generate. But as the pitch in the blades is increased, the drag on the blades as they move through the air also increases. To compensate for this drag, more power is required to maintain the same speed. Helicopters can slow to a hover and rise vertically into the air because the pitch in the blades can be increased to create greater lift. But, to maintain rotor speed, this takes more engine power and therefore the need to control the engine throttle in coordination with the application of the collective control. The control of the throttle is much more than a minor aspect of the process of coordinated vertical flight.

Therefore, throttle control is always a challenge for the novice helicopter pilot. Coordinating the use of the other controls already seemed to me to demand an exceptional level of concentration and was by no means, intuitive or automatic yet. That hover button seemed a long way off as I began to try and master the helicopter's all-important throttle. Throttle control was simple in theory but hard to master. As you lift the collective, you had to *roll on* the throttle. You also had to apply left pedal to counteract the torque effect of the engine that tried to make the nose of the helicopter turn right. As you lowered the collective, you had to *roll off* the throttle and ease up on the left pedal and push in the right pedal to reduce the effect of the tail rotor in countering the engine torque. Did I mention the tail rotor?

Once Mr. Lee had confidence that I could adequately control the machine at a hover, we began to practice lifting the machine off the ground and setting it down again. While this may seem a simple task, the coordination of power, rpm, and lift via the collective, heading control via the pedals, and attitude control via the cyclic was a major challenge that required utter concentration. This concentration was so intense that my undershirt would be soaking wet in a matter of minutes and my face would drip with perspiration. But slowly I could do this more smoothly and with the control movements less erratic.

Control of the throttle and maintaining the correct rpm for the engine and the rotor blades was more art than science. After a few frustrating sessions of trying to synchronize my employment of these various control devices, suddenly it all seemed to work! It actually surprised me. What is this a new sense of awareness of the aircraft? It was beginning to seem so automatic. Hey, this is not that hard! What had happened? Suddenly, quite unexpectedly in about the eighth hour of my flight training experience, it all seemed to click. I had found the elusive hover button. Now, I assure you that I was not anywhere near the league or talent level of Mr. Lee, but I could do it and do it naturally, without the level of intense concentration required in the early hours of my effort. With each hour of flying this beast, I was getting more comfortable, more confident and, more importantly, more competent.

Soon we began to work on autorotations. Mr. Lee had already demonstrated them several times and I was comfortable with the flight profile—that is, dropping like a rock, albeit a guided one— and the controlled cushion at the bottom to make the landing less dramatic than a crash. These became somewhat fun to do as I became more familiar with them. Soon, Mr. Lee and I were competing, to a small extent anyways—he always was much better than I—to see how close we could come to landing on an exact spot as we came down the very steep glide angle of the autorotation's descent and then, at almost the last second, applied up collective to cushion the landing, and left pedal, as the rotor blades traded energy for lift so that the actual landing was as soft as a powered landing, just with a bit more slide across the ground upon touchdown.

These flights were fun, and I found myself sometimes wondering about being paid to do this. We also learned the techniques for safely landing in the event of an engine failure while at a hover, referred to as a *hovering autorotation*. In this case, if the engine failed, as you feel the aircraft suddenly settle toward the ground, with very careful timing you apply up collective just prior to touchdown to trade rotor system energy for increased lift to cushion the landing. The instructors were so proficient at these exercises that they could rapidly roll off throttle, allow the aircraft to fall, then apply up collective with such precision that they could preserve enough rotor system energy to not only cushion the touchdown, but return, if only for a few brief seconds, to a near-ground hover and set it back down again softly. It was some time before we developed the needed sense of touch and control over the aircraft to do this ourselves.

Hovering autorotations and those from higher altitudes became a routine part of nearly every flight. These maneuvers were made with both air recoveries (that is return power to the drive train, above ground, and return to level flight) and unpowered, full autorotations to ground landings. The more we did it, the more proficient we became. The more proficient we became, the more the instructors stretched our skills and precision with the controls.

Soon, I was the master of the traffic pattern and local area flights between stage fields and the main heliports, like Dempsey. I was the master of the hover. I was the master of the liftoff and landing of the TH-55 onto the earth. I was proud of myself until, at about the twelfth hour of actual flight training, Mr. Lee decided that I should do this alone, without his powerful presence near the controls. Indeed, he proposed that he would watch from the ground as I made my first solo flight in a helicopter. Oops, where did that sense of mastery suddenly go? *Me . . . alone . . . fly this thing . . . without you?* On the outside, I was all confidence. You understand that we helicopter pilots have an image to maintain, of course. He knew I had the technical ability, and I knew that I could fly this machine, but flying solo was a big step.

When I learned to fly planes under Captain DeAngelis during college, I soloed within about ten hours. That was about normal for a new fixed-wing pilot. I easily mastered the technical aspects of basic flying back then. The coordination requirements were minimal, and self-confidence was never an issue. I was eager to solo and become a real pilot. Now, with the ante much, much higher, the coordination requirements an order of magnitude greater and the potential for disaster even greater, the probability of success was not quite assured. Suddenly, the pay did not seem enough.

Mr. Lee directed me to the ramp on the stage field, where we landed. I rolled the throttle to idle and as the blades spun down, he announced on the radio to the control tower, and all at the stage field, that his student was about to conduct his first solo. He looked me in the eye for a second and asked if I thought I was ready. I answered yes and he got out and walked toward the operations building. I rolled the throttle back up to recover engine and rotor rpm and then I called for taxi clearance. The tower cleared me to air taxi (moving over the ground at a hover) to the departure end of one of the several lanes used for takeoff, landing, and autorotation practice. I hovered into position and awaited my takeoff clearance.

I checked everything twice and then a third time, using the pretakeoff check list. Seat belt and harness, doors secured, engine rpm, rotor rpm in the green, oil pressure, engine cylinder head temperature, radios, caution lights, and I then cleared myself overhead and to the sides. With the takeoff clearance from the tower, I pushed the cyclic forward and accelerated down the lane at about four feet off the ground. As my airspeed rose, I felt that now familiar bump and jostle of the airframe as the helicopter moved through translational lift and the rotor disk itself began to act like a wing. I climbed up to the traffic pattern altitude and began to prepare to turn on crosswind as I headed away from the axis of the takeoff lane. Once well clear of the stage field lanes, I turned left and headed onto my downwind leg. As I flew along parallel to the stage field lanes, I marveled at finally being up there, alone, at the controls of a helicopter. Not the kind of aircraft I had expected to be flying in the Army, but nonetheless an accomplishment demonstrating how far I had come as a pilot.

The turn onto the base leg of the traffic pattern around the stage field and the call from the tower that I was cleared to descend to land at a hover came almost too soon for me. I was enjoying this, just as I had enjoyed that first solo flight back at PG Airpark in the DC suburbs of Maryland in 1969. I made two more trips around the pattern on that first solo flight and then returned to the stage field ramp to land and shut the aircraft down. I was elated at my successful solo and that I had now earned the right to wear a full set of student pilot wings on my white hat. After landing, Mr. Lee, of course, gave me a rather critical debrief on my pilot technique, my hover altitudes during the solo flight and my "sloppy" corners in the traffic pattern. Then he held out his hand and congratulated me on becoming a real helicopter pilot. "Hoover Hoffman" had soloed!

My reference to "hoovering" early in our flight training was actually a joke on my part when trying to lighten the mood one day. Dusty then dubbed me with the nickname, and it stuck.

There were several others of our class who soloed that day.

Some had already soloed, and some had yet to solo. Then there were a few who would never solo. For those unfortunate guys, this was the end of the line. If you do not solo within a specific period of time, you are out of the school. We had both Army and Air Force officer students in the class who did not make the cut and were gone at the end of that week. This was normal attrition for the program. It is far better to make the determination at this early point than to try and give them more opportunity to become the subject of an aviation accident board later in the school. We would have enough of those anyway, even with otherwise very capable pilots.

A tradition at fort Wolters in those days was to have "solo parties" on the evenings that class members soloed. These were held off post at a local Holiday Inn with a pool. These were generally beer parties right after the end of training for the day that ended up with all newly soloed pilots being tossed into the pool with their flight suit still on. We all, of course, operated strictly by tradition, so it was off to the pool that night. I drank more than one beer and was in the pool more than once that night. The next day I was back on the flight line, ready to fly again.

As we took turns flying our aircraft in the pattern and building time, and as Mr. Lee helped us expand our experience with the nuances of helicopters and their flight characteristics, our confidence in both the machine and ourselves grew. These machines were very basic helicopters. The cockpits were small and cramped. I was one of the larger members of the class at seventy-three inches tall, with a large build and just over two hundred pounds. When I flew with any other larger student, we were near our maximum payload. Calculating weight and balance for the aircraft was just as important as with any fixed-wing aircraft.

The best way to describe a helicopter is as follows: several hundred thousand small moving parts flying in close formation and occasionally bumping into each other. They were weird, complicated, noisy, sometimes uncomfortable, and full of vibrations, but they flew, and they flew pretty well. Well, at least most of the time they did. While we all experienced some form of instrument, engine, or system malfunction at some point in our training, they were normally not serious or catastrophic. Yet we did have some instances that were. One day, while flying in the training area with our instructors, we were instructed to return to the main heliport and land. Once back to Dempsey Army Airfield, we were informed that there was an aircraft missing and presumed down.

We were paired with an instructor and sent back out to search individual search boxes in an attempt to locate the downed bird. About one hour after we got airborne and began searching our assigned area, the crew in an adjoining box spotted the downed helicopter. We flew over to take a look. There on the ground was a shattered TH-55 without its rotor blades. Both student pilots were killed. All aircraft were immediately recalled, and we were then told all TH-55 helicopters would be grounded temporarily for special inspection—once an initial assessment of the down aircraft's condition and discern any possible malfunction was completed—to check the entire fleet for any indication of a similar problem. This resulted in several days of no flying.

The accident board later concluded that the crash was caused by separation of one of the rotor blades from the rotor head. With one blade missing, the rotor system would be in an out-of-balance condition and would come apart quickly. With no rotor blades, the helicopter became a rock and fell from the sky. It was a sad, dark day at Fort Wolters. Aircraft accidents and mishaps are not uncommon in the military flight training community. Military aviation operations are inherently dangerous and unforgiving of mistakes and neglect. Aircraft component failures, pilot errors, and ground crew inattention are perils that all new pilots face. There is a lot going on in the cockpit and a lot of information to absorb: flight environment, instrumentation, weather, the radios, and your flight plan that must be assimilated by your brain, processed, and acted upon. Even then, with the pilot doing everything correctly, sometimes, though rarely, the machine simply fails to fly due to a catastrophic system failure.

As a new pilot, you are concentrating on many aspects of your pilot duties and the control of the aircraft. It is easy to miss key information, overlook an important task or get fixated on a single issue or problem in the cockpit. These are the most common causes of accidents and fatalities in military flight training. Hence, the flight training curriculum is long, intense, and demanding. The intent of the flight training program is to build your experience base so that what should be automatic, nearly involuntary pilot functions, become so. They are intended to expand your vision, your awareness of your environment, and your ability to keep your head both inside and outside of the cockpit at all times. It worked and the US Army turned out thousands of highly qualified, experienced pilots who proved their value, expertise, daring, and unique flying skills every day in Vietnam.

Mechanical or structural failures also are a risk but are less often the cause of serious accidents. In this case, it was the aircraft that failed, not the pilots. It was a sobering time for all of us in Class 71-30. While these students were in a class ahead of ours, the loss had a dramatic effect on us, our instructors, and the school. As is always the case in life, these experiences also prepared us to face the risks of flying even more complex and, potentially, more failure-susceptible aircraft, such as flying a combat-damaged or degraded aircraft out of harm's way. It also had the side effect of preparing us for the loss of friends and comrades in combat.

The loss of that student crew served for some time as a daily reminder of the dangers of our endeavors to both students and wives. There were several small gatherings with our classmates and wives in the following weeks that had a more somber tone than the carefree, joyous gatherings of just weeks before, when simply being in flight school, the fun of flying, the evening and weekend home time, and the new family financial improvements, all contributed to a sense of satisfaction and enjoyment unfettered by such awareness.

Not all mishaps were mechanical. Some were indeed mental failures of one sort or another. We had a few in our class, but none that were fatal or serious. All, however, were educational for the rest of us. For some, however, the mental challenges were incredible. Take, for example, our Vietnamese Air Force (VNAF) student pilots. With the expectation that Vietnam would take on a more prominent role in helicopter support to combat operations, as the US military presence was reduced, groups of South Vietnamese Air Force student pilots were also training within the US Army aviation training system. These were intelligent and capable young men, taken from a simple, bicycle-technology-level environment and thrust into advanced systems, all taught in a new language. This always struck me as a monumental hurdle. These guys had guts, were obviously pretty smart, and, in many ways, committed in a manner we could not appreciate. Yet, these cultural traits and their perspective of the world often got in their way, sometimes bringing great humor to all of us and unjustified humiliation to them. It was both the language problem, even though they had learned classroom English, and the cultural differences. The result was that flight training for these brave young student pilots was made even harder. We Americans viewed their accomplishments with awe.

Once beyond our solo flights and into limited cross-country trips with our instructors and, of course, hours and hours of time in the traffic pattern, we began two new areas of flight training. The first had to do with maintaining control of the aircraft in the event of sudden loss of visual reference to the horizon. The TH-55 helicopter is not equipped for operations without reference to the ground, such as when you are on the inside of a cloud. This limitation means that it can only operate under visual flight rules (VFR), where you can see the ground and the horizon. Those aircraft that can be operated employing instrumentation inside the cockpit only, and without reference to the ground or horizon, can operate under instrument flight rules (IFR). The TH-55 was a VFR only aircraft. It lacked the instrumentation for IFR flight. To safely fly it, day or night, you had to have the ability to see the ground or the horizon in order to maintain the correct orientation of the aircraft, which is with the ground below the cockpit and the rotors above. If you found yourself with the rotors between you and the ground, for any reason, you were going to have a very bad day.

However (and there is always a *however* in flying) the one thing we cannot yet control is the weather. Weather forecasts are just that. They are not fact, and they are often not even close to what will become fact. In my experience, being a weather forecaster is about averages. This being the case, you can never assume that the weather will be as forecast. Often you can takeoff under clear blue skies and then find yourself, less than thirty minutes later, scooting under a rapidly developing cloud layer, running through heavy rain, and bouncing along in twenty- to thirty-knot winds. Such conditions can quickly reduce your visibility and make it nearly impossible to maintain ground references and correct aircraft orientation. So, you had to learn to use the limited instrumentation that you did have in the TH-55 to maintain, or recover to, your correct flight attitude.

To train you to be prepared to deal with an inadvertent IFR situation, the instructors put us through attitude recovery drills. In these training sessions, the instructor would put the aircraft into an unusual attitude, often nose down and banked severely to one side, while you wore a hood to limit your ability to see outside and limit your view to the floor of the cockpit. Then he would instruct you to look up at the instruments and recover the aircraft to level flight, looking only at the instruments and without looking outside the cockpit at the ground or horizon. For many, this was a real make-or-break skill to learn. To those of us with previous flight training, this was less of a challenge. But that is not to say it was easy, particularly when the instructor began to take away instruments. Normally one had reference to an attitude indicator (wings level and nose pitch up or down indicator), a turn and bank indicator (indicates whether the aircraft is turning left or right, the degree of turn, and whether you are in trim or not—flying with the tail directly behind the nose or skidding to one side or the other), a rate of climb or descent indicator (indicates the rate, in hundreds of feet per minute that you are climbing or descending), and an airspeed indicator (how fast you are going through the air—falling airspeed normally indicated a climb and rising airspeed indicated you were going down faster and faster, usually not a good sign!). With all of these instruments, you had immediate indication of your attitude, airspeed, and situation relative to climbing, falling, or turning. But to keep the training interesting and challenging, the instructors would cover one or more of these instruments during the unusual attitude recovery drills to see if we could interpret the information from the remaining instruments sufficiently to return the aircraft to straight and level flight.

Why, might you ask, would the instructor be so abusive to his students as to take away perfectly good instrument indications and make life so difficult for we novice rotor heads? Well, the answer is simply Murphy's Law, a premise that seemed to stay not far away from me throughout my flight career: what can go wrong, will go wrong. A corollary to that is the saying that when one thing breaks, something else is sure to follow. Therefore, a good pilot must assume that at precisely the time that the weather goes "stink-o" on you, one or more of your instruments will fail at the exact same moment for no other reason than Murphy's Law and its chief corollary!

My US Army flight training was far more extensive than what I had undergone with Captain DeAngles back in college and it proved invaluable to me later. Unusual attitude recovery was a skill that was essential for combat flying, as well as instrument flight because you never knew what a sudden gust of wind, or the effects of an exploding anti-aircraft round or bomb detonation near the ground would do to the flight condition and orientation of your helicopter. Therefore, this skill was practiced throughout the remainder of my flight training at Fort Wolters and, later, at Fort Rucker, Alabama.

Captain Arnold "Dusty" Holm explains his flight plan to a fellow student pilot (or, more likely, tells a war story).

The other area of new training was in operations away from traditional airfields and stage fields. This training was to introduce us to the fundamental value of helicopters to the US Army, the capability to operate anywhere. To do this successfully, you must be prepared to land in places where there is no large open runway, heliport, or even open, level ground. To be ready to meet the mission needs of military operations, helicopters must be able to operate into and out of very small areas, often lined with trees, telephone poles, and antennas, land and takeoff from the very tops of high mountains, mountain ridges, buildings, and even moving ships. These operations are referred to as *confined area and pinnacle operations*. With the ease that one witnesses such operations by helicopters nearly every day, whether in person, on the news, or in movies, one might think that this is a simple, routine activity for helicopters. If one thought that, then one would be very, very wrong, indeed. These operations are never simple, never easy, and rarely without some level of increased risk compared to normal flight operations.

Confined area operations present several unique safety problems. First, there is the issue of inadvertently striking the obstructions (hopefully light shrubs or tree limbs and leaves and not steel or concrete) with the main rotors, the tail rotors, or the tail boom. Any strike is hazardous, but the more durable and solid the obstruction, the more catastrophic the result of the contact. A further complication to the problem, however, is wind. Wind is very unpredictable stuff. It flows over, around, and through things in strange ways. It is the focus of much study by people with pocket protectors and computers. The more they study it, the less they seem to know about it. For pilots, understanding wind and how it acts around obstructions, mountains, buildings, and trees is more art than science. It is more about feel of the aircraft as it moves through the wind; it is about how the leaves are swaying and how smoke curls than hard science. Judging how the wind will affect you as you cross over a building, a high wall, or fence or over a line of trees as you descend into a landing area is something you learn to do with experience, not with a book or in a simulator. So repeated flights into and out of confined areas, surrounded by a wide variety of obstructions and in even greater variety of wind conditions, is how you gained the skills you would need later in flying combat missions into and out of hot, confined landing zones (LZs). After many weeks of landing at designated LZs that surrounded the flight training area in Central Texas, we gained a bit of that essential skill set.

These LZs were not, for the most part, on Fort Wolters property. Most were out on farms and ranches where the Army made a deal with the landowner to allow student pilots to land and takeoff from these designated landing sites. How such issues as legal liability and the potential for property damage were worked out, I never knew. I simply knew that these landowners understood our need and wanted to help train us. These remote landing sites were studied, exercised, and checked regularly by flight school instructors. They were marked with tires to indicate the skill level needed by the pilot to make a landing at that site. There were white tires for new pilots, yellow tires to indicate LZs for more experienced student pilots. And there were red tires to indicate locations where only instructors were allowed to demonstrate the more difficult confined area landing operations. We made almost-daily trips out into the Texas countryside to practice our confined area landings. Most were uneventful trips and were even fun most of the time.

This is not to say, however, that the weather was perfect for flying at all times in this region of Texas. Indeed, it was not. The very sudden arrival of extremely powerful thunderstorms in this area of the country is common. These storms, with their very powerful winds and heavy, heavy rain, even hail, can literally swat a TH-55 from the sky. Our unusual attitude recovery training and a watchful eye on the clouds and winds were the means to survive. That was normally accomplished by a quick landing at an approved LZ (though the parking lot of a gas station or store often worked just as well), a quick tying down of the blades and a long wait in the cockpit as the storm passed over. This became a common afternoon experience for all of us.

During this phase of the training we also learned pinnacle operations. These were landings and takeoffs made to and from LZs located on the very top of hills, ridges, and low mountains. Pinnacle operations present unique problems for the new pilot. Again, there is the wind. The wind at higher elevations blows with more force than near the ground. The wind that strikes these tends to ride up the structure and, after joining the wind blowing horizontally across the top, it can boil over the top with unpredictable patterns and widely varying forces and directions. This makes landing on such LZs difficult and dangerous, even in the best of conditions. Add fire, smoke, and the heating of the air by the sun and you get an environment that can make your hand sweat profusely as you strangle the grips on the cyclic and the collective.

Then you must overcome the natural psychological reactions that result from the visual cues you are presented as you make your approach to the LZ or as you takeoff. As you descend to land on a pinnacle LZ, the point of intended landing is rising at one apparent speed, as the surrounding area below the pinnacle rises to you at a different apparent speed. This can rapidly confuse your brain into interpreting that the LZ is flying at you or moving itself. Then there is the loss of surrounding ground horizon references as you near the landing point on the pinnacle. What is up, down, and level becomes difficult to interpret until you gain experience in trusting your instruments, the relative location and approach speed to the LZ itself and in discounting the contradictory visual cues you get from the terrain away from and below the pinnacle itself. These confined area and pinnacle operations were serious challenges to our primitive rotary-wing skills but we overcame by repetition and competent instructors to gain the needed skill sets and confidence in our own abilities.

By April we were beginning longer cross-country trips to continue building flight time and gain navigation experience. These trips took us to such exotic places as Oklahoma and Amarillo, Texas. The weather in central and northern Texas is good for flight training with generally clear air, fewer storms than much of the country, and great visibility. As I had already developed competent aerial navigation skills before arriving at Fort Wolters, these trips were less about confidence building for me than gaining more experience at the controls of a rotary wing aircraft and appreciating the extraordinary perspective one has of the countryside from such a platform and its huge, clear front plexiglass bubble canopy. I had the sense of sitting on a small balcony overlooking the terrain, as I maneuvered over and around the countryside. There was no ride at Disneyland to compare to this sensation! These trips took us nearly to the end of our VFR fuel loads and resulted in a new level of backside numbness. The cramped seats, combined with the constant high frequency vibrations of the aircraft transmission left us with levels of discomfort that one does not experience in fixed-wing aircraft. To make matters even worse, a few of the aircraft in our training fleet had vibrations in the tail rotor system that caused the pedals to vibrate to the point that it would put our feet to sleep as well.

And then there were the buzzards! Flying in Texas is a special experience in many ways and buzzards are one of those experiences that one never forgets. They were everywhere. Sometimes they flew in great flocks, particularly when they sensed lunch was available somewhere along the highway or out on the range where a cow or deer had encountered some fatal misfortune. Generally, they stayed clear of our small helicopters but sometimes we got in their way, or they got in ours. Such was the case one sunny Texas afternoon when 71-30 classmate Mike O'Byrne and a very large buzzard tried to occupy the same air space at the same time. This was a relatively (for a TH-55 anyway) high-speed encounter that was fatal for the buzzard. Mike fared better, but you would never know that at first glance when he landed! The buzzard had flown directly into the plexiglass front of the aircraft, under the rotor disk. A blade strike on a large bird is bad enough, and can disable the aircraft or damage a blade, perhaps resulting in a fatal crash. But to take one through the plexiglass at high speed, right into your lap at a closure rate of about 100 mph is something else altogether. This is what happened to Mike. The buzzard impacted the plexiglass and it and the bird disintegrated. The resulting mix of shattered buzzard and plastic fragments then impacted Mike in the legs, chest, and face. Fortunately, he had his helmet visor down and his eyes were protected from the incoming fragments. Mike was in serious trouble, but he kept his wits, stayed cool, kept control of the aircraft) and he headed back to the main heliport to land.

What we all saw upon his landing was a sight from a Hollywood movie scene. The entire inside of the cockpit, along with Mike, was covered in bird guts, bird shit, bird bones, bird feathers, and bird blood. Mixed into this were fragments of the plastic front of the cockpit. Mike was a mess but very happy to be on the ground. Upon first look, with the blood and gore everywhere, the rescue crew thought he was very seriously injured. But upon cleanup and a thorough medical check, all he had were a few cuts and bruises. The real damage was to the TH-55 helicopter that Mike was flying. This was the source of much humor and jibes for Mike for the remainder of flight school.

Even with these minor discomforts, the flying at this point in the training was more like a flying club than a school. While we still underwent flight evaluations and tests, most of our flying was designed to give us airtime and build experience. These trips out over the Central and West Texas countryside were sheer joy. That part of Texas is gorgeous. The rolling hills, the cattle ranches, the tree-lined deep cuts across the landscape that contain the fast-running rivers and the small game and the running deer made each trip out in our flying machines a special experience that was unique to this school. Flying at Fort Rucker later that year was never like this. So out of April 1971 and into May we flew over the Texas countryside. During this period of unrestrained joy in flying, I gained for the first time a true sense of the meaning of the famous aviator's poem by John Gillespie McGee, pilot officer, No 412 squadron, RCAF, killed on December 11, 1941 during the Battle of Britain, entitled "High Flight."

I grew up with this poem prominent in our household, as it was a favorite of my father, but I never really understood or appreciated it until this time in my life.

But as with all good things, this too came to an end. After months of learning new skills, day after day of sweat filled flight hours, check rides, daily evaluations, and long hours in classrooms and the stark realization that this was, after all, very dangerous work, we graduated from the US Army Primary Flight School in May 1971. We traveled to Fort Rucker, Alabama, for Advanced Flight Training to complete the requirements for graduation from the US Army Rotary Wing Flight Training Program and to earn our wings as Army aviators.

My Dad in World War II on Tinian with his P-51 named for my mother, Anne Hoffman.

The move to Alabama was quick because we had to be back in class within a week. That meant that Karen and I had to pack up our Mineral Wells apartment, ship our household goods, drive to Alabama, find a place to live, move in, then in-process to the post and be ready for the start of the next phase of our training. After our arrival at Fort Rucker, we found that there was no on-post married housing available, and we would have to find an apartment in town. This meant Enterprise, Ozark, or Dothan, Alabama would become our new temporary home. After a check of local listings, we found a second story walk-up apartment in Enterprise, a typical Southern farming town with some local industry, but whose main economic engine was the sprawling military complex to its northeast, Fort Rucker. This was a town founded originally on cotton, devastated by the boll weevil and by the 1970s a town dependent upon the peanut and the US Army. To ensure that everyone who visited Enterprise, Alabama knew this history, there is a large statue that honors the boll weevil in the very center of the town.

The new apartment was tolerable, the drive onto post short, and we were now near family in Pensacola, Florida, where my grandparents lived in the same house where my great grandfather, grandfather, and father had been born. This house, built of ship's timbers in the mid-1800s, was the summer gathering point for our extended family on my father's side for several generations. The beaches of the Florida panhandle are unique in the world with sand so white, it looks like sugar. Being so close to Pensacola was a perk that I valued greatly during my time at Fort Rucker. As an officer, most evenings and weekends were mine. So, Karen and I traveled regularly to Pensacola and Panama Beach to go camping and swimming in the Gulf of Mexico and to see my family.

At Fort Rucker everything was very different from Fort Wolters, from the flying weather, the countryside, and the atmosphere of the school to the aircraft we would fly. Gone were the enjoyable days of our Texas flying club. Here was serious training intended to get us prepared for combat aviation operations in South Vietnam. Later we would all come to call this post "Mother Rucker," as it is the official Army aviation schoolhouse and source of nearly all US Army aviation doctrine. After our in-processing, we quickly began intense instrument training, both in the classroom and in the air. The classroom training was reminiscent of my prior instrument training and presented no real challenge. The flight training part, however, was, well to be blunt, a real bitch! Instrument flight training at Fort Rucker in the early 1970s was conducted in the TH-13T helicopter. This was the original bubble helicopter so ubiquitous in the 1950s, 60s, and 70s across civilian aviation, in Korea, and in the early stages of America's involvement in Vietnam. But it was not well suited to being an instrument trainer. It was underpowered, overequipped and it vibrated like a rattlesnake. This helicopter was equipped with a large horizontally opposed piston engine that had a supercharger added to it to enable it (barely I must add) to carry the weight of the two pilots and the heavy, somewhat antiquated instrument and navigation package needed for instrument training duty.

The high heat and humidity of Alabama, with a density altitude (the relative density of the air, with air temperature and moisture content factored in) that was often equivalent to flying at six to eight thousand feet in the tropics! In such conditions the TH-13T did not perform well. We were always flying these machines at the very edge of their safety and performance capability.

Yet for day after day and hour after hour, we flew these machines to gain more experience in IFR conditions. We once again wore the hood to shield our eyes from the outside world and we lived entirely inside the cockpit as we learned the intricacies of rotary-wing instrument flight. My lack of confidence in this aircraft, combined with the poor overall performance of the machine led me to fear this aircraft in a way I never feared any other aircraft in my life. There were frequent precautionary landings for mechanical failures, there were numerous engine failures that resulted in emergency autorotations, and there were many days where we had our flights delayed for hours while the maintenance teams tried to render the machine safe to fly in the first place. This training continued for two months as we gained the skills to employ the instrumentation on the helicopter's instrument panel to maintain level flight and learned to navigate using the limited Army radio navigation aids, such as non-directional beacons and ground-controlled approach (GCA) systems to aid in landing in bad weather. All of this training was not intended to give us student pilots a full Army Aviation Instrument Rating. No, this effort was devoted to ensuring that we could, at a minimum, recover from and safely land in the case of inadvertently encountering IFR conditions. The result was that we were given a tactical instrument rating, not a full instrument rating for helicopters that would allow us to plan for and intentionally fly in IFR conditions. This seemed like a lot of wasted effort, adrenaline, and fuel to me. Why go halfway when, for a little bit more effort, you can get the whole enchilada! I found that this was often the route taken by the Army. This simply proved, to me anyway, the old financial doctrine that said a half-assed investment would only yield a half-assed dividend. I wanted the whole thing (and I got it later on my own accord).

Flying TH-13s was the subject of much discontent in the class. Most of us felt that the TH-55 had been a far superior machine. It was much newer, had better payload and could be equipped, as the civilian models already were, with lighter, more modern instrument navigation equipment. But this was a case where the Army had what it had on hand and would, by God, use it until it was worn out. Well, it (the TH-13) was already worn out by the early 1960s. But no one had apparently told the Army chief of staff! So, every day was a crap shoot of sorts. We got the needed instrument flight training hours in, but only with patience and a great deal of anxiety in the process. This was the only part of my flight training that I truly disliked.

Once we had completed the required curriculum for the instrument training phase, we left the TH-13 for good (as the Army finally did a few years later) and we moved to what was referred to as *contact training*. Contact training was our introduction to and initial contact with turbine (jet engine) powered helicopters. In this case the UH-1B Iroquois, often called a "Huey" by both pilots and the media. It was manufactured by Bell Helicopter Corporation. Large numbers were produced, along with the OH-58 turbine powered light observation helicopter (that had replaced the OH-13—combat version of the TH-13) and the AH-1G Cobra Gunship, also called a "Snake," that also became famous during the later years of the Vietnam war. Now *these* were aircraft with plenty of power, the reliability of turbine engines, and the payload we needed to properly train in combat helicopter operations.

The UH-1B was the helicopter also used to create the first

gunships, known as a UH-1C. This aircraft had a larger engine than the UH-1B and D but it had limited range and really was not suitable as a capable gunship. These original helicopter gunships were simply Hueys with additional guns and rocket pods added to them. The Hueys without guns or rockets were then referred to as *Slicks*, meaning the sides had no external rocket pods and therefore had slick sides. The term stuck and was used in RVN for all UH-1s that transported troops and cargo even after the AH-1G Cobra or "Snake" was deployed to Vietnam.

This training also included an entirely new ground school on modern helicopters. We learned about turbine engines and how they function, we learned about hydraulic control systems, self-sealing fuel tanks (that will not leak after a bullet passes through them—as long as the bullet is not an incendiary one, anyway), semi-rigid rotor systems, and engine torque. No more rubber bands! Wait, torque? What torque? Oh yeah, I knew engine torque from my fixed-wing days, but how would this apply here? I had a lot to learn! This was very fascinating to me. I have always loved technology and how things work. I get this from my dad, the West Point engineer, fighter pilot and tinkerer.

I grew up taking things apart to see how they worked. Aircraft powerplants (engines), airplane components, and how systems functioned were of great interest to me. Now I was getting the kind of systems and maintenance training that I really could get my teeth into. Not all of us in the class were into this part of the training. Many simply wanted to learn to fly these machines, while myself and a few others not only wanted to fly them, but to understand how they worked. This was a knowledge base that would serve me well later.

Flying a jet-turbine-powered helicopter is much different than flying a piston-powered machine. The two most important differences are available power and automatic control of engine rpm to maintain rotor rpm. In a turbine-powered helicopter the fuel control unit will automatically adjust fuel flow to the engine and adjust engine rpm, so one does not have to manually control the throttle on the end of the collective. This meant you had one less control to manage in-flight. You could just roll the throttle control to full on and leave it there and the fuel control system then managed it from there. While we did train to manually control it in an emergency, I never actually had to do that after flight school. This was a major reduction on the span of focus required inside the cockpit for the pilot. That, in turn, meant that you could refocus attention elsewhere, such as outside the aircraft and its flight environment and, yes, on your use of engine torque. Engine torque was a new control requirement that is vital in managing engine power in a jet-turbine-powered helicopter.

Lesson: if the Army gives you a break on something, expect to pay for it elsewhere.

With the availability of all this vast engine power, the torque that the engine can produce can, quite literally, damage the helicopter's systems. To help the pilot manage torque, there is a torque meter on the instrument panel to aid you in monitoring the torque you are pulling from the engine so that you can keep it below fifty pounds. Above that level you risk damage to the entire drive train of the helicopter. But learning to manage torque output was a small price to pay for not having to manually control the throttle and not having to rely upon rubber bands!

These helicopters were much larger than the small training machines we had been flying. With the helicopter's large cargo and passenger compartment, there was room for your stick buddy to ride in a jump seat when you were in the right pilot's seat and the instructor was in the left cockpit seat. While the machine was generally easier to fly, the new heavier feel of the control, the slower response of the controls, and the hydraulic assist within the control system gave the machine new handling characteristics that took some time to become comfortable in our hands. My contact instructor was Chief Warrant Officer 2 Fromme, an experienced IP with several combat helicopter tours in RVN already. He was as a good instructor with the same pilot touch and teaching ability as Mr. Lee and one of those skilled warrant officer pilots I mentioned earlier.

Contact training was in the UH-1B helicopter, and a few modified versions with bigger engines and newer rotor system, identified under various suffix codes, such as UH-1M. This brought to us a reintroduction to everything from preflight inspections to pre-takeoff checks to flight operations themselves, prelanding checks and postflight inspections. We had to learn the techniques for takeoff with a turbine engine, different mainly in power available and control response. Autorotations were now even more exciting because the aircraft was heavier and you dropped with a faster rate of descent, but maintaining rotor rpm in the descent was easier. However, applying collective to cushion the landing required a new sense of timing, as the control inputs lagged over the rapid response of the TH-55. On the other hand, there was much greater energy stored in these larger blades and you could set the aircraft down with much greater precision. Hovering autorotations were also different because of the aircraft was heavier and the rotor disk energy higher. The contact phase of training passed quickly, and we were soon into our initial tactical training phase.

UH-1D Training Helicopter at Ft. Rucker, AL in 1971.

Cockpit instrument panel of the UH-1D Helicopter.

This brought us to a newer version of the UH-1 helicopter, the UH-1D, and a larger, more capable helicopter. The UH-1D had a larger cargo compartment, could lift a greater payload, and had newer systems and engines. We also were given some flight time in the newest Huey of the day, the UH-1H model, the most common UH-1 then in use in Vietnam. This is the point in our training where we began to learn about US Army helicopter tactical operations doctrine and helicopter operations in support of ground combat operations. All our instructors were veteran helicopter pilots with one or more tours in Vietnam. These guys were very good, as well as being very frank about what actually did and did not work in combat operations, US Army aviation doctrine notwithstanding. We practiced formation flight almost every day. Our formations ranged from two to twelve ships flying cross-country missions across southern Alabama, Georgia, and the Florida panhandle. We practiced confined-area and pinnacle operations, both single ship and in small formations. We flew troop lift missions at Fort

Benning, we learned external load operations, utilizing the hook on the bottom of our helicopters. We flew practice instrument missions and simulated radar-controlled approaches. We flew nearly every weekday from late June until the beginning of September, developing our skills and experience in the UH-1 series helicopter and building flight time. Our goal was two hundred hours of total flight experience by the time we graduated from the program.

A special thrill that I looked forward to from my first arrival at Fort Rucker was the mission every flight school class undertakes in support of the Ranger camp at Eglin Air Force Base in Florida. When I had been in Ranger school more than two years before, we had participated in several airmobile operations flown by student pilots from Fort Rucker. Shortly after these student pilots picked us up on our first lift, they handed out snacks and candy. These were a big hit with us, when I was in Ranger School, but we knew we had to eat them on the aircraft because the Ranger instructors knew the gambit and would conduct an inspection to confiscate any pogey bait shortly after we landed. So, we wolfed the snacks down with great enthusiasm and appreciation for these thoughtful crews. Now it was my turn. This custom was well known at the school. However, there were only a few actual Rangers in the class. We made sure that our mission to support the Rangers was well supplied with snacks and candy. The mission went off without a hitch, but I suspect that the maintenance guys at Fort Rucker continued to find candy and snack wrappers in strange places all over those helicopters for years.

Another phase of training during our time at Fort Rucker was Escape and Evasion Training. This is mandatory training and is intended to acquaint all Army pilots with the potential psychological and physical demands of surviving a crash in enemy territory, avoiding capture and, if captured, what it might be like and what your Geneva rights and obligations are. It also attempted to represent to each student how one must conduct oneself while in captivity and how, knowing the disregard for the Geneva convention displayed by the North Vietnamese and their Russian mentors, what we might expect in captivity in Vietnam. While much was known within the US military about how the North Vietnamese abused, tortured, and killed captives, the American public did not learn about all of this until some of our captured soldiers were released in 1973.

For me this training was an instant Ranger Challenge. While in Ranger training, you not only learn how to survive and evade, but you also learned that sometimes the best defense is, indeed, a better offense. If you are in danger of being captured, then a plan to make it impossible for the enemy to capture you, by either defensive or offensive action, may be your best bet. That seemed to be the case here. The training scenario that was briefed to us was straightforward. We would be dropped in pairs in the ground training area. We would be expected to move cross-country on foot to a rally point where we would be "rescued." However, there would be a "bad guy" force operating between the drop point and the rally point that would try to capture us and deliver us to their prison camp for interrogation. They were permitted to use force, but nothing lethal or harmful. No rules were specified for us except that we would not carry weapons or food, only water. The whole event was to last about twelve hours, over the course of one night.

I decided, along with Dusty and a few others, that we would not subject ourselves to capture, and we would, if possible, see that others in the class were not captured as well. Our plan was to locate and proceed to the prison camp, recon it thoroughly, then decide whether to set up ambushes of the bad guys to free anyone they captured or, if the camp security was lax, simply capture the camp and shut it down for the night, take their trucks and pick up our classmates and drive them to the rally point. Upon being dropped, we proceeded directly to our own rally point we had set up in advance near where we thought the prison camp was probably located. We had done a thorough map recon and talked the situation over with others from classes ahead of ours. After a rather short recon effort, we located the camp. There was almost no security around it. Most of the "bad guys" were still there, as they wanted the trainees tired from many hours of walking before they went out to police them up. They assumed, incorrectly, that most of these officer students could not read a map well from the perspective of an infantry soldier or grunt.

Our plan, formulated rather quickly from an overwatch position, was to simply waltz right up to the prison camp entry point and take down the two guys on sentry duty. That took about fifteen seconds. They never saw us and did not know what was happening until they realized they were blindfolded, hog-tied, and stacked behind a tree. We took parts of their uniforms, weapons, and gear and took control of the entry point. We then walked in and took two trucks back out the front entry and parked them in the trees. We now had mobility, the bad guys also were short two of their own and now knew that they did not control their own camp and could put fewer folks out on patrol for the students. We then simply watched the camp. As it turned out, most of the class made it to the rally point safely. We released a few who were captured when they were being escorted past us on the way to the camp. This also put more bad guys out of the exercise.

The result was that the night's exercise was a failure from the academic point of view. But we had accomplished our mission. The next day, the school commandant was not happy at all, we were so informed by our student company commander. Yet there was little that could be done about our actions that night. What were their options? We had prevailed in the exercise, we got to our rally point, along with most of our class, and we had used our own Army-taught skills and initiative, just exactly what Army doctrine preaches. They seemed pissed outwardly, but inwardly they must have been both pleased and disappointed. Pleased that a few high-initiative students had succeeded in their mission, but disappointed in the sloppy, low-caliber effort by the training team and staff that operated that E&E training event. We learned later that month that the entire E&E training program was reworked and improved.

Lesson: Sometimes, despite the risk, pushing the envelope can make a huge difference in your success and staying "on the reservation" is not always the best choice. The trick is determining the optimum alternative outcome and developing a plan to achieve it.

We participated in an extended tactical exercise near the end of our UH-1D tactics training that presented us with all the missions and tasks that characterized an air-mobile combat operation. This included multi-ship formation flights during the day and at night. It included simulated medevac missions, command and control flights, and resupply missions with cargo carried internally and externally on our cargo hooks and operations from unimproved, hastily improvised airfields and rearm and refuel positions. It also included an introduction to gunnery operations. Even UH-1 helicopters are armed. There is normally an M-60, 7.6- mm machine gun mounted in the after-compartment on each side of the fuselage. The flight engineer and a door gunner man these guns. These enlisted crewmen also trained at Fort Rucker and during our tactical training, they would fly with us on some of their gunnery training missions. These guns provide suppressive fire into and around an LZ when the helicopter is landing in a *hot* LZ where the enemy is contesting your landing, something I would appreciate in the coming year.

Lesson: ladies and gentlemen, please keep your arms and legs inside of the aircraft when the door gunner has live rounds!

Training hours during the last six weeks were very accommodating to our officer class. Generally training began at noon on Mondays and finished at noon on Fridays. This gave us three full days for almost every weekend. That meant trips to Panama City and other nearby places were easy and became the rule. We did a lot of camping and partying on the beaches. The training itself was great and fun. Most of the time the living, the money, and life was very good. Of course, we all knew this was going to end in the near future, and our prospects were for a long plane ride west unless there was real progress at the peace talks in Paris. We knew this but took the attitude that we would enjoy life while the living was good.

One of the last flight-training activities before graduation was the *nap of the earth* flight. This was a tactic, then in development, to enable helicopters to operate close to the ground at actual treetop and bushtop level, so as to make them less vulnerable to anti-aircraft fires, particularly to missiles, which we knew the Russians were deploying within their army and, it was suspected, in the North Vietnamese Army. This was seen as a good defensive tactic in Europe for those pilots headed to NATO assignment and a good way to avoid ground fire of all types in Vietnam. When you fly at high speed very close to the ground, it is difficult for those on the ground to determine which direction you are approaching them from and where you are, if they cannot actually see you. Their line of sight to you is very short and it is hard to track an aircraft below the jungle tree line from that vantage point. Several of our instructors had experience in this mode of flight and they took us on long, sweat-filled cross-country trips where we flew from treetop to treetop, often not twenty feet above the ground at eighty to one hundred knots airspeed. That is more than 115 miles per hour, twenty feet off the ground!

Nap of the earth is fun, exciting, and a great skills builder as you dodge obstacles, trying to keep your eyes outside the cockpit. Your copilot must watch the instruments and systems indicators for you—you cannot safely look in and out of the cockpit at that speed and that close to the ground. Things happen way too fast at very low altitude! This training helped build your confidence as a crew working together and learning to navigate when you can't see much farther than you could if you were standing on the ground. This navigation aspect is particularly hard. Learning to understand a map and the terrain takes on a whole new meaning at that speed and altitude. Trying to determine your best route toward your destination and avoiding obstacles as you flew along hugging the folds of the earth or those of the forest and vegetation, all while not getting lost can be a real challenge. For most of us, getting lost at least once or twice was the norm and how we learned. Flying in southern Alabama meant simply climbing up to get your bearings and then returning to nap of the earth flight mode and continuing on your way. Later in Vietnam, getting lost was not an option. If you did and you tried to climb up to find your bearings, it could mean an immediate hail of anti-aircraft fire targeting your bird. At that altitude, you are well within the range of everything from 57-mm anti-aircraft guns to a 9-mm pistol, any one of which can bring you down if the hit is in just the right spot. Once we got the hang of it, nap of the earth was great fun, and those last weeks went by fast.

As September and our graduation date neared, our final check rides were looming. We also had to complete a few final academic requirements and plan for our postgraduation leave period—our last before most of us would be sent to Vietnam. I had performed well in academics. The last few check rides, however, would determine my overall final standing in the class. This was important to me because if you finished in the top 10 percent, you often, not always, but often had a choice of aircraft transition training immediately after flight school. This normally meant Cobra transition or even fixed-wing transition at Fort Stewart. On very rare occasions, if you finished very high in your class and the instructors felt your pilot skills were good enough, you could get CH-47 Chinook transition. The CH-47, a very large, multi-engine, twin rotor-system helicopter, was the most sophisticated of Army helicopters at that time. It was the cargo and external-lift workhorse of the Army.

Unlike the Huey and Cobra, built by Bell Helicopter, the CH-47 was built by Boeing. Boeing only built big aircraft. As I had progressed through flight school, I had decided that, given the chance, I would pass up Snakes for the Chinook. I figured that after the Army, training and experience in multi-engine heavy helicopters would be a more useful resume item than a gunship. However, I did not expect that I would get such an opportunity. I figured that the need for Huey drivers was greater and the only transition option most classes had been afforded before ours was Cobras. After my final check ride, I was advised that I would be an honor graduate from the US Army Flight School. Not bad for the son of a WWII fighter pilot, but about what he expected, I supposed.

The next thing for me was to find out was where Dad would be in September and see if he could come to Fort Rucker to pin on my wings at graduation. I had written him a letter in August, letting him know about the plan for graduation and my wish that he could attend and pin on my new wings. I brazenly assumed, at that point, that I would graduate and become an Army aviator. In early September I called Mom and asked her to find out from Dad if he was coming. He called me a few days before graduation and told me that he would be back in the US from South Vietnam and planned to attend my graduation. I was thrilled, to say the least!

My Father Flew back from Vietnam to pin on my new Army aviator wings at Ft Rucker, AL in 1971.

As we neared graduation date, updated orders came filtering in for my classmates. A few of us were told that once the final grades were processed, we would find out about our standing in the class and whether we had qualified for an immediate transition to Cobras. About two weeks before the actual graduation ceremony, we found out who got the transition opportunities. I was told that my option was Cobras. I wanted Chinooks. I pressed my case and was told I would need a check ride with a Chinook IP first. I took the check ride and the Chinook IP told me I would get the Chinook transition. Not only did I get the CH-47 transition but one other in the class did as well. I was very happy for a variety of reasons. One, it meant that my departure for Vietnam would now be delayed another two months. It also meant that Karen and I could stay in Alabama for another two months and we could spend even more time with my extended family in Pensacola.

Captains Hoffman, Kelly, and Dusty Holm, 1Lt. Schafer and wives upon graduation from US Army flight school in September 1971.

Graduation day was September 21, 1971. Dad arrived the day before and was present for the ceremony and got to pin on my wings. I doubt that he fully understood what that meant to me. Growing up around the elite of the Air Force fighter community and living with a man who lived and breathed aviation leaves a mark on you and a desire in some, even if unrealized until early adulthood, to fly. Now I was a military pilot. I was about to learn to fly the biggest the Army had. I was good at it, I had fun doing it, and they paid me well to do it. It does not get much better than that.

After flight school ended and we out-processed from the program, I had a short period of leave before my CH-47 flight training program began. Karen and I spent time in Florida, in DC visiting her family, and a short trip to Dad and Mom's home at Wright-Patterson Air Force Base in Ohio where Dad had just become the director of international logistics at the Air Force Logistics Command (AFLC). This was a job with worldwide responsibilities but one that also kept him focused much of the time on issues and requirements in Vietnam. It would also often place us together in RVN in the year to come.

Our holiday was much too short and passed far too quickly. When I got to the first day of the actual CH-47 transition training program, I was surprised to learn that all but two of the pilots in the class were very experienced pilots, with RVN tours already under their belts. I was one of two who were new aviators. It was both humbling and a bit intimidating because the others in our class were all far more experienced pilots than I.

The training began with a ground school on the CH-47C, the model we used for the transition and the newest model in the Army's CH-47 fleet at that time. Here was an aircraft with complexity that exceeded many current Air Force and Navy fighters of that time. With twin jet-turbine engines and tandem rotors, the aircraft had enormous power. This power was not designed for speed, though it was the fastest helicopter in the Army inventory in level flight at that time. Instead, it was designed for brute lifting strength. The C model had upgraded engines and could lift up to twenty thousand pounds on its single hook.[6] The CH-47's two engines drive a combining transmission that, in turn, drives a forward and an aft transmission. These two transmissions transfer the motive power to the forward and aft rotor systems. Because of the tandem rotor arrangement, the CH-47 does not require a tail rotor.

The cockpit of the CH-47 is far more complex than that of a UH-1H due to the more sophisticated dual engine control systems and monitors, as well as more advanced avionics and flight navigation systems. When I first sat in the cockpit of a CH-47, I was bewildered with the massive array of gauges, knobs, switches, circuit breakers, navigation instruments, radios, dials, and caution and warning lights. I once again had the sick feeling of a mountain before me that was simply too tall to climb. My instructor must have seen that look before. He simply said, "It will all come to you in time." In time, it indeed did.

The first thing I attacked that night when I got to our apartment was the CH-47C–10 manual. Every machine used by the Army has an operator's manual called the –10 series manual, spoken as "dash ten." This includes jeeps, trucks, guns, artillery, and helicopters. Most are about a quarter- to a half-inch thick. The –10 for the CH-47 is two inches thick! There are also corresponding –20, –30, and –40 manuals, but these address higher and higher levels of maintenance, from basic crew level maintenance to depot overhauls. We, as new CH-47 pilots, were charged with mastering the –10 and the –20 manuals. That first night, I focused on a complete review, cursory to be sure, of the –10. Several things struck me as odd with this first look. There was no collective. No, the CH-47 has a *thrust lever* in place of a collective. This was a Boeing influence no doubt. After all, big iron produces thrust, it does not collect it.

The second thing I discovered was that one controlled the engines with two *beep* switches on the end of the thrust lever that you adjust with your thumb. These switches enable you to control engine rpm. Then there was that small notation that if you had a complete hydraulics failure, because the entire control system was controlled by hydraulics and could not be manually operated without hydraulics, the only approved emergency procedure was to "exit the aircraft." What? Exit the aircraft? How and with what? I had never seen parachutes for crewmen in Army helicopters. I did not show Karen that part of the manual. Lastly, I was astonished at the extent and complexity of the aircraft's hydraulic system. It was a maze of pumps, pipes, valves, pressure reducers, actuators, accumulators, hoses, fittings, and sensors. Golly, what a vast amount of technology, all of which is subject to failures of one degree or another. No wonder there are so many caution lights in this beast! But this too was taken in, chewed over and, in time, completely digested. I did, however, begin to wonder about the concept of the brain becoming too full and things starting to leak out your ears as you shoved more information in! Somehow this all got in and even today I remember more of it than I will ever need to know.

Along with the classroom instruction and homework, we flew. We flew these monsters every day that the weather permitted. We flew in varying load and fuel conditions. We flew with internal and external cargo. We flew with vehicles inside and vehicles hanging outside, underneath on the cargo hook. As we gained experience and control touch with the CH-47, the instructors added more weight and more weight. As you added cargo weight on the hook, the aircraft became more and more sensitive to flight-control inputs. If the load was not aerodynamic, it would try to fly or oscillate in the wind. The heavier the load was, the worse the oscillation would get.

With our novice CH-47 touch combined with a very heavy load, sometimes simply a ten-thousand-pound block of concrete and a little choppy wind, you could get the aircraft into a serious oscillation that was sometimes difficult to dampen out without slowing almost to a hover. The more we flew, the more proficient we became and the finer our touch on the controls. About halfway through CH-47 transition, while riding in the jump seat between the instructor and another CH-47 transition pilot, I marveled at the power and capability of this huge machine. Here I was learning to fly the Army's most sophisticated operational helicopter (the new Cheyenne attack helicopter was in development at this time but would never progress to production), and just a few short months ago I was with Mr. Lee just learning the controls of the TH-55 one at a time! Surely the Army had this training process figured out to a degree I did not appreciate until this time.

Soon my days in CH-47 transition came to a close, and I was awarded the CH-47 qualification. There was no real formality to the conclusion of this course. You had a final check ride with an instructor pilot and you either passed or failed. If you passed, they shook your hand, completed the paperwork, and sent you on your way. For Karen and I, this meant packing up our belongings, arranging for a mover for our new bedroom furniture (the only actual suite of furniture that we owned) and arranging for it to be shipped. Karen's family lived in DC, and we decided that we would find an apartment for her in the area while I was deployed.

I was entitled to a month's leave between my flight training and my departure for Vietnam. So, we planned to spend that time in the Washington, DC area finding an apartment and getting moved in. This took about a week. We then traveled to see my mother and siblings at Wright-Patterson Air Force Base in Ohio and then spent the next three weeks with Karen's family and our friends from the DC area. The apartment was a third-story walkup just opposite Georgetown University, across the Potomac River. It was very convenient to the military facilities of Fort Myer, such as the commissary, the PX, and the medical and dental clinics. This proved fortunate because this leave also resulted in a surprise nine months later—our daughter Lynn Kelly Hoffman, the first of our three children born over the next few years. I have always believed that this was a successful and happy leave, just what one would like before departing on a dangerous adventure.

CHAPTER FIVE
WELCOME TO THE REPUBLIC OF SOUTH VIETNAM

MY ORIGINAL VIETNAM port call date, the date you are to show up at the port (in this case, the airport) of embarkation for overseas duty, was December 11, 1971 at McGuire Air Force Base, New Jersey. But I got a call and then a follow-up letter confirming a change in the date. This change allowed me to stay home an extra two days. While this may seem like a minor delay, any delay in deployment to a combat theater is a major delay, and it certainly was a welcome one for Karen and me. On the morning of December 13, 1971, Karen and I drove to McGuire Air Force Base to meet my 1500 hours port-call time. We were instructed to fly in Class A uniform. This seemed quite absurd to me. Why ride in a packed transport plane in Class A uniform for more than twenty hours? But orders were orders and we all showed up for the flight in those more formal uniforms. We had little baggage, as we did not need much. Just one bag containing our olive-drab fatigue uniform, boots, belts, fatigue hat, some jeans and a shirt, tennis shoes, shorts, two towels, olive-drab underwear, shaving kit, and a few books.

When I got to the terminal, the place was quite crowded. The many families and friends of departing soldiers filled the snack bar, the check-in area, and the waiting areas. After checking in for the flight, dropping off my one checked bag and getting my seat assignment (a middle seat), Karen and I said our goodbyes and I proceeded to the boarding gate. This was no doubt a tough day for Karen. She was sending me off to a faraway war to fly helicopters. And the media portrayal of the survivability of Army helicopter crews in Vietnam did not paint a very good picture. I felt terrible leaving her on her own like that.

The plane was an older, stretched DC-8 with every seat filled. This was not a load of happy campers. Many were returning for second, even third tours of duty in Vietnam, and it seemed the vast majority were either pilots or aviation crewman. The plane was hot and poorly ventilated with typical contract airline food. The food was not just crappy, the meals simply sucked. It was not even Air Force box-lunch quality. It was some kind of cross between airline food and a prepackaged box lunch that was ordered for use in 1945. I suppose this was an omen on the food rations in my future. Indeed, once in Vietnam we often found ourselves eating C rations dated from the early '50s.

The flight to Saigon was long and very uncomfortable. The aircraft was set up for maximum seating, so the seat back did not tilt much and it was narrow. I was a big guy, at six feet, one inch and 205 pounds. While I had a reasonable waist, at just over thirty-two inches, I wore size forty-eight jackets. My shoulders could not rest square in the seat back. I had to sit canted toward one side or the other. In our three across seating, on each side of the center aisle, my two seat mates quickly fell into a coordinated shoulder overlap arrangement that we alternated in unison about every hour or so. The flight was long, hot, and boring. There was no movie, no music and, as the cabin noise in this old bird was so bad, any conversation was tough. I read the two paperback books I brought with me and then I traded them with my seat mates for new ones.

We flew to the West Coast, refueled, and then took off again.

They did not let us get off the plane to stretch or get any snacks. The crew told us that they had been instructed to keep everyone on board, but they were given no reason why. We then flew to Hawaii, where the plane was serviced again, with us still having to remain on board the entire time. Next, we flew to Japan for our final stop prior to arriving in Saigon, South Vietnam. At each stop the stewardesses changed. The first crew we had was young and tried to help make the flight as tolerable as they could. The crew that got on in California was decidedly older and less enthusiastic, but they were helpful and joined with us in our disgust with the chow they had to serve us. In Japan, they finally took us off the plane so that it could be cleaned. By this time, almost twenty hours later, the inside simply stank. The toilets had all overflowed. There was trash on the floor because the trash containers were all full. I am certain that our own body odor made the stench even worse.

At the base in Japan, we were allowed to go to the PX near the terminal because the plane needed some maintenance, in addition to fuel and cleaning. I had the opportunity to buy a new watch, something I had planned on doing when I got to the first PX in Vietnam (or *in country* as we referred to being in Vietnam itself). This was a very nice, self-winding job that seemed to fit the part of a dashing pilot's chronographic wrist adornment. It was a Seiko, which Dad had told me to purchase because they were great watches and very inexpensive at the PX. I paid the princely sum of twenty-nine dollars for this watch, and it was a good buy. I still have it and it still runs—fifty years later!

We took off from Japan with another new crew. On this flight I discovered where all the old, worn-out but still active cabin crews go when they are no longer welcome as young and attractive representatives of the airlines. They go to contract charter operators and fly missions into places where they can get hazardous duty pay, a tax break, and no one on board really worrying much about what they look like. More important, with their experience and older demeanor, no one on board will give them any guff! The average age of this cabin crew was clearly over fifty and the average weight of these crew members suggested to me that the fuel load for the trip into Vietnam had been substantially reduced. Passing one in the aisle was simply not possible. But getting up and moving around did not seem like a good idea anyway because once we were airborne again, the head stewardess told us over the loudspeakers to "stay seated, shut up and we won't have any problems!" These gals seemed like graduates of some austere confinement facility. The final leg of the trip was only a few hours, but it was deathly quiet inside that cabin. No one had much to say to anyone, so perhaps the stewardesses had flown this leg long enough to know that a bit of intimidation and gruffness was the right way to set the tone. There wasn't any service on this leg anyway and we had all just eaten in Japan. So, I decided to try to get some sleep. I failed.

I arrived at Bien Hoa Air Force Base on the afternoon of December 15, 1971. Our original destination was Da Nang, but somewhere along the way that changed. We were told that when we arrived, we would be taken by bus to Long Binh for in-processing and initial in-country training. After we landed, the pilot of our stretch DC-8 seemed to be in a rush as he turned onto the taxiway. We were sliding on the asphalt as he made careening turns onto a ramp and then locked the brakes so hard that we were thrown forward in our seats.

That was when we first heard the very loud and very close sound of impacting rounds. "What was that?" someone asked. Others said loudly "Holy shit! Incoming!" With that, the aircraft door was thrown open and a huge, burly US Army NCO stepped into the aircraft and began yelling "Get the fuck off this airplane right now and run for cover in the slit trench near the edge of the ramp!"

Run? Run where? What slit trench? I grabbed my hat and ran off the plane, while trying not to be run over by those behind me. Instead of the slit trench that already looked quite full, we were herded into a building just off the ramp and were directed into an interior hallway and told to get on the floor. There were no more sounds of rounds impacting but the staff in the building was quite tense. The major sound for the next few moments was simply breathing.

The first thing I became acutely aware of as we departed the plane, after the sounds of explosions, was the rank, humid air. It seemed that every breath had passed through a sewage processing plant. What a noxious stink! I thought maybe we were near an open sewer line. As I parsed the smell, I thought it seemed to be mixture of exceedingly unpleasant odors. Each breath was a shock to your system. I asked about the stink and an MP in the terminal said, "You're just smelling Vietnam!" He was right. That smell was the smell of Vietnam. This smell was a combination of human waste, animal waste, rotting fish, and, in my mind at least, the smell of death. It permeated your clothes and your gear, but after a while, say about a month, you did not notice it much, except when eating.

Soon things eased up. The primarily US Air Force staff in the terminal building began to return to normal activity and we moved to the baggage area to get our gear after it was unloaded. I do not think that the doors on our arrival DC-8 were all closed before it taxied to the runway and took off. Apparently, we had arrived just in time for a mortar or rocket attack. I would later learn that they occurred now and then and were not that big of a deal, but it was quite an arrival ceremony for us.

From this Air Force terminal building, I and a small group of other army pilots were assembled, along with our gear, and then loaded into two trucks and transported to Long Binh and temporary quarters. We were delivered to the US Army replacement depot at Long Binh Army Base, the headquarters for the US Army in the Republic of Vietnam. This was a huge base, located on a dusty plain outside of Saigon.

Most of the buildings we passed as we were driven across the base were small, mainly single-story wooden WWII Pacific War-style construction with a solid covering of plywood on the lower half of the walls and screen for the upper half. The roof was typically corrugated metal. Most had a stack of wooden ammunition boxes, filled with sand, stacked around the buildings up to the height of the screens. Between most were small structures that looked to be outhouses. There were also small mounds of sandbags here and there that appeared to be the tops of bunkers or bomb proofs. There were also a few buildings that looked like they had taken a direct hit from some relatively modest indirect ordnance[7], but with gaping holes in the roof and blown out sections of side walls. This aspect did not make one feel optimistic about peaceful sleep any time soon, even with our severe fatigue and jet lag. There was also the frequent sound of distant gunfire that reinforced your awareness of being in a combat zone.

A final reminder of the danger all around were the impact craters scattered around the billeting area. These often filled with about a foot of water and smelled awful.

My first hootch in RVN at Long Binh in Dec 1971. Note the blast shielding with sand-filled barrels and rocket boxes.

This huge base was the Vietnam headquarters for the US Army forces supporting the fight against the attempts of the communist North to take over South Vietnam. In its large, multi-storied headquarters complex, at the center of the base, was Military Assistance Command Vietnam (MACV) headquarters. This is also the location of the 1st Aviation Brigade, the headquarters, by that time, of nearly all US Army aviation in country. It was also obvious that this base was in some phase of a draw down. We passed many long rows of empty buildings and facilities on the way to the replacement center. Some looked as if they had been thoroughly ransacked by someone. We unloaded and an NCO greeted us and told us that we were at the 90th Replacement Battalion. He pointed out the barracks building we were assigned to occupy, how to get to the officer's club and then where the PX and barbershop were located. I was, of course, very glad that he had his priorities straight. I needed a beer and, hopefully, about thirty-six hours of sleep. The barber and the PX could wait.

Our temporary barracks had simple cots and wall lockers but no bathroom, sinks, or showers. Instead, there were outhouses, and a communal shower house serving several barracks. There were bugs everywhere. Of the assortment of insects that scurried across the floors and that were on the walls, what most impressed me were the cockroaches. These bugs were the largest I have ever seen in my life. Then there were lizards on every wall and up in the ceiling. They were noisy but turned out to be welcome barracks occupants as they ate the mosquitoes. Here we would wait for our orders that would dispatch us to our assigned units out in the field.

We threw down our gear and headed to the o' club for a meal and a beer. I had one beer and felt that I was about to pass out from the combination of fatigue and the alcohol, so I went back to the barracks and fell onto a bunk. I woke up the next day to the sound of a chief warrant officer letting us know that there would be an indoctrination brief after morning chow, the uniform was class C and "by the way, what in the hell are you guys doing in class A's anyway?"

The first thing they told us at the brief was that we would be shipping out within forty-eight hours to our units. Orders would be delivered to us, along with our transportation requests (TRs), for movement on Air Force transports by tomorrow. They gave us a list of gear we needed and told us to go directly to the Central Issue Facility to draw it after the brief. We were told to stay in the compound and to always keep our flak vest and steel pots handy because *Charlie* was dropping calling cards every few hours into Long Binh. What helmets and flak vests? None had yet been issued to me. Lastly, the guy briefing us again asked why we had arrived in class A uniform. He told us to go to the post office and send them home before we left Long Binh, or we might not ever see them again. As officers, we had to pay for our uniforms and Class A's were expensive. Mine were custom tailored and they were too expensive to end up as lost mail from some remote base camp out in the bush.

The United States Military Assistance Command, Vietnam (MACV) Headquarters at Long Bin

The trip to CIF, as the central issue facility was called, was a bit of a flashback for me. As we went down a line of counters, all manner of stuff was dumped into our arms, from flight suits and boots to underwear to helmets (both steel pots and flight helmets) to flak vests, web gear, packs, canteens, mosquito nets, poncho liners, and first aid kits. It all fit into two large duffel bags. But no weapon or ammo was issued. Those would be issued to us by our new units.

Here I also ran into several flight-school classmates. It was great to find other white hats here, even if only a handful. It seemed that about half of my officer class was arriving at just about the same time. A good chunk of the class never got orders into RVN, but as the next year rolled along, about two-thirds of the class arrived in country for the last year of combat by US Army forces. Dusty Holms was already up north. Fred Suttle, Mike O'Byrne, Alan Tigner, the Smiths (Ted and Norm—not brothers but they could have been!), Forest Synder, Dexter Florence, and a few others were in various stages of in processing into other units around RVN. Unfortunately, we never had a chance to get together and catch up as a group and, worse, some I would only see briefly ever again. I am, however, often reminded of all of those we lost, as are many others when they see their names on old unit orders from Vietnam, documents we may have saved from flight school, or carved in stone on the Vietnam War Memorial.

That second day in country we went to the PX to buy shipping materials and then to the Army post office to send home my Class A uniforms and postcards announcing my safe arrival in country to Karen and Dad and Mom. The week before I left, neither Karen nor my mom were handling my departure well. For Karen, it was unknown territory. She was apprehensive of the future and the news on TV, with its reports on American casualties, downed helicopters, and poor progress in Paris. For Mom, this was unwelcomed but familiar territory, and she did not like it in the least. Not only had my father already had two yearlong tours in Vietnam, now I was there for a year, and Dad was in an assignment that carried him in and out of the country on a nearly monthly basis.

Late that second night in country we were awakened by several incoming rounds. They sounded small, so I assumed they were 60-mm mortars impacting in the distance but clearly inside the security wire on the vast perimeter of the Long Binh base. There was no more sleep that night for me. After the all-clear sounded, I returned to my bunk and simply waited for the next sound of incoming. Obviously, that was the point of the exercise for the bad guys: the People's Army of Vietnamese (PAVN) from North Vietnam. For me, it would be something that took some time to get used to hearing. Later during the next year, there would be times when the only way I could get to sleep was to have a familiar sound in the background, such as a radio playing softly. Other times, I would be so exhausted that I would fall asleep at the very first opportunity. But not this night. I had no radio and, while I was still tired from jet lag, I could not relax sufficiently to sleep.

The next day I got my transportation request and orders from the 1st Aviation Brigade Headquarters for my assignment to the 203rd Assault Support Helicopter Company (ASHC) at Marble Mountain Army Airfield, near Da Nang, in I Corps up north. Marble Mountain? Why does that ring a bell? I thought about this name for a moment, which seemed harder than usual in my sleep-deprived state. Then I remembered. My cousin, George Dewey, had been flying out of Marble Mountain in a Marine CH-46 when he was killed in 1969. Not a good omen. I decided that communicating my new assignment location to the family back home would not be useful. Little did I know that Dad already knew my initial in-country unit of assignment. A reality that began as a bit of a game, then a routine.

The 203rd was a Chinook outfit that had once been a part of the famed 1st Air Cavalry Division. Although they were flying relatively old A-model aircraft, flying Chinooks was fine by me. That was what I had hoped for. Plus, Da Nang was supposed to have cooler weather and great beaches. Seemed like things were going okay so far. I decided to try and put a call home to Karen to let her know I was okay. I went to the o' club of the 90th Replacement, where they said you could put through a MARS call to the States. Now I had no idea what a MARS call was, but a call was a call.

At the club I was told I could request a time for a MARS call, but the waiting list was long, and I would probably be in Da Nang before I even got a time slot for a call, so I asked what a MARS call was. I was told it is a link between the military communication guys and HAM radio operators in the States who would place a collect call from their location to whoever you wanted to call. Sounded worth a try, but obviously not any time soon. I then asked about a regular phone and the possibility of a collect call straight to my home. Yep, I was told, you could do that but not here. I was then told that the Red Cross office in Saigon had phones, the Red Cross office at Ton Son Nhut had phones, and the R&R Center in Vung Tao had phones, but you couldn't get there from here. And, they told me, the cost is a bit steep for the other end. How steep, I had to ask. The reply was that it costs a lot, a whole lot, so it had better be an important call! So much for calling home.

I decided to try and get a haircut and then see a movie at the o' club. After my haircut I went to the club to get some chow and watch the movie they had advertised for that evening. I needed to kill some time and fight the boredom of waiting and I was tired of reading. I got a rusty can of beer, a Carling Black Label, and a burger and went to a table to await the movie. When it started, I sat back and quickly became engrossed in an old B western. About ten minutes in, the film seemed to run out, to a loud flapping sound. The lights came on, and the projectionist, an NCO with the club, told us to give him about two minutes and we would be back in business. Sure enough, in no more than two minutes the film resumed. The only problem was that the film did not restart at the same place it had stopped. It restarted somewhere else in the film. The movie then went fine, albeit in a different part of the story, for about another ten minutes.

Suddenly the image dropped off the screen, we had the same flapping noise, and the lights came on. Once again, the projectionists asked us for two minutes and then he got it going again. This time the story seemed to be at about the same point, it was just slightly later in the story, due, no doubt, to some missing section of film. Then the movie went another fifteen minutes or so and the entire process started again. This time, when the movie resumed, the story was at an entirely different place again. Obviously, the film had been damaged and broken in several places, probably from repeated use and shipping. And just as obviously the pieces of film were not all in the correct order. I had lost all track of what was going on and I gave up. I went back to the bar, got another beer, and sat down to watch the Armed Forces Network Vietnam on the TV and the news from the States.

The news was mostly politics, why Republicans are evil, why the Army is evil, why the Democrats are evil, and how industry is just trying to screw everybody. Then there was news of marches, burning buildings on campuses, and why no one will be buying anything for their kids this year because everyone is broke and Santa Claus is generally, the news report suggested, just too pissed off at the world! There was little about Vietnam. Only a brief statement from some Defense Department wag about the need for patience on the peace talks and a college professor who asserted that he was God's gift to the nation and knew all the answers that were important. So much for the news. When the beer was done, so was I.

On the morning of the sixteenth of December, we received our flight manifest, and we were loaded onto trucks for the trip to the flight line on Ben Hoa AFB and a ride in a C-130 to Da Nang. Now I knew that things in the Army could run efficiently sometimes and that planning ahead was always a good thing to do. I did not realize how gifted the folks in the 90th Replacement Battalion were at that. Indeed, they seemed, like much of the Army in the coming months, to be doing things before they happened and move people about either before or after they actually moved them. This must be a place where the Department of Defense had figured out time warps or something. There in my hand was a flight manifest for a flight that day, yet it was dated the next day. If that does not make sense to you, it did not make sense to me either. This was certainly an omen, but I did not know it at the time.

Lesson: when things do not make sense, the folks in headquarters may or may not know what they are doing . . . proceed with care.

The trip north to Da Nang was noisy but smooth. The air at altitude was cool and smelled fresh, with none of the stink I smelled on the ground at Long Binh. We landed at Marble Mountain, which I found out later was unusual. We deplaned into a bright sun but a comfortable temperature. But, damn, there was that stink again. We unloaded while the bird was still running, dragging our gear along with us down the back ramp. Normally, such flights land at Da Nang Main Air Force Base and new aviation personnel arriving at the 22nd Replacement Depot are then trucked to Marble Mountain Army Airfield. I never did get an explanation for this departure from normal procedure, but I was grateful to have avoided another ride in the back of a deuce-and-a-half truck. We were met on the ramp by a representative of the 11th Combat Aviation Group. He escorted us to an area in front of the 11th CAG headquarters where we waited for our units from on base to come and police us up. A quarter-ton truck came up from across the runway and took me over to the 203rd Assault Support Helicopter Company (ASHC) area.

The 203rd ASHC was equipped with medium lift, A-model CH-47 helicopters. These aircraft provided lift support to artillery units, moving guns and ammo, and to infantry units to lift troops and to provide resupply. The 203rd also supported engineer units to move equipment and supplies. The 203rd occupied hangars on the ocean side of Marble Mountain Army Airfield with its aircraft parking ramps on the east side of the runway. The runway ran almost north and south along the coast, just to the east of the main Da Nang Air

Force Base. Marble Mountain Army Airfield supported, in addition to the 203rd, three assault helicopter companies, equipped with UH-1H and AH-1G helicopters; two air cavalry troops; a CH-54 heavy-lift company; an OV-1 Mohawk reconnaissance airplane company; and an assortment of support, fueling and maintenance units, all under the command of the 11th Combat Aviation Group (CAG).

CHAPTER SIX
THE WILDCATS

AS A NEW CH-47 driver with so few hours of actual flight experience in CH-47s that they did not count, one does not have much standing upon arrival at an experienced unit such as this former 1st Cavalry Division Chinook Company. As the former A Company of the 228th Chinook Battalion, 1st Cavalry Division, there was a lot of experience in heavy lift operations in combat within this unit. It had a storied and gallant reputation and was one of the last remnants of the 1st Cavalry still in RVN. Equipped with older A-model aircraft, these 203rd helicopters had a very limited lift capacity in the heat and high-density altitude environment of Vietnam—read moist, thin air[8]. They were all well-worn, but serviceable airframes that were no longer front-line machines. Indeed, Chinooks, at this point, were now in their third iteration with the deployment of C models, with bigger engines, more lift, and more sophisticated systems. But these A models would suffice for the present and they did not fail our crews. They could lift five to seven thousand pounds on the hook, depending upon the density altitude and temperature on the day of the mission. On most days in that hot, humid environment, they could lift a 105-mm howitzer, just barely, but could not also lift the A22 ammo bag that normally was lifted with the gun. That meant one had to make two lifts instead of one to move a single gun, crew, and ammo. These aircraft were quite well-suited for the other combat support missions of the unit, such as moving supplies and ammunition to fire bases in the area, moving PX CONEXs (medium sized shipping containers used as mobile Post Exchange shops) between firebases and Da Nang AFB and for transporting casualties.

The 203rd was commanded by Major Theo Epperson. He was an experienced pilot and a good commander. He greeted me and Lt. Smith, a former flight school classmate, warmly. He gave us a short brief on the unit's current missions and then told us to find our new platoon leader and get settled. And, he added at the end, stay out of the way and out of trouble and learn the ropes as fast as you can. The company XO was Bill Schmidt. Both were good leaders who took care of the troops and always tried to make the best of a bad situation. Everyone in the unit appreciated their leadership and devotion to the men.

After signing into the unit and meeting the company first sergeant, we went to our respective platoon areas and found empty hootch space and dumped our kits. My hootch was made of rocket boxes stacked about eight feet high with a simple truss roof covered in corrugated steel sheets for rain cover. There were no real windows, just gaps in the framework and boxes that were mostly covered with screen in a failed effort to keep bugs out. Speaking of bugs, it became clear right off that we shared this living space with more of the giant cockroaches. If anything, these were bigger than the ones I saw in Saigon. These guys were so big that you could, and this is a real "no shit" story, shoot a hole in one with a .45 and it could still crawl away.

This was also my introduction to *jet fuel shitters*. That is just what they were. There were simple wooden out houses for doing one's business. But instead of a hole in the ground underneath, there was the bottom half of a fifty-five-gallon drum, filled halfway with JP-4 jet fuel. This was the same fuel used in our helicopters. When a drum was too full of human waste, unit members had the unpleasant, rotating duty of pulling this drum out and burning off the JP-4 and the waste therein. It was a stinky, unpleasant task that made the entire air base stink of burning human waste. Yuk! Only recently have the adverse health effects of such practices been recognized.

Defensive positions and watch tower along the beach front at Marble Mountain Army Airfield, RVN in 1972.

After I got settled, I met my hootch mates, the company maintenance officer and a warrant officer pilot who was one of the unit's aircraft commanders (AC). Both were friendly and helped me get settled that night. I then went off to meet the unit's XO, Captain Bill Schmidt, so he could fill me in on what to expect and what I needed to do next. Bill was a friendly, cigar-smoking pilot who had been around for a while and knew the unit so well that he ran the administrative side of everything. The CO ran operations and was in command, but Bill made the unit function. He became a good friend and was great help to me. The 203rd ASHC aircraft parking revetments and maintenance hangar were situated on the east side of the central airfield runway. That put our hootches and company CP on the ocean side of the airfield. The cool ocean breeze and the smell of salt water took a bit of the edge off the heat and the stink. The ocean side had a road that ran along the perimeter wire between the beach and the first row of structures. Along this road, facing the ocean was a series of sandbag and timber bunkers and gun pits. To their front was row upon row of concertina wire almost down to the high tide mark. There was one small area, between two large bunkers, where a small, cleared area near the water served as the designated swimming area, when it was considered safe to be on that side of the wire. The rest of the area along this oceanfront was mined and booby-trapped to keep enemy sappers (infiltrators who try to blow up things) from swimming in at night and trying to get into the base from the ocean.

Beachfront wire defenses at Marble Mountain Army Airfield near Da Nang, RVN in 1972.

The airfield also had a small but well-appointed officer's club with a nice ocean view patio. The beverage fare offered was very limited: sodas for a nickel, beers for a dime (or, if the can was really rusty, a nickel) and sometimes, not always, liquor drinks for a dollar. The only food normally available was hot dogs, sometimes French fries and popcorn. But I found that a beer and hot dog was often more satisfying than anything available in the mess hall. There was also music from a record player, a TV set, a movie screen and, about once a month, a small USO troupe would play live music for us.

This is the last photo, just as we abandoned the base, that I took of our small officer's club at Marble Mountain Army Airfield. This was where I had many enjoyable times with Dusty and our fellow pilots. The club's patio was surrounded by a low wall in the foreground. One or two occasions, I hid behind that wall as incoming mortar rounds impacted on the airfield. But I never dropped my beer in the process.

The 203rd was, by this time in the war, a bit of a lash up of a unit. It did not have a full complement of CH-47 aircraft and was not fully manned. There were only a few CH-47 A model aircraft still in the Army inventory. At any one time, the unit had ten to twelve that were flyable. The unit used parts off of aircraft that were not flyable to keep others operational. This was partly due to the fact that the unit was flying older A-model aircraft and partly because there was a drawdown of US forces in country underway that directly impacted the logistic system in a less-than-positive manner. The unit had three flight platoons, a maintenance platoon, and a headquarters and operations section for command and control. I was somewhat disappointed not to get assigned to a unit with newer, better C-model Chinooks, but I quickly learned that this unit had grit and lots of very experienced pilots. This would be important in the days to come.

The first step for newbies in an aviation unit is to get unit qualified as a peter-pilot or copilot. This means an initial unit instructor pilot check ride. Then you must get familiarized with the area of operations and the unit's missions. You do all this riding in the right seat, on rare occasions getting to touch the controls until the instructor pilot knew and trusted you. So, after my initial check ride, I started flying as a peter-pilot on local area administrative missions and training flights. Then I slowly moved up to flying right seat on combat support missions to outlying firebases and to other field sites and airfields in I Corps. I often found myself as the alert-crew peter-pilot, which meant sitting around all day waiting to fly, if needed, which was not often at first. I did not get a lot of flight time in December 1971 and January of 1972. To further reduce actual flight time for many of us new guys was the fact that the 203rd was training Vietnamese Air Force (VNAF) pilots to fly Chinooks and they got to fly as copilots on many of the 203rd ASHC missions during January, February, and early March 1972.

So as not to let me get bored, Major Epperson did assign me to an additional duty for the unit. I was designated as the keystone officer for the 203rd. Keystone was the name of the overall drawdown of US forces operation across South Vietnam. That meant that I was responsible for the administration and management of the stand down of the unit and the transfer of its aircraft, maintenance support systems, spare parts, and most other unit assets to the VNAF. I was also responsible for the inventories of all weapons and other sensitive equipment not going to the VNAF, their accounting and transfer to other units or for shipment stateside. I also had to arrange all unit personnel transfers home or to wherever they would be assigned after the stand down of the unit.

Then the cold rainy season came in on I Corps. I spent a lot of time outdoors doing inventories and inspecting gear to arrange disposition. I also spent a lot of time doing preflights of aircraft, often in the rain, as an alert crew but not much actual flying time. What I did get was sick, very sick. What started as a cold in late January turned into full-fledged pneumonia by early February and I found myself in 95th Evac Hospital (China Beach) recovering.

Dad and I in front of his BOQ quarters on Ton Son Nhut Air Force Base in RVN in 1972.

When I first arrived in country, one of the many forms I filled out was my casualty notification card. This card was used to prescribe who and when anyone was to be notified if you are sick, injured, wounded, or killed while in country. I elected not to have my wife Karen notified if I was sick or wounded but retained in country. I listed my father as the person to be notified if I was wounded <u>and</u> evacuated or killed in action (KIA) or missing in action (MIA). Therefore, when I got sick, no one was told. No big deal to me, as my mail continued. I sent letters home and generally did not let on to anyone that I was anything but healthy and safe. Big mistake! I soon discovered that Dad, on one of his many trips into Saigon as the chief of international logistics for the Air Force Logistics Command, tried to get in touch with me at Marble Mountain. However, much to his consternation, I was not there.

"Well, where is he?" asked my concerned father of the 203rd ASHC first sergeant. The sergeant dutifully answered, "Why in the hospital, of course." I, as you can surmise, did not actually hear this conversation, but I did hear a loud rumble coming from the direction of Saigon, some several hundred miles away just about that time. I was briefed on the conversation several times in the following weeks. First, I heard about it over beers at the Marble Mountain Army Airfield Officers Club by the first sergeant and Bill. Then later at the Da Nang Main Officer's Club over dinner I heard about it in full and loud detail from Dad, who was once again in Da Nang on one of his many inspection and coordination visits. From that point on, during my entire tour of duty in Southeast Asia, an almost daily call was made by Dad's office in Saigon to my unit's top sergeant to ascertain my overall health, location, and duty status. This continued until I was back in the United States for good in December of 1972.

My dad, Colonel George E. Hoffman Jr., on one of his many inspection tours of USAF assistance programs to the Vietnamese Air Forces. Dad is leading his team, holding the camera. Dad was serving in a brigadier general's assignment as he awaited his US Senate confirmation as a general officer, which never came.

This was not the only interaction between my father and the 203rd in early 1972. No indeed. Dad liked to occasionally *bring smoke* on folks to keep things moving and transparent, and you never were quite sure when he was joking and not joking until you knew him well. One day, while on a visit to his staff at Da Nang Main Air Force Base, he decided on a side visit to my unit at Marble Mountain. At this point the 203rd was actually working for him. The overall push to *Vietnamize* the war included training the Vietnamese Air Force (VNAF) pilots to fly Chinooks and then to turn over many early model US Army Chinooks to the VNAF. Hence the 203rd was training Vietnamese pilots flying as copilots on various missions, as a part of my father's program.

So, one day Dad arrived with his small entourage at Marble

Mountain Army Airfield to visit the 203rd and inspect its progress in training VNAF pilots and its preparations to turn over its aircraft. No one in the company had ever actually seen him in person before. Further, they did not know that the Air Force officer from Wright-Patterson Air Force Base in charge of the US Air Force Vietnamization Program was my father. After formal introductions and a tour of the unit, Dad paid an office call on Theo, our CO. While in with the CO, Dad proceeded to complain about seeing a US Army captain, wearing a 203rd unit patch, over on Da Nang Main with a disheveled, unkempt flight suit that badly needed to be washed and pressed (pressing was something you did not do to Nomex flight suits!) and, oh by the way, "sporting the most God-awful mustache" he had ever seen on a commissioned officer. Dad asserted to Theo that as a West Point graduate with an Army background during WWII, he was offended by this officer's appearance. Dad then informed Theo that, if he did nothing else during the remainder of his tour of duty in the Republic of Vietnam, he was to get that ugly mustache off the face of that Captain Hoffman. He turned on his heel and walked out of Theo's office and returned to Da Nang Air Force Base, or Da Nang Main, as we called it. Shortly after I returned from flying a mission out to a firebase west of DaNang, I was summoned to Theo's office.

Just what in the hell, Theo asked, had I been doing over on Da Nang Main that had pissed off the Air Force full colonel who was overseeing the entire 203rd ASHC project with the VNAF? He was genuinely upset and concerned that there was trouble with the Air Force over whatever I had done. Well, I did not know whether to laugh or try to act concerned. I heard a slight chuckle coming from behind me and I turned to look at "Top," our unit first sergeant. He was clearly about to lose it. He had recognized Dad's voice and knew then and there that this was humor on the part of my father.

Theo looked at his face and realized this was some kind of joke that he was not privy to. He looked at me and asked what was going on. I asked him what the name of the Air Force officer was.

He hesitated and then the light came on. Hoffman, his name was Hoffman, he said and then grinned. He then told me to shave off the mustache and laughed. Then Top asked me how I came to be in this unit. I told him that it had nothing to do with my dad. "Right," he said. Honestly, I protested. I was CH-47 qualified out of flight school and this was the unit I drew. "Right," he said again. "No one gets CH-47 qualified right out of flight school," he protested. "I did and several others did, too," I replied, not bothering to add why, as it would have made no difference to him at that point.

The truth was that I had the ugliest, most irregular looking mustache in the entire US Army aviation community. It was the butt of jokes the entire time I wore it. Yet no one in that community, where mustaches were almost de rigueur, ever would have suggested I shave it off. What this mustache did reflect was my distant Spanish heritage in a manner more fitting for Hollywood humor than anything else useful.

What did come of this funny confrontation and the new "monitoring" was a good back channel for the unit to the Air Force. No one at Da Nang Main or from 7th AF HQ in Saigon could really screw with us much from that point on. Nor did we hear much from 1st Aviation Brigade HQ or from the 11th CAG beyond mission assignments and, on occasion, mission debriefs. We flew our missions, we got the job done, and everyone was happy. At least until March of 1972.

I had the occasion to catch a C-130 flight to Saigon in mid-February to address some administrative tasks for 1st Aviation Brigade HQ. This gave me a chance to visit Dad during one of his inspection visits to Vietnamese Air Force units and attend a New Year's party with him on the VNAF side of the Bien Hoa Air Force Base near Saigon. I often had missions or tasks that took me to Saigon, though sometimes I assumed that there was some cause and effect in play with these tasks. When Dad was in country, he would usually stay at Ton Son Nhut AFB in BOQ #1, which had numerous rooms off a central great room with a kitchen and dining area, along with a large sitting and TV area. It was quite nice and had flush toilets! Once in a great while I would be there overnight and would stay with Dad in this Air Force lap of luxury. Dad's frequent trips in and out of country afforded me with a unique package delivery system that succeeded in resupplying me with homemade cookies (not all dried out and crumbled as those were that arrived via conventional Army postal channels), popcorn, and cans of Mexican food, all of which was always a great hit after weeks of C rations and the reconstituted, very bland stuff that the mess halls served.

Another great thing about BOQ #1 was that it was directly across the street from the main Ton Son Nhut Officer's Club. This was a great place for dinner, Sunday brunch, or just to sit in the bar and listen to the live music. Eating there was like being back home in the States for an evening out. There was nothing else like it in all RVN.

I was on this trip south to also complete an investigation of some irregularities in accounting for some mess hall expenditures at a unit near Saigon—yep, I asked the same question myself, why me? There were several valid reasons, of course. One, an officer was required to investigate; two, the unit in question was a 1st Aviation Brigade unit; and three, I had the military police investigative experience. So, there I was at Dad's BOQ front door again. "Any booze in there or wild women?" I asked when I arrived at his door. No women, but there were lots of refreshments. I decided this was the place to relax and catch up. Since I was going to be in Saigon for the next two days, I just stayed in dad's BOQ. Of course, I had to marvel at the facilities, flush the toilets several times to simply watch technology function, and get a shower where there was unlimited hot water! Dad invited me to attend a party that the VNAF was putting on at Bien Hoa the next night. Party? Sounded good to me . . . I should have known better!

This event was for the benefit of the VNAF itself in the Saigon area. It was attended by a mob of Vietnamese officers and senior NCOs. There were only a handful of Americans present and it was all traditional Vietnamese cuisine, including a roasted water buffalo and native venison. It was quite a spectacle with some amazing entertainment and more food than I had ever seen in Vietnam. The party started in the late afternoon and lasted all evening. We traveled over to Bien Hoa in dad's C-47, as this was an official function for him and his staff at 7th Air Force Headquarters in Saigon. The food was okay, but I should have known better than to eat water buffalo and local deer meat. But, hey, when in Rome

My dad and his team in Saigon at the 1972 VNAF New Year's party at Ben Hoa Air Force Base. This was a party he and I both should have skipped!

As the evening wore on and the time neared 2200 hours, Dad decided that it was time to *sky up* and get back to Ton Son Nhut. The C-47 was parked nearby, and the crew was standing by to leave. As we walked out on the ramp and were within about 100 feet of the aircraft, all hell broke loose. Machine gun bullets with red and green tracers were flying across the ramp, mortar rounds and rockets began to impact on the flight line and the runway. Dad yelled at the major flying the C-47 to "fire it up! Let's get the heck out of here now!" The engines were coughing to life as we jumped in the cargo door. As soon as we were inside the door, the crew chief followed with the wheel chocks through the main cargo door and were we rolling down the taxiway. The tracers were flying by the windows and open door and the air vibrated with sounds of gunfire and the sounds of incoming mortar rounds impacting on the airfield. I was still standing just forward of the open cargo door when I realized that the aircraft was at full power and the tail lifted off the ground as we rolled down the taxi way. The pilot decided to takeoff from where we began to roll and not bother with the runway. Dad made some remark about how the VNAF sure knew how to close a party.

Seconds later we lifted into the air. I was still standing by the open door—no seat belt, no safety harness, nothing but my hand holding onto a tie down panel in the aircraft side wall as the aircraft bumped through the rough air that was rolling and buffeting us around. I was watching out the door at the amazing light show around and below us as tracers streaked through the sky, mortar rounds exploded and 122-mm rockets impacted on the airfield, when I realized my potential peril. I quickly climbed into a seat and strapped into the seat belt. Cool light show, but a bad time to be watching it and a bad place to watch it from!

Lesson: They make seat belts and safety harnesses for a reason!

The trip back to Ton Son Nhut AFB was quiet and sobering. Whatever alcohol I had consumed, actually only two *33* local Vietnamese beers[9] over the entire afternoon, was processed and gone from my system and brain. I was stone cold sober and alert during that short plane ride. Ton Son Nhut AFB was quiet, and the air was clear of tracers and flying death. I slept okay that night but was still a bit unnerved the next morning. It had been a close thing because the next day we found bullet holes in the fuselage of the C-47, from the cockpit to the cargo door. I finished my report, turned it in, and left for Da Nang on a C-130 hop that afternoon. Later that day, both Dad and I began to feel sick, though we did not know then about each other. Dad got so sick, he was medevac'd back to the States within twenty-four hours. Back at Marble Mountain there was no doubt in my mind that I had eaten something very, very bad in Bien Hoa that night. What the bullets and mortar rounds did not do that night, some evil bug tried to do over the next few days as I fought off Ho Chi Minh's revenge. I was out of action for about forty-eight hours. I learned later that dad was seriously sick for two weeks. I suppose my constitution was more in tune with the local pathogens than was Dad's at that time or I was simply in better condition to overcome the pathogen's effects. Turned out that all the US military officers present at this event became very sick. I assumed that this was no accident. I have always considered that to have been an intentional use of biowarfare targeting senior American officers who were supporting the VNAF. I was back to work and flying again by the end of the week.

In February, the 203rd was tapped to fly a USO show out to the Navy carrier USS *Kitty Hawk* (CV-63), then off the coast of Vietnam just east of Da Nang. I was assigned as peter pilot for the mission. The day of the mission, we flew over to Da Nang main for the pickup. The USO troupe had just finished a show for the Air Force and was packed and ready for us when we landed. As soon as the performers were loaded, our flight engineer called on the intercom to advise us that one of the performers wanted to ride in the jump seat in the cockpit. I told him to send him up. As we readied the bird for departure, into the cockpit steps Sammy Davis Jr.! *Cool!*, I thought. What a thrill to meet one of the famous Rat Pack. He sat down in the folding jump seat and the crew chief helped him strap in and get set up on the intercom. He greeted us with thanks for the ride and then sat quietly as we received our ATC departure clearance and taxi instructions from the Da Nang AFB tower.

Soon we were airborne and headed east out over the ocean. As things became routine in the flight and we had time to converse, we introduced our selves to Mr. Davis. He immediately began telling us one-liners, commenting humorously on everything from how complicated the instrument panel looked to the color we had selected for our aircraft. He was a real gentleman and very personable. He made us feel at ease talking with him and he put us in stitches several times with his constant stream of jokes, sometimes to a point where it was hard to fly the helicopter! Soon we had the carrier in sight, and it was time to focus on landing.

Aerial operations on and off a Navy carrier are as seriously dangerous as they are challenging. Such landings were not routine for US Army pilots. Mr. Davis got up and went to the cabin to sit with his crew of musicians and dancing girls. We shot the approach to the carrier and its forward deck area from the side because they were just finishing aircraft recoveries on the stern and angle deck. As we touched down, our flight engineer lowered the back ramp and Mr. Davis immediately ran down the ramp on the carrier deck, followed by his troupe of young female entertainers.

Apparently, the sudden arrival on deck of Sammy Davis Jr. and his show girls was enough to momentarily distract the Navy deck handlers who were supposed to chock and block our aircraft and tie us down to the deck. It was at this point that good ol' Murphy and his law showed up. Just after I pulled the flight condition levers back to *ground* as a part of the post landing checklist, the utility hydraulics system on our CH-47A failed. Apparently, some seal or valve had picked that precise moment in time to stop performing as intended. Murphy's Law! The first thing we saw was that we had no brakes and had begun, ever so slightly, to roll forward. As soon as this happened, I threw the condition levers to *flight* and began beeping the engines and rotors up to flight rpm. In a matter of seconds, PriFly, the control tower on a carrier, thinking that we were rolling uncontrolled on the deck and not in a flight configuration told us to abandon the aircraft as they were sending "Tilley" (a huge deck tractor on a carrier) to push our aircraft over the side to protect the other aircraft on the flight deck.

"Like hell," I said, knowing that the Air Force would be very unhappy, to say nothing of Dad, if we lost one of the CH-47s intended for the VNAF. I saw that the USO passengers had all departed the helicopter and were clear. The flight engineer, now standing on the carrier flight deck but still plugged into the aircraft intercom through his long walk-around-wire was yelling that we were rolling. No shit! As we had reached flight rpms, the aircraft commander (AC) pulled thrust, and we rolled forward, then up and off the end of the carrier in flight, and we climbed away from the carrier and turned toward Da Nang. On the radio the Navy air boss was screaming at us for taking off without clearance and for not letting Tilley push our multimillion-dollar helicopter over the side and into the South China Sea. "Well, fuck him," I told the AC as we headed to Marble Mountain. At least we did not lose the helicopter as the result of the lack of attention to procedure on the part of the Navy deck crew. The Navy would get over our disrespect of their tradition of destroying expensive US Army aircraft because they didn't trust Army aviators.

That was not the end of the issue, however. The air boss on the *Kitty Hawk* filed a complaint about our actions and failure to follow his orders with 1st Aviation Brigade HQ in Saigon. They sent an Army Colonel and one from the Air Force up to Da Nang AFB to investigate. The air boss demanded that the commanding general of First Aviation Brigade conduct a flight evaluation board (FEB) to strip us of our wings. The investigating colonels met with us and asked if we had saved the aircraft and we replied that we had. Then one asked if we broke any airplanes or other Navy toys on the carrier and we replied that we did not. He then asked if we were sorry we had disobeyed the Navy air boss and we replied, "No, we are not." The Air Force colonel smiled and said, "I do not see any basis here for any further action on this matter. You clearly saved the United States government a very expensive aircraft due to your quick thinking and obvious pilot skills." He said he would tell the Navy that they did not understand the orders under which we were operating, nor the value and importance of the aircraft involved. Finally, he said that he saw no basis for any punishment, and that we took quick action in responding to an onboard emergency that could have resulted in catastrophic damage to our aircraft and those on the carrier's deck. We had not endangered the carrier or anyone or anything on that carrier. That was the last we heard about the matter.

Lesson: If you disobey orders, there had better be a significant upside for everyone involved.

As we progressed into March of 1972 it became clear to us in the 203rd ASHC that there was something in the wind and it was not good. Getting flight time was soon no longer a problem, but getting the keystone duties accomplished was about to become a major problem as the war spun up again. I noticed many indicators that something was afoot.

1. The intel types at Marble Mountain all disappeared.
2. We kept hearing that the peace talks in Paris were making "progress," but nothing else was ever announced.
3. The MPs caught a hootch maid pacing off distances between the sleeping hootches.
4. Many hootch maids and contractor cleaning staff were no longer coming to work.
5. The Zoomies (Air Force types) were saying over beers in the club that there was a lot of convoy and armor traffic by the NVA north of the DMZ.
6. We doubled the number of daily artillery resupply mission up in Quang Tri province in support of the ARVN.
7. Finally, but not least, we heard that the F-4 fighter Zoomies were planning to relocate their primary operational base from Da Nang Main AFB to Thailand.

Now, I may not have been the sharpest knife in the drawer, but I knew intelligence indicators when I saw them. Indicators combined with rumors usually meant something. While we had the occasional 60-mm mortar round land out on the airfield proper and even had a few 122-mm rockets fired at Marble Mountain Army Airfield since I arrived, none did much damage, and they were classified as harassment fire. Now even that had stopped for about three weeks . . . things did not feel the same. Time to ask questions and investigate how to stay safe if this all did change for the worse.

I looked around our hootch area at the airfield and realized that there was no convenient bunker to crawl into if some bad shit started repeatedly falling out of the sky during the night. It was time to dig a hole. After a discussion of indicators and an explanation of why a good hole is better than no hole, I enlisted the aid of my hootch mates to dig one. We began digging one afternoon and dug for about a week. When we were done, we had a good-sized buried bunker with a concrete floor, solid walls, zigzag entrance, and good overhead cover built between two of our hootches. Of course, the construction effort was not without the usual local disrespect, insults, and hoots from others who did not seem to understand or care about indicators. We designed the bunker for about six folks. Six of us built it and six of us planned to employ it for protection, if and when bad shit began to fall from the sky.

As March 1972 neared its end, the indicators got stronger. As we worked on our bunker, others began to rethink the bunker idea and asked for advice on building their own. It turned out that since the US Army had taken over the Marble Mountain airfield several years before, it had only been directly attacked with a few mortar rounds every month or so and only the very occasional 122-mm rocket.

Captain Hoffman supervises bunker construction just prior to the Easter Offensive of 1972 in RVN.

These are big weapons that can move a lot of earth in a split second. Assuming you are not close enough to be killed or badly wounded and tossed through the air or flattened into the ground, you still both feel and hear its impact. The feeling you get, when you are far enough away from the impact point to not get badly wounded, is like a shock wave hitting you, even 500 meters away from its impact point. You feel it in your chest, as if something soft but powerful slams into you and stops your breathing for a second or two. You also feel it in your head, as if your ear drums have been hit with a hard smack of compressed air—which is due to the compression of the air around the impact point that then moves outward, at least at first, at near supersonic speed. That shock wave can knock you down even a hundred meters or more from the impact point.

The sound is a combination of both a sharp, loud crack and a deep but very strong low frequency, elongated combination of a thud and a thump sound that stretches over two seconds and can make your head feel like sound is a physical thing that has hit you hard enough to rock your brain and take your breath away.

These 122-mm rockets were most likely the occasional rockets fired at Da Nang AFB that had overshot the mark and fallen on or near our airfield. The few 60-mm mortar rounds lobbed onto the airfield had done some minor damage to a few aircraft. But there had never actually been a serious attack of any kind on the airfield since the Army had taken it over from the Marines several years before. There were bunkers on the wire. There were several operations bunkers around the airfield and a few slit trenches for personnel to use when the occasional mortar round came in. But like lifeboats on the Titanic, there was not sufficient bunker space for everyone.

Our bunker was built and ready and others were soon trying to duplicate what we had. Of course, as the number of bunkers under construction rose, the availability of bunker building supplies correspondingly dwindled. Soon, the best most could do was dig a slit trench and put a poncho over it. Ours, on the other hand, had interior lights (as long as there was electricity), a concrete floor, two layers of twelve by sixteen-inch timbers across the roof, two layers of PSP over each layer of timbers, and about three feet of sand on top of all of that. Electricity meant we could also listen to the Armed Forces Vietnam Radio Network[10] or AFVN as we called it, in the bunker if we decided to bunk in there. It was a good bunker. It would serve us well.

On March 30 there was another but seemingly far more urgent call for moving some artillery and ammo to the north. The ops folks put out the call to wake the crews and report to operations. I was not on crew alert that night. Indeed, I was focusing most of my time on my keystone duties for the unit. The alert crews, both American and Vietnamese, all reported to operations, along with most of the rest of us to find out what was up. The word was that the NVA had crossed the DMZ with massed tanks formations! So much for the peace talks in Paris! And so much for the indicators that no one else, like 1st Aviation Brigade in Saigon, seemed to see. This was, it was reported, the real thing.

What, wait . . . *tanks*? The NVA are attacking with tanks? It was confirmed, we were told, this was a major armored attack across the DMZ and south along Highway 1. NVA forces equipped with T-54 and T-55 (nearly state of the art at the time) Russian tanks were on the move south. This was the first real NVA offensive with major unit formations since 1968, almost four years! This time, the reports indicated that the NVA was attacking with tanks and armored vehicles, and lots of them. Now how, in a time when we were flying regular reconnaissance missions all along the DMZ and to the north and west, could our intel pukes and the command in Saigon not know there were major tank formations massing north of the DMZ and moving down the Ho Chi Min Trail and poised for attack? Obviously, they did. But no warnings were provided to us.

Initial reports from Marine advisors on the ground at Dong Ha, up north, were that this was a major attack and the Vietnamese Army forces in the areas would be unable to stop it. There was an immediate need to move additional artillery north to support South Vietnamese defense efforts and our own personnel along and just south of the DMZ. So, the 203rd Wildcats began to plan missions to do just that. But before we could start such missions, assuming the needed artillery could be freed up for movement northwards, the call came down for evacuating what artillery there was north of Quang Tri. Oh shit! This was the real deal and things did not look good. We had just moved from holding and support operations to full-scale combat operations to support a large-scale tactical withdrawal in the face of a major enemy armored attack.

When the first attacks began up north and out west, we experienced our first real targeted mass indirect fire attacks on Marble Mountain. By the second day of such attacks, we were scrambling to keep birds flying and to protect ourselves and our equipment. The evening of the first heavy indirect fire attack, the incoming-fire warning siren sounded and I ran out of our hootch toward the airfield and our alert bird in case we were ordered to sky-up. As I ran across the PSP-covered flight line, an incoming 60-mm mortar round landed behind me. I then had close up experience with an impacting 82-mm Russian mortar round. While not as strong a sound or impact as a 122-mm rocket impact, when you are too close to a mortar impact the effect is similar but with the disadvantage of being thrown through the air. In my experience that night in April of 1972, I was thrown into the air and injured, though not seriously. I was incredibly lucky! The sound was so loud that I thought my eardrums had been ruptured. When I got my wits back a second or two after hitting the PSP on the ramp, all I could hear was a loud whistling sound combined with a high frequency ringing in my ears. It was very weird and disorienting.

Near miss on the Marble Mountain AAF control tower by an NVA launched Russian 122-mm rocket in April 1972.

I thought I had been hit in the back with a large chunk of something absolutely solid when the round impacted. At first, I could not suck in any air, as my chest seemed to have something sitting on it. It seemed it took a few seconds after I hit the ground before I could suck in any air. The initial sound was so loud that it seemed to shut my hearing off for a second or two, after the initial very loud, high frequency crack sound of the explosion. I still hear that sound in my head every day, all day and all night.

The explosion of the round blew metal fragments out and a shock wave that hit me in the back and threw me forward more than twenty feet across the PSP onto my hands and knees. One second, I was running and the next I was flying through the air flailing my hands and legs like a dog paddling in water. I hit the PSP hard, landing first on my knees and hands. Then I was pushed flat into the PSP. For a moment I was stunned and disoriented.

But someone ran up to me to see how badly wounded I was and asked if I could stand up and move. I understood, even with my ears ringing, and I stood and said I was okay. He told me that I was not okay and that I was to head to the flight line medical aid station at once. I Looked down and saw blood on my torn flight-suit pants. Then I saw the blood from the cuts and scrapes on my hands. I started to walk and suddenly my knees seemed to scream out in pain. I paused to lean over to look at my knees when my lower back felt like there was a knife in it. "Oh, this is not good," I thought to myself. My fingers and palms ached and were bleeding a lot, as wounds to the hands often do.

To this day I do not know who it was that came to check on me. People were running all around me. I could not hear much noise, just a loud ringing sound in my head. I knew I was too disoriented to fly and that my hearing was badly compromised, so I stumbled to the flight line medical clinic to see the flight surgeon. I walked in, looked around and my wits returned quickly. There were kids there with real serious wounds, unlike mine, which were, I was sure, superficial. I had blood on my hands, back, and legs. My flight-suit pants were ripped up and my back hurt, but I seemed intact. A medic led me to an exam table, and I sat. He looked me over, cut away my pants and took off my flight shirt. He told me that I had no serious wounds that a few stitches would fix it. The main thing, he said, was the risk of infection and that I would need a tetanus shot, some antibiotics, and to have my wounds cleaned. Fine, I said, give me the tetanus shot and sew me up. He did it right then and there, with no anesthetic or waste of motion.

As I was well into some level of shock, I did not feel much. He then asked me "Do you want a Purple Heart?" I looked around at the real wounded, those with serious shrapnel wounds, broken bones, and in real pain and I thought that he had real work to do here. I also thought that having him stop to do some paperwork instead of treating the wounded would be real bad karma! I told him to be sure to put this in my medical records but worry about the Purple Heart paperwork later and asked for some antiseptic and bandages. Then I got out of the aid station as quickly as I could. How I did not get more serious shrapnel wounds is beyond me. I was running less than fifteen feet from where that mortar round impacted in the metal surface of the PSP. I can only assume that in this case the PSP attenuated the shrapnel effect because the round, while it did penetrate the PSP, was relatively small and the PSP was very heavy. I never got any of my medical records after my final return from Vietnam. I never saw that Purple Heart either, but that was not an award I coveted at any level.

Rounds continued to hit all around the base on and off over the next forty-eight hours. One 122-mm rocket impacted just below the airfield tower but did not damage it. Obviously the NVA had us targeted accurately and were close. The mix of rounds coming in over the next few days showed a good coordination of fires and accurate adjustment. We needed the area around Marble cleared of potential enemy forward observer locations and we needed better counter-fire capability. What we did have was a special counter-fire and observation post up on the Marbles (the top of the western most Marble Mountain to the south of the airfield at an elevation of about 1,100 feet). This team of American special forces soldiers had some unique toys that they put to work. Once they were beefed up with additional personnel and weapons, they did a great job for us.

Whenever a mortar round was fired, they could see it and the mortar tube. They would then fire a special .50-cal rifle at the guilty mortar tube location. The first round they fired would pierce the tube and render it useless. The second and third rounds would go through the mortar crew. The same would be done for anyone launching a 122-mm rocket. Indeed, the guys were so good that once they detected a rocket being set up, they then waited. They would wait until just before it was ready to fire and then they would shoot a .50-cal round through the warhead and detonate it. Soon the attacks on Marble Mountain became rare. Because Da Nang Main AFB was closer to the mountains, the bad guys had more cover to fire from and it was more difficult to interdict them. But at Marble Mountain, we were in pretty good shape for the next few months.

Captains Gary Garczynski and John Hoffman on Marble Mountain AAF in 1972.

Just as this new Easter Offensive of 1972 was spooling up, I again ran into my Georgetown University classmate, Gary Garczynski[11], who was an artillery forward observer with the remnants of the 196th Infantry Brigade, still operating in I Corps. Gary was spending a lot of time flying in the back seat of aircraft from Marble Mountain providing artillery fire support to both American and Army of the Republic of Vietnam (ARVN) forces operating against the North Vietnamese in and around Quang Tri Province, to our north. It was great to run into Gary again and share our experiences as well as regain a sense of home life and stateside friendships. We have always had a lot in common and have remained strong friends over the years. As 101st units withdrew from Vietnam and the NVA offensive grew in our region, Gary found himself functioning for several months as one of the principal American artillery support officers for the ARVN ground forces in I Corps, so he was on the go all the time, bringing *smoke and fires* upon the NVA. The artillery dudes were very popular with us because they often were the first to return fire against enemy indirect attacks on our base and they were the primary means for us to suppress enemy anti-aircraft when we were operating over or near the NVA. I still owe him and his fellow forward observers some beers!

It was soon clear that the NVA were attacking in multi-division strength from the north and from the west. There were NVA armor forces, supported by heavy artillery, attacking into I Corps and II Corps to the south from Laos to the west, as well as south across the DMZ. This meant that significant Russian-supplied armor and artillery was moving through Laos and Cambodia and attacking into South Vietnam to support the NVA attack across the DMZ and to try and divide the ARVN and US response. Fortunately, US air power, both Air Force and Army, were in positions to assist in interdicting these NVA avenues of attack. But this also portended the potential for more enemy forces to come into the fight.

View from the cockpit while on approach to land, with only the rear wheels on its helipad, to deliver cargo to the firebase on top of Hill 350 west of Da Nang Air Force Base in a 203rd ASHC CH-47 helicopter in 1972. The Chinook was too big to land all four wheels on the small landing area in the middle of this firebase.

With this renewed NVA offensive, suddenly there was now a lot to do, and crews became a problem. The VNAF pulled away some crews and sent us others as new pilots. They were fine for local area missions, but not combat missions. We often found ourselves flying several lengthy missions a day. We flew ammo north and west. We flew casualties south and east. We moved 105-mm artillery tubes between firebases. We flew flame-drop missions where we dropped a homemade version of napalm on enemy bunkers and ammunition and logistics sites. We flew some very difficult missions into the mountains west of Da Nang into an area called the Banana Valley and out to such locations as LZ Siberia, to the southwest of Da Nang in the mountains that border Laos. These were hot areas where the

NVA was moving in large formations of infantry and light armor. We began encountering numerous anti-aircraft weapons, including the shoulder fired SA-7 GRAIL (NATO designation) or 9K32 Strela-2 Russian anti-aircraft missile. The *Strela* or "arrow" in Russian, was first used in large numbers in Vietnam in 1972.

On a mission to resupply Fire Base Siberia in the mountains southwest of Da Nang one day, we had to contend with weather, anti-aircraft fire and a mountain. This was a typical cargo-haul mission with a large net loaded with ammo, rations, and supplies on our cargo hook. The AC was our maintenance officer, and I was peter-pilot. The route in was hot as we passed up a mountain valley with bad guys in the hills on both sides. There was a broken cloud deck hanging just at the tops of the mountains.

On the way in we took some fire but no serious hits. We made a very steep, hot approach to the pad with the load. It was our plan to put the load on the center of the pad, punch it off (release the cargo straps on the hook) and then pull up into a steep, sharp climbing turn between the mountains on either side of the LZ. We wanted to climb up into the clouds as fast as we could to reduce the time the NVA could see us and shoot at us. The approach went smoothly, if a bit dicey. We were heavy. The air was cool and that helped, but we were dropping so fast, we were committed to the pad because we did not have the power to pull up without punching off the load. If we dropped it early or late, it went to the bad guys who would simply use it against our ARVN buddies in the firebase. Down we went with the rate of descent indicator showing about one thousand feet per minute rate of fall. As we neared the pad we began to pull in thrust and reduce the rate of descent. I looked between my feet and saw the ground coming up as fast as any autorotation I had ever ridden through. The ground was coming up, the enemy tracer fire was streaming by the cockpit, and the bird was heavy and falling. Just as we neared the ground, with me *beeping* the engines to max power, we slowed to about one hundred feet per minute and I felt the AC punch the load.

203rd ASHC flightline at Marble Mountain AAF in 1972.
Note the blast walls around each CH-47 parking spot.
The Chinook on the left has its forward rotor head and housing
removed for maintenance.

Free of the five thousand pounds of dead weight, we sprang up like a rabbit taking flight from the hound. The AC pitched us forward slightly; I was controlling the engine rpms and torque and watching rotor speeds as we clawed for altitude. The wind coming over and around the mountains grabbed our aircraft and the ride became a bit wild for a few moments and almost immediately we went into instrument metrological conditions (IMC) in the clouds and lost sight of the ground, the cliffs around us, and the bad guys. But we were also in a climbing turn to the right as I told the AC to tighten the turn back toward the LZ to stay away from the *cumulo-granite* around us (this is pilot slang for a cloud with rock in it). He did. Just then the clouds suddenly parted a bit and there directly in front of us was a solid rock wall. Holy shit! "Turn right!" I yelled on the intercom, but he was already turning the aircraft onto its side and adding thrust to pull us through the turn as tightly as he could. Because we were already in a tight turn to the right, we were quickly turning away from the rocks, and we rose away and above the cliff. Tight pucker factor there, for sure! We flew on for a few moments in silence. There was nothing to say. We had survived and we had succeeded. That was what counted, nothing else.

Lesson: Carefully plan your exit out as you make your approach in and expect the unexpected.

And another lesson: The mountain wave effect on the aircraft, even one this big, can give you a very wild ride. Plan for it and deal with it, even in the face of fire from the bad guys!

The next few weeks were a blur of missions to firebases and equipment inventories. I had lots of paperwork to do between missions and lots of missions between the paperwork. We flew to Fire Base Sally with supplies. We flew to Hill 350 with ammo for our 105-mm howitzers up there. We took parts to units north of Hue and we took casualties back to Da Nang. The NVA were moving south toward Quang Tri, and it did not look good. We had reports of Russian officers being sighted but none had been captured yet. All the while, the brass told us that this was not a major attack. They told us the NVA did not have the numbers of tanks that were being reported. They told us that this simply could not be a major offensive. For us, it did not matter what they thought. We knew what we knew. It was time that some folks in the basement of the White House (where it seemed to us someone was trying to run the tactical fight) needed to get their heads out of their collective asses and look around. This was a major fight, with tanks the NVA supposedly did not have coming south into I Corps from north of the DMZ. It turned out that this was not the only avenue of attack by the NVA armor. They were also attacking from Laos and Cambodia into South Vietnam in a multi-pronged assault to try and break South Vietnam. They assumed that the Americans would break and run and not step up the fight to support the VNAF and ARVN. They assumed wrong.

The firebase on Hill 350 west of Da Nang AFB was typical of
the firebases that supported American and South Vietnamese
ground forces across South Vietnam during the war. Each Firebase
contained a least a battery of three to four howitzers. In this case,
M102 105-mm guns.

Our resolve to fight was hardened by a sight I cannot get from my
head even fifty years later. Shortly after the fall of Quang Tri, a large
city just south of the DMZ, the population attempted to flee south
along Highway 1 toward the city of Hue, still in ARVN hands. The
NVA and their Russian support elements set up on the hills on the
west side of the highway and massacred the entire civilian population.
Reports of the massacre dribbled into ARVN and American forces
from a few survivors. But it was the US Air Force pilots who reported
seeing and smelling the aftermath from their planes as they flew over
that brought the truth home about the 'Highway of Death" in I Corps.
We discovered this for ourselves on later assault missions north as

we moved to retake the area south of Quang Tri. This tragedy of massive civilian loss of life was to be repeated on a far more immense scale in 1975 and 1976 as communist forces seized South Vietnam and Cambodia after the United States abandoned the fight under a fraudulent peace accord in Paris in January of 1973. At this time, however, our own reaction was disgust and anger and it made clear to all of us why we were there!

I recalled then my time as a teenager, living in France, when I had the opportunity to watch and be an extra in the filming of the movie *The Longest Day*. I not only had the opportunity to speak with many of the actors, including John Wayne and Sal Mineo, I also had the chance to talk to the technical advisors from the various countries with forces in the actual battles. I recalled the comments of that former German Army officer, who had been with the German coastal defense forces in Normandy on D-Day. He had explained what it was like to look out over the English Channel waters that morning of June 6, 1944, and see all of those Allied ships coming out of the mist on the Channel waters coming straight at him, ships his brass told him that the Allies did not have and which were full of weapons and troops his brass also told him the Allies did not have.

Lesson: When the intel pukes pack up and leave the area while telling you all is just fine, take note and prepare. This was not a good omen! And when the intel pukes tell you that the bad guys do not have something . . . they got 'em!

Here I was a decade later hearing that story flying north on resupply missions in Vietnam, and looking out across a battlefield full of NVA tanks and trucks moving south that our brass had told us the NVA did not have! To this day, there is no way that our intelligence pukes did not know this was coming. There was simply too much advance warning and too many indicators. I do not know the why or wherefore of this situation. But I did quickly come to grasp that, even if they were dead wrong, it would not matter. The rate at which these NVA armor vehicles were being killed told me that, while they may gain some ground, they would not hold it long. The shear intensity of the US Army, Air Force, Navy, and Marine air power coming down on them was astonishing. But I also noted that there seemed to be a very high kill rate for our Air Force that we did not understand, yet.

The view looking down through the *hell hole* in the floor of the CH-47 directly over the external load hook. You can see the cargo net of drums filled with jellied gasoline on the hook of a 203rd ASHC CH-47 during a flame drop mission against NVA ammo storage site in the mountains west of Da Nang, RVN in April of 1972.

One of the things that our CH-47s were well-suited to do was destroy North Vietnamese Army supply dumps. These were located by scouts and recon flights, but as they were often hidden on hillsides and in caves in mountains, it was hard for the Air Force to get at them. But a large helicopter with a sling load of jellied gasoline was just the thing to smoke out these positions and destroy the weapons and ammo stored there. We flew many flame-drop missions on NVA ammo storage and supply bunkers and improvised, well-camouflaged resupply sites. We had a pretty good hit rate, not perfect, but much better than the Zoomies! To do this successfully and survive, you had to have a pair of Snakes (AH-1G Cobra gunships) with you and good overhead air cover and air-to-ground fire support from the Spads (A-1E Skyraiders[12]These were certainly hairy missions with a very high pucker factor, and we rarely came back without a few holes in the bird. The CH-47 was a tough, well-built machine that could stand punishment and numerous hits without a major mechanical failure—just as long as nothing critical was hit—because there was a fair amount of armor plating in strategic locations on the aircraft.

We also were supporting a substantial buildup of ARVN forces coming in from the south, and we learned that there was a major fight in the Kontum area to the south and west but that, after some initial loses, it also was not going badly for the ARVN now. Then things settled down again to a routine slug fest, albeit with a higher operational tempo and higher pucker factor routine than previous two to three years in South Vietnam. We stayed very busy, and the time went by rapidly. Missions went out every day and every night. Resupply, equipment movement, personnel movements, and downed aircraft recovery became daily tasks. The Chinooks held up well for such old airframes.

As the fight grew in intensity, and our lift capability was becoming a key defense resource, the Command in Saigon decided to stand us down and turn over the aviation assets of the unit and its mission to the VNAF. Shortly thereafter we had our official stand-down date on April 30, 1972. At this time, all aircraft and equipment were to have been transferred to the VNAF and all personnel sent home or reassigned to other units. Further, we were to maintain mission status until the latest possible time, but at least until mid-April. *What?* I thought. *Are these guys on something? Are there any spare head-doctors that we could send to Saigon and conduct fitness evaluations down there? Well, at least this is a quick ticket stateside for most in the unit, so why fight the program?* It was tough to fly combat missions and conduct unit wind-down operations at the same time and, many felt, with considerable unjustified risk. We were flying in a combat zone with no US combat units on the ground, though there were a number of US advisors with the ARVN units. This continued as the daily routine for all of us until the last week of April 1972 when we began equipment and aircraft turnover to the VNAF pilots. The message from on high in Saigon was that this defensive fight was to at least appear to be a VNAF show. The VNAF and the ARVN were trying, but they were facing a huge struggle that only our firepower, cunning, and creativity was going to overcome! Little did I know then . . .

203rd ASHC CH-47 sling loads a freshwater buffalo out to a firebase. Safe drinking water was often a problem for remote firebases and troops in the field. CH-47s were often the primary source of fresh water along with ammo and rations.

Lesson: sometimes the big picture is bigger than you actually think, but it is usually also just as distorted and out of focus as you think it is.

These South Vietnamese forces were facing an enemy force that was way beyond any insurgency, any simple terrorist effort. The guys were pawns in a world political struggle and the Soviets had just raised the ante! The question was how far the US would go to call their bluff. The presence of that French gal from the World Peace Council with Jane Fonda two years before had not been lost on me. There was a larger Soviet stratagem in play here.

The transfer of equipment to the VNAF presented no major problems. They wanted the aircraft and gear as soon as we would give them up. The harder part was what to do with the many years' worth of unit-accumulated stuff that was not on any unit property book. For example, we had a true museum of weapons in our arms room. We even had WWII German, 9-mm submachine guns. We had twice as many M-16s as were on the books. We had more .45-cal Grease Guns than all the rest of the units in the 1st Aviation Brigade combined. We had AK-47s, we had Chinese carbines and we had rifles of all makes and sizes. We had Colt .357-cal revolvers that were not on any books. We had Colt .44-cal revolvers that were not even in the US Army inventory. We even had a few Gyrojet rocket pistols, but no ammo for them. It seems that the unit had collected weapons from the battlefield and from former unit members who brought personal weapons to the war but could not take them home. We had weapons purchased in Vietnam by unit members for their own use but left in the arms room when they DROS'd (Army slang for *departure and return from overseas station*).

We even had a small M114 armored personnel carrier that was not on the books of any unit at Marble Mountain! There was a rumor that this was left over from the Marines, but there was absolutely no paperwork of any kind that I could find. It had a 5.56-mm minigun mounted on top and was a lethal defensive platform.

So, I gave this to the 48th AHC for continued use on the perimeter defense when we stood down. I did not want to bury the various extra weapons we had in case someone found them, dug them up, and used them against us or the ARVN. We took all these extra small arms and put them in a locked CONEX and proceeded to carry them out over the South China Sea to see if any nearby Navy ship wanted them because I sure did not want to be responsible for them. But the damn hook on the bird carrying them out over the South China Sea failed somehow and they fell to the bottom of the sea, CONEX and all, where they no doubt remain today. I, of course, was going to initiate a collateral investigation but the unit would cease to exist in a few days and there was no time. Funny how things just seemed to work out.

On April 9, a few weeks before we were to stand down the last of the 203rd ASHC, we were awakened by a loud roar that just seemed to grow louder and louder over Marble Mountain Army Airfield. As we listened, many possible explanations went through our heads, from a Russian air strike to an incoming ICBM! It was like nothing any of us had ever heard. We grabbed our helmets, flack vests, and rifles and ran outside and looked up. Just then a giant B-52 strategic bomber passed overhead at about five hundred feet above ground level (AGL). We looked up into the night sky with astonishment. Incredibly, the B-52 had an intact, unexploded Russian SAM II anti-aircraft missile imbedded in its right wing! As we watched wide-eyed at this spectacle, the plane began a long, flat turn toward Da Nang Main Air Force Base where it landed. The next day, we flew over to Da Nang Main to transport some equipment to the VNAF, and we saw that the B-52 was sitting on one of the two parallel runways and the missile fuselage had dug a long trench down the side of the runway where its tail had dragged as the B-52 had landed and rolled to a stop. Amazingly the missile never detonated. The Air Force mechanics were already hard at work to remove the entire wing of the bomber so most of the aircraft could be saved and returned to service. The Air Force flew in a new, fully built-up wing complete with engines, along with a Boeing technical team, the next day. The fully operational bomber flew out of Da Nang less than thirty-four hours after the arrival of the new wing[13]. The Explosive Ordnance Detachment (EOD) folks then deactivated the missile warhead while it was still embedded in the old wing. The missile was then removed, and the area was cleared to bring the runway back into operational status. While that B-52 sat on the Da Nang runway, it was an incredible target for the NVA, so there was a massive security operation in and around Da Nang to reduce the potential for a rocket or mortar attack while it was being repaired and returned to flyable condition.

As we got back to the business at hand we also had to put up with a lot of very silly shit from the facilities folks in Saigon. Here we were, on a base that was slowly closing, with buildings that were intermittently being blown to scrap by incoming fire, and no one to move into the buildings we were leaving. Yet, in the infinite wisdom of the Army, some jerk field-grade schmuck somewhere among the idiots in Saigon told us that the buildings had to be clean, serviceable, and all damage had to be repaired and ready for inspection prior to having them cleared from the unit's stand-down list. What? Most were not even real buildings! How can a pile of sand-filled rocket boxes with a makeshift truss and corrugated metal roof be a building? Just because someone had put a number on it at some point didn't make it a real building. Hangars and offices I could understand. Our hootches? What a joke and what a waste of time during open warfare. Who were they kidding? Well, we cleaned them, and we patched leaks in the roofs that had never been patched before. We swept out the sand and we took out the trash. Then I told everyone to just close the doors and sky-up out of there. Screw it, what were they going to do to me, send me to Vietnam or something? So much for building clearance. Some weeks later, while I was out on mission with the 48th, some staff puke came looking for me about the condition of the old 203rd sleeping "buildings" (as in hootches). He left a note for me to call him at Da Nang Main. I never did. I never got a bill for cleaning from anyone either.

The last remaining vehicles went to the VNAF during the last week, except one jeep that was not on anyone's books. I kept that one so I could get around and so I could drive Major Epperson to the Da Nang air terminal for his DROS flight home. When I dropped him off at the terminal, I went in with him to make sure there were no hitches in his orders or flight arrangements. I walked him out to the plane. It was tough to see nearly everyone else go home, yet I had to stay in country and report for reassignment to the 48th Assault Helicopter Company (AHC), where I would become a slick driver again, "slick" being the nickname we used for our UH-1 Huey helicopters. As Theo boarded the plane, he stopped and turned back to face me. He pointed to my upper lip and said, "This is an order, shave off the damn mustache!" He laughed and climbed up the stairs to the plane.

With Major Epperson gone, I simply had to mail the final unit documents to St. Louis and turn over the last buildings we had occupied to another unit. That done, I drove over to the headquarters for the 48th Assault Helicopter Company and reported in for duty. "Oh, by the way," I said to the unit XO, Captain Larry Wilson, as I reported into the 48th, "I come with my own quarter-ton!"

CHAPTER SEVEN
THE BLUE STARS

I REPORTED INTO the 48th AHC as a Chinook driver who had some flight school time in various models of the UH-1. I was knowledgeable of the area of operations (AO), and I had my own jeep. Further, I had given some cool "toys" to the 48th in the previous weeks as I liquidated the assets from the property books of the 203rd ASHC. The most popular of those assets were vehicles, maintenance equipment, and part of the contents of the arms room. This arms room was unique in that it had more weapons in it that were not on the unit's property book than it had that had been authorized. And, of course there was ammunition of all kinds to share as well. Not a bad development for these units as the combat operations intensified.

I was instantly welcomed and absorbed into the unit by the 48th's commanding officer, Major Dan Kingman. I was made a lift platoon section leader and given a check ride that day in a UH-1H Huey. I was soon flying as a peter pilot (copilot once again—I did not have sufficient time in the UH-1H to be an aircraft commander) out on combat lift missions and resupply flights. I also flew *nighthawk* missions and helped with logistics for the unit. The unit commander, Major Dan Kingman, was a charismatic and capable leader. The XO was Captain Larry Wilson. Larry was a capable leader as well, but his roll was admin and logistics, and he did not fly often. Larry's plate would become very full in the next few weeks.

One night in May while pulling security duty with some of our unit's enlisted force on the perimeter, (yes, the Ranger Tab indicated ground warrior talents that few aviation officers were assumed to possess) the TV was on in a beach-side defense bunker. On came a story about Jane Fonda in Hanoi that showed her sitting in an anti-aircraft gun pretending to shoot down American planes. Here she was, not just consorting with the enemy, but, by any definition of the phrase, giving aid and comfort to an enemy in a time of war. I was so pissed I could not talk at first! Here was this espoused peacenik, against all war and all violence by anyone (according to her statements in my presence at Fort Hood in 1970), clearly enjoying the opportunity to pretend to be a soldier and inflict harm on her American countryman. She was obviously—then and now—a media prostitute out for coverage more than any principle.

Jane Fonda talking with a North Vietnamese anti-aircraft gun crew, Hanoi, July 1972. By Pictures from History/Getty Images.

Of course, I already had a fair sense of who she really was. What a despicable person and what an insult to every American who answered the nation's call. This was not about imposing our will on the poor Vietnamese. Vietnam was not about trying to dominate the world; it was about countering Soviet efforts to do just that. Even the Red Chinese got it. They even went to war with the Russians and the NVA after we pulled out. And what about the more than eight million who were summarily put to death in Southeast Asia after we left?

I don't believe any of this, not a wit, mattered to Jane Fonda then or now. Jane Fonda is about Jane Fonda, period, end, full stop! She wanted anything that would gain her additional notoriety, anything that got her on the front page. It mattered not to her whom she stepped on or whom she abused. It was, and remains today, all about her and her perception of her personal influence and standing. Principles, death, suffering of others, and destruction of cultures and values mean little to people like her.

Lesson: arrogance and the thirst for self-recognition are symptoms of the same disease so common in the political world—lust for power and position.

Since early April 1972 flight operations for the 48th AHC had escalated from routine patrol and supply missions, along with the occasional nighthawk flights around the base for night security, to twenty-four hours per day, seven day a week, full-out combat flight operations to support the ARVN ground forces in their efforts to stop the NVA armor drive south. The NVA had taken Quang Tri by April 30, 1972, and were moving down Highway 1, the main coastal movement corridor in I Corps, at a deliberate but slow pace. The mass of armored vehicles coming south seemed endless and the average ARVN soldier may have become disheartened, just as the NVA leadership and their Russian advisors had no doubt planned. For the first month or so, the NVA made progress south along Highway 1 but were stopped north of the Imperial City of Hue. Then stalemate set in for a period of time. But the ARVN commander in

I Corps was changed. Lt. Gen. Troung took over and things quickly seemed to turn around.

48th AHC Slicks returning to Marble Mountain AAF near Da Nang, RVN, after a combat mission up north.

The mission of armored forces everywhere in any offensive is: smash your way through with brute strength, run over the defense, and scare the crap out of everyone in your way! But the ARVN soldiers moving into defensive positions north of and around the old Imperial capital of Hue began to show some real grit and defiance in early May of 1972. At the same time, US military air power and naval gun fire began to take a major toll on the NVA forces. In a straight up, head-to-head contest with our guns, the Russian armor was not looking too good at this point. This was part of the morale boost for the ARVN. Suddenly the NVA were paying a heavy price. The wreckage of Russian armored vehicles, T-55s, a few T-60s, PT-76s and other assorted armor, including old American tanks and APCs, captured in previous engagements by the NVA, were beginning to stack up along their movement axis north of Hue. In one case two PT-76 light armored vehicles were killed with the same bomb and became known to all who saw them as the "Humping PT-76s." They became a navigation reference point for some time after that.

Russian built PT-76 light armored vehicles destroyed in the fighting along Highway 1, north of Hue City in May of 1972. Both vehicles were "killed" within moments of each other and one drove up on top of the other just as it was hit. The "humping" PT-76s became an aerial navigation reference point for many weeks after their destruction.

The main US effort was to cut off the North Vietnamese supply line to stall their operations. After the war, it was reported that the United States had carried out 14,621 air strikes and 836 naval gunfire attacks against North Vietnam in the period between May 9 and June 15, 1972.[14] By mid-May 1972, this was clearly having an impact on NVA tactical operations in I Corps!

This situation was helped by US Air Force F-4 fighters that

began to engage the NVA armor forces with the new "smart" bomb technology that dramatically improved their accuracy and vehicle kill rate. In one case, a Gunfighter F-4, flying out of Da Nang AFB that day, engaged a tank just south of Quang Tri, north of the My Canh river on the east side of Highway 1. He was using a new guidance unit that put the image of the target on a small TV monitor in the cockpit. The pilot or weapons officer in the back seat could then send steering commands to the bomb's guidance unit in order to "fly" the bomb into the tank. In this case, as we watched from our cockpits, the bomb missed and hit just to the side of the tank. This was a two-thousand-pound bomb, I was later told, and the impact was huge. Dirt flew into the air in a huge umbrella shaped cloud. When the dust and smoke cleared a bit, it was obvious that the tank was more or less in one piece and the bomb had indeed missed. However, the tank was not much use to the NVA at this point because it was upside down on the edge of the bomb crater with the main gun barrel wrapped up along one side of the vehicle. So, while this was not a kill in the sense that this armored vehicle was destroyed, it was certainly a mobility and functional kill, and the tank was out of the fight. Obviously, it was not a good day for its crew.

Later that night in the Gunfighter o' club on Da Nang AFB, where we managed to get some chow on a supply mission from Marble Mountain, we happened upon an argument between F-4 jocks as to whether that tank was or was not hit and whether it was a kill or not. As we had witnessed the engagement, we offered that the bomb had not hit the tank, but that the tank was a mobility kill because it was upside down and the main gun was destroyed. The two crewmen from the Gunfighter F-4 were relieved to hear our perspective and the crew ultimately got credit for a mobility kill. The Air Force crew then offered to buy us a round of drinks, but we could not accept as we were still on duty and about to fly back out to Marble.

This is the result of a near miss by a two-thousand-pound smart bomb. This Russian T-55 tank was rendered useless when it was flipped over in the explosion and its main gun was wrapped around its hull. The USAF pilot received credit for a mobility kill.

But not all our challenges at this time were created by the enemy... at least not the North Vietnamese enemy forces. Often weather was our nemesis. It complicated everything. It was hot, it was wet, it was overcast with five-hundred-foot ceilings, and it was windy there on the coast of the South China Sea. Did I say it was hot? Sometimes the weather, the terrain, even the whole environment in that part of the world would complicate our lives. Take, for example, the night that a report came in from the Navy of a tsunami approaching Da Nang. Those of us not on night missions were awakened by the airfield sirens. As we crawled into our gear, we assumed that a mortar or rocket attack was imminent. As we ran outside, we immediately noticed that we could not hear anything unusual, no sounds of impacts or the hollow pop of 60-mm mortar rounds being fired at us. The word was quickly passed to report to company operations as fast as we could. We ran across the runway to the west side of the airfield and into the Blue Star Company HQs command post. There the unit XO told us of the report of the approaching fifty-foot-tall tidal wave in less than forty-five minutes. The report, he told us, came from a Navy destroyer about one hundred miles offshore that was almost turned "turtle" by the massive wave.

Our first response was: "What the hell can we do about it?"

The XO said, "Nothing—except launch as many birds as we can to save them and then get everyone else to higher ground fast."

"Well shit," someone yelled out. "The only high ground around here is Monkey Mountain to the north of the airfield, and it's controlled by NVA and the Marbles are to the south. Both are too damn far away to be much help!"

Luckily the concrete *wonder shelters* that housed our maintenance operations were about fifty feet tall, so we assigned crews and launched everything that was flyable as fast as we could. Several of the remaining officers, including myself, had to stay behind to coordinate the effort and take care of the troops who could not ride out in the aircraft.

About one hundred of us grabbed our weapons, radios, and survival vests and donned our *water wings* (personal flotation gear for over-water operations) and climbed up on the top of the shelters. When we got up on top of one of the hangars, I looked around and saw a small gaggle of troops on top of nearly every hanger on the airfield. About this point in time, the sirens sounded again and this, we were told, would signal the arrival of the wave. We looked out over the beaches toward the ocean and waited. Nothing happened for a few minutes, and then we saw an unusually large wave come ashore and wash up into the wire along the top of the tide line and then recede back into the surf. That was it. Some tidal wave! We were both relieved and disappointed that nothing happened. Strange way to feel, but somehow it was an interesting diversion from our usual risks and activities.

Once the all-clear was passed around, the recovery of the aircraft began. I went back into company operations and tracked the return of our platoon's birds. After a bit, one of the "Joker" pilots (the call sign of the gun platoon flying AH-1G cobras) came in to report that all the Cobra guns were back on the ramp. He looked and me and began to laugh. I asked him what was so funny, and he pointed to my undeployed water wings under each arm and asked, "Just what the fuck good do you think those would have done?" I had forgotten I still had them on. Rather sheepishly I explained that we thought that if the water got too high, we might be able to float up and, at least, stay on the surface and not drown right off the bat. He laughed some more, and a new source of humor became institutionalized in the 48th.

As the fight intensified north of the Imperial City of Hue, the leadership in Saigon realized that the propaganda war in the US and Europe was being won by the North Vietnamese and the Russians. We saw this on the news each day when AFVN would rebroadcast the evening news from the major US networks from the night before. In these news reports we would learn about battles we had lost, and aircraft lost that simply had not happened. North Vietnamese propaganda reports seemed to have become a primary news source for US TV networks and we all very much resented it.

My wife and I exchanged cassette tapes that we recorded for each other regularly. In these taped letters, Karen expressed great concern about our losses and the consequences of the much-anticipated North Vietnamese victory that was expected within weeks. None of that was true, I assured her. But I am not sure how much she accepted as true from any news source, including me.

This willingness to report fiction from the aggressor forces from the north in lieu of the real news from their own reporters in country mystified us and their own reporters on the ground. They would respond to our questions about the stateside reporting with answers like, "our news reports do not fit the reports they want to make." At the same time, the stalemate on the battlefield was not seen as a defensive victory for the South Vietnamese forces, which it clearly was, but as a perceived inability of the South Vietnamese Army to gain the upper hand on the battlefield. This was having an impact in Paris at the peace negotiations.

In this context, the ARVN commanders decided, no doubt with some input from our advisor cadre in Saigon, that it was time to kick butt and take Quang Tri back. There was no question that we could do it, if we were given the green light and the resources. We could now kill every piece of enemy armor on the coastal plain battlefield in I Corps and probably sweep them into the sea in a matter of weeks. Those in the remote mountain havens who could run and hide in Laos were, of course, another story. But even they could be kept at bay if we were given that green light. But the plan and resources needed were not forthcoming at this point.

A few weeks after my assignment to the 48th, Major Dan Kingman, our company commander was to lead a lift mission in support of an ARVN force that was attempting to retake key terrain on the coastal plain to the north of the city of Hue. These limited missions were intended to minimize the advances of the NVA, make any effort to gain more ground by the NVA costly in terms of manpower and equipment, and, of course, buy time to build up the ARVN counterattack force for I CORPS. Where possible, efforts were mounted to retake support and overwatch positions around the battlefield to aid in any future counterattack to the north by the ARVN. With the probability of another major armor battle brewing, taking key terrain features to employ as fire support positions was vital. On one of these missions, we were putting up a two-platoon lift, supported by our gun platoon, the Jokers, in support of ARVN infantry.

May 24, 1972, Lt. Bruce Kline came to me to ask that he be taken off the missions for that day. I was scheduled to fly with the CO for that day's mission in support of ARVN forces fighting north of Hue. He was scheduled to fly on a lift bird as the peter pilot. He was genuinely terrified of the planned mission. I told him that I would switch seats with him and fly the lift. So, he flew with the CO that day. The CO's slick, the command-and-control bird for the 48th's mission that day, was hit with an SA-7 shoulder-fired anti-aircraft missile of Russian manufacture just north of Hue. The crewmen were Specialists (Fourth Class) Bausch and Monkelbann, with whom I had flown many missions already. The aircraft literally fell from the sky and impacted into the soft coastal plain soil, nearly disappearing. Several days later we recovered the crew from the deeply buried wreckage. The bodies were in such a poor state that we had to sling load them out in a net and back to Da Nang to the guys at Graves Registration. It was a difficult task for all involved. The odor of death permeated everything that came near the aircraft that day and it cast a pall over the unit and our morale in a way that only the loss of a trusted commander can do in combat.

As the result of the political position back in Washington, DC, his loss was initially listed as an "air crash." Even though we recovered the aircraft wreckage and the remains of all of the crew and the cause of the loss was obvious to the investigators, no reference was made, officially, that it was hostile fire until sometime later. At this point, we were told all operational missions in the defense of Hue were strictly by the South Vietnamese and no US military units were involved. Well of course this was horseshit! And this posture further undermined our own unit morale.

The introduction of these small Russian shoulder-fired, heat-seeking anti-aircraft missiles was a significant, historic, and deadly development in the war. This gave the NVA ground forces, at least initially, a temporary edge against our aircraft and made our missions much more dangerous. Over the course of the next few weeks several US Army helicopters, including a CH-47, were shot down with the complete loss of each crew. It did not take us long to figure out, however, that by flying low along the nap of the earth in the treetops, these weapons were ineffective against us. We immediately began to fly just through the tops of the trees at seventy and eighty knots, sometimes even one hundred knots of airspeed. While this increased the challenge of navigation, it made our lives much safer. This change completely befuddled the NVA and the Russians. The SA-7 Strela was the Russian copy of the US Redeye anti-aircraft missile. But it was a poor copy for the most part. It was only really effective if you flew about one thousand feet AGL and were flying straight and level. In that case, it was deadly. They still tried to shoot at us and wasted hundreds of these expensive weapons. Even when we flew over open ground, if we were flying fast and low, the missiles could not lock onto the heat signature generated in the exhaust of our turbine engines.

The Army wasted no time in fielding a heat signature reducing kit for our aircraft. It consisted of several heat dispersion shields over hot exhaust vents on the bottom and top of the aircraft along with a strange, toilet-looking heat deflector that clamped onto the engine exhaust. This simple device redirected the turbo-shaft jet engine exhaust straight up into the rotor wash. This effectively dispersed the heat signature and made it very difficult for the SA-7 to lock onto our aircraft at any altitude. However, as you can appreciate, we were still reluctant to fly at any altitude above treetop. This mode of flying became institutionalized in our units across Vietnam by the late spring of 1972.

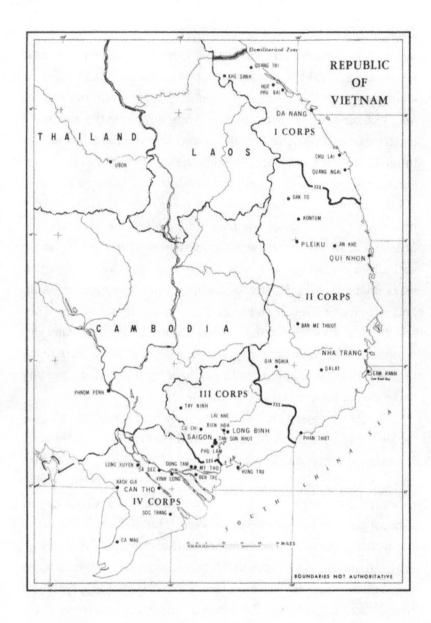

US Army report on US Military communications in RVN during the war.

Of course, we had to ask: "Where did these ready-to-install kits come from on such short notice?" Clearly, DOD knew of this threat and had prepared for it. Deploying them a month or so earlier would have saved a lot of lives. Why did that not happen? Our speculation at the time was that DOD knew of the expected introduction of the SA-7 into the battle in South Vietnam and of the new NVA offense that would exploit its use. Fielding the IR suppression kits would have revealed to the North Vietnamese that we knew what was coming. But if this were true, why did no one prepare us for what was coming? I have never read or heard of any explanation beyond that this was a "policy issue." My father's explanation was that the negotiating team in Paris led by Henry Kissinger, was calling the shots.

Captain Harvey ("Larry") Wilson was forced to quickly step up to be a combat commander. He did this with amazing skill and dedication to the unit. He transformed himself from our chief administrative and logistics officer to an effective tactical commander overnight. For me he was a study in leadership, command, and adaptability in the face of hardship. Loss of one's unit commander, especially one who is competent and well-liked, is tough on all the unit members and has a very negative impact on morale, motivation, and unit combat effectiveness. Yet Captain Wilson, supported by the senior subordinate leaders, also captains, quickly focused the unit on its mission and reestablished both an effective command climate as well as the unit's mission performance resolve. He was respected and well-liked already, and this helped all of us in this difficult transition of command. I do not believe that Larry ever got the appropriate recognition he deserved for his outstanding, extraordinary leadership and grit under these most trying of circumstances.

The unwillingness of the US Military Command in Saigon to allow military recognition of any kind for outstanding combat or leadership performance and for the sacrifice made by so many American soldiers during this period was both unconscionable and ultimately disrespectful to men like Larry Wilson. The effort to create a fraudulent appearance of independent ability and success on the part of the South Vietnamese forces did not serve them or any of us still in deep and dangerous day-to-day fighting with the

North Vietnamese and their Russian advisors. The official response from Saigon for any recommendation for awards or recognition of individual valor or achievement was always the same after April of 1972: "official US Army records do not reflect that any US Army personnel or forces were engaged in combat operations in the Republic of Vietnam on the date and time cited in the recommendation." The result was a misunderstanding of what was actually happening on the part of the South Vietnamese leadership, US political leadership, and a realization by the North Vietnamese and their Soviet supporters that the US had no intention of supporting the South once we disengaged.

Lesson: at that point in the war, when you heard from the senior command in Saigon or Washington, and their lips were moving, they were lying.

Another lesson: as a senior commander, if you are dishonest with your troops and subordinate commanders, no good will come from it.

This ill will from the troops still in combat in RVN at that time persisted in the US Army for more than a decade and resulted in a collapse of respect and confidence in many senior general officers then on active duty. It was such a problem later that in the early 1980s the Army leadership and the senior military educational institutions had to directly address the problem with a renewed effort at building and sustaining integrity and moral conduct. Added to this quandary, for those of us at the operational and tactical level, were the clear indications that our very tactical operations plans were being compromised in advance of our missions. This clearly was from US channels and was a point of significant concern within senior military channels back in the United States[15]. We became very careful about what planning we shared with anyone for our assigned missions.

The week I joined the 48th, the NVA had reached Quang Tri and had surrounded the second ARVN Division command post in a vast bunker complex at an airfield south of the city at a location

we called Five Star Pad. This was because there was a helipad above
the bunker. In this bunker were both Senior ARVN officers and
American advisors. As the NVA closed in on the bunker site, many
ARVN officers chose suicide over the prospect of capture, much to
the surprise and disgust of their American advisors and liaison teams
with them in the bunker complex. The call went out for immediate
extraction of these Americans. Both our unit and the Navy aviation
units offshore were tasked to attempt the extraction. The Navy and
Marine CH-53 helicopters supported by US Army gunships were
dispatched at the same time that the 48th AHC launched UH-1H
helicopters from Marble Mountain. A quick extraction and support
plan was developed and coordinated with the Navy over the radio.
We flew north as planned and flew over NVA armor forces on the
way to our link-up point along the coast. We got hosed with anti-
aircraft fire several times but did not lose any aircraft or crew. As
the Navy and Marine aircraft arrived first, our gunships moved up
to provide the Navy CH-53s with fire support and the extraction
began. Three Marine CH-53s got to the pad on the bunkers and
two of these aircraft loaded the evacuees: the ARVN commanders,
their surviving staff, and the US advisors. Upon departure from
the Five Star helipad one CH-53 had a mechanical failure and was
forced to land along the extraction route to the east. Our 48th AHC
Cobras provided air cover while the other empty CH-53 landed
and picked up the evacuees and the crew and flew them to safety.
The Marines lost one CH-53 on the mission. The 48th provided
backup and recovery support but only our Cobras actually engaged
the enemy forces on the ground on this mission while supporting
CH-53 aircraft.

In the end, our slicks were not needed, though our gunships
were vital to the mission, and we all were deep behind enemy lines.
So, we flew out over the ocean and back to Da Nang empty but
relieved. It was a hairy flight, but it was a great recon of part of
the enemy occupied area we would be back over in the coming

weeks, and it gave us a good look at the enemy on the ground we would engage. We learned later that the CH-53 crews were all awarded Distinguished Flying Crosses for executing the mission. Upon inquiry, we found out that the US Navy and the US Air Force were indeed officially engaged in combat operations in support of the South Vietnamese. But there were no US Army units directly engaged in combat operations in South Vietnamese that day. This event was also controversial for years later due to the fact that these stranded, nearly overrun US Advisors who were rescued asked the command in Saigon: "Where was the Army?" Small wonder DOD had both credibility problems in the ensuing years and had issues, in the opinion of many, with ethics and integrity on the part of senior leadership after the Vietnam War.

Captain Hoffman awaiting for a 48th AHC combat assault mission to begin in the spring of 1972.

In the period between early April and late June 1972, there was intense fighting between the NVA and the ARVN forces supported by US air power to include US Army aviation. We were in the thick of this fight every single day, flying mission after mission, day and night. As allied forces slowly pushed the NVA back to the north from the My Canh River, their southernmost penetration along Hwy 1 to the north of Hue, we found that the NVA had been killing the civilian populations en-masse. They overran and laid waste to every building and everything they overtook. It was a slaughter of unbelievable proportions that our leadership in Saigon seemed to feel was not all that important in the larger scheme of things. To me it was reminiscent of the stories and scenes I saw and heard as a young teenager living in France and traveling in Europe in the aftermath of World War II. How was such indiscriminate slaughter of civilians okay? Where was the appropriate outrage in the media back home? Apparently, no one cared about the conduct of the NVA and Russians or the safety of the local Vietnamese civilian population caught up in this battle. Apparently for the NVA and their Russian advisors this was just business as usual for them. This was, and is, the Russian way of war.

During this period, I was flying missions north along Hwy 1 as we supported the ARVN troops trying to stop the southward movement of NVA tank forces. One day while flying support missions to Fire Base Sally, just north of Hue to the west of Hwy 1, we took some serious hits in our aircraft and were forced to make a precautionary landing at Fire Base Sally.

Captain Hoffman standing on top of a Russian built T-55 tank destroyed by a US Army LAWs rocket at Firebase Sally in May of 1972. Note the small penetration hole at the base of the turret, just above the destroyed external fuel tank. Typically, the LAWs rockets were effective only against light armored vehicles, such as a PT-76. This "kill" was an unusual result for a LAWs rocket hit on a main battle tank. It suggests that the steel used on the T-55 tank was not consistently of high quality.

When a round hits your aircraft, there are two distinct sounds and feelings you have as a crewmember in the helicopter. This is because there are three types of surfaces that are most often impacted in the fuselage. The first sound is a round that just hits the skin of the aircraft and passes though. This feeling feels like a subtle, but very noticeable sharp but short vibration combined with a bit of a *thunk* sound that you may or may not hear, depending upon where you are sitting and where the round impacted on the aircraft. These impacts may be the result of a rifle or machine gun bullet hitting the aircraft or a piece of shrapnel from an exploding anti-aircraft or flak round that was far enough away to not actually hit you with the explosive but only hit your aircraft with metal fragments from the exploding shell. When you do feel such a hit, you keep a wary eye on the master caution panel to see if anything is amiss.

The second sound is from a more consequential impact such as when a projectile impacts something solid in the helicopter, such as the transmission casing, the engine, or the protective armor covering some of the aircraft components, like the engine area or your seat armor. You feel these impacts much stronger, like someone kicking your seat or yourself in the butt or back. The sound is much stronger as well, regardless of where you are sitting in the aircraft. When you get such a hit, you know you have damage. You just don't know what is damaged and how bad . . . until the master caution light comes on and the warning segments in the caution panel start to light up with indications of problems in the main transmission, the engine, the fuel system, etc.

The third impact type is to the helicopter rotor blades. If a main rotor blade takes a hit and does not simply come off (always a very bad thing), you feel it in the cyclic control as a jerk on the stick and then a side-to-side vibration that does not stop. Depending upon the severity of the hit, the vibration most often stays constant. That usually means you can keep flying but need to land as soon as it is safe. I had this happen many times, when either a bullet or a chunk of shrapnel hit one of my main rotor blades. I even landed in some cases at a safe place, and we would wrap heavy tape, we called *100 mph tape*, around the blade at the hole and then continue to the mission. Sometimes it seems to get worse. If that happens you must land immediately, regardless of where you are, because you are most likely going to hit the ground soon whether you want to or not.

Or you might take a hit in your tail rotor blades. You often feel this both in your feet on the pedals and because, most often anyway, such a hit can momentarily cause the helicopter to slew sideways for a second or two. Depending upon how bad the vibration was in your feet, you knew how bad the hit on the tail rotor blade or blades was. I never lost the tail rotors completely, as some others did, but I did get hits there and flying back to a safe and secure landing area was never fun.

This photo shows the mix of NVA armor that was destroyed near Firebase Sally along HWY 1 north of Hue. In the foreground is a former ARVN US manufactured M-41 tank that had been captured by the NVA and put back into the fight with an NVA crew. They did not fare too well in the subsequent battle.

Firebase Sally was an ARVN 175-mm artillery battery firing in support of ARVN forces just to the west and north, who were then trying to attack the west flank of the enemy advance from the north. These US-provided 175s were simply huge guns! However, they were not as accurate as our newer artillery weapons and were adjusted by three hundred- to five hundred-meter increments by the forward observers. But they were pretty effective against enemy armor formation. The fire base had US Marine forward observers (FOs) advising the ARVN artillery teams and to help with naval gun fire support from the US Navy ships offshore when needed. But do not misunderstand the value of the 175-mm guns. If three of these shells hit in your grid square, it was not a good day for you. So, the NVA wanted these guns taken out and they mounted a major assault to capture or destroy them. We had picked a bad day to visit.

The fire base was assaulted by a formation of NVA armor made up of a mix of T-54 and T-55 Russian tanks and old US Army M-41 tanks, captured from the ARVN earlier in the offensive. The real threat were the T-54s and T-55s because we could kill the older tanks with a shoulder-fired LAWs antitank rocket. Not so the more modern Russian tanks. Or so we thought. When the assault got intense, the ARVN 175-mm gun crews maintained fire support to the forward forces while the remainder of the troops in the firebase defended the position against the enemy tanks, and the US Marine FOs brought naval gun fire directly onto the attacking NVA forces and tanks. The infantry and artillery support personnel within the fire base operating as base defense volley-fired LAWs and 106-mm recoilless rifles at the advancing NVA tanks. Our crew initially stayed out of the way in a bunker. But as things got heated, we decided to help the perimeter defenders. Our sidearms were of little value. We did find, however, that the base was well-equipped with LAWs rockets. So, we contributed to the common defense by firing these small rockets at the enemy tanks, for whatever good that might do in slowing them down. We were astonished to find that the metal on these Russian tanks was not of consistently high quality.

One T-55 took several hits from LAWS rockets directly on its main gun turret and one LAWs rocket penetrated the turret and incinerated the inside of the tank by igniting the powder in one of the tank's own main gun rounds inside the turret, knocking it out of the fight. This was a major flaw in Russian built tanks. The ready rounds awaiting to be fired were stored along the inside of the turret. If you penetrated the turret from the sides, at the turn plate, or from above, the crew inside was instantly incinerated. Often the turret would unseat from the hull, as intense fires from the burning rounds brewed up, often coming completely off the hull of the tank. I saw these tanks as mobile crematoriums. I would not want to have been a Russian or NVA tank crewman. Apparently, this was a common sentiment among NVA tank crews as we found that many dead tankers in these Russian tanks were chained to their positions inside. Soon accurate navel gun fire and at least one round of direct-fired 175-mm ammo killed many others. It was also not a good day to be an NVA tanker, and the attack failed with huge losses for the attacking NVA unit.

The NVA got no farther south along Highway 1 after that day, and they lost the initiative in their offensive in the I Corps eastern areas near the coast. From that day forward, they lost ground almost every day as they were pushed north by determined ARNV forces, backed by US air power.

In the meantime, the tank battles continued and NVA assaults from the west continued to be a significant problem for the ARVN in I and II Corps and threatened the security of the ground that had already been retaken by the South Vietnamese forces.

Between May and July of 1972, I spent a total of four weeks on nighthawk duty conducting nighttime aerial patrols around the outskirts of the Da Nang area to interdict enemy night action against our bases, such as mortar and rocket launches, night sapper operations, and even all-out attacks on our outlying security posts and fire bases to the west of Da Nang. The flights were, to say the least, exciting.

Today US Army aviation owns the night by employing a variety of night-vision devices that turn night into day and employing highly sophisticated navigation and flight management systems. In 1972, we had none of that. We only had the Mark One Eyeball (as in our own eyeballs) and pilot skill, that was it. Yet we operated very successfully at night over hostile terrain and against a determined enemy who thought it owned the night in Vietnam.

These operations required that all crew members night adapt for two days before commencing night operations. We took turns, operating for two weeks as night pilots or, as we sometimes referred to this duty, as vampires, living and operating during the night and sleeping in darkened hootches during the day. We never saw the sun for the entire two-week period. We planned our missions at night, we pre-flighted our aircraft at night and we flew only at night. These missions were very successful, and we interdicted hundreds of enemy night attacks in the Da Nang area. We found mortar and rocket launching sites at night and we found spider holes that were only open and visible at night from which the enemy infiltrated our lines and launched attacks. We also found enemy supply operations out in the open on several nights. We brought destruction upon the enemy in each case, and we denied the enemy the cover of darkness for their operations around Da Nang. But lacking the technology of today, this high successful approach only extended to our local area where we had overwhelming backup. Out on the major battlefield areas, nighthawk missions were far too dangerous and unsupported. Out there, the enemy did own the night . . . unless "Specter" was in the area. Specter was a US Air Force C-130 that was armed with some serious, computer-controlled firepower on board, and sophisticated night-vision capabilities that operated day and night over the battlefield. The enemy was easy pickings for these US Air Force crews because they did have the technology, targeting, and navigation systems we lacked in the Army at that time. They could hit virtually anything on the battlefield at that time.

As the battles of May, June, and July 1972 raged on in I Corps, a variety of aircraft were supporting this defensive effort against the NVA forces. These, in addition to our US Army aircraft, included a wide range of technologies and generations. Some were World War II aircraft such as C-47s. Another WWII USAF workhorse in Vietnam was the Douglas A-1E that sported a giant 1940s-era radial engine, and could carry the same ordnance load as a WWII B-17 bomber! They provided some of the best and most accurate air-to-ground fire support that we saw in I Corps. The A-1E pilots could get right down in the dirt and stick it to enemy ground units of all types, even NVA anti-aircraft elements. We also had support from the latest fighters and aerial weapons platforms in the US Air Force inventory as well as those amazing Specter gunships. The various jet fighters could drop smart bombs and provide intense tank-killing 20-mm Gatling gun fire. The Navy and Marine Corps jets provided responsive and accurate fire support on short notice when needed, particularly the small A-4 attack jets. US Air Force F-4 fighters, based at this point in time in Thailand, flew scheduled, preplanned sorties over the battlefields targeting enemy formations of troops and armor. But they also would orbit, when their fuel state permitted, to attack targets of opportunity that we developed as we supported the ARVN or when we came under intense anti-aircraft fire ourselves.

The most effective aircraft in providing our nighthawk operations overwhelming support on a ground target at night were those Specter and the older C-47 Spooky gunships. The modern Specter bird was equipped with a row of 20-mm Gatling guns, a 40-mm gun, and a computer-controlled 105-mm howitzer gun that could put a round through the engine block of a truck or tank on the ground using infrared targeting. The older C-47-based Spooky was armed with a row of 20-mm gatling guns and some night-vision targeting capability. These birds frequently played a major role in disrupting NVA attacks on ARVN forward operating bases and fire bases. They provided extraordinary fire support to our Nighthawk operations in and around Da Nang. They were often the first response with counter battery fire when NVA forces would launch heavy 122-mm rockets or mortars on friendly positions or when the NVA employed Russian 152-mm artillery to fire on our positions, bases, or LZs. They were also very helpful with counter anti-aircraft system support. When a ZSU-2, equipped with 23-mm guns, or other heavy machine gun AA sites were encountered or located, they could make short work of them, adding to our safety on missions.

When one of these birds engaged their 20-mm Gatling guns, the sound was deafening and, no doubt very frightening to those under the effect of these awesome weapons. When the guns were firing, it often looked to us like red water pouring from the sky onto the target area. As it hit, the rounds would often ricochet out from the initial impact like a wave of water flowing outward. When the smoke cleared, the result was utter devastation in the impact area. The effect of the 105-mm gun on board the C-130 Specter was just as devastating to any target, including tanks. We always felt safe and protected when one of these aircraft was operating over or near our area of operation.

Another key aircraft in the fight were the airborne forward air controllers (FACs) flying twin engine O-2 Cessna or the North American OV-10 Bronco observation aircraft. These brave US Air Force pilots would orbit battlefield actions and coordinate the ground support strikes by the various US Air Force, Navy, and Marine jets that played such a key role in stopping and pushing back the NVA armor forces. These planes operated at relatively low levels so that their pilots had a clear view of the friendly forces on the ground as well as the enemy forces to be targeted. This put them in grave danger from ground fire and SA-7 missiles. Through skill and defensive technology, such as heat signature reduction and the use of flares to confuse the missile tracking systems, they generally escaped these dangers but not always. Many of us owed our own survival to their quick intervention when the bad guys got us in a corner or when one of our aircraft was downed and we needed to rescue the crew. In such cases these FAC pilots, at great risk to themselves, would coordinate available ground attack fighters, mark ground targets with smoke rockets, and direct aerial attacks to hold off the enemy while we executed an extraction of the downed crew. They also provided air support to our many assault and reconnaissance missions. These unsung US Air Force heroes were rarely adequately recognized for their contribution to the success of our missions or for their ability to save our asses on so many occasions.

In many cases North Vietnamese Air Force aircraft came south across the DMZ into I Corps to engage our Air Force, Navy, and Marine fighters that were providing air-to-ground fire support and interdicting the attempted southern movement of the NVA armored forces. The enemy pilot's primary tactic, long used over North Vietnam to inhibit effective air strikes by US attack aircraft, was to initiate an engagement with our fighters and then break off once our fighters had dumped their ground attack ordnance to prepare for aerial combat. This only worked a few times during this NVA offensive. Our tactical air support, wise to the tactic, would always operate with fighters set up for air-to-air combat, not ground attack. This usually paid off with one or more enemy fighters shot down or damaged and chased off. As a result, the enemy had little success challenging our air superiority over the battlefields of South Vietnam during this period of the war.

We even had the occasional Russian helicopter, such as a Mil 4 or Mil 6, show up in our area. They did not try to challenge or engage us and generally scurried off over Laos when we discovered them. The real threat to us remained anti-aircraft fire from ZSU-23-2s and dual- and quad-mounted .51-cal machine gun trailers, and the occasional SA-7. On rare occasions, the NVA would fire SA-2 anti-aircraft missiles at us or through our helicopter formations at our overhead fighter cover. These rarely had any effect, but there were quite unnerving to watch fly up past us.

R&R in Hawaii . . . and loss of a good friend

Each soldier assigned to a combat area is normally authorized a one-week period of rest and recuperation, known as R&R, outside of the combat area. Some took the leave stateside, some went to Australia, some went to Thailand, and others to Hawaii. I decided to go to Hawaii to meet Karen for my R&R from June 2 to June 10, 1972. We booked rooms at the Coco Palms Resort on the Island of Kauai (of *Blue Hawaii* fame) for the week because Dad and Mom had stayed there in the past, including on one of his R&Rs from RVN and they knew the owners. I contacted them to make arrangements and they could not have been more generous or accommodating. We had a truly wonderful time there and were treated like family.

We took long walks on the beaches, swam, attended a luau almost every night, explored the wonders of the island and slept, which I seriously needed. We also spent two days in Honolulu and stayed at the Hilton Hawaiian Village. That was a nice place, for sure, but they did not think much of a soldier staying there at the time. I was quite taken aback at this attitude. While I would not want to speculate too much on the reasons why, the front desk did not want to honor our reservation because I was a soldier. It took a near showdown with the hotel manager and a call to the US Army Recreation Center at Fort DeRussy to get this fixed. This experience left several questions in my head over the next six months. These were questions that I got answered over the course of the following few years.

Lesson: The American media, for whatever agenda motivates it, frequently focuses adverse public opinion on those least able to defend themselves. In the early 1970s, it was the soldier.

The R&R was all too short, of course, and on June 12, 1972, I was back in the saddle with the 48th AHC at Marble Mountain AAF and ready to sky up. I had a lot of time to go in Vietnam, a year can be a long time!

I had originally departed for my year of duty in South Vietnam on December 13, 1971. Upon arrival I had fifty-two weeks and one day to go. That I would serve a one-year tour of duty was itself a new development in combat manpower sourcing for the United States Army. In past war situations, soldiers had served in the military for the duration of the conflict. United States soldiers in all previous wars in the twentieth century had served in combat as needed, not for a set period of time. Soldiers and their units operated where and when needed. Periods of rest, recuperation, and rebuilding did occur, but these were mainly a means to conserve combat power and then the soldiers could be redeployed and reengaged in combat operations at some other point as needed until the war was over. Air Force aviators and air crews were the exception to this general practice. They typically were rotated off combat missions after a set number of missions. In Vietnam, that was 100 missions. Army aviators and crews had no such perk. We flew and flew and flew, day after day, until our year was up.

Yet in Vietnam, most served in country for one-year tours and then were returned to the United States. For large numbers of soldiers once that year was completed, if they survived or were not returned home due to injury or combat wounds, they were discharged from the military shortly after their return. They were then backfilled with new enlistees or draftees who could expect the same year of training and then a one-year assignment in Vietnam. Sure, those who were career officers or NCOs who reenlisted in the Army or Marines could expect to return to Vietnam for additional one-year tours. And so it was from 1964 until early 1972. Then things changed and few replacements were sent to fight in South Vietnam. The few who did come into country were individuals with specific experience or skills needed by the few remaining combat units still fighting.

This one-year rotation gave rise to the *short-timer's calendar*. Soon after you arrived, someone would give you a copy of a graphic picture that was composed of 365 small squares, circles, half-moons, and other assorted shapes. The shapes used and the graphic image they made up depended upon the talent, or lack thereof, possessed by the original author of the graphic. Each shape in the graphic contained a number from 1 to 365. Most often this larger graphic was some obscene image of a woman, but some were cityscapes, country scenes, or cars. As each day passed, you would color in the shape that represented the day just completed. The calendar was your countdown record as you progressed through your one-year tour of duty in Vietnam.

When you first arrived in country for your first tour of duty, typically you did not pick up your calendar until several days after you arrived. Once you had yours, you quickly shaded in the spaces for the days you had already been in country. At first it seemed this year would go by quickly. You would, of course, be wrong. The days seemed to drag by slower and slower. On those days when things were hectic, when you were on patrol in the boonies, repulsing a ground attack on your position, flying combat sorties, or hunkered down in a bunker as incoming rounds shook the ground under and around you and blasted your ears with that crunching loud boom, those days did not seem to speed up. On the contrary, they seemed to go by ever slower.

But go by they did and soon you saw that you had thirty or fewer spaces in the graphic remaining to be checked off. That is when you sensed at the core of your being the closeness of that time when you would board that *freedom bird* and leave that sweltering hell of terrible smells, broad suffering, and lethal winds, and return to the real world. But this same realization of the few spaces left on the calendar also made you acutely aware of how dangerous that place could be and the seemingly growing risk to you personally from some stray bullet, a shell fragment, or the possibility of being in the killing zone of that highly inaccurate and unpredictable 122-mm Russian rocket or Chinese 82-mm mortar round. You became cautious to a fault. This presented its own risks both to yourself and your buddies and was very hard to manage for most.

For me at the near midpoint in my tour, the war just continued on, day after day. That DROS date was a long way off and not thought about too much. My focus was to do my job and survive. My DROS would arrive in due time. I just had to watch my back, along with my front and my sides. I had to be conscious of my risks and wear all of my survival and protective gear every day, on every mission. No exceptions. No complacency. And I cut no corners, even to the chagrin of my fellow crewmates.

One of the most storied events of this period in South Vietnam was the search and rescue effort for "Bat 21," the call sign of the specially equipped EB-66 recon and electronic warfare aircraft that Lt. Col. Iceal "Gene" Hambleton had ejected from and landed behind enemy lines. A mission was laid on F/8 Cavalry and the 48th AHC to support the US Air Force rescue teams who were trying to recover him. Much has already been written about this event and Hollywood even made a movie about it. Unfortunately, little was reported or documented about the effort on the part of the US Army aviation units involved. The truth is that many of us put in many long hours flying and searching for him over very hostile enemy forces and one crew from F/8 Cavalry was lost in the process.

As with this rescue effort, the truth was that we did have losses all too frequently. The day after I returned from my R&R in Hawaii, June 11, 1972, my old stick buddy from flight school "Dusty" Holm, Blue Ghost White (White was the designation of the cavalry unit's aerial recon platoon leader) was lost flying his OH-6 Little Bird while on a recon mission with F/8 Cavalry west of Camp Eagle in Northern I Corps. His aircraft was reported to have exploded while low to the ground, but there were conflicting reports about his loss or capture. Those who witnessed the event believed that the aircraft was hit by an SA-7 missile. Enemy fire was so intense that the other aircraft who tried to get in to rescue Dusty and his gunner were also hit. Another OH-6, flown by First Lieutenant Jim McQuade was also shot down while trying to aid Dusty. I took Dusty's loss very, very hard. It was, without doubt, the single biggest morale buster I experienced in Vietnam. My motivation was crushed with Dusty's loss.

For the next week, the 48th AHC and F/8 Cavalry mounted several search missions to try and find Dusty and his crew because we did not know if they had survived the crash or not. We never found them. There was little to go on and both aircraft were destroyed. The truth was that the area was too hot to recon on the ground, and we did not know for sure what happened to them until an MIA recovery crew working with the Vietnamese government in 2007 found the crash site and returned the remains to the military identification lab in Honolulu for examination. In 2009 we received word that Dusty's remains had been positively identified. In 2011 surviving members of F/8 Cavalry gathered with Dusty's wife Margaret and his family on November 9 at Arlington National Cemetery for the burial of Dusty Holm, his crew chief, and gunner with full military honors.

Dusty was a close friend and I think of him often. Dusty and I had been very close in flight school. We were both experienced captains We both had a family and we both loved flying. Seems neither of us could keep a stick buddy early in the training because they had all fallen out of the program. That was, until we were paired up to fly and train together. We built a bond of trust and respect in each other. We knew we were both headed to Vietnam after graduation. But we did not expect to serve in any close proximity once in country. When we both found ourselves assigned to Marble Mountain, even though in different units, we were living and working fairly close together. And down time was often spent together at our tiny o' club on the beach on the east side of the base. I watched a few sunrises on that patio with Dusty drinking beer, laughing, and lamenting about where we were and what we were doing.

When Dusty was killed, I was devastated from his loss. He knew my unit, at that time the 48th AHC, was standing down soon and he wanted me to join his cavalry troop as the Blues platoon leader. They needed a Ranger-qualified captain for that position and one who had some experience with small-unit ground operations. He felt I would be a great fit in the unit. He said I would like my assigned call sign for that position, "Blue." He had convinced his troop commander, Major Jack Kennedy, to request my reassignment to the unit. I had mixed feelings about this, of course. I would be eligible to return home when the 48th stood down, as a new policy implemented in early June allowed for those who had been in country more than six months at the planned time of a stand down.

I made no commitment to Dusty or Major Kennedy. If I could return home to my pregnant wife, I planned to do that. Amid all of this, Dusty was shot down and killed. It hit me hard. No one else in my unit at that time really knew Dusty and they did not understand my reaction to his death. Particularly since we had lost Major Kingman in May. My usual energetic demeanor seemed to vanish, or so I was told by several other unit members as well as by Captain Wilson, now the CO. This was not good. I knew that attitude and mental focus was the key to both mission effectiveness and individual survival. I had to get my shit together ASAP. It was a struggle and I probably drank a bit more than I ever had done. One morning, I had a pretty painful hangover when I found out I needed to fly. That moment seemed to snap me out of the depression over the loss of Dusty just enough to become combat effective again.

As with Dan Kingman, Dusty was initially simply listed as MIA, even though many had witnessed his downing. After the loss of Major Kingman, this angered me terribly and it affected my attitude about many things from that point on in my tour. Loss was not new to me, nor was a combat loss of family or close friends. That was the way things were during that period of war for our country. I had lost my cousin, George Dewey, in a Marine CH-46. I had lost friends from high school. I had lost fellow unit members to hostile fire. I lost a mentor from my Georgetown ROTC training days. I lost classmates from Georgetown and had already lost other friends from flight school, but this loss was different to me. It felt different and looked different. I was more angry than sad. I saw this one as shear waste more than any other during Vietnam. I was angry that he was gone. I was angry that he died because the United States political leadership at that time clearly thought we were simply expendable. I was angry that we would never fly again together. I was angry that he would not ever get home to his wife and daughter. And I was angry that I would never spend another sunrise on the porch of the o' club with him. His loss haunted me for the rest of my tour, as it has for the remainder of my life. There was nothing to do but keep flying and fighting my part of the war. I tried to compartmentalize it. I tried to push it back in my mind to some closed space where it would not bother me so severely. I carried on, did my job, and watched my back and those around me. But he was never far from my mind, and he still isn't.

Whatever PTSD that might plague me, and I really have no idea whether I would be categorized as having it or not, it is as much from my survivor guilt over his loss as it might be from any of my many very frightening experiences in combat. Yes, I have some sleepless nights where some aspect of my experience in Vietnam pops into my head and I still sometimes overreact to a sudden perceived sense of danger or even senseless absurdity, but mostly I think I am bothered by Dusty's loss.

I know others from F/8 Cavalry troop feel that same way. I knew Dusty to be one of the most dedicated, professional, and courageous individuals I ever met. He and his crew demonstrated through their sacrifice, as did others that day and during the entire time that the Blue Stars and the Blue Ghost flew over Vietnam, if I might paraphrase, that uncommon valor was a common virtue.

His final homecoming decades later and the moving burial ceremony at Arlington was more than just another soldier returned home. It was the return of a national hero, the return of a long-missed, loving husband, father, and grandfather to his family. And it was, with the return of these three fellow aviators buried together in one grave, the return home from a long-forgotten battlefield of comrades and brothers. It was closure for many of us of unfinished business as members of F/8 Cavalry and the Blue Ghost family.

This was evident to everyone at Arlington that day when they saw how many unit members were present after so many years, to both honor these three brave young heroes and to support their families. Those attending included former F/8 Cavalry members from 1972, to include a former secretary of the Army, and many distinguished career officers, flight school classmates, successful scholars, entrepreneurs, and government officials. For those former F/8 Cavalry unit members and former flight school classmates no longer with us or who could not be there in person, their presence was both deeply felt and was well represented by those that were there to honor these brave heroes.

On June 13, 1972, I received word that another flight-school classmate, Captain Fred Suttle, had been killed near Kontum while riding in the front seat of an AH-1G Cobra. It was a dark time for me and made readjusting to being back in Vietnam and back in combat very difficult. Fred was killed by ground fire when he was struck in the chest with a .51-cal Russian machine gun bullet. I was told at the time that he was not wearing his chicken plate. I knew that he did not like to wear it because he felt it got in his way while flying and was uncomfortable.

Lesson, or rather a lesson reinforced: I had already learned in my previous career as a fireman that you wear every bit of the safety and protective gear you are issued and anything else you can get your hands on that will add to your protection! I was one of the few pilots in the 48th and later in F/8th that wore it all, every day, every time. I know that my gear saved my life more than once!

Homesickness following my return from seeing Karen on R&R combined with the loss of Dusty and Fred put me, on some days over the next month, in such a foul mood and depressed state that I even surprised myself. I had experienced loss before. I had seen death, touched death and had my own escapes from death. It was not fear of my own mortality or coping with the dangers to me or that which I might bring to others. It was more a feeling of waste, that same feeling that every soldier in combat, I suppose, experiences to one degree or another after the loss of close and special friends. The utter waste of humanity that I had seen in the war, the extermination of the population of the City of Quang Tri by the NVA and Russians, the devastation of every village and town along Highway 1 as the NVA moved south and the incredible destruction of the NVA armor force as it neared Hue, all contributed to this sense of waste. Motivation sometimes came hard those next few weeks.

It also gave me, as it did many others, a deep frustration with the processes in Paris. Clearly the United States was seeking a solution where the fighting could stop, and a more peaceful approach taken to resolving the issue of whether the two halves of Vietnam could or even should ever unite. Just as clearly the North Vietnamese, no doubt at the behest of their Russian mentors, wanted to stall any real progress in hopes of a battlefield victory that could enable them to dictate terms and, just as clearly, for the US to be humiliated. Yet this awareness on our part did not affect our resolve, one way or another, to perform our missions. Quite the contrary, the loss of Major Kingman and the loss of Dusty, Fred, and Jim McQuade seemed to deepen our disgust with the situation and our anger at the NVA and Russians from starting this Easter Offensive during the peace talks in Paris. We did see ourselves as expendable pawns on the battlefield, yet if we frustrated the Russians and the NVA, we felt it could have a positive influence in Paris, even if no one else ever really knew. That might save some lives down the road.

Despite North Vietnamese and Russian propaganda intended to cause US soldiers still in South Vietnam to desert, none had any such inclinations, particularly after what the NVA did to the populations in I Corps that they overran. Any propaganda-constructed perception or assertion that the NVA were liberators was fully dispelled in March and April of 1972. The reality of the true intentions were then reaffirmed in 1975 and 1976. I wonder how well those slick, selfish politicians in the White House, US

Congress, and the media at the time now sleep at night. I suspect their demons far outweigh and outnumber those we Vietnam veterans have had to manage in our lives.

When the NVA Easter Offensive period began, the 48th AHC Blue Stars got several new toys to even up the fighting. We needed new toys because our seventeen-pound 2.75 Folding Fin rockets that the Cobras could fire were less than worthless against anything but a PT-76 (and there were lots of those) and the NVA-operated old, captured US tanks. Early in this NVA offensive, the Russian ZSU 23-2s, a mobile, armored anti-aircraft system, and the T-54s and T-55s were eating our lunch, to say nothing of the SA-7s, and we had to resort to trickery and creativity to stop them!

The 48th AHC initially got the French-made SS-11 guided missiles. It was great fun to shoot, but more as a toy than a combat weapon. These were mounted on older B-model Hueys that were adapted to be M-models with more powerful engines and larger rotor blades. The SS-11 was very hard to use against anything but a stationary object, like a bunker or an already immobilized armored vehicle. They had a great wallop when they hit and did a lot of damage to those on the receiving end. However, against moving Russian tanks with 12.5-mm machine guns on top, they did little good, and frankly they got us into situations where we took lots of hits! Both Joker and lift platoon pilots got checked out in these, because we did not want to sacrifice any gunship availability for our missions. To fire the SS-11 you had to manually guide the missile to the target using a small joystick by trying to keep the flame of the missile's rocket engine between you and the target and then trying to guide it by flying that exhaust flame into the target. Imagine doing this when you are moving, the target is moving and seemingly every North Vietnamese AA weapon in South Vietnam is trying to shoot your bird out of the sky. This is because the NVA knew that once an SS-11 missile is in the air, if they can kill or distract the launching bird, the missile will miss. In truth the SS-11 had limited value and was very frustrating to use. Our confidence in the weapon and our enthusiasm for it was not helped by the fact that we had firsthand evidence that France was also selling weapons and supplies, even these same missiles, to the NVA!

Early in the tank battles of April 1972 we quickly discovered the key weakness in the T-55 Russian tank: their fuel tanks were external and exposed on the left and right rear deck. This made the tank very vulnerable to fire.

But the Joker guns learned fast, adapted to opportunities, and did a pretty good job with a field expedient antitank solution with the Cobras. We discovered that rockets loaded with *nails* (antipersonnel flechettes) and *Willy Pete* (white phosphorous) could be very effective against the NVA armor because their Russian supplied tanks carried external fuel tanks. This was a new version of *shake and bake* and was very useful! We often flew with Cobras armed this way accompanying our M-model equipped with the SS-11 missiles. This was a productive combination of firepower, if not an ideal antitank capability.

One night in early June 1972, some strange folks in civilian clothes showed up at our company operations room. We were told to gather those of us that were flying the SS-11-equipped helicopters, along with a few more, and that we were to have a middle-of-the-night briefing on a new *Star Trek*-like weapon. We were told that what we were about to learn was top secret, and that we could never, ever talk about the existence of this new weapon. Then they told us that we would now be using a weapon where we did not have to guide the missile itself, like with the SS-11. For this new weapon you only had to point a sight system that you held in your hands at the target and keep the target in its cross hairs. This missile, they said, would go wherever the sight was pointed—yeah right! And oh, by the way, they told us it had a magnifier built into the sight and that every shot was recorded by a gun camera! At the time we all thought "Oh shit, now they will be grading us like the Zoomies!" The new weapon was called a TOW missile. Its designation was BGM-71. TOW stood for tube launched, optically tracked, wire guided. Now that was a mouthful, no wonder it had the simple operational name of TOW.

The next day they took us out to show us these flat-black painted helicopters as they arrived (they looked like they had been hastily painted with a brush and a can of cheap spray paint). We quickly discovered that "some assembly required" was the first major problem. Once again, the two birds that were delivered were a variation on the B-model UH-1 helicopter. They looked like overweight, tired old slicks. Oh joy, ain't we got fun! These same aircraft had been operating, we were told, in the Kontum area where they had proved their value. We had heard rumors of a new antitank missile, but the rumors had been considered just that.

We also noticed that these had no aircraft identification numbers on them and no "US Army" on them. There were also no hand receipts or documents to sign for them. They did not belong to our unit. At first, they did not seem to belong to anyone. I was interested in this small detail because I had just been designated the unit keystone officer. This meant that I was now in charge of figuring out what stuff the unit had in total, and preparing to turn it all in, as we were now slated for stand down sometime within the next ninety days (we had no specific target and I later learned that the time was to be determined by our casualty rate, as we would get no more aircrews or aircraft).

UH-1B TOW Missile Ship that operated from the 48th AHC at Marble Mountain Army Airfield. It brought incredible tank-killing ability to our fight against the NVA armor forces in 1972.

These birds did appear to have what looked like *Hughes* painted on the tails in small letters but that had been painted over with black spray paint. The missile launchers were mounted on pylons on either side of the aircraft and each mount had a cluster of three launch tubes housed in an aerodynamic fairing. Given the slow speed of these birds, I never understood the reason for the fairing, as any aerodynamic advantage they offered was minimal while the added weight was significant. These fairings simply got in the way, but it made the bird look more lethal, I guess. These TOW missiles were designed to kill all known armored vehicles. Sounded pretty good to us, if true. Accompanying these two aircraft was a major and a few warrant officers, a couple of enlisted crew members, and a couple of Hughes technical representatives who were experienced with the aircraft and the missiles. These pilots said they were from a unit stationed at Fort Bragg, North Carolina and introduced themselves as the 1st Combat Aerial TOW Team.

Our first question to these new friends was: "How do these TOW missiles actually work?" They seemed knowledgeable and very, very confident in this TOW missile system and its ability to kill tanks but would not tell us a lot about the system due to what they said were security classifications. We had to learn on the job how to help this small team prepare their aircraft and to unpack these new, rather thick, bulky missiles and assemble and load them into the launch tubes. They were larger and seemed more powerful, from their looks, than the older SS-11s did. This was pretty much a do-it-yourself situation as we had no trained ground crews or ammo handlers in our unit who knew this system and how to help this small team. We were told that we had to help them target only enemy tanks so as not to waste the missiles unnecessarily because each missile cost as much as one of our helicopters! That seemed a bit extreme—using a half-million-dollar missile to kill a hundred-thousand-dollar Russian tank? Hey, if it worked, we were not paying the bills . . . well, maybe we were, at that.

When we helped to load the first missiles on the two ships for their first mission with us, I was struck by the dates on the inspection stickers on the missiles. They were less than forty-eight-hours old! Boy, this was hot shit stuff, coming right off the assembly line and being flown directly to us. I asked one of the tech reps how many birds there were like this and how many missiles we would get. I told him there were thousands of tanks headed into RVN from the north and there were only these two birds and a total of twelve missiles sitting on the ramp. He told me I wasn't allowed to ask that. I then asked if we would get more missiles. He replied that we would get as many as we could shoot.

Well, after getting our clocks cleaned trying to stem the initial tide of new Russian tanks, anything would help, but this seemed a bit light for the task at hand. We were told we were going to stop the tanks using these missiles and some new smart bombs the Air Force was bringing in. One tech-rep told us in April, about a month into this NVA offensive, that the US Air Force had bombs with TVs in them. We all laughed . . . yeah right, and what do they watch during the bomb runs, soap operas? We didn't believe it until the first time we saw an F-4 drop a single bomb and get a direct hit on a T-55 tank.

Anyway, off the first TOW flight went with a total of twelve missiles. This first mission was accompanied by some Joker guns and one slick as command and control and observer. I flew in the C&C bird on this first sortie with the TOWs and, frankly, I did not think this would amount to much. Most likely more of the same: run in, fire, get the shit scared out of you, and haul ass. Well, we located several NVA tanks and directed the TOW ships to the targets. The real challenge when employing this weapon was getting close enough for the missile to get to the target before the guiding wire broke. The TOW did not have a seeker head like a heat-seeking missile. In fact, all of the guidance for the missile's flight was provided through the wire to the missile. After some maneuvering into position and at the correct distance, the first missile went down range and BLAM, the targeted tank just blew into pieces in a huge explosion. In fact, the turret popped right off the top of the tank. *Well*, I thought, *that was weird. Why did the turret pop off so fast?* It had happened in just a second or two instead of the agonizing time it took the French SS-11 missiles to reach their targets. The second bird fired his first missile but missed. Then they both fired again and got two more tanks, again in huge explosions (this was the missile's very large shaped charge detonating, penetrating the tank's armor and causing the tank's internal ammo load to also detonate, in what seemed like one big explosion). That, I realized, was why the turret separated from the tank's hull so quickly. The ready-to-fire ammo in these Russian tanks was stored inside the turret with the gunner and tank commander and this amplified the destructive power. Very cool for us but a very bad day, finally, for those tankers! As to the miss, we later asked what happened because the missile seemed to fly off on its own. I was told, "Well, the wire probably broke."

Lesson: watch your turns and do not break the wire when employing this system.

We drank some beer that night as we celebrated our new team members and their amazing weapon system. Now we had the ability to really hit back, after taking it on the chin for months and after losing our CO and some fine crews. Hot dog, we sure had something here. We could now kick ass and do it so fast, we really had a chance to kill all of those "motherfucking Russian tanks." That is, if we could get a lot more missiles. Well, that tech rep had been right; we had all we could shoot, as they came in by the C-130 or C-141 load every day over at Da Nang AFB.

These missiles, combined with the smart bombs the Air Force was using, turned the area north of the city of Hue into an armor junk yard of monumental proportions. It was indeed fair play. You see, after the initial invasion of Quang Tri, the NVA and the Russians had slaughtered nearly the entire population of that city. Obviously, they never expected that we would get back in there to find out about this war crime, so confident were they of their Russian armor and advisors. The location of this pointless slaughter of innocent men, women, and children was an indicator of what was coming once we left RVN. But now we had our own instrument of death for Russian armor and our own revenge for that day. Highway 1 and the entire flat coastal zone from the DMZ south to Hue became the new highway of death for NVA armored vehicles.

After about two weeks, any tank that moved was dead meat,

either from our TOW missiles or from the Air Force. We used
the Jokers and their AH-1G Cobras for anti-aircraft suppression
using nails and 40-mm chunkers, and we used Slicks to seed the
areas with Willy Pete grenades and used their M-60 machine guns
to suppress small arms. We had fires burning in tanks across the
I Corps battlefield nearly every day. Anything that moved and we
could see was targeted with the TOWs. Soon we owned the sky and
the terrain . . . well, at least by day.

At night it was totally different. Yes, we had the Specter aircraft.
But their area of operation was much larger than ours and priorities
often took them away from our battle area. While flares helped
us with targeting, it was far more difficult to detect and hold a
target in sight from a moving bird, unless you were flying nap of
the earth. We had no night sights and the sights on these systems
were not night vision systems as we have them today. Our starlight
scopes were too poor to use for targeting from the air. I flew a lot
of nighthawk missions where we tried to use flares to help aim at
moving tanks, but it was not nearly so effective. We did kill a lot of
NVA infantry at night, however, using the nighthawk birds to call in
naval gunfire, artillery, and Air Force Willy-Pete, iron bombs, and
sometimes napalm missions on enemy supply concentrations. But
during the day, we were solidly in control.

In July the 48th AHC was running out of everything. We had
suffered far fewer casualties after May of 1972, but we were losing
crews to DROS and to wounds. Plus, our aircraft were getting
broken and worn out faster than the parts came in to fix them
(except for the TOW ships), so we soon received our orders to stand
down the 48th AHC. In late May of 1972, when we received our
warning order for the imminent stand down of the unit, Captain
Wilson called me into his office. He told me that as the only one in
the unit with keystone experience, I was now officially designated
the keystone officer for the 48th AHC, something he had told me
once before to expect. I was to plan and execute the stand down

of the unit starting immediately. But I also had to continue to fly combat missions because we did not have enough pilots to fill all the seats as it was. So, I began working with the administrative and logistics components of the unit that night. There was little time for sleep or recreation, just flying and working on the stand down. The next three weeks were hectic and tiring for me. I assumed that once we stood down the unit, I would rotate home with the rest of the unit members. So, I fixated on getting the job done to get home.

Then on June 28, 1972, amid preparing for its stand down, the 48th was called upon to also prepare to participate in its final major combat air assault. This air assault, a part of the South Vietnamese leadership's first major counterstrike against the North Vietnamese Easter Offensive and planned by Lt. Gen Ngo Quang Truong, was the key component of a plan referred to as Lam Son 72. This South Vietnamese operation was a plan to take back Quang Tri and called for several air assaults deep into the North Vietnamese rear, north of the Imperial City of Hue in into Quang Tri Province. The planned air assaults would require close timing between a ground push west of Hue and an amphibious landing along the coast, east of the planned landing zone for the air assault forces, by South Vietnamese Marines. Given the enemy armored, anti-aircraft, and infantry forces between Hue and Quang Tri, this was a daunting tactical decision, even if it made strong strategic sense in the face of the ongoing peace negotiations in Paris. The Lam Son 72 operation, to be decisive during a stalemated armor battle, would have to be an air assault deep into the rear of the enemy forces' position to the north of Hue. The plan initially called for a heliborne air assault of South Vietnamese Marines conducted by US Marine CH-53 helicopters along the coast, east of Quang Tri city. Once that air assault was completed and the South Vietnamese Marines were in place, a much larger follow-on air assault would be conducted to penetrate deeply into the North Vietnamese army's rear on the south side of Quang Tri.

There was excellent intelligence on the ground coming from

within the Quang Tri city area from South Vietnamese military elements who were still in the area. The problem was the airlift resources needed for the South Vietnamese troop forces to be inserted during the assault. This would have to be a low-level helicopter assault. The sea landing and its supporting air assault, flown by the US Marines, were not sustainable that close to the DMZ with the extensive Russian artillery firepower that could target the ships, landing craft, and the coastal air assault LZ. This sea-based assault was planned as a feint to confuse the NVA and draw off a part of its combat power, but one that could help retake the initiative on the battlefield from the North Vietnamese.

A traditional airborne assault with paratroopers was also not practical due to the extensive anti-aircraft weapons deployment around Quang Tri and behind the main NVA line of contact to the north of Hue. Besides the South Vietnamese Air Force simply did not have enough aircraft to stage such an airborne operation.

But a successful assault to retake Quang Tri would cut off supplies and stymy the continued attack south by the NVA. The NVA armored force north of Hue would then be caught between two large South Vietnamese forces and under the direct attack by US Naval gunfire, US Air Force bombers, and the VNAF. It would be both a significant tactical and strategic victory for the South Vietnamese. It would also have a significant impact on the peace talks in Paris. But doing it would be a hard and potentially a very costly task. The downside, if the mission failed, was probably the immediate failure of the South Vietnamese government. Such a failure would be a strategic victory for the North Vietnamese and the Russians, whose main goal in all of this was to achieve a warm water naval port on the Pacific Ocean. Of course, helping to defeat a US ally would be a significant strategic bonus as well.

The only practical way to carry off such an assault was with helicopters. While the VNAF had a significant number of UH-1D and H helicopters, most were already in the field and not available, some were ultimately committed to the operation but not enough. Clearly the leadership was also concerned about the experience, talent and, in some circles, the commitment needed on the part of the VNAF air crews to plan and pull off such an attack. This would be the largest VNAF air assault that they would ever try to accomplish. So, the decision was made to commit fifty US Army UH-1H Hueys as the lead lift element in the assault, escorted by eighteen US Army AH-1G Cobras. Planning for this massive air assault began at 1st Aviation Brigade HQ in Saigon. However, the real experience for such an operation was at Marble Mountain in I Corps, considering that most of the experienced air operations talent at the higher headquarters had already been sent back to the States with the withdrawal of the last of the 1st Cavalry Division and the 101 Air Assault Division. So actual tactical-level planning for the mission fell to the leadership teams in the four US Army aviation units still located at Marble Mountain Army Airfield outside of Da Nang. These were the F/8, F/9, and F/4 Air Cavalry troops and the 48th AHC.

This was to be a massive effort but very, very dangerous. Deploying fifty Hueys on one mission, all in one lift, with sufficient maintenance spares, along with eighteen Cobras meant that the maintenance teams had to pull off a near miracle with less than a week's notice—all the while maintaining ongoing operations against the still potent NVA armor force to the north. We also had to maintain operational security around the planned massive air assault. The less that higher headquarters in Saigon knew about the actual plan, the better. So, they only knew very basic information through normal reporting channels. Only when senior folks came to Marble did they learn the actual air assault plan and its exact date. No doubt that the NVA knew something was brewing. But, as it turned out, they misjudged the information they did get. This combat air assault would prove to be an event of many firsts.

In truth, only the US Army aviation forces in I Corps had the aircraft on hand and experienced crews needed to make the initial penetration through the NVA front line. The most experienced South Vietnamese helicopter lift squadrons were deployed and badly needed in other operations to the south of I Corps, so they could only provide a limited number of troop lift helicopters, mainly for follow-up operations.

With a little over one week's operational planning time, four US helicopter units would provide the fifty Huey troop-lift helicopters and eighteen Cobras on July 11, 1972. And the 48th AHC, who would provide 50 percent of the aircraft for this mission, was now scheduled to stand down and be redeployed to Germany by July 30!

This mission became known as the *Fifty Ship Mission* for the US Army forces involved. It would prove to be the largest single formation air assault of the war. While past air assault operations had involved more aircraft, none ever flew that many helicopters in a single lift and a single air-assault formation into on LZ at the same time. And no one up to this operation had ever attempted a massive helicopter air assault over a conventional armored enemy forward battleline with in-depth anti-aircraft formations, and deep into the rear of enemy held territory. This was a stretch of then current US Air assault doctrine.

The plan was for the fifty Hueys, loaded with South Vietnamese Marines and infantry, along with the eighteen Cobras, to depart the forward pickup zone (PZ) north of Hue but south of the line of contact. Our intent was to launch as a single, tight, coordinated liftoff and fly in a compact high-speed single formation at treetop level directly across the front line of contact into the enemy rear and toward our landing zone (LZ) just south of Quang Tri city itself. We would be followed by up to one hundred assorted VNAF helicopters transporting the follow-on forces. It was a gutsy plan. And it would only work with massive air and indirect firepower to prepare the battlefield and suppress enemy air defenses along the route of flight and on and near the LZ. And it needed surprise. Of course, the likelihood, in the view of the North Vietnamese and the Russians, that such an air assault could even be mounted was low. The assumption was that the enemy would believe, due to pending stand downs of US aviation units in I Corp (which they likely knew about), conducting such a large-scale offensive operation was all but impossible.

We knew, however, at treetop level the NVA had not proven adept at bringing effective fire on American helicopters and we were confident that we would have the element of surprise. After all, despite tactical helicopter doctrine then still evolving, no one had ever actually tried to do this anywhere before on a conventional battlefield during a war. Such operations had been rehearsed in the past in Europe as part of defensive planning against any possible Soviet invasion of Western Europe. But this had always been just an exercise and in smaller lift numbers. It had never been done, even in Vietnam, with such a large, single formation of helicopters.

Brief but intense hours of planning ensued with the final approval of the plan from brigade headquarters coming only a few days before the actual operation. It was going to be a dangerous mission and we expected significant losses. The key was coordinating the US Air Force and US Navy fire support. The only US artillery left in I Corps was supporting security operations around Da Nang Air Force Base, and they would not be available to support our mission. The US Navy and Marines did have artillery liaison elements with the South Vietnamese and Marine fire support elements on the ground. These units would be helpful in targeting and suppressing NVA anti-aircraft elements near the front line at our planned crossing corridor. But for in-depth fire support on our flight route north into Quang Tri Province, we needed extensive naval gunfire support and precision attacks with smart weapons from US Air Force assets. Arc Light missions of B-52s would be ideal to suppress the overall enemy response, both around the intended LZ and along the route of flight.

This seemed a challenge to secure and coordinate. In reality, it was very straight forward. The Navy liaison officers told us they had "lots of guns and lots of ammo" that they wanted to use. They did not want to go home with it. Much of it was WWII naval ammo that needed to be expended and there would be no shortage of it for the mission. Now, I was not a strong believer in flying helicopter formations under overhead naval gunfire, which would be needed in this case. Typically, we avoided flying under the gun-target line because a short round could ruin your day. For this mission, the Navy would need to be able to fire in front of us, on either side of our line of flight and even behind us, both on the way into the LZ and on the way back south to Da Nang. This indeed was going to be tricky to coordinate operationally. The Air Force liaison simply told us that we need not worry about suppression of enemy air defenses and the potential for a rapid enemy counterattack on the LZ. The request for Arc Light strikes to support the operation was already in.

There was little time to rehearse the operation. Operational security also dictated that no hint of what exactly was planned must reach the North Vietnamese. However, it was a given that the North Vietnamese spies on the ground in the DaNang area would learn additional South Vietnamese counterattacks on Quang Tri were coming. Each US aviation company participating in this massive assault put together its own planning cell to create the conditions needed to have its aircraft ready and on station at the pick-up zone on time. We had to depend upon ad-hock planning and employ our own extensive experience and competence in operations like this. This was an example of "come as you are" military operations. This is how battlefield operations doctrine is developed and tested in real life! This type of novel tactical operation is difficult, dangerous and, of course, failure prone. But it was, we then hoped, a validation of the evolving, if untested, helicopter operations doctrine, some of it still only theoretical. But it was a tribute to the skill of our aircrews, maintenance support, and logistics that made this short-notice, high risk operation even possible.

For the US Air Force fighter cover needed for precision attack on enemy targets, we had the air liaison officers, or ALOs, who already worked with us on a regular basis from Da Nang Air Force Base. They were from the Gunfighters, an Air Force F-4 squadron that supported us and whom we supported often and FAC units based there. The Army, Navy, Marine Corps, and Air Force interservice tactical collaboration and support was long in place and a given for this operation. We US Army aviators all knew how it worked and how to use it. Shortly into the planning effort the support with Arc Light missions was confirmed. This was great news and brought an additional degree of confidence in the probable success of the mission. This was tactical offensive destruction on a scale new to mobile warfare: massed B-52 bombers flying in tight formations and able to deliver precision bombardment strikes, up to fifty-eight thousand pounds of bombs per aircraft, that effectively suppressed most of an entire grid square. A grid square is a box one thousand meters on a side. The strategic bomb planner's intent was to create a rolling carpet of destruction on enemy anti-aircraft capabilities forward of our flight path all the way to the LZ to assure our successful penetration into the objective. As most of this area had already been utterly destroyed by the North Vietnamese forces during their advance south from the DMZ, there was little threat to civilian populations or infrastructure in the combat assault corridor we would use.

My immediate thought as I listened to these gray-headed US Air Force briefers, was *Holy crap! This will be something I will never forget but will be the scariest day of my life.* I then wondered which of these guys had flown B-17s or B-24s twenty-five or so years before as young Army Air Corps lieutenants over Germany or Japan trying to do this exact thing! I remembered living in postwar Europe in 1960 and the vast destruction that still remained even then from the massive bombing raids in 1944–45 to protect the advance of the Allies into Germany. I suppose they were somewhat weird thoughts for me to have at that exact moment, but such are the ways our own experiences and history influence our perspective throughout our lives. After all, these gentlemen seemed to be about my father's age. And my dad was at that moment in his office in Saigon. He had flown P-51Ds over the Pacific Ocean escorting B-29 strategic bombers on missions over Japan in 1944–45.

This is a B-52 strategic bomber making a run over a target in South Vietnam. Normally, such sorties were made by flights of three B-52 bombers who dropped their bomb loads in unison on the target. The resulting destruction on the ground was massive. The B-52s employed in Vietnam normally carried eighty-four 500-pound bombs internally and twenty-four 500-pound bombs externally. Each aircraft's 108-bomb load put 54,000 pounds of bombs on the target.

This mission would have many firsts. According to several sources, in addition to being the largest single formation assault by US helicopters during the war with sixty-eight aircraft flying in a single formation, it was the first time the strategic bombers were used to directly support a single US Army combat air assault in a tactical operation in real time since WWII. It was also the first time in the war that all the US military lift and assault aircraft in such an operation were reported by the US headquarters in Saigon to be only South Vietnamese aircraft being flown by South Vietnamese pilots. While this was all nonsense, the propaganda value for the population of South Vietnam was enormous. Potentially, just the perception of such a South Vietnamese military capability might have an impact in Paris. But we knew that once the mission began, the NVA and their Russian advisors only needed to look up to know this was an American-led mission, flown in US Army aircraft with US crews. This likely irrelevant effort to deceive the NVA, the American public, and most of its political leaders also meant no official recognition of the sweat, hard work, and valor of the US aircrews involved from the US Army. Such was the level of politics and, indeed deceit, on all sides of this conflict. But one had to keep things in perspective as, to paraphrase, war at this point in Vietnam was indeed nothing more than a violent extension of political theater. The problem was that people were getting maimed and killed.

This was one of the most frightening, unnerving operations I flew during my time in Vietnam. The morning of the mission, July 11, 1972, there was little discussion. Everything seemed to be handled as if this were just another day on the line flying in support of the defense of Hue and Da Nang. But we loaded extra 7.62-mm linked ammo for our door M-60s. We each had a string of baseball hand grenades strung behind the pilot seats in our aircraft. Each pilot and crew member wore all our ballistic protection and survival gear, along with extra flares and ammunition for our side arms and Car-15s, which was a short-barrel and smaller shoulder-stock version of the M-16 that fit well in the cockpit. We departed Marble Mountain in unit formations before sunrise. For the 48th AHC: two flights of slicks and guns, and we flew west from the airfield. We then turned different directions, some initially south, some east and some north, to confuse any NVA intel assets watching and reporting on US aircraft operations in and around Da Nang. We all eventually flew north of Hue to a very large pick-up zone situated on dry rice fields and a vast cemetery near a US radio research station complex on the west side of Highway 1. While it looked very large to anyone on the ground, to us it looked to be a very tight PZ, and an excellent target. It took about an hour to get all our birds on the ground and in position for the precision departure we planned.

Our concern upon landing was the numerous 130-mm guns that the North Vietnamese had in range of this PZ and whether they would discover our operation and location. The longer we were in the PZ the greater the chance that this would occur. We landed just after first light, as planned, in the formation needed for the assault. We must have covered more than three hundred acres over the countryside and none of it was a prepared landing area. We landed in farm fields and among large burial structures, common in that part of the world, near small Vietnamese villages and near a large school. Operational security was a major challenge while we are on the ground in the PZ.

The ARVN and South Vietnamese Marines were already in place and distributed along the aircraft parking lines in groups ready to load. They were heavily armed and did not look very happy. As with any soldier about to embark on a dangerous combat operation, I cannot imagine there was much enthusiasm for the undertaking ahead of them. They knew it would be a dangerous flight into the LZ and an even more dangerous fight retaking the entirety of Quang Tri Province. I did not envy their task. Those firsthand accounts by D-Day veterans I had heard as a teenager briefly came to my mind. I felt a chill on that hot, sweaty, dusty day. This was going to be some real shit to go through—even for us.

We waited in the PZ sitting in our aircraft ready to go with little information available as to what was causing the delay, all the while waiting for the first NVA round to impact in our PZ. We were covered in sweat as we sat in our hot aircraft cockpits in full combat gear: all leather, rather heavy combat boots, flight suits, Kevlar body armor, survival vests, flight helmets, gloves, and a nervous gut. We waited and waited. It got hotter and more humid and yet we waited.

But soon we could hear a continuing deep, throbbing rumble off in the distance to the north. Somebody was getting it bad. After about two hours, during which time no enemy indirect fire found us, we finally got the word to launch.

48th AHC and F/8 Cav UH-1H Slicks await in the PZ for the initial Air Mobile assault to take back Quang Tri.

I never heard why we had the lengthy delay, but I suspect it was coordinating the naval gunfire and the Arc Light strikes as we could now clearly hear munitions going off to our north but far closer than I would have liked. Finally, the word came to load up and crank up. Load and crank we did in a matter of a few moments. We brought the systems up to speed and sat light on our skids, as planned, to make the lift off more efficient and synchronized. Then came the countdown to pitch pull . . . five . . . four . . . three . . . two . . . one . . . GO! We lifted off as a single entity. It was an amazing thing to see from the cockpit of a Huey in the midst of such a large aircraft formation. Birds to front and side all rising and tilting forward to gain airspeed in a seemingly single motion and as a single formation. It was as if we had a rigid bar connecting each aircraft. The danger of what we were doing was real and painfully obvious, but it worked. It worked because of the skill and experience of every pilot and crew member on those helicopters.

Our C&C ship, flown by the commander of F/8 Air Cavalry Major Jack Kennedy, had given us the pitch-pull count down and we launched together into the clear skies of I Corps. Just as we launched, despite the initial loud noise and vibration of the massed helicopters and their screaming engines and throbbing blades, spinning and churning the air, we heard and felt a loud and a very deep, rumble to our front that overpowered our own takeoff-generated noises.

When B-52s drop their massed ordnance, the vast number of explosions from their impact on the ground creates an expanding concussion bubble that both pushes the air outward and creates a sonic wave that moves out from the blast. When you are close, this blast wave of air can be deadly. At distances of even several kilometers it can knock you down and take your breath away. Even at the distance we were from the front lines and the impact zone of these strikes, about ten kilometers, we could feel and hear the impact of these very destructive attacks against the NVA positions. While ominous to us, we were told to expect an Arc Light just north of us directly upon and to the immediate rear of the NVA front lines just before we launched. This was expected to be the area of the most intense concentration of effective anti-aircraft fires from the NVA, so they needed to be knocked out to prepare our safe passage over the line of contact. As we lifted to treetop level and pushed the cyclics forward to accelerate as one body, low level north across the landscape, all of that distant rumbling sound was dimmed a bit in the noise of our transmission scream and the rotor noise.

As we lifted to about one hundred feet above the dry rice fields around us, the munitions we heard became visually apparent to us as we looked north along our route of flight. There were dark roiling clouds of smoke and debris rising high into the sky to our front. They were angry, fast rising clouds and to our surprise there was what appeared to be lightning in them. "Into the gates of hell we ride," someone said on the radio. But that is what it appeared we were doing, rising into hell . . . or at least into a hell of a fight. I felt my ass tighten on the seat and my hands were sweating in my flight gloves as I gripped the cyclic stick and the collective. As we neared the angry clouds and smoke, we felt the air tumble and quake around us. It was like riding a horse at a gallop and the analogy was not lost on any of us. Below us as we crossed from the friendly defense line to the NVA forward positions was utter destruction. Enemy soldiers were running around like lost crazy people. Vehicles, tanks, trucks, armored personnel carriers and what looked like small cars or tracked vehicles with guns or tubes on them, were destroyed or flipped over, though a few were driving around but with no obvious purpose. Once we flew right over a large missile launcher, the missile was partly destroyed but it was huge. I suspect it was a SAM-2 anti-aircraft missile, but I could not figure out why it would be so close to friendly artillery. Surely it was a target.

In many cases the crews of the NVA tanks would abandon their vehicles when confronted with TOW missiles, attacks by helicopters, or when ARVN forces brought effective fire upon them. This resulted in scores of captured T-54s and T-55s by the South Vietnamese ground forces in the first few months of the Easter Offensive by the NVA. As a consequence, by June of 1972, the NVA commonly chained their tank crews into their tanks.

Our PZ had seemed serene and peaceful with no sign of war. As we flew forward over the enemy forward positions, we saw considerable destruction ahead of us. Our planning efforts had identified an area where there was a thinning in the enemy lines. The US Air Force had flown those planned anti-aircraft interdiction missions to locate and destroy any heavy anti-aircraft guns that they could find but there was no guarantee that new guns had not been moved up or that they had been hidden and not targeted.

As we flew forward, we could clearly see that the assault was indeed being conducted behind a rolling Arc Light. The massive B-52 bombing technique was successfully clearing a path in the enemy anti-aircraft shield all the way to the LZ south of the city of Quang Tri.

Soon the smell hit us. We were flying at 100 knots. The air turbulence from the aircraft to our front and from ordnance detonating at a close distance made the flying challenging. There was a lot of smoke and airborne debris all around us. We continually *jinked* and *jockeyed* our aircraft to stay in tight formation. But now we were also flying a few feet above the ground here. We were dodging the remains of trees, buildings and destroyed fortifications and bunkers. That smell was the one we all knew too well—death. A dead soldier's body turns ripe very fast in that heat. This smell combined with that of burned flesh sears your nose and is a smell that stays with you for a long time. If you ever smell it again, the images of those days leap into your mind. Smell is a powerful thing. The memory of it is the same.

On we flew, just to the west of Highway 1 on one of the most incredible missions of the war for me. This first wave of the larger air assault mission involved more than 100 aircraft, ours and a variety of different South Vietnamese Air Force helicopters that followed us, but in much less disciplined formations. In addition, Air Force, Marine, and Navy helicopters were involved to lift follow-on ARVN Marines out on the coast. VNAF Chinooks, several former 203rd ASHC aircraft, flown by South Vietnamese pilots followed with support artillery and additional infantry into the LZ to support the coming ground fight for Quang Tri.

I was flying as a peter pilot in a UH-1H Huey in the lead assault flight section within the larger US helicopter formation. As we flew, we could hear the occasional small arms round hit the aircraft. It makes a distinct sound, and you can feel the impact of even small arms rounds hitting anywhere on the airframe. We repeatedly asked the crew for damage reports, but none seemed serious. Not surprisingly, the small-arms fire from the ground was ineffective. On we flew toward the ever-growing angry clouds to our front. The bucking and jinking continued. The ground fire diminished about thirty minutes into the mission. There was still some ground fire coming up and we saw missiles fly overhead, including what appeared to Strelas, but they flew over the top of us off into the distance. None hit any of our aircraft. So much for that vaunted Russian battlefield technology.

While we could not see them nor hear them on the radio, as radio silence had been ordered on the initial flight northward until we neared the LZ, we knew that behind us was the second large formation, made up of the VNAF helicopters, from UH-1s to CH-47s, that would proceed into the LZ once the area was secured by the ARVN marines and soldiers we had inserted. They were depending upon us to succeed, or their mission would be lost.

The ground force that would follow the air assault was a massive ARVN armored force that was already lining up along Highway 1 just forward of our PZ. I was very impressed when I saw it.

The pre-assault and attack route bombardment we were witnessing from B-52s, naval gunfire, and close air-support aircraft, as it was later reported during our mission debrief, exceeded in volume, intensity, and destruction the single day bombardment before D-Day on June 6, 1944!

US Army helicopters lead an air assault north along HWY 1 in I
Corps during the initial counterattack on Quang Tri. Note the
Russian-built PTS-76 in the upper left, to the right of the small tree in
this photo. It was a bad day for that NVA PT-76 crew. Note also the
utter destruction of the countryside in this area as the result of the
NVA advance south in the spring of 1972. Just months before this
was a green and vibrant area. This is the only photo of that mission.

As we continued to fly north, we observed an even larger gray-
black seething wall of dust, debris, and smoke to our front. It was
so intense and roiling that it contained intense cloud-to-cloud
lightning within it. The rumbling sounds grew louder in our helmet
headsets. Now it had a strange screeching sound as well. It was an
intimidating site, into which we were flying! But as we progressed
north, flying nap of the earth just west of Highway 1, the wall just
moved forward ahead of us. As we continued flying over the impact
area of the bombardment, we noticed the massive destruction of
military equipment and units under us. While not all the villages and

buildings were destroyed or even hit, the Russian military vehicles and equipment we could identify were, for the most part, destroyed. There were NVA soldiers stumbling about here and there, but very few. In one case a lone surviving Russian PT-76 turned toward us as we approached at better than ninety knots and raised his main gun, a 76-mm weapon, and fired as if the gunner hoped to hit a helicopter in flight with a fantastically lucky shot. He did not, but it was the last thing the crew of this thin-skinned, light-armored vehicle ever did. Within seconds, at least three AH-1G Cobras engaged the vehicle with rockets and 20-mm cannon fire. It quickly erupted in a ball of fire as we flew past it.

On north we flew into the mist and now thinning debris cloud as the naval gunfire and Arc Lights moved well north ahead of us and coastal winds dispersed the debris cloud and smoke to our front. The noise remained so loud from the bombardment, concussions, and secondary explosions to our front that we could still hear them through the noise of the helicopters themselves. It was awesome to see and very frightening at the same time.

Occasionally we would see the odd NVA soldier stumbling in shock, both from the traumatic experience of being under the intense bombardment and shelling, as well as from our sudden appearance overhead. We did not engage these poor souls unless they attempted to fire at us. Few did. Most just stood and looked up in shock or amazement. Several had the presence to drop their weapons and raise their hands in the air.

On we flew toward the LZ just south of the city of Quang Tri. Suddenly we were over the original highway of death area on Highway 1 and the stench was so strong we gagged, even this many weeks after these hapless residents of Quang Tri were murdered by the NVA. Below us were bodies strewn everywhere, destroyed vehicles of all kinds lay in piles and their possessions, from furniture to suitcases and bundles, lay all about in scattered tatters. What a horrific sight. What a sad commentary on the state of things in the bipolar world of that time and upon the nature of those who were trying to seize this land out of greed, political advantage, and strategic ambitions.

We approached the LZ as one tight formation of helicopters. Unlike some formation flights, we had to maintain a nearly identical altitude due to the low height above the ground at which we were flying. So, the formation around us looked like a flat, tight layer of aircraft approaching as one large machine coming down from the sky. Ground fire picked up for a short period of time as we descended to land. Our door gunners poured fire on any target that seemed to threaten us. Given the tight formation and the number of M-60 door mounted guns firing on any NVA soldier who took aim at our aircraft, any overt offensive movement was the immediate recipient of a hail of bullets. Add to this the effect of the chin-mounted miniguns, 40-mm Chunkers, and the rockets coming from the Cobras, and the effect was devastating on the already confused and disoriented enemy. The result was that the enemy soldiers on the ground stopped engaging us and raised their arms in surrender, though some just took cover. We approached a scene of utter devastation. I had landed near this very site months before and I could barely recognize where we were. I thought that perhaps there had been an Arc Light here, but we were told that would not be the case as the area would be far too dangerous to land in after such a strike. Instead, this area was prepared by US Air Force fighters with precision strikes on any enemy position identified. What we later learned during our mission debrief was that the NVA and Russians had shelled Quang Tri and its surrounding communities to near total destruction during their invasion.

Enemy fire was intense as we approached the LZ. There were enemy soldiers on the LZ and off to the north firing at us with a variety of weapons from AK-47s to .51-cal Russian machine guns. But the fire was strangely ineffective and quite uncoordinated. Clearly these were shelled shocked troops without effective leadership at this point and they were firing at us because that was what they were trained to do. But their fire was much more frightening than actually effective. The "pucker factor" was still quite high. A few Strela missiles were loosed in our direction, but they flew overhead and off into the distance with no effect. A few mortar and artillery rounds fell before we landed but none as we approached the LZ.

As if on some magical puppet strings, the formation of fifty UH-1H helicopters that made up the American only first formation to land raised their noses in unison and slowed to landing speed as one great body. As we settled to the uneven ground some of the Vietnamese troops began to jump out even before we touched down. These were experienced air assault soldiers, and they knew that the arriving helicopters were the targets that would draw the most enemy fire, if there was any. The ground we landed upon was turned over like a newly plowed field but without the correctness and neatness of a farm field. As we settled to the ground a very small amount of dust rose up around us and then dissipated almost instantly. As it cleared, a lone NVA soldier rose from a hole in the ground to our right front, about ten yards from us, and raised his AK-47 to fire directly into our helicopter. But almost the very instant he raised that assault rifle and aimed at us, multiple door gunners opened fire on him, and he disappeared in a sudden burst of red mist and was gone. Not a single enemy shot was fired into the LZ at us while on the ground during this first insertion of the assault. All of the enemy fire passed harmlessly overheard. It was surreal.

We were on the ground but mere seconds. While we wanted to get the troops off the aircraft and takeoff as soon as we could, most of these troops had jumped from the aircraft before we even touched down in the LZ. Helicopters are always targets, big targets you do not want to be in or near if they get hit. We also wanted to get the hell out and away as fast as we could move because we wanted to clear the LZ as fast as possible. The result was that the order to again pull pitch and depart the LZ came within seconds, and we climbed up, again as one tight formation, and out of the LZ in a climbing turn to evade as much enemy fire as possible. With the aircraft now much lower on fuel and not transporting the weight of the eight or nine troops, the birds seemed far more eager and agile as they leaped up and around for the low-level but fast trip home.

The problem we then faced on the return trip was, of course, that we had to fly back over, though briefly, some of the same basic path we came in on for part of the flight. However, most of our route home took us south and then east over the water. The South China Sea was US Navy territory and was a far safer route home flying what we referred to as *feet-wet*. So, the only challenge was to get to the water. Apparently, the NVA were eager to see us go as well. They were already having a very, very bad day. None stuck their heads up to become targets below us as we flew away. The ineffective enemy fire overhead continued for the first few minutes and seemed to melt away.

Of course, as we rose from the LZ on our departure, we saw the approaching formations of VNAF aircraft in the distance to the south heading north toward the same LZ. We knew there were more flights of VNAF helicopters behind us, so we had to clear the area quickly. Part of the Cobra force stayed behind to give the VNAF formation gun cover as they came in to drop their troop loads. As there was little opposition, they soon followed us feet-wet and south back to Da Nang. A quick head count from each unit showed we had lost no aircraft, unlike the US Marine air assault a few days before, when two aircraft were reported downed. None of our birds took any serious hits that day, and we had no mechanical issues to force any aircraft down. I was astonished to hear this. The whole operation was a surreal, strange experience for those of us who had been in country for a while. We had assumed a 25 percent aircraft loss rate from enemy fire and mechanical problems. The anti-aircraft fire suppression was far more effective than we expected. The Arc Lights had done their job of preparing the path before us on the flight into the LZ. And our aircraft mechanics had also done their job just as well. We owed the maintenance team our lives! Without their dedicated and skilled labors our aircraft did not fly. This day they proved their worth once again.

We returned to Marble Mountain to refuel and stand by to be called back into the fight if needed. We landed just as if it was any other day, flying any other combat assault mission in Vietnam. But it had been far from it, and we all knew that. It had been a textbook operation and opened the door for the South Vietnamese to retake Quang Tri. Over the next few days we flew resupply and assault missions in this same area as more and more ARVN forces were pushed north to exploit the successful air assault of July 11th and into the outskirts of the city of Quang Tri itself. The 48th flew several medivac missions in the following days. In one case, a Blue Star UH-1H successfully landed in an LZ near Quang Tri in what was referred to as a blizzard of enemy anti-aircraft fire and successfully rescued fifteen badly wounded South Vietnamese Rangers. Unfortunately, this also resulted in the final combat casualty for the 48th AHC when the aircraft's door gunner was hit and killed. The South Vietnamese troops finally retook the entire city more than a month later after a long and bloody fight. But the ARVN forces were never able to return any farther north. They never retook their old defensive positions on the original DMZ.

This air mobile operation was a tribute to the tenacity, skill, and technology of the Americans as well as to the skill and drive of the ARVN soldiers, ARVN marines, and VNAF airmen that executed the majority of the mission. It seemed to us that if we could continue to provide the needed technology and air support to the Vietnamese, they could stand up and hold off the NVA, even with the Russians supporting them. But it was just as clear that if we did not continue to support our Vietnamese allies, they could not withstand a determined future offensive by the NVA and Russians.

We had accomplished something during this fifty-ship air assault over a modern enemy armored force that, as far as we knew, had never been done before. We had done it with success and precision and had sustained no casualties. At least not until the psychological one hit all of us. Upon the start of the mission debrief we were informed that no one was to write home about the mission. There would be no awards, no decorations, and no recognition of any kind for participating in or for outstanding performance in the any phase of the mission. The stated reasoning for this had two parts. First, this was officially an all-South Vietnamese military show and, second, no American ground or US Army units of any kind were officially involved in the mission. The only US involvement was supporting Naval gun fire and Air Force precision munitions support and, of course, the Marine helicopter unit, who got all the glory and official recognition of their skill and valor. We were simply ghosts who had appeared and then disappeared from the battlefield.

We had been hearing this for several months when coming back from operations. The big lie in Washington, DC leading up to the 1972 elections was that the US Army combat units were no longer involved in the war in Vietnam. After Dusty's loss, this did not do much for my morale from that point on during the rest of my tour. At the debrief, one clearly more aggravated and angered pilot than I blurted out to the dude in the suit from the Embassy who was briefing us on our "official non-participation."

"What the hell would you have said if we had lost an aircraft and crew?"

The suit responded, "That didn't happen, as we expected, so it is not an issue."

Not an issue my ass!

Lesson: No good deed goes unpunished!

Then we got into the meat of the debrief with the US Air Force ALOs and a Marine gunny sergeant from an Air Naval Gunfire Liaison Company (ANGLICO) unit on the ground. Those who witnessed the takeoff and flight of the fifty-ship formation during the mission had been astonished at what they saw. They had never seen Hueys fly in such tight, low formation and move over the ground as if it were one giant machine. They described our flight as if we had flowed over the ground and through the ground fire unaffected by its intensity. Intensity? This was news to us. It certainly did not seem as effective or intense as we usually see on missions north into the main combat zone. But then these were ground troops whose perspective is a bit different than ours, to say the least. Yet, we pilots and crews had to wonder that day: *What did they see that we did not?* I suspect it was a combination of two things. We were so intent on our flying, navigating, and keeping the formation that we may not have realized what was happening around us. Second, most of the enemy ground fire rose behind us and was ineffective. We were so low and so fast, the enemy gunners could not track us. No doubt they, themselves, learned a new lesson that day.

The post mission effects on our conduct of operations going forward were quite significant. Our units were soon moved out of Marble Mountain Army Airfield. The 48th was immediately stood down and F/8 Cavalry, the Blue Ghost moved over to Da Nang Main Air Force base.

We no longer flew large formation missions. We now limited our operations mainly to unit-level recon, rescue, and fire-support missions when needed by any US advisors or downed aircrews. There were a few exceptions during the remainder of 1972 but generally we also no longer took the chances we once did unless it was for an American in danger. The message from the Embassy had been received loud and clear. We were leaving South Vietnam and the American public thought we had already left. Of course, our friends and family knew better. As my dad told me "Son, your job is now to survive this assignment, do your job, and get home safely." He was blunt about our status in country at this point.

It is interesting to note that, according to the *Green Book*, which is the official US Army history publication, all US Army combat operations in South Vietnam were terminated after June 1, 1972, and only unit security and withdrawal operations were undertaken.

This was not true and has never been corrected. The result is that many records for US Army soldiers who served in South Vietnam during this period have never been corrected and their service not correctly recognized. Even the personnel records, called the *201 file*, for nearly all US Army soldiers in country during this period were never returned home and were never found. This has plagued many deserving Vietnam veterans who have had benefits denied by the Veteran's Administration as a result. That is more than just a shame and the cause of unnecessary suffering in some cases, it reflects very badly upon the Department of Defense, the VA, the Nixon Administration, and upon Congress, who refused to address this failing of our government. Lt. General Jack Hennessy told me many years later, when I was trying to get some of my own records corrected to reflect my assignment to F/8 Cavalry as their last Blues platoon leader (August–December 1972) and was denied by the Board of Military Record Corrections, "John," he said, "this will never be corrected until the last senior official of the US government from that time is dead."

Following this mission, I turned my attention to the task of standing down the 48th AHC as keystone officer. Essentially my task was to account for all the unit's property and assets and arrange for their turn-in for transfer back to the United States or local disposal. The 48th AHC had also been in country for many, many years. While it had most of the items it was authorized under its table of organization and equipment (TOE), it did not have everything. Plus, much of what we had as unit equipment, from tents to vehicles, was only marginally serviceable, except for the aircraft, and was suitable for disposal. Most everything else was to be transferred to the VNAF. Having done this before made the job a little easier for me. I knew what to do and how to do it. Of course, even with most of the US Army command structure at Long Binh and in Saigon already stood down, there were still those facilities people who wanted everything in full spit and polish for turn in, particularly our hootches. So, once again, we *turned-to* with all available hands to remedy deficiencies in our buildings and facilities at Marble Mountain for turn in. Most in the unit understood the utter waste of time involved but we played the game as required and got through the process.

In the 48th AHC we also had a lot of gear that was not on the books. So, this time I took early steps to parse the weapons and gear into *valuable, useful,* and *useless* piles and began distributing it to worthy and willing recipients around Marble Mountain. This time I had to dispose of, once again, the M114 armored personnel carrier with a battery operated 5.56-mm mini gun mounted on top that had been used for perimeter defense. It was on no one's books, not even the mini gun. Obviously this valuable and deadly minigun had been recovered somewhere back in time from a combat-downed and written-off Cobra and never put on any unit books. It was quite an effective perimeter defense weapon that was highly prized for its ingenuity and effectiveness. Such a system for ground and surface defense is common today but back in 1972 this was radical innovation! All we could do was strip the M114 of everything, including the minigun, render the vehicle unusable, and leave it in place on the perimeter of the airfield. The minigun went to F/8 Cavalry, the Blue Ghosts.

As we neared the estimated stand-down date, I was officially informed that the unit was, indeed, to be transferred to the American forces in Germany. Oh boy, we thought, Germany here we come. Then we found out that only the unit books, records, and flag were going to Germany. Everything else, save the aircraft, would transfer to the Vietnamese and our personnel would DROS to the United States. The only one who as going to Germany for the official transfer of the unit was the company commander, Captain Wilson.

We ceased our last combat operations in mid-July. Unfortunately, because we flew missions supporting the South Vietnamese forces fighting to retake Quang Tri right up until the aircraft were turned in, we did suffer one more casualty. One July 13, 1972, Specialist (Fourth Class) Michael A Hill, was hit by ground fire while serving as an aircraft crew chief. He was hit by friendly fire from South Vietnamese troops as his aircraft conducted the rescue of the crew of another downed US aircraft in the midst of the fighting around Quang Tri City. He succumbed to his wounds that day. At the time, his death was listed by DOD as a "non-battle casualty." Really? At least he was posthumously honored with a promotion to Sergeant.

Orders for executing unit TOE equipment transfers began arriving along with individual transfers for the unit members, and most of the unit members began to rotate out immediately. When my orders came, I was not happy. I was to ensure that all assets were transferred, all personnel signed out and routed to their new assignment, unit records closed out and mailed to the Department of the Army (DA), and then I was to report to the commander of F Troop, 8th Air Cavalry for duty as the unit's new Blues platoon leader.

Well crap! I closed out the unit and signed the last official 48th AHC unit morning report in RVN as the last member of the unit in country on Aug 10, 1972, and, as acting CO for one day in RVN, put the unit personnel and other administrative records in the mail back to the United States. Captain Wilson carried the other necessary unit command and organizational documents needed for transfer of the unit's flag to Germany. I mailed the last pouch of documents and records back the US at the Da Nang Main AFB post office on 12 August 1972.

I have read very little about this period in any books or histories, or about the brave contribution made by the Blue Stars during the Easter Offensive of 1972. The TOWs were only a small part of that story. Yet all I ever read about now is the Marines and how they "won" the battle of the Easter Offensive at Dong Ha and south of Quang Tri. Well, I can tell you that the only fighting Marines were the Marine advisors *we* pulled out from the DMZ area of operations. After that, only ANGLICOs and Marine Jolly Greens

(CH-53 helicopters) to support their carrier-based aircraft were still in the fight. This was a US Army aviation and US Air Force fight that helped South Vietnam take back Quang Tri. In that period from April to August of 1972 we kicked some serious ass. Yet there were no individual citations, no unit citations, no official recognition, and no written history of all of this in the Army Green Book even today. To this day, officially, no US Army combat units were engaged in combat operations during this period.

When I came home, I read about the TOW missile system in the *Washington Post* in January 1973. So much for security!

CHAPTER EIGHT
THE BLUE GHOST

THE DAY AFTER I signed the last morning report for the 48th AHC,
I reported to Major John Kennedy, troop commander of F Troop, 8th
Cavalry. I originally signed in as the lift platoon leader on 11 August
1972. This assignment was changed on 20 August 1972 to fill the vacant
Platoon Leader position of the Aero Rifle Platoon within F/8 Cavalry.
I was one of the very few from the 48th AHC who did not get sent
home with the unit stand down. I asked Major Kennedy if he knew
why, and he pointed to my Ranger Tab. "Enough said," I replied. I
already knew from my coordinating with the personnel pukes at brigade
headquarters in Saigon during the stand down of the 48th AHC that
few new personnel were coming into country, and no new ground
combat officers were arriving. I was the only captain-Ranger-aviator
available in country. The vacant platoon leader position in F/8 Cavalry
required an Infantry officer who was Ranger qualified. That I was also a
pilot was a bonus because I could also lead the lift platoon. Those with
experience and specific skills were to be kept in country. So, I was the
"one" in this case. Well, I would do my best as a Ranger and an aviator.

I now knew a small bit of how those brave soldiers and sailors
must have felt on Bataan and Corregidor in the Philippines in the
winter and spring of 1942. In high school my father gave me a book
by W.L. White entitled *They Were Expendable* published in 1942.

It was a fascinating look at the very real but challenging concepts of duty, honor, and country. This story was later made into a movie starring John Wayne. While none of us were, by any means, like the fictional main character of that movie, those of us left in Vietnam during a time when our presence as combat soldiers was not officially recognized understood the concept of being expendable in a context few will ever have to experience.

It was a time of very mixed emotions and uncertainty for me. Not being able to return home, of course, was, at least initially, foremost in my mind. But arriving in F Troop, 8th Cavalry with Dusty gone was very saddening to me. Somehow the intensity of activity within the 48th AHC after his loss in June had dulled the sense of loss as June turned to July. Now, being in F Troop, where he had tried to get me assigned since the spring, without him there to greet me, struck me quite hard. I missed him, and I missed our sessions over beers, our jokes retold on the flightline, and our laughs about his Superbird and how he was going to enjoy that car. I missed his ever-present jovial mood and his talk of the future. What a loss to his wife Margaret and his baby daughter, as well as his many friends, the Blue Ghost family, and to the people of the United States.

Dusty was a gentleman, a soldier, and a patriot. We are the poorer for his loss, as well as the loss of others from Flight Class 71-30 and all of our cousins, fathers, brothers, sons, and friends who died in RVN trying to do the right thing. This is a debt we can never fully repay but must always honor. While it may sound corny to some, it was with these emotions that I embarked upon my final chapter of combat in the Republic of South Vietnam. I felt that I was one warrior who had to do my best to keep up the honor of his unit and to help make the unit safe and successful, whatever the future held for us.

I also saw two messages for me upon reporting into the storied Blue Ghost Air Cavalry Troop. First, having a Ranger Tab and seven months experience in country was not a combination that yielded a ticket home at this point in the war. Second, this whole shebang was going to shut down soon, so whatever I needed to do, I needed to do it carefully and safely. My task, as Dad had frequently pointed out, was to do my job, survive, and get home in one piece. With the very small number of actual US combat forces left in country and the scale of NVA and Russian operations at this point, staying safe just might prove to be hard to do.

Major Kennedy, who was a decent, very competent commander with a lot of experience, told me shortly after my arrival in the unit that Dusty had recommended me to him as the best guy for the Blues platoon in the entire brigade. Then he said nothing for about two to three minutes, and I simply said, "Yeah, Dusty told me that he did that . . ." There was nothing else to say. I sure wished Dusty were there then. I would have given him a piece of my mind for roping me into this, but then I would have told him that if we got to serve together, then it was okay by me.

So, I settled into new digs with F Troop. I met my new platoon members, both the aircrews and the blues—our ground infantry troops. My platoon was referred to as the "Blues." And now for the first time in RVN I had my own personal call sign: "Blue." The use of colors in the US Army Cavalry to signify function has a long history. The Cavalry has always seen itself as something different and apart from the rest of the Army. Cavalry operations in the United States Army began, in an organized way, in the Civil War and matured as a component during the Indian Wars in the latter half of the nineteenth century. The mission of the cavalry operations in Vietnam in 1972 was to act as the eyes and ears of the maneuver units or units like the 1st Aviation Brigade. Our mission was to find the enemy, fix his location, and facilitate the interdiction by larger ground and air forces. However, by this time in the conflict, our troop mission had evolved into a far more significant role in support of the overall US strategy in the war. Our role was shifting to that of security and interdiction of Soviet-supported NVA operations targeting both US and South Vietnamese defensive operations. The strategic objective was to hold ground and blunt NVA offensive movements to create negotiating space for the US in Paris. As each day passed after August of 1972, there were fewer and fewer US combat and force projection resources in country. The clock was ticking down.

The troop was composed of a headquarters, an airmobile infantry platoon composed of three squads of infantry, nine UH-1H Huey helicopters, and a leadership team, at this time in Vietnam all called the "Blues." The troop also had a reconnaissance platoon composed of small, armed OH-6 observation helicopters, referred to as the "White." Then there was the troop's real firepower, the guns platoon composed of AH-1G Cobras, armed with 20-mm and 5.56-mm Gatling guns, 40-mm automatic grenade launchers (Chunkers) and 2.5-inch folding fin rockets. This platoon was referred to as the "Red." In addition, the troop had large aircraft and vehicle maintenance teams and its own logistics capability that provided everything from chow to communications to supplies and ammunition. The troop was organized to operate independently for extended periods, as was the case for all cavalry units. In combat power, operating footprint, and in sustainment capability the troop was more like a mini-battalion than a traditional aviation company. F/8th Cavalry had been in country since 1967 and would be the last to leave South Vietnam in April of 1973.

As I got settled into the troop and my new assignment, I began to use my own call sign within the troop: "Blue Ghost Blue." We started planning the next few days' missions from the flight ops boards and began an inventory of equipment and supplies. The platoon sergeant was a squared-away fellow and things seemed to move as they should. The infantry platoon members did few actual air mobile missions. Their primary job was perimeter and site security for the troop and doing occasional bomb damage assessments (BDAs) on engaged targets. The Blues also conducted counter operations patrols to prevent enemy elements from penetrating our base or mounting a successful attack. The one other task that they took to with eagerness was ground security out in the field whenever we or another unit had a bird and crew down and they needed help to protect and recover them. These guys were good and mission focused. Unfortunately, the American troopers that made up my infantry platoon were pulled less than thirty days later. In September of 1972, the president stated that there were no US combat troops remaining in South Vietnam. Within twenty-four hours, our infantrymen were pulled from the troop and sent home.

In October of 1972, we were given a platoon of Chinese Mung mercenaries to serve as our infantry element. They also served primarily as our perimeter security and counterattack force in the coming months. While we still mounted security and extraction missions out in the field when needed, this platoon carried out very few counter-action patrols outside the perimeter wire surrounding our small base. There were two reasons for this. First, they were not equipped or trained for this and, second, other units were then assigned this mission. Besides, I was a good foot taller and half again wider than all of them and I was reluctant to take them out of the wire myself unless it was mission essential, as I would always be the primary target of any enemy sniper or ambush force, and we were already short of pilots.

One of the onerous tasks that fell upon all of us on a regular, if erratic basis in the Blue Ghost, as with my previous units, was the piss test. Because there had been many cases of abuse of illegal substances in RVN over the years, along with the fact that you could not rely upon or trust a buddy in combat that was high, there was a rigorous, unannounced spot-testing program that required every soldier to pee in a cup or bottle in front of a senior unit officer. We all understood the reasons for the testing, and we all agreed that clean and sober soldiers were less dangerous to themselves or others. The onerous part was that, as a captain in the unit I sometimes had the testing supervision duty myself. This meant that I had to sit or stand and watch trooper after trooper pee in front of me. Yuck!

My first Blue Ghost missions were from Marble Mountain Army Airfield, before our move to Da Nang Air Force Base. These first missions were simple visual reconnaissance (V/R) missions and some hunter-killer missions to the north and west of Da Nang as security operations. I, of course, knew the AO well, having been flying in and around this region of I Corps for more than seven months at this point. I was given a check ride in the unit's UH-1H helicopters and designated as an aircraft commander or AC. It took only a short period of time to get used to using my new call sign, usually abbreviated as simply "Blue." Within a few days, however, we were told to pack up and prepare to move to what we called Da Nang Main. Marble Mountain Airfield would be shut down and turned over to the ARVN. Marble Mountain airfield had originally been built by the Marines in the mid-1960s. It served as a forward operating base for a variety of Marine helicopter squadrons, including the CH-46 unit that my cousin George Dewey had served in when he was killed. Moving the unit to Da Nang AFB was a big deal, indeed. This was the land of a very big PX, a real restaurant on base, larger, air-conditioned quarters, electricity that was on all of the time, and toilets that actually flushed! Wow, we were going to be living high on the hog for a change.

The flight line we moved to over the next few days was large and well equipped, with heavy revetments and concrete hangars. Our quarters were small ranch-style homes. This base had been a regular Air Force base for a while and these quarters were nice. We had regular bedrooms, kitchens, living rooms, and bathrooms. What luxury! The rooms were not full of sand, there were no bugs to speak of, and the refrigerator not only worked, but it probably could hold six or eight cases of beer. Such were our metrics of luxury at the time.

Moving bases did not mean a stand down of operations or any reduction in intensity. Indeed, the pace was fast, and we flew a lot of missions. Our blues, until they left us, joined in supporting the overall security force for the base and we conducted only a few actual ground reconnaissance operations. Mainly we conducted aerial enemy interdiction missions to protect Da Nang from direct armored attack. Scattered small-unit NVA armored operations continued around I

Corps and the fighting, while of a lesser intensity than earlier in the summer, was still often challenging and dangerous across our AO.

It was around this time that we learned that several ground TOW systems, mounted on quarter-ton jeeps were now in country and several were with ARVN forces in the area. As these were a very valuable and still classified weapon systems, we were told to be prepared to retrieve or destroy any that might be in danger of capture. We were told that the Russians had placed a bounty on them. We all assumed that this meant destroy more than retrieve because if one was in danger of capture, we had little capability to land and fight off a major attacking force to recover a system. So, this may not be good news for the TOW system's crew.

One night we nearly lost one of the mounted TOW systems on Firebase Lion, near Hill 55, southwest of Da Nang. Its loss could have been a real serious threat to our forces and a major compromise of sensitive technology. The presence of Russian advisors with the NVA was common knowledge, by this time. ARVN and American aviation units had already killed and retrieved the bodies of several. We knew that the Russians badly wanted one of these systems and would mount an all-out effort to capture one. They did that one night against an ARVN fortified position, Firebase Lion. This small base was a critical defense position and firebase for the security of the sprawling US air base at Da Nang. Its loss would create a real threat to the big base because it overwatched approaches to Da Nang from the south. Its elevated position made it ideal for anti-armor defense. As a result, mounted TOW was placed there to help defeat any armor threat coming out of the hills to the southwest that might threaten Da Nang. Given the sometimes-poor operational security within the ARVN forces, it was no surprise that the NVA learned of this weapon system and they went after it.

The NVA mounted a major assault one night on Hill 55 and Firebase Lion. They were able to overrun it before a relief force of ARVN could get there. The ARVN did successfully surround the NVA occupied position, but not before the TOW was lost to enemy control.

An emergency call went out from I Corps headquarters to destroy everything on the position as fast as possible to prevent the Russians from removing the TOW to the mountain safe havens the NVA controlled to the west. We launched the nighthawk team and an additional heavy gun team from Da Nang AFB and flew the relatively short distance to Hill 55. When we got there, we observed a serious firefight underway on the sides of the hill and were immediately greeted with lots of small arms anti-aircraft fire coming up at us. It was clear the bad guys had control of the top of the hill, where the TOW had been located. We quickly rolled in hot and blasted everything on the top of the hill. As soon as we had some good secondary explosions going off on the hilltop and some large fires burning, we backed off to allow a flight of Navy jets to hit the hilltop with some heavy ordnance. This took only a matter of minutes. Once the explosions died down a bit, we returned to the hilltop and flew over. The top of the hill had seemingly been dropped a good ten feet. There was debris everywhere and no return anti-aircraft fire from the hilltop, though there was still a fight underway along the slopes of the hill and down at the base of the hill on the north side where some of the ARVN had initially retreated. They now smelled blood and must have wanted revenge because they were clearly trying to fight their way back up into the main defense position on the hilltop, or what was left of it.

We felt the hilltop was relatively secure and the orders were to put troops on the hill to locate the TOW. We then landed an assault team comprised of our blues from two slicks. My blues lieutenant reported that there were dead NVA everywhere and that the very top of the hill was secure. Then another bird from Da Nang AFB arrived and landed a tech team to look for the TOW. They not only found it and destroyed it, but they reported over the net that there were what they believed to be two dead in Russian military uniforms among the debris of the TOW. They said that it seemed to them that the Russians were trying to dismantle the TOW because there were tools and satchels lying among the debris. They were suddenly told to switch frequencies and go *green*, meaning switch to a secure radio. That was the last we heard from them. We recovered our blues as ARVN soldiers returned to the top of the hill to reoccupy what was left of the position. At debrief, we were told that word had come down that we could not discuss what we had heard or what we had done that night because the TOW system was classified.

After about a week, I found out that I would be eligible for a second one-week R&R leave because of my rotation through three units so far. I asked for a one week leave stateside the first week of September, as Karen was expected to deliver then. To my surprise, and directly as the result of Major Kennedy calling in a favor, I got it. I had three weeks to get everything set up. Arranging a ticket home on Pan Am was the first problem. It seems that most non-military Americans and other Europeans in Saigon and the other big cities had seen the handwriting on the wall and wanted to get out of Vietnam, so seats were a premium on outbound flights. The personnel folks then gave me an R&R chit that gave me a priority on seats, so I was able to land a ticket and seat on a flight out of Da Nang, to Saigon. The wait for that flight seemed liked months, not weeks. I was hoping that I could get back to DC before the birth of our first child, but I knew it was very unlikely that I would have such luck. I flew only a few missions that last week before my departure on leave because Major Kennedy always seemed to have something for me to do.

When the time came to leave, I was nearly incoherent, I was told later. All I wanted to do was get on that flight and get the fuck out of Dodge and get home for a long week of leave. I did not even think about coming back, which seemed remote and irrelevant to me at that time. Yes, I had a round trip ticket, back on Pan AM through Saigon, but somehow that did not seem to matter.

Once on the plane out of Saigon, I seemed to get home very quickly, and I honestly cannot recall much of the trip. I think I slept the entire time. I did not realize just how tired I was. I got home to Dulles International, and Karen picked me up. She was huge! She looked like she was going to pop any second. We got back to our small apartment and we took a nap. I was still tired, and she was tired from being very pregnant and from anticipating my return. Asleep with Karen in my own bed was amazing. We awoke sometime later and made lunch or dinner or breakfast, I do not remember what time it was there, in Vietnam or anywhere. I was home, hungry, and with Karen and we were about to have a baby! Then Karen told me that she felt funny and was having contractions. We tried to relax, of course I had been gone the entire time of her pregnancy, and I had no real idea of what she had been through or was feeling. I did know about childbirth, the delivery process, and what the clinical situation was, after all I had delivered my share of babies as a fireman and paramedic during college. But this was very different. This was *our* child and I had missed almost the entire pregnancy—but I was home now and would be there for the delivery . . . or so I thought.

Karen soon went into serious labor, and we were off to the hospital in suburban Maryland where Karen's doctor would meet her. We got her checked into the maternity ward and I was immediately relegated to a waiting room. No ifs, ands, or buts. That was where I was to stay—hospital policy. But, but, but . . . like they said, no buts! So, she was on her own and I was stuck in waiting room—damn it to hell! Many hours later, out came a nurse to tell me everything was fine, not to worry, and just relax. Maybe, she said, I should just go home, and they would call me. I asked how long this might take and she said it was going to be a while so I should just go home and relax. I ended up going over to the nearby home of another college classmate and close friends, Hank and Suzanne Pramov, to catch a nap since my body clock was still out of sync, and I was stressed over the impending birth of my first child. I slept there for a short while and then went back to the hospital to continue the vigil.

Late on September 4, 1972, Lynn Kelly Hoffman was born,

and the doctor brought her out to me. He looked at me, then at Kelly, and said flatly: "Well, boy, there is no denying that this is your child!" As if I thought something else? I was, of course, elated, thrilled, amazed, and all those things that new fathers are. I was not, however, at all clued into what Karen had been through after almost a full day of labor. When I finally got to see her, she was comfortable and full of a new mother's joy, holding Kelly, but she was exhausted. I was wasted emotionally and as physically as she was. This new mother and father stuff was tough!

Holding my first child, Kelly, in September 1972 just before I had to return to Vietnam. That was a difficult departure from my family and a tough flight back to Saigon.

Two days later, we were back at our apartment and suddenly there was much to do. I needed to get to work on the list of things that Karen needed my help with. Plus, we had family and friends coming in to visit. It was a hectic but joyous time for the next week. Then it began to sink in. I had to go back to Vietnam! Given Kelly's arrival, I decided to check in with the Red Cross to see if I could get an extension of my leave. Miraculously, they arranged a one-week extension. However, I did learn that I now belonged to some unit at Fort Bragg, North Carolina (what the heck?) and they required me to go back to F Troop in Vietnam when that week was up.

Those last few days at home were tough on all of us. It was nearly impossible to get up and leave at that point, but duty called. That flight back to Vietnam was difficult, to say the least. The flight to Hawaii was crowded but uneventful. The flight from Hawaii to Saigon was utterly empty. I had most of the economy class section to myself, until one of the stewardesses invited me to come up to first class. There I found only a few other military officers and other some government officials. It was probably easier for the crew to look after and feed the few of us in one section of the plane. It was a long and very quiet flight. Few of the passengers had much to say. We landed in Saigon around midday, and I caught a C-130 hop back to DaNang AFB.

Upon arrival, I reported into the unit and Major Kennedy seemed shocked when I walked into his office. I asked him why and he said that he had never expected me to return. He assumed that I would work out an arrangement to stay home. I asked him how I might have done that, and he had no answer. He also knew nothing about any assignments or transfers to units at Fort Bragg.

So here I was, back in country again. I was quickly back in the saddle with F Troop and flying missions as the air mission commander (AMC), to the southwest of Da Nang looking for and engaging enemy that might threaten the base. We were on call nearly twenty-four hours a day, seven days a week and often sleeping in the aircraft. About ten days after I returned and was back out on missions, we received a request to fly an Air Force radar system component out to the *Kitty Hawk* for repair in their avionics shop. I was given the mission and we loaded the faulty radar part and took off for the carrier, then located about 100 miles offshore. The flight out took about an hour and a half of quiet, peaceful flying tuned into the AFVN playing Elvis songs. We landed and the Navy deck crew immediately secured the aircraft and put wheels under it to move it below deck, as we were to wait for the part to be repaired and then fly it back to Da Nang main. My crew was taken below. My peter pilot (a CW1) went to the area of the ship where warrant officers live, and the enlisted crewman made their way to the enlisted mess.

I was directed to PriFly, up on the superstructure of the carrier to report to the air boss. I was hoping that he was not the same air boss from February . . . thank goodness he was not. He looked at me and said, "Captain, you smell bad and look like shit!" I apologized and pointed out that I had been in the same flight uniform for a week and had not been able to get a shower in several days due to the mission load we had been flying. He told me to follow a crewman who would show me to a shower and have my flight suit cleaned. Then I was to join him for dinner in the Wardroom. I had nothing else to do but wait, so I followed the crewman to an officer's stateroom a few decks down. It was so small that I could not bend over to take off my boots without hitting my head on the door and my butt on the bed frame. But I noted that the bed had clean sheets and a regular blanket. It was then that I noticed that the stateroom was air conditioned and quite cool. *Boy*, I thought, *these Navy types have it made.*

The crewman turned out to be a steward for the officer's mess. He returned to the stateroom for my flight suit, and he brought me a clean towel and soap. When he left, he also took my boots and socks and underwear. He told me to shower down the hall and then come back to the stateroom to wait for my clothes and dinner. He also told me that I could take a nap on the lower bunk because it was not occupied. I took my shower with hot water! Wow, it was nice on this ship. I went back to the stateroom, passing several other junior-grade officers in the passageway who looked at me as if I were some intruder. I just ignored the looks and went back into the small stateroom to catch some sleep. Lying there I had to wonder why this bunk was unassigned at this time. Had the previous occupant been transferred, promoted to a larger stateroom or . . . had he been a casualty of this conflict. It seemed like only a few minutes later that I was awakened by a knock on the stateroom door. I got up and opened the door to find the steward with my flight suit pressed, starched, and folded. On top of the flight suit was my OD underwear and socks, also pressed, starched, and folded. On top of those were my boots, all shined and bright. *Wow, these Navy types really do have it made*, I thought. Then I tried to put on the clothes.

Have you ever tried to break starch in your socks? Have you ever put on starched boxer shorts? I never had and will never, I hope, do so again. Worse, when I put on the starched Nomex flight suit, I could barely walk. I was like Gumby, trying to bend and walk. When I did walk, the starched pants made a sound like two combs rubbing together. It was embarrassing. I proceeded up to the Wardroom for dinner with the air boss and some of the Navy pilots on board. I found an ornate room with a large U-shaped table covered in green felt and a white tablecloth. On the table were real china place settings with real silverware. Talk about upscale—this was unlike any Army mess I ever ate in! Dinner was outstanding and the desert was ice cream, three flavors! We never saw ice cream in Da Nang.

After an excellent meal, I was told the radar was fixed and loaded in our helicopter. I asked about bringing the helicopter up onto the flight deck and I was told it was ready to go with my crew waiting for me. I went up on the deck and started to preflight. My copilot then told me the preflight was done and we needed to clear the deck ASAP. Just then the flight deck PA came to life and the air boss directed us to start our engine and prepare to depart as quickly as possible. We were soon in the air and on the way back to Da Nang main. A few bright stars were just becoming visible in the early evening nautical twilight and Otis Redding's "Sittin' on the Dock of the Bay" was on AFVN. Funny how you remember some things, like what song was playing at a certain time in your life.

As we leveled out for the flight back across the South China Sea to

Da Nang I asked the crew how they were treated by the Navy on the ship. They all said, nearly in unison, that their flight suits had been washed and that they had ice cream for dinner! It was not a bad afternoon for any of us. Certainly, it was not a typical afternoon in Da Nang.

Flying as the air mission commander in the left or aircraft commander's seat, I am coordinating an air strike on NVA armor positions in October 1972. This photo was taken by Richard

Blystone, then with the AP.

Note that I am wearing the full survival and blast protection kit while my copilot is not. We had trouble getting some pilots to wear all of the personal protection gear in those days. It was a practice not enforced then and it cost us many good pilots and crewmen.

About a week after I got back, a mission came down to relocate a portion of the troop to Chu Lai so we could run missions over southern Quang Nhai Province from the old Chu Lai airfield, about a one-hour flight south of Da Nang Main AFB. I was designated as one of two AMCs, for the mission. That airfield had been abandoned by US forces earlier in the year. Now it was simply a refuel and rearm point operated by the ARVN but had a small special forces detachment assigned there as well. We took two heavy gun teams, and a portion of the blues platoon down there and set up shop at the old Rosemary's Point Coast Guard Station. It turned out that there were some nice homes out on the point that were just like stateside beach houses, complete with driveways off a cul-de-sac, all overlooking the South China Sea from high on a bluff. There was a reasonable club of sorts run by the ARVN and some US special forces operating in the area that served decent food, and the fuel and weapons and ammo storage was secure. We set up shop in the beach houses and parked our aircraft in the driveways in front. We operated from here for the next two weeks, flying out over the southern half of the province, conducting interdiction operations against NVA forces and screening the areas south of Da Nang. There were several heavy engagements during this period, one of which changed my view of the media forever.

While out one day conducting air cavalry screening operations, we flew near a small village that was not on the map and that hadn't been there the week before. As we approached, the tops opened on several of the thatched hootches and out popped anti-aircraft weapons, several 14.7-mm machine guns, and a 57-mm anti-aircraft gun. They had us dead in their sights but with some some fancy, nap of the earth flying and some effective nails and Willy Pete, we shut down this trap fairly fast. These traps were becoming quite commonplace and usually meant that there was something significant for the NVA in the immediate area. When this engagement was over, there were just some smoking holes left. Upon our return to Chu Lai, we were greeted by a news team from a US network. After shutting down our aircraft, they approached with their film camera rolling and began to ask questions. This was very unusual, to say the least. Few news teams had the ability or authority to roam the area, but these guys apparently did.

We almost had our clocks cleaned that day in that anti-aircraft trap. These news guys had apparently seen the action while flying into Chu Lai on another bird. Their first question of me was, "How many babies do you think you just killed in that village?" I was a bit stunned. There was no village, there were no babies, and several of us had almost bought it. I wanted to take that camera and shove it right up the ass of that network nitwit, but I thought better of it. I simply said, "None. It was not a real village. It was an NVA anti-aircraft trap." I said nothing more and refused to talk to them any further.

It was about a week afterward that Richard (Dick) Blystone from the Associated Press office in Saigon (years later the CNN Bureau Chief in London) showed up at Chu Lai. Here was a newsman of another flavor. Dick turned out to be a straight shooter with a cool head. He had a French photojournalist with him, and they spent about a week with us and turned in several great feature stories on our team, our assignment, and some of our missions. Dick took a lot of great pictures during that week. He even gave a camera to two of our gun pilots, Mike Austin, and Dwane Shirley, to take pictures on missions.

Now how was it that the Associated Press could cover some of the combat missions that we were "officially" not flying? No one back at Da Nang had an answer. Some of the pictures that Dick took of us he later gave to me in Saigon when we went out for dinner one night.

He was quite fearless and flew with us on night missions and during some hairy daytime missions into the western mountain areas. On one flight, we were tasked to provide escort to two Vietnamese Air Force helicopters that were resupplying a surrounded ARVN firebase in the mountains. We linked up at a forward ARVN firebase on a hill southwest of Da Nang. There I briefed the pilot in command of the two VNAF slicks. They clearly thought it was too dangerous to fly into this firebase because there were reports of NVA still in that area. I explained to them that the firebase had reported that it was cut off and surrounded, under sporadic direct and indirect fire, and that is why we were needed to fly in the replacement soldiers, ammunition, food, and medical supplies. We discussed this mission for about an hour until I convinced the pilot that he could follow me into the firebase and that our guns would stay with him all the way in and back out. Finally, he agreed and off we went. During the flight we took some ground fire, but the return fire from the Cobras and fire from within the firebase itself suppressed it enough for us to get in and out again in one piece. Dick Blystone took an interesting photo of me discussing this mission with the VNAF pilot. He later gave me the original photo.

I explain the plan for a resupply mission into a hot LZ to a less than enthusiastic VNAF pilot. This is another photo taken by Richard Blystone.

The days flying out of Chu Lai were a welcome change of pace. The missions were a bit hairy, but the only aircraft we lost was my own. On one mission near the end of our time flying out of Chu Lai, we took on a small NVA armor force due south of Da Nang. The force consisted of several Russian PT-76 light tanks, a few trucks, and at least one towed 57-mm anti-aircraft gun. The PT-76 also had 14.5-mm heavy machine guns mounted on top. We took on the force with a heavy-gun team and called in an air strike. In the process of the engagement, our guns expended their rockets and 20-mm ammo and I remained overhead a bit longer to coordinate the Navy air strike we brought into the fight. Once the bad guys realized the guns had pulled off, they must have assumed what was coming. They also must have realized that the slick which was still nearby was coordinating the impending air strike. So, what did these gomers[16] do? Well, they all, at once and together, began shooting at that one remaining nearby American helicopter—us! Needless to say, the pucker factor was up as all the NVA anti-aircraft fire in southern Quang Nhai province, it seemed, suddenly began to come straight at us. The guns saw what was happening and rolled back around to fire with their miniguns and 40-mms to help draw off the fire. We managed to get the air strike on target and get headed back north. Of course, the intense anti-aircraft fire helped the Navy pilots acquire the target area and aided several NVA in meeting their maker, probably along with a few Russians. Usually when the NVA did something well, it was under the direct tutelage and intervention of their Russian advisors.

To describe the effect of being hit with anti-aircraft fires that include flak, think of all of my previous descriptions of the sound and feeling of things hitting my helicopter at the same time. Now add to that the fact that you are also impacted with both the shock wave of the exploding shell and the noise of the close-in explosion. This was not fun. Of course, if the anti-aircraft round was a direct hit on the helicopter, which was actually rare, you likely feel nothing, at least not for very long. But if it was a near miss, as was the case this day, it will still cause a lot of damage and you may or may not be able to stay in the air. I was in close proximity to several such flak explosions where we were hit with lots of shrapnel but could continue to fly the helicopter.

The effect of such rounds exploding is to both cause a serious shock wave to hit the helicopter, sometimes making it difficult to recover control of the aircraft, and then the impact of the many, many pieces of shrapnel thrown out by the exploding flak projectile. This is the main point of such weapons, as actually getting a direct hit on a helicopter is difficult unless you use a guided weapon, such as the heat seeking SA-7 Russian shoulder-fired missile. It is the shrapnel thrown out from an exploding shell that most often causes fatal damage to any aircraft.

Upon getting north of the target area, one of the guns calmly pointed out that there was smoke coming out the back of our aircraft. Just about that time the Master Caution light came on, followed by several warning light segments. One indicated that there might be a fire in the engine area. I knew we had just screwed the goose. It was time to land somewhere. However, all the area below us at that point was potentially controlled, or at least patrolled, by the bad guys. So that did not seem like a good option. There was no major fire visible as yet, but we were leaking fuel and the fuel gauge was dropping fast. We had a transmission warning light, a fuel pressure warning light, an engine warning light, and one or two others. But the rotors were in the green, there was no serious vibration, and torque was good. So, I elected to head straight north into Da Nang Main AFB which was only about ten minutes north of our position at that point in time. I declared an emergency and we got a clear shot at the left-hand north-south runway. As I approached the airfield from the south, one of the guns reported that we had fire visible in the engine area. The crew chief leaned out for a look and confirmed that we had a torch shooting out the engine exhaust. Not good! I made a running landing and told the crew to grab their gear and jump from the aircraft as soon as it was moving slow enough to get clear without getting hurt. I was afraid that the aircraft would be consumed in fire any second. I shut down the engine and killed the master switch as soon as we were sliding down the runway on the skids. The bird slowly rotated sideways and came to a stop and I rolled out the side of the aircraft onto the runway and scrambled to the grass along the side of the runway. The fire trucks were on scene by then and hit the aircraft with foam. Only then did I realize that the engine compartment was fully involved in fire. We all got out of that bird as fast and safely as we could. The landing was good, and no one was hurt. The engine fuel control, the transmission, and the fuel bladder were all hit. So much for this nearly new UH-1H. It was likely a total loss. I doubted the resources were available in country to rebuild it. It may have been sent to the States for rebuilding but I never found out. We were debriefed at the unit and then I picked up a new aircraft and we flew back to Chu Lai. Before we left, the CO informed us that no US aircraft were engaged in combat operations anywhere in I Corps today. Screwed again. No point in writing up the crew, once again!

We operated out of Chu Lai for another few days, then we were recalled back to Da Nang Main for a troop meeting in mid-October. When we got there, we learned that we were moving south to Saigon—all of us. Cool! We were all excited. Saigon was the Paris of the Orient, a city of lights, a city with a really big PX, and, most importantly, the home of the DROS bird back home!

"Where in Saigon?" someone asked. Then the balloon popped. Lassiter LZ was the answer. It was like someone had just farted a big one in the room. That answer stank.

Many of us knew that Lassiter LZ was at Bien Hoa, not Ton Son Nhut. Bien Hoa air base was closer to Long Binh, the former location of the US Headquarters in Vietnam. However, Long Binh had been shut down during the summer and abandoned. The US Air Force had by and large pulled out of Bien Hoa and consolidated on Ton Son Nhut Air Force Base. That meant that we would be the only Americans on Bien Hoa, save for a few US Air Force advisors and logisticians. Further, it was a long, very unsafe drive from Lassiter to the city of Saigon. So much for living it up in Saigon. Over the next few days we packed our gear and prepared the troops for the move. Our departure from the I Corps area would mean that there would only be one Air Cavalry troop left in that region. Many Americans in the Da Nang base area were not pleased that we were being pulled out. The Air Force personnel remaining at Da Nang Air Force Base were very concerned that 50 percent of the Army security force for the area was departing with a major NVA force, which included armored units, still in the hills to the west and north of the base. While true, they still had enormous combat capability and firepower in the Air Force, Navy, and Marine fighter units stationed nearby in Thailand and on carriers just offshore. When the day to depart Da Nang came, we packed our personal gear in our aircraft, took off, and formed up for the long flight south. The Air Force moved the rest of our unit equipment and personnel to Bien Hoa. As we flew south the automatic direction finder (ADF) was tuned to AFVN radio, and we heard the Animals singing "We Gotta Get Out Of This Place." This song had become the unofficial song of our cavalry troop, and years later became that for the Vietnam Helicopter Pilots Association (VHPA).

The move to Military Region 3 or III Corps, as it was also called, went smoothly. We settled into our new facilities with little problem. However, our accommodations left something to be desired. We were once again in huts of different sorts. We had jet-fuel shitters again, we had limited running water, and even more limited shower capability. No laundry, no PX, no o' club, little pavement, and lots of mud. We did have dry sleeping areas, we did have good bunkers, and we did have good wire. We were also inside the greater Bien Hoa Air Base perimeter, so NVA coming into our wire defenses was unlikely. But we also had a rather steady diet of incoming rockets and mortar fire, so sleep was difficult, day or night.

One evening not long after our arrival, I was dead tired and sound asleep when the crap began to fall upon us again. It seemed that I was getting more and more tired, as we all were. We had long, tiring days and nights of flying combat missions. We were getting only short naps for sleep. On this occasion I did not wake up when the sirens started or when the first rounds impacted. I was dead to the world. My flight platoon sergeant did a quick head count in the bunker and realized I was missing. He took off from the bunker amid the incoming rounds impacting all around the airfield and came into my hut and picked me up, threw me over his shoulder and carried me out the door. I woke up to loud noises and his big hands holding me up—it scared the crap out of me. To think that I could have slept through the attack and exposed myself to incoming fire like that was very sobering indeed. After that night I never slept in the hut alone, just in case. I tried to write him up for valor and saving my life but was denied.

Flying out of Lassiter was less scenic than Marble Mountain. The area was more heavily populated, with little farms and fish camps with small ponds all around the area. The area also stank of human and animal waste, both of which were used as the primary fertilizer for local farming. There always seemed to be a brown, smoky haze over the entire region that smelled of sewage and death. The people in the area seemed resigned to war as their daily lot.

Shortly after moving to Bien Hoa, I had a chance to catch a lift over to H-3 (called Hotel-3), the main helipad at Ton Son Nhut Air Force Base. I was at that point technically grounded because I was over the allowed number of flight hours in the past thirty days, so I could not fly missions for forty-eight hours. We were allowed up to accumulate up to 120 hours of flight time in thirty days. This was to prevent crewmembers from becoming too tired to safely fly. If mission demands and the tactical situation dictated, the flight surgeon could wave the rule for up to another twenty hours, or 140 cumulative hours of flight time in the past thirty days. You could only fly more than 140 hours if it was an emergency, and the CO approved the flight. I was routinely hitting 140 hours in a thirty-day period at this point in my tour.

When I got off the slick on which I caught a ride over to H-3, I was asked for my base ID. "What the heck is that?" I asked. The operations officer at base operations informed me that all personnel on Ton Son Nhut now required an installation ID to move about the base due to the possibility of infiltrators gaining access. I showed him my US Army ID and told him I was headed to BOQ #1 to see Colonel Hoffman. He was most happy to send me on my way.

This temporary administrative grounding was an opportunity to catch up with Dad that evening. I walked to his room, knocked on the door, and heard someone say "come in," so I walked through the door and saw a star—as in a general's star. I figured this must be the wrong room or that Dad had moved. Then Dad walked out into the living room area from one of the bedrooms and the general turned so I could see who it was. It was Brigadier General Chuck Yeager.[17] Though I had not seen him for many years, I quickly recognized the most famous pilot in the free world and old friend of Dad since his WWII days! What a treat to see him again. Dad told me to throw my gear in his room and offered to make me a drink. This was just like being back home.

My father was on the Air Force list for brigadier general himself at that time but waiting for his Senate confirmation. Because the Senate was squabbling with President Nixon and were loudly pissed-off at what was then referred to as the "Lavelle Affair,"[18] they were refusing to promote any senior officers in the Air Force. Once again, the politicians were screwing the members of the military over their civilian political beefs.

The Air Force, of course, knows how to live. They are not like us Army pukes living in the dirt, with minimal creature comforts and only occasional hot chow. No, the US Air Force does it right. Here we were in Vietnam, a combat zone, and they lived well, as always.

The place was a real palace. No one came and hauled off the smelly buckets containing a mixture of jet fuel, urine, and crap to burn once a day—no, not here.

After taking a leak and watching the toilet flush about three times, I headed out into the living area and Dad handed me a drink. Real bourbon, real ice, real glass, and a real comfortable couch on which to rest my tired backside. Ah, what a life! Yep, I should have been a Zoomie!

I then asked Dad about this new installation ID for Ton Son Nhut AFB. He said not to worry, he would arrange one for me in the morning. Indeed, the next morning I went over to base HQ to ask about getting one of these new IDs and was told to see the security office. I went to security and everyone in the office stood up, including the much older Air Force captain at his desk. He stuck out his hand and said, "Yes sir, we have your new ID right here. Please sign it before you put it in your wallet." I asked everyone to please relax and have a seat. I thanked the captain and left. I do not know who they thought I was, but, what the hell, I now had a Ton Son Nhut AFB base ID. Now I could come and go as I needed.

My Ton Son Nhut Air Force Base ID card.

While my father and I stayed in touch via field phone or messages via his office in Da Nang while I was in country, it was great to see him whenever I could. Dad and I had always had a very close relationship. This shared experience during a time of war, with its daily risks and extended separation from home and family, brought us together in a way I would not fully appreciate until much later in life.

That night in his BOQ room, after a couple of drinks and catching up on Mom, my brothers, and sisters, and talking about Karen and our baby, Dad asked just what in hell were we doing at Bien Hoa and why was I not back in the States. He had not seen me since I had returned from my R&R home and Kelly's birth. He was not at all happy that I was back in Vietnam. He knew that I was only going home on leave and had to return, but with the precipitous draw down then underway, he had hoped that fortune would smile, and my orders would be cancelled. "No such luck," I told him.

It seems that no new combat-arm types could be sent into country, I explained, so if I did not return, the troop would be short a Ranger and aviator-qualified Blues platoon leader. This was, of course, despite the fictional or perhaps alternate reality being played from the White House that no US Army forces were then engaged in combat in the Republic of South Vietnam. "No," I told Dad, "I understood the conditions when I went home, and I am just thankful that I got to see Kelly the day she was born. But it sure was tough to pick up and head back here and leave Karen and Kelly in DC. It sucks," I said.

"Yep, it really sucks," said Dad. We had another round of drinks.

Then we decided that we needed to have some dinner. The Ton Son Nhut Officer's Club was just across the street. The food there was renowned, and I was up for some great chow. But I also was feeling no pain at this point. Dad suggested that we have some pizzas delivered.

"Delivered?" I asked. "What the hell? You mean the Air Force has delivery pizza here?"

"Of course," said General Yeager. "We have certain standards of living, after all!"

"Fucking amazing, just fucking amazing!" I replied.

So, the general and Dad worked up a list of what we wanted and called it in on the phone to whoever ran the pizza concession. Had I considered this for more than a few moments, I would have asked for a beer delivery, but the bourbon was going down just fine, so I said nothing.

We ordered five pizzas, each with different toppings. Apparently, ordering more than one pizza was a new concept for this concessionaire. When the pizzas arrived, there were, indeed, five pizzas. The only problem was that all five were in the same box, one on top of the other! We put the box on the kitchenette counter (this place even had a fucking, no-shit kitchen, complete with oven, sink, refrigerator—it also made ice—and the usual pots, pans, dishes, and silverware). I thought we might be able to separate the pizzas onto separate plates. Unfortunately, all five were glued together with the pizza sauce and cooling cheese. Consequently, what we had was a five-layer pizza cake. It was good anyway and we ate every scrap of it.

Then out came cards and more drinks. It is rough duty having to spend the evening with a full-bird colonel and a world-famous brigadier general! But I made the best of it. Over the next few hours, I told a few war stories, some that dad did not want to hear, and they told me their own, covering three wars in the process. It was interesting to sit there and hear these two reminisce about their own experiences as aviation warriors in World War II, Korea, and now Vietnam for Dad, and Pakistan for General Yeager. It was humbling and awe-inspiring at the same time. Both began flying in airplanes covered in cloth and powered by round engines and flying with little more than a turn needle, trim ball, an altimeter, and an airspeed indicator as their only flight instruments (hence the old aviation term: "flying by needle, ball, and airspeed"). From there they progressed to such historic aircraft as the P-40, the P-47, the P-51, and the P-39 during WWII. Then both transitioned into jets and multi-engine transports and bombers. In the case of Chuck

Yeager, of course, he went on to transition into rockets! He broke the sound barrier in the Bell X-1 and flew the X-15 to the very edge of space. It was this topic that quickly became the center of the tales being told. Dad was delighted at my steady stream of questions fired at the general and grateful to be talking about something other than what we were all doing at the time.

The general related his experience with the X-15 and his frustrations with the Department of Defense and the DC policy makers for holding back the manned rocket-plane approach to space, which can fly there and then return and land on earth to be flown again, in favor of the one-time use, very expensive, vertically launched semi-guided multi-stage rockets of the Mercury, Gemini, and Apollo programs. His view was that this unreasonable focus on reaching the moon as the primary space goal was missing the larger goal of conquering, living in, and then exploring space itself. He spoke with frustration, and at times, near rage in his voice about the political controls on the X-15 program, its ultimate cancellation, and the cancellation of the X-20 program, which were, in his words, criminal. He felt they were all sacrificed on that altar of moon-landing politics. He was blunt. He said that any other space program or initiative in the 1960s, whether by DOD or any other agency, was seen as potentially undermining NASA's sole mission of landing on the moon and as a competitor for funding. The result was that all other programs were either frozen in time or cancelled outright.

"What is the X-20?" I asked him. Out came pencil and paper and he drew a picture of what I would later come to know as the Space Shuttle. Of course, at this time I had never heard of the X-20 or the even the shuttle concept. I thought the way to space was sitting on top of a big roman candle and shooting dice with providence.

"There is a better, safer way to do this. Of course," he pointed out, "all systems that one might use to fly into space are inherently dangerous—as is flying itself—but flying there makes much more sense than being blasted there!"

He told me that there was a flight article built under the X-20 program (engineer talk for a flyable prototype). He said it was scrapped on orders from the politicians in Washington in case it might become a distraction from the "real space program"—the Apollo moon mission. He then said, "Son, just you wait! They will go back to the X-20 at some point because it is the only way to really go out there and explore! This" he said, "is the business of astronauts who are real pilots!"

Many years later Tom Wolfe wrote the book *The Right Stuff*, where this history and these differing approaches to the conquest of space are explored in much greater detail. But this was 1972. This was just three years after the first manned landing on the moon. This was so utterly foreign and contrary to my understanding of the space program, how it worked, and why, that I was both amazed and shocked. It was a very unusual discussion, a welcome evening's diversion from the real world outside, and a significant education for me.

Somewhere late into that night I slept soundly, as though I were somewhere else and in another time. The next day brought reality crashing back and I was back at Bien Hoa planning missions for the next few days.

Waking up to enemy incoming was a nearly regular occurrence, one that we almost, but not quite, got used to. Keeping us awake, on guard, and scrambling seemed to be part of the NVA's psychological operations program. It was rare that they did a lot of damage, but we did lose some sleep. But it never really seriously wore on us or interfered with missions the way our own operational tempo itself did at that time. The rocket and mortar attacks seemed such a waste when you consider that some poor NVA conscript had to walk all the way into North Vietnam, to some Russian ammo deport, pick up four to six rounds of 60-mm mortars and walk back down the Ho Chi Minh Trail to Southern Vietnam, only to have it wasted during one night's useless, ineffective mortar attack and then have to make the long hike, all on foot, all over again and again.

Lesson: when you have unlimited manpower and no consideration for losses or morale, you can build, move, and shoot virtually anything whether useful or not.

Something that did have an impact often was the use of improvised explosive mines along the major roadways. These mines were usually command detonated by an NVA observer as one of our units passed nearby. These were constructed from all manner of explosive charges from C-4 to Semtex to old artillery shells and aircraft bombs. They were powerful, deadly, and did a lot of destruction to the road networks in the south of Vietnam. Today we call these improvised explosive devices (IEDs). Vehicles that took direct hits normally had few survivors. As a result, we avoided surface transportation situations as often as we could. It was a rare day that we drove off Bien Hoa AFB. When we did, it was with an ARVN Military Police escort, along well-traveled and surveilled roads.

Needing transport in and around Bien Hoa Air Force Base itself quickly became a major problem for us after our arrival. We had few items of rolling stock that were not purpose dedicated at all times. Having a truck to haul pilots, crews, and gear to and from the flight line was a major need for the unit. Luckily, one day I discovered a truck that had been abandoned by a contractor who had left the country. Everyone had assumed that it was broken and had ignored it. I found that with some rather simple maintenance it ran just fine. It was a small flatbed truck with a cab that accommodated three. This old truck served us well until I left.

Lesson: never assume anything and waste not, want not.

On October 29, 1972, a flight-school classmate was killed in I Corps while flying for D Troop, 17th Cavalry and doing something we all knew better than to attempt. He decided that he would try to rip an NVA flag from the flagpole in an NVA position as a souvenir. This had been done so much in the past that by this time in the war, the NVA were attaching grenades to the flagpoles as a booby trap for daring American pilots. He paid for it with his life. In his case, he paid slowly because he died nearly a month later of burns from the crash of his OH-6.

Lesson: Burns were one reason I wore every bit of protective clothing and gear I could. I had seen fire, touched fire, and seen fire kill. I did not want to meet fire again, if there was anything I could do about it.

Life at Bien Hoa was not all bad. We had okay food (just okay, mind you), semiregular electricity, and we were not the primary target of the frequent mortar and 122-mm rocket attacks on the base. Plus, we were a short hop by helicopter from Ton Son Nhut Air Force base. We were able to visit there often, either for logistic runs or to pick up or drop off VIPs. We did a fair amount of VIP transport in and around Saigon, as we were one of only two US Army aviation units left in that area. The other was another Cavalry troop, F/9th Cavalry. One day we received a mission order to fly an Air Force VIP out to some VNAF bases for inspection and coordination visits. I was assigned the mission. The VIP was an Air Force colonel who turned out to be my father. In fact, on two occasions I found myself flying my father around the area as he visited VNAF bases.

I also had the chance to get into Saigon itself several times. On one visit I was able to visit Dick Blystone at his Associated Press office in downtown Saigon. We had dinner at the old Intercontinental Hotel in Saigon and caught up on developments for us both. I also had the chance to have dinner in downtown Saigon with Dad on several occasions. One such dinner was at a very good restaurant in Saigon run by Koreans that served French food to mainly Americans. What a city!

As our combat air patrols out to the west of Saigon continued, we ran into all manner of NVA units and formations. In one case, out near the Parrot's Beak area along the Cambodia-Vietnam border we happened upon a full battalion of NVA infantry crossing into South Vietnam on foot, carrying supplies and bicycles, moving east through an extensive system of rice paddies. Here they were, out in the open, directly in front of us. It was one of those surreal moments in war when you know what is going to happen, but it just seems not to happen for long time as each side waits to see what the other will do. After what seemed like ten minutes but was probably only one, a few of these NVA soldiers put their hands up like they were going to surrender. Almost at the same time, several of them brought their AK-47 assault rifles to bear on us and began to fire. Having no real choice in the matter, we simply opened up on them with the two M-60s on our two slicks, the side-mounted M2 Browning .50-caliber machine gun on my ship, the miniguns, and rockets from the Cobras.

It was not a fair fight, but war rarely is. Many of the NVA fell where they stood. Others ran in different directions but did not get far. A few others just seemed to melt away. After only a few short minutes, the battle was over. There were bicycles and NVA supplies heaped haphazardly across the rice paddies. Bodies floated in the water in growing red plumes, and it was suddenly very quiet. The battalion-sized force was decimated and dispersed. No doubt most of their survivors regrouped and returned to the Ho Chi Minh Trail over in Cambodia but they were no longer an effective fighting force and no longer a factor in the battle for III Corps. Interestingly, this action was observed by the US Air Force forward air controller who was standing by to help us if needed. He was not needed but he apparently wrote up the incident. A year and a half later, when I was back at Fort Bragg, I was notified that the Vietnamese government had awarded me the Cross of Gallantry with Gold Star for this action. The irony was huge of course, but the award was, at first, obstructed by the Army staff in Washington. The award came down to me through Air Force, not Army, channels.

The Army's position was not to have my immediate superior headquarters endorse the award down to me because, I found out, I was "officially" not in Vietnam at that time and, therefore, was ineligible for the award. The commander of my unit at the time at

Fort Bragg, Major Neil Paxson, knew the truth and arranged for the presentation of the medal. After some years, the Army gave in and put the medal into my official records. On the official US Army microfiche of my personnel records, there is to this day a letter stating that my whereabouts from June 1972 to December 1972 were unknown to the command to which I was assigned at that time: 18th Airborne Corps at Fort Bragg. But there is also now, in my meager, mostly empty official personnel file relating to my service in Vietnam, this combat award from the South Vietnamese government. Go figure.

Lesson: If you tell a lie long enough, it can become fact. If you tell two contradicting stories long enough, they both become fact despite the obvious conflict with reality. Such is the body politic in America. Of course, the simplest escape from this obvious historical conflict is to simply erase all the records. This is, apparently, why I and so many other Vietnam veterans from that period of the war, July to December 1972, have so few actual military service records for their time in Vietnam at the St. Louis Military Records Center.

As often as not, in combat I found out things, usually some period of time after landing from a particularly difficult, event-filled mission, that would scare the crap out of me—after I thought about the possibilities and what had happened. Many examples of this presented themselves to me during my time in South Vietnam.

Shortly after the move to Bien Hoa, I and two others from the unit were asked to attend a mission brief over on Ton Son Nhut AFB. The brief was held in a secure room that was guarded by Air Force security. We arrived and had our IDs checked against a log and we were told that we could not bring cameras. Cameras? Who brings cameras to Air Cavalry mission briefs? Once in the room and seated, two briefers, who were in suits, not uniforms, stepped to the front. There were some Air Force–types just watching the brief. There was one representative from 1st Aviation Brigade and one person who was identified as being from the embassy.

The brief began with some small talk on our move to our

new airfield. Then one of the briefers, neither actually identified themselves by name, stated that it was time to begin discussing why we had been "brought down here." That struck me strange. Did he mean why we were brought to this briefing or why we had relocated the entire troop to Bien Hoa? There was no clarification. But I think that became clear as the mission was briefed. Next, one of the briefers stated that I was to be the air mission commander for this operation and that we were not to disclose to anyone not in this room what we were briefed on that day or on our actual mission. That was strange. We asked how we could plan and mount combat air operations without telling anyone in the unit about it or getting clearance for flights into the area of planned operations? Not a problem, said the briefer. Then he said that we were to explain our operations as simply security operations around the west side of Saigon out to the border.

We were then shown what was reported to be US Air Force aerial reconnaissance mission images of tanks and heavy equipment moving south in dense trees on what looked like a dirt road. The briefer stated that these images reflected NVA movements on the Ho Chi Minh Trail along the extreme western edge of Vietnam in the I Corps region. In the images, while a bit grainy, were clearly tanks, trucks, and some artillery. Then they put up an enlarged but even more grainy image of the artillery. "Holy crap," I muttered. Those were Russian towed 130-mm artillery tubes.

These were long-range guns that would reach out to nearly thirty kilometers. We knew there were numbers of 152-mm and 130-mm Russian guns supporting the NVA armor, along with rocket launchers and lots of anti-aircraft systems up in I Corps from mountain positions and some down in II Corps, again located in mountainous terrain. The briefer then explained that they had not been seen in III Corps but that was where the intelligence suggested they were headed. He explained that the assessment was that the NVA and Russians were going to try to insert these guns close enough to Saigon to bring it under indirect fire. The 130-mm

Russian M-46 towed gun had a range that could target Saigon itself, if the NVA could get them well into III Corps. Our mission was to find the Russian 130-mm towed artillery, "the Saigon Guns" as one staffer referred to them, that were now believed to be somewhere in the western regions of III Corps.

The NVA wanted to try, according to these intel types, and put the city of Saigon under indirect fire from heavy artillery as a means to break the will of the South Vietnamese, and to impact the peace talks in Paris. If the NVA was successful in directly shelling downtown Saigon, it would be a game changer in Paris. Our task was to find and destroy this artillery if indeed it was somewhere out in that area. The South Vietnamese military was certain that this was not a real threat, that such artillery was nowhere in III Corps and that the NVA could not get them that close to Saigon anyway. Our Air Force–types were not nearly as confident of that as the ARVN seemed to be.

Well, if these mission briefers are right, that would certainly not be good, I thought. But III Corps was very open, with limited cover to hide big guns and their prime movers, like it was in I Corps and II Corps to the north. Particularly III Corps, to the west of Saigon, was mainly open rice fields and lots of compartmentalized terrain, not suitable for moving artillery clandestinely off-road. This would not be an easy move for the NVA. They would have to move at night and then camouflage the guns and their prime movers, along with the ammunition trucks needed to support the guns, every day. Camouflage was something the NVA did very, very well. So, finding them, even in this relatively open terrain might prove challenging, if they really were out there.

We were told we would have at least two sets of *Buffs* (each set was a flight of three B-52s, endearingly called "big, ugly, fat fuckers" by the Air Force) on call to support our team and a priority for additional fighter-bomber teams on call during this mission. In this case they were to be Navy A-4s (pretty good shooting air-ground assets, from my experience). At this point in the war, there was already a practice in place of having sets of B-52s on station and ready to engage targets as they were developed. We were assured that if we confirmed the presence of the suspected Russian 130-mm guns in the search area, we would have immediate priority for the next available set of Buffs on station. We had no idea how long or how far we would have to search to find these "Saigon Guns." There was a lot to think about for this mission and it would need a lot of careful planning and coordination. But we could not tell any else why.

When I looked at some of the photos during the briefing, they seemed very unusual to me. These were close in, grainy images that were very vertical . . . all across the image. Not the normal oblique or slant-view images we normally used for imagery analysis or the near-vertical images we used for targeting. Simply put, they were too vertical. Objects at the outer edges did not lean away from the center of the image as they do in aerial photography. Yet they had been distorted in some way and did not look quite right, just as if they were bad images in some way. After looking at the one image on the briefing wall for a moment I realized what was wrong with the general perspective of the image: it was indeed far too vertical and one image seemed to cover an area far greater than what an aircraft-mounted camera might collect. It did not look like a composite image, but it seemed to be a single image. Strange!

I had been an avid photographer since I was ten years old. I had employed imagery in previous military duties, and I had some imagery interpretation background. These were not run-of-the-mill US Air Force reconnaissance images from a plane. These were taken from way too high up.

Afterward I asked one of the intel briefers, "Where was the guy who took the picture standing, on the moon?" He looked at me with a face that stated loud and clear: *shut up, sit down and never, ever ask that question again.* When the meeting concluded this same suit stood close to me and then repeated what I already understood.

I was to never discuss what I had seen that day, to never ask such a question again, and to just get the job done and forget about the entire package of images they had shown. He then suggested that there was a cell at Fort Leavenworth with my name on it, if I ever violated those instructions. I didn't speak of this again for more than twenty years.

Lesson: Sometimes you can learn too much between what you know and what you are told. It is best to keep mum! There is more going on in this world than you will ever know or understand. And there is some really strange shit out there, so go slow, be deliberate and be very, very careful. If we have it, then the bad guys probably do too. Keep your options open and always plan a way out!

We knew the intelligence on these guns was now somewhat cold. By that I mean more than a few weeks old. In truth we had no idea how old those images actually were. But we also understood that there had been other, more recent reports that these guns had been seen moving south on the Trail. So, we had a rough idea where to look. What I did not know at that point was that these guns had apparently been picked up on Corona images moving south some months before and our guys only had intermittent data on them as they were moved toward Saigon. The area we were looking into was on the extreme edge of the 130-mm's range for hitting Saigon itself. Needless to say, this was a priority mission.

Corona images[19] were the most heavily guarded US national security secret at that time. Corona was the name of the satellite system that was used for overhead reconnaissance imagery from the early 1960s until 1972. Later in life I would walk into the Moscow offices of the very organization that planned and executed Russian space reconnaissance operations and learned that they had similar capabilities almost as early in the space race as we did, thanks to captured German World War II technology.

As we carefully planned our first mission to actually look for these big guns, I had a map grid from the briefing around which to begin our search. This was based upon estimates, we had been told by the intelligence briefers, that the Air Force recce folks had created. The Air Force intel folks had estimated when and generally where those guns might arrive in the III Corps area based upon calculated movement times for such equipment on the Trail, the terrain and potential movement corridors that the NVA would likely employ. The timing of this mission assignment was based upon those estimates.

We also knew that the NVA had brought additional anti-aircraft systems into the western III Corps region, right into our planned AO for this mission. We expected that, if there were 130-mm Russian artillery pieces in that area, the NVA and Russians would go all out to protect them with everything they could. But we did not know what such defenses might be until later. What we expected were single-mount 14.5-mm machine guns mounted on top of armored vehicles, .51-cal machine guns, lots of small arms and, perhaps, more SA-7s. What they had in the area, in addition to the shoulder-fired SA-7s, were large SA-2 anti-aircraft missiles (really big stuff!), 57-mm radar-guided AA guns, 14.5 quad-mounted AA gun trailers and the new ZSU-23-2. These self-propelled anti-aircraft gun systems were equipped with two guns then but were later modified by the Russians into ZSU-23-4s. Both were and are real dangerous stuff for helicopter operations.

On the first day of our search for these guns, I led a heavy-gun team into an area west of Nui ba Din, the Black Virgin (a big, solitary mountain northwest of Saigon), on the first of a succession of missions into that area. There were no Americans left in this part of South Vietnam; we were on our own. To ensure security of what we were doing and to prevent the Soviets, who were providing signals intelligence to the PAVN command, we conducted all communications via our onboard KY-28 secure communications units. It was us and the bad guys and a very few widely scattered friendly ARVN outposts, though none of these were actually near our search area. We flew at treetop level, breaking branches with our chin bubbles and skids. And we had to climb up slightly to cross most of the dykes around the rice fields we flew over. Initially, we were taking some sporadic ground fire, but it was erratic and stayed well behind us, just what we might expect flying in this AO just west of Saigon. So, we continued west toward the border area with Cambodia, known as the Parrot's Beak.

Into this very contested border area of III Corps we flew, my slick now packing a 5.56-mm six-barrel door-mounted minigun and a .50-cal M2 Browning heavy machine gun mounted in the opposite door, along with assorted M-79s and grenades (yes, we used to throw grenades from our birds all the time . . . sounds silly but it was effective when you are only from ten to thirty or forty feet in the air going at 100 knots!). I had one little bird, an OH-6 and three heavily armed AH-1G Cobra gunships. One Snake had a 20-mm Vulcan and the others had 2.75-inch folding fin rockets sporting a combination of nails, Willy Pete, and high explosives (HE), along with chin-mounted miniguns and a 40-mm automatic grenade launcher in a small turret below and forward of the aircraft's cockpit. The Cobra's rockets were for marking targets and starting fires. We were confident that we could really bring some smoke on this NVA heavy artillery, if we could find them.

They found us first. On one of the early missions into the targeted AO, as we closed on the border itself, we flew into a real wall of pure shit! Flak was going off all around, anti-aircraft fire of all kinds was flying through the air, and they were firing SA-7s like they had thousands of them. We started shooting at everything in sight because everything in sight was shooting at us. We crossed a small *ville* and the tops of the hootches opened to reveal numerous anti-aircraft emplacements! The Snakes nailed them first and then laid on WP and HE. Both of my door gunners were firing nonstop. I was marking what I saw on the map so I could accurately identify targets while I was calling for the rest of the cavalry that was supporting us. Shit was hitting the aircraft as we raced through the treetops on a route straight out of there and back to the east into relatively safe areas.

My right-side gunner suddenly yelled "SAM, SAM, SAM!" and began hosing something with the minigun out to our right side. He was screaming and firing, and I quickly turned the helicopter in his direction and put us into a steep nose tuck to try and break the IR lock on our engine exhaust, if the missile had indeed acquired us, and to get away from whatever he saw. There was a loud bang in the back of the airframe and the aircraft shook a bit, slewed sideways slightly then straightened out, but all seemed okay, and I had no lights on the caution panel.

Each of our aircraft had put a lot of ammo out and started some good fires and had gotten some small secondaries. Once out of the direct line of fire, I guided the Marine A-4s in and then passed the grids to the Air Force FAC controlling the on-call Buffs so they could slam the area where we had encountered the heavy anti-aircraft fire. We were about fifteen kilometers beyond any friendly positions.

That characterized this entire mission. We were well into bad-guy country when we were searching for these guns. In fact, even though we were only searching areas about forty to fifty kilometers from Saigon, we were out of friendly controlled areas when we flew just twenty kilometers west. The areas we were searching were generally clear of locals, except right around actual villages. This was because the NVA tended to impress locals into the service of the PAVN when they were discovered out in the countryside. Where we found small villes that were not on the map, they were nearly always fake, hiding logistics or anti-aircraft sites created by the NVA. When the roof pops off of a grass roofed hut and .51-cal or 14.7-mm fire erupts, it is a dead giveaway.

So, I was not worried about any civilians in that AO because of what we saw, realizing that these grass hootches were, once again, actually fake. I wanted the area plastered so we could use it as an alternate safe route back in or out later. I expected we would do bomb damage assessment, or BDA, and would then have a relatively safe route into and out of the area. A three ship, or even a one ship Arc Light drop, accurately delivered, as they generally were at this point in the conflict, was great for suppressing and clearing paths thru AA concentrations, even if a bit expensive! Our current mission gave us some priority for such support, particularly given how far into bad guy territory we were operating. There was little prospect of rescue by anyone other than ourselves if something went seriously bad. This was a high-risk, high-pucker-factor mission.

At first, as we flew clear of the enemy fire, no one seemed to have taken a serious hit as we got clear, an absolute miracle! But I knew we had taken some damage. Soon every bird reported caution lights for something, though most were minor, and low ammo levels. We flew back to Bien Hoa AFB to rearm, refuel, and address repairs to the aircraft. We had lots of targets identified on our maps that we needed to pass to the intelligence folks. We examined our bird for damage. There were holes in the bottom of the aircraft and in the transmission well area just aft of the main cabin and along the tail boom. Maintenance was not happy. I then asked the right-side gunner about his SAM report. He said he saw the guy launch it and he hosed it with the mini gun as it came toward us. Another of the gun pilots said he saw it launch and figured we were goners, but he never saw an explosion and thought that it must have missed. We also had an Air Force FAC pilot flying above us, and he had also reported a launch over his radio net we later learned, though we did not hear that call on our secure radio net.

So, we looked at the right side of the aircraft to see if there was any evidence that perhaps it had detonated early or behind us. All we found was a very large dent in the aft section of the engine cowling. Was it from an airburst shock wave or did the gunner kill the SA-7's seeker or damage the detonator in the rocket as it came at us? Had an SA-7 bounced off of our bird as a dud? We will never know but I still figure that gunner's quick reactions saved us. We did have the IR suppression kit on the aircraft so it was very unlikely that the SA-7 could have locked onto us at that low altitude. But there were reports of the NVA volley firing them at helicopters in order to try to get a ballistic hit, when they knew they could not get a lock on an IR-signature-suppressed, low-level aircraft.

Lesson: quick thinking, having a plan in mind, and executing it automatically can save your life.

After examining the aircraft and reaching no definitive decision on what had or had not hit us, we debriefed our actions that day and then planned our operations for the next day.

The following day we launched midmorning and headed east with the same team structure. The pilots knew the basic mission— searching for and eliminating NVA artillery in western III Corps. Why we were doing this and why we were searching a specific area was not shared with everyone. It was just another security mission around III Corps to keep the NVA on the defense and to destroy their firepower when we could find it.

Back out in the AO nearing the border, but in new grid squares, we saw lots of rice fields and open terrain. But we also observed mostly empty roads and that was unusual for this area. There were some small forest areas and long tree lines along many of the roads, but concealment that the NVA could exploit was very, very limited. As we neared the end of our fuel loads, we did find a small group of NVA soldiers moving along a footpath between rice paddies. As we flew over, they jumped into the water trying to hide. They were not a useful target for us. They were just doing their jobs and were no threat to us. It was time to return to base as we neared low, ("Bingo") fuel status. Just then, a few of the NVA soldiers began to fire at us and they got a few hits.

As we formed up, with me flying lead and my slick at 100 knots through the treetops, I asked for a visual check as we crossed some trees along a road between rice fields. Suddenly the aircraft was slammed sideways violently, and we heard a loud bang and a brief sound like pebbles in a shaking tin can. Then suddenly there was a lot of AA fire clawing at us. This was not time for a fight. We just flew away to the east. One of the other pilots asked, over the radio, if we were okay and I said I thought we were, and I asked if anyone saw what that initial explosion was. As we quickly cleared the enemy fire, one of the gun pilots came on the net and said that something seemed to just explode right next to us. One of the guns came along side and told me to stand by as he checked us for visible damage. After a few moments I asked if he saw anything. He very calmly told me to slack off on the speed and be "real gentle now" with the controls. I was in no mood to slow down, as I was getting us the hell out of there and back to safe ground so we could regroup and figure this out.

He then said, "I can see daylight through your tail boom compartment." At that point my peter pilot told me we were losing fuel. Daylight through the fuselage . . . oh shit! That tail boom better stay on! It was more than twenty kilometers to any friendly ground! The aircraft was holding together. We were in no mood to walk back and rescue on the ground by friendlies was unlikely.

That was a long sweaty flight back to Lassiter! When we landed and I shut the engine down the fuselage groaned a few times as it sat on the pad and then it settled about twelve inches too low as the damaged skids spread apart. I unstrapped and jumped clear, yelling for everyone to get out and get clear in case there was a fire. I walked back to look over the aft of the aircraft. I just about crapped in my flight suit. The entire tail boom was shredded. The access panels to the transmission well were blown off and all kinds of shit was leaking from everything. The engine compartment had holes in it and the tail rotor driveshaft had cuts in it that went almost halfway through. When something hits the rapidly spinning drive shaft, you don't get a single hole, you get what looks like an elongated cut the width of the projectile. There was more than a dozen such cuts. The tail rotors were blasted to hell and torn up, and I don't know how they were working.

As the other crews shut down and came over to look us over,

we were speechless. How in the hell did that aircraft stay together and get us home? Not only had we taken a lot of small arms and flak damage, but we realized that we had likely flown through a claymore mine set up in the trees! This was a tactic by the NVA that was being reported around heavy NVA positions. This meant that we were on to something.

Lesson: Clearly the NVA believed that we flew our aircraft at the textbook airspeed of sixty to eighty knots on missions and set these mines accordingly. We did not; we normally flew at speeds over 100 knots and often just short of our maximum safe airspeed.

The claymore trap was obviously set to kill a helicopter flying at lower speeds. So, the blast from the mine in the trees mainly missed but some of the small projectiles in it had hit the tail boom but not the main cabin/cockpit portion of the fuselage. The maintenance officer told me that I ought to be put in for a Distinguished Flying Cross or something for bringing that bird back in, more or less, one piece, but the word from 1st Aviation Brigade was, once again, no awards or decorations for anyone for anything. "No US Army personnel were engaged in combat operations on the day in question" was the constant response at this point in time. There could be no recognition for actions in combat because no American units were in combat. It was not that our operation was classified, it was that the operation was simply not officially taking place.

A few days later, after another debrief with the suits at Ton Son Nhut Air Force Base, some of the Air Force FAC pilots ran into us over at the o' club. When we could, we would grab lunch there, as it was better than the cold sandwiches and fruit juice lunch back at our compound. The Air Force pilots asked if we knew who was flying the AMC UH-1 out west the day it had flown through a trap and had the SA-7 launched toward it. I told them that I was the AC in that bird that day. They looked at me in amazement and then they all stood up and told me that they had something to give me. One of them handed me a red and blue patch for my flight suit that had sewn on it: *SA-7*

Flight Examiner. I thanked them and asked why they were giving it to me? One of them told me that he had seen the SA-7 launch that day and we had managed to survive. That, he said, was why.

My SA-7 patch. This was presented to me by some Air Force pilots who witnessed the near miss in III Corps when we were on the mission to find the Saigon Guns.

There were too many holes to count in my aircraft after the claymore hit us. It was a total loss. It was almost new and had less than three hundred hours on it! But it had gotten us home. "Ma Bell" sure made good, solid helicopters! I tried to sleep after our debriefing because I was exhausted by sundown. I was too keyed up, scared, excited, and shocked to sleep, so I got back up and went to our little self-built *bar hootch* that served as our communal o' club and found the rest of the team there. We shared some bourbon shooters and beer. Bourbon can be a wonderful sleep aid, occasionally. The next thing I knew it was morning and I had a mild hangover. And it was time to go at it again.

It's a fate thing . . . and a positive attitude thing as well. But there is a lot of luck in the mix, and no one wanted to cash in the chips with the end of this war so near. The Paris talks were continuing and both sides were suggesting progress, but no peace deal was at hand.

But luck is a valuable thing. That and focus and a positive approach to every challenge and every crisis, whether in the cockpit or on the ground, enables the otherwise well-trained and motivated individual to keep it together, make good decisions, and survive. The lesser-trained ones, or those who give up, don't. "Ah, but the one, one is a warrior, and he will bring the others back." But Ernest K. Gann said in his book of the same name, "Fate is the hunter." Just some food for thought.

So, we went back into the wild, hotly contested spaces of western III Corps, along the edges of the Parrot's Beak. We flew this region repeatedly over the next few days. It was certainly clear to the NVA that we were searching for something, I have no doubt. On the other hand, that searching probably was an incentive for the NVA to keep the guns hidden and not operational, in hopes we would give up. If we quit looking, it was likely the guns would be deployed to firing positions and Saigon would have a very bad day.

After a general search over the entire area over more than a week turned up no evidence of Soviet artillery, we began to seek out specific areas where these large guns might be hidden. We were looking for places where there was sufficient cover and concealment to protect equipment as large as these guns. This really did narrow the potential locations we needed to search that were within or near the range of Saigon: between twenty-five and fifty kilometers out from the edge of the city of Saigon itself. This Soviet M-46 artillery gun has a range of over twenty-seven to thirty kilometers, so we assumed they would want to locate these guns somewhere that would be close enough that they could move within range at night, fire, and then withdraw back to their concealed location. The gun is huge. Even put into towed-travel configuration, it is over thirty-five feet long, almost eight feet tall and weighs more than eight metric tons. Therefore, it requires a heavy truck, or prime mover, and good roads to move it around.

The entire configuration of the gun and its prime mover would be around fifty to sixty feet in length. They would also have to be concealed in a configuration that would enable a rapid movement to a new location if they were in danger of discovery, so we assumed they would be hidden in the travel configuration. As a result, hiding them would require some serious work, lots of camouflage, and a unique environment. All we had to do was find locations in the area that provided sufficient such concealment for several of these truck and gun combinations. We realized that the unit was probably deployed and hidden in battery configurations of three guns each. So, they may be placed some distance apart, perhaps up to a kilometer. But they could not be too far apart due to command and control needs and for communications with their fire direction center.

Finally, a few days later in late October, we hit pay dirt. We were examining some small clumps of dense forest about forty kilometers from downtown Saigon. The pilot of our OH-6 scout helicopter that day reported that he thought he saw what looked like several tires or wheels under some brush just inside a modest, wooded area. It was one of several small woods in the search area that day but not big enough for an entire artillery battalion. But it certainly was large enough for a full battery. This sounded promising. He made another pass by the wooded area but got no reaction from anyone who might be in there and lost sight of the wheels he thought he had seen earlier.

We had a FAC, call sign "Covey," on station and we had bombers on call. I figured that we needed to do a little more fishing to see if anything was in there. We had a lot of firepower available and if there was something there, we needed to take advantage of what we had on hand and not miss an opportunity. However, I did not want to waste our heavier ordnance on what might be nothing at all. The little bird pilot was very nervous and said he had a bad feeling about these woods. An experienced *loach* driver, as we called OH-6 pilots, can "smell" the bad guys. Those that survived this unique aviation mission of searching at low levels through all kinds of environments, gained a very real sixth sense for danger. Further, they flew so low and so slow that they could, sometimes, actually smell the enemy. It seems showers or any kind of bathing was far less regular for the NVA than it was even for us.

I decided to make a low pass and fire up the woods where he had seen the tires with our .50-cal M2 machine gun to see what might happen. Often a simple reconnaissance by fire can cause the bad guys to return fire or give away their position. I brought the ship around and made a high-speed, low-level pass, about twenty feet off the ground, past the area where the little bird pilot had said he saw the wheels. My door gunner fired, and the rounds went into the woods and came right back out past us at all different angles. *Holy shit, what is this?* I thought. The ricochets were so intense that only some kind of heavy metal could reflect back that many rounds. The FAC pilot, who was watching this entire process, screamed over the secure radio net for us to pull out because we were under heavy fire, in case we did not know it. Well, we knew it, but I also realized that this was our own rounds coming back at us. So did the door gunner as he swept the barrel toward our rear to keep the rounds behind us.

Clearly, whoever was in there, and there was certainly something—trees do not cause ricochets— had very good fire discipline. They did not want to return fire on us and give their position away at that point. To me, it was already given away. Either this was NVA armor hidden in the woods, or it was the 130-mm towed guns we were looking for. The 130-mm had a large, slightly

V-shaped front armored shield, which was tilted backward to protect the gun crew. Assuming that several of these guns were generally pulled into the wood by the trucks and parked with the shield and barrels pointing outward, this would account for the deflected fire we observed. If it was armor in the woods, we would get the same effect. Either way, this was a serious threat to Saigon itself.

I called our guns to engage the target area. With everyone watching us, there was no question as to the exact location of the suspected guns or armor. The guns rolled in hot with nails and HE, along with 20-mm cannon fire. The effect was to strip away the tree limbs and the concealment that they bad guys had enjoyed until that very moment. As the initial blast smoke dispersed, there they were, whether the politicians in Saigon or the ARVN commanders wanted to believe it or not. There, in those very woods, were three 130-mm towed artillery tubes and several other support vehicles that we could clearly see.

With their cover blown, the NVA let loose with all they had. Then anti-aircraft fire came out of two of the small, wooded areas nearby. The sky was suddenly filled with flying steel and smoke and bad shit of every make, model, size, and configuration! I called everyone off the target, which was, of course, now well-marked for all to see. I called up the Buff controller on the secure net and requested an immediate Arc Light on these woods. I also asked the FAC to bring in whatever immediate fighters were nearby so we could pin down this crowd of bad guys and destroy them. We did not want them to disperse and escape with the artillery tubes. If that happened, I expected that we would need to track down each gun individually. We began to circle the woods at a small arms stand-off range, but at nearly ground level, to keep tabs on anything that tried to come out of the woods. Such very low-level flight over the rice paddies prevented the NVA from employing their SA-7s, if they had any. But these bad guys were firing .51-cal machine guns and rocket-propelled grenades at us, but to no effect. About five minutes after we pulled back, the first Navy A-4s rolled in on the woods from the clouds.

These were great ground-support aircraft, and they lived up to their reputations that day. All their bomb loads went directly into the woods. The initial explosions were large, as expected of the five-hundred-pound bombs they had dropped. But the subsequent secondary detonations of what must have been the stored 130-mm cannon ammo on the NVA trucks were simply gigantic. The shock waves caused our aircraft to rock and roll as the wild winds and concussive forces generated from the massive explosions hit us. It was all I could do to retain control of our UH-1H. This close to the ground, in nap of the earth flight, a sudden pitch of the nose or roll of the aircraft could cause a ground strike by the rotor blades. The outcome would be very, very bad. I struggled for a few seconds and then pulled up and away from the area. Surely, if anyone had any idea of running from these woods, they would be no threat to us at that point and it was very unlikely that any vehicles would manage to escape intact from these nearly constant, rolling secondary explosions. Just then the Buff controller called on the UHF and asked if I could confirm big guns on the target location. I answered, "Roger that, these are the big guns!"

Shortly after we regrouped away from the target, the Buff controller reported that the first Arc Light bombs were in the air. We did not see the B-52s dropping these bombs, but we also heard the standard Arc Light warning to aircraft on both the VHF and the UHF frequency, and we immediately pulled farther away from the woods. As we looked back, we could see the first strings of bombs rain down directly onto these small areas of woods. The resulting detonations made those from earlier seem like firecrackers going off. The air over the target seemed to momentarily compress into a series of semi-opaque black domes that were followed by huge discharges of trees, dirt, metal objects, and then actual gun barrels separated from the gun carriages, all flying up and out from the woods. It was an amazing sight to see, but I knew that we were in for another wild ride when the accumulated shock wave from this massive strike reached us. I turned and accelerated and began to climb with our entire formation in tow. A few seconds later the compressed wind wave hit us, and we bounced and rolled in the turbulence. The effect was very brief because we had put some three to four thousand meters between ourselves and the woods, but it still rattled our teeth and shook us up pretty well. Wow, what a ride. That was the closest I ever was to an Arc Light strike. I never want to be that close again.

Lesson: When someone says Arc Light, or you hear yourself saying Arc Light, get the fuck out of Dodge as fast you can! You do not want to be within five grid squares when one of these strikes goes in, period, amen, over and out!

The US Air Force put at least two more Arc Light strikes on this location during the next twelve hours. The secondary explosions continued for two full days. We maintained a surveillance patrol on the target area for the next few days, watching the fires and explosions and to ensure that nothing came out that was not intercepted. The South Vietnamese put an ARVN infantry force on the ground to surround the location after the secondary explosions ceased and then did a detailed search of the site. I doubt there was any EOD team clearing the site first. They just went in to assess the extent of the force we had engaged and to confirm what we already knew. This was the NVA battalion of Russian M-46 artillery guns that had been trying to get close enough to Saigon to target it. We later learned that they positively identified at least four individual cannons in the debris of the first wooded area we engaged. After that we heard nothing more about the air strikes or what was in the other wooded areas. Of course, the official record only reflects that we found and destroyed a cache of 130-mm artillery rounds[20]. I am not sure of the logic here as these rounds had no military value without the guns to fire them, but such is the nature of the politics surrounding the peace negotiations in Paris at the time.

This was a near thing. These guys were close enough to the

Saigon area to have done serious damage with fairly accurate indirect artillery fire. With each gun firing up to eight rounds per minute, just four of these guns could have put thirty-two rounds per minute into the city. Assuming a reaction time of at least ten minutes for counter battery fire to commence, they could have expended their basic load on the city before anyone would have been able to react. But even a ten-minute response was not likely for the ARVN artillery, and we had no US artillery left in the area. A response from the air, either helicopter or fighters, would have been at least fifteen to twenty minutes. The damage done during those ten minutes of firing would have been horrific in the densely populated city of Saigon, even if they only reached the suburbs!

Clearly the NVA knew they would sacrifice this force in the process, but if they could have hit Saigon with such massive weapons before being detected, it would have had a major impact in both Saigon and Washington, to say nothing of Paris. Even with the tip-off from the intelligence folks that these guns were in the area, it was a huge area to search. We were incredibly lucky to have found this force with nothing more than a few Mark-One human eyeballs!

When we got back to Bien Hoa, I went to the company CP to report in and to recommend that we request that the little bird pilot be put in for a Distinguished Flying Cross for his fearless search work and for detecting this monumental threat to Saigon itself. We got a response from brigade HQ that night—no dice. The operation out west had been an all ARVN and VNAF affair and the US Army forces had officially played no role in the action. It had been the same old story since the start of the entire 1972 NVA Easter Offensive. Only the Navy, Air Force, and Marines were "officially" in this fight along with the ARVN and the VNAF. Why? Because President Richard M. Nixon said so, that is why.

Lesson: always assume politics will trump the truth.

As with the fifty-ship mission to help the ARVN retake Quang Tri, as with operation out of Chu Lai where we almost lost it all, and now this major and very hairy operation . . . we were not there. Any official recognition of the valor and dedication for the men who executed these missions by our own higher headquarters, in this case the US Embassy in Saigon, was denied on the grounds that no US Army personnel were "engaged in combat operations on the dates in question." [21]

This had been a stressful period for all of us in F/8 Cavalry. The Easter Offensive had been a period of sustained and very intense combat operations on both sides since it began on March 29, 1972. But it had been a clear failure for the North Vietnamese and the Russians. While losses had been significant for both North and South Vietnam, the scale of loss and destruction for the NVA was horrific. For the South Vietnamese, supported by the US military air operations, this nine-month campaign to defend their country from an invasion by the North Vietnamese was a resounding victory. While not reported as such in the United States media then or now, the facts tell the story.

The South Vietnamese suffered eight thousand killed in this period, with approximately twenty-four thousand wounded and thirty-five hundred missing in action. The North Vietnamese suffered more than one hundred thousand casualties with around forty thousand killed from an invading force of approximately two hundred thousand! The NVA lost more than half of its tanks and artillery during the invasion and the fighting that followed. It took the North more than three years to rebuild its twenty-division army with major funding and equipment provided by the Soviet Union. And General Vo Nguyen Giap found himself eased out of command of the North Vietnamese Army. [22]

The North Vietnamese claimed that the 1972 Easter Offensive was a resounding success. The Russians claimed that America had been defeated on the field of battle. Seems a difficult argument, if we were not there! Clearly the NVA suffered debilitating losses during the invasion and had very little to show for it[23].

I was tired, very tired at this point. I had been in country for a year and was operating at a day-to-day physical op-tempo that was unsustainable. I found myself making small, stupid mistakes while flying and I realized that we all were worn out from the stress of flying combat missions day after day after day. At this point in time, November of 1972, the flight surgeons were long out of the picture, and we only had ourselves to monitor each other. It was apparent to all of us that we could not go on without relief and that was not going to happen. Our only hope was progress in the peace talks.

December 1, 1972, while on another search and recon security mission west of Saigon, I felt the thunks on my slick as it took several rounds through the floor and the master caution light came on, causing my eye to automatically look toward the caution light panel. Crap, hydraulics failure! Almost instantly the controls seemed to lock up and were very hard to move, after seeming so effortless to maneuver just moments before. Flying that wounded bird suddenly became a real challenge, as the bird wallowed through the air with the controls barely responsive. I needed help with the controls and told my peter pilot to get on the pedals and keep this bitch in trim while I fought the cyclic control stick. It was a sweaty, arduous, and tension filled thirty-minute flight back to our base near Saigon. As we neared the field, I declared an emergency to the tower at Bien Hoa. I lined up with the runway, sort of, flying slightly out of trim. We were already at near nap-of-the-earth altitude, and I remember that smell assaulting my nose as we crossed the runway threshold at ten feet above the concrete. I made a running landing back on the short runway.

As we slid down the runway the aircraft began to slew around to the left as our main rotor system lost lift and the tail rotor control lost effect. I killed the engine to reduce the chance of fire. We were on a runaway slide down the runway. I just held on and hoped the bird did not roll over. That would have been very, very bad. Finally, it stopped. There was complete silence for about five seconds and no one in the crew spoke. I was unbuckling and looked back in the cabin. I saw eyeballs and white teeth yet again. And once again,

I yelled "Let's get the hell out of this thing before it burns from leaking fuel!" It was my last month in country, I had twelve days to go until my original one-year anniversary in country and my expected DROS. In early December of 1972 it was reported that the negotiators were near a deal and a cease fire was near. Shortly after that, on Dec 10, 1972, I was told to prepare to stand down and pack my gear because I was going home in the next week or so.

CHAPTER NINE
BACK TO THE REAL WORLD

Photo taken by my father of me flying as an AC when I flew him on an Executive Transport Mission one day out of Ton Son Nhut Air Force Base in late 1972.

IT SEEMED THAT real progress was being made in Paris, though none of us had any illusions about the integrity or intentions of the North Vietnamese and Soviets. The NVA was bent on conquering the South and the Russians wanted access to and use of the bases in South Vietnam. We understood that the North would do, say, and agree to anything to get us out so they could move south and take control. With the proposal for a commission dominated by Warsaw

Pact nations to enforce any peace deal, the fraud planned was clear. One must wonder about the honesty of the American negotiators toward the American public. While there was little doubt then or now about the integrity of Richard Nixon, I, for one, expected more from the likes of Henry Kissinger. Even with the hard stance by the American side to force some kind of agreement that would allow the United States to withdraw from the conflict, they obviously knew that a complete fraud was being perpetrated in Paris. That said, we also wanted out of this place. If the politicians in the United States were writing off the South Vietnamese anyway, it was time for us to cut bait and get out.

After my return from Vietnam, the Paris Peace talks finally resulted in an agreement of sorts. This and the introduction of the Four-Party Joint Military Commission intended to supervise compliance with the terms of the peace accord, offered no prospect of protecting South Vietnam from being invaded again by the North in its effort to reunify the country under their communist government. But it is worth noting that the destruction the United States military had wrought upon the North Vietnamese 1972 Spring Invasion force had been so complete that it took the Soviets two and a half years to rebuild the North Vietnamese Army. Only after it was reconstituted, and reequipped with replacement Russian armaments, could it remount the offensive and then march on an utterly defenseless South Vietnamese. The Four-Party Joint Military Commission was powerless and utterly melted away before the rebuilt North Vietnamese invasion force in 1975.

I was told about twelve hours before I left country that I would be returning to the States the next day. I had just come off another rather bad, very scary mission where I brought back another badly damaged slick, to be told after my debrief that I was done and would be sent home immediately. Little did I know what lay ahead at that point. I assumed it would be a somewhat triumphant return home to family and friends, as I had survived! Yet my return was a journey unto itself.

It was harrowing and was as bad as any combat mission I had flown as a helicopter pilot in Vietnam. It was also an embarrassing, personally repugnant trip home. It was truly an insulting process for me and every soldier on that Pan Am contract flight home.

When I was told to report to Ton Son Nhut for my DROS, I was most eager to get aboard that "freedom bird" and fly east. The morning I was to leave Vietnam, December 11, 1972, I turned in my unit gear and weapons to the troop supply and packed my few personal belongings. These consisted of a Yashika 35-mm camera, a few rolls of exposed film, my watch, one custom-tailored tropical-worsted khaki uniform, a few pairs of civilian pants and shirts, a shaving kit, my personal notebook, my flight logbook, and a few local trinkets as souvenirs. All this fit into a small bag I had picked up in Saigon. I signed out of the unit without copies of my unit-level records, not a normal procedure but I was told they would be forwarded to my next gaining unit of assignment. I then waited for the next bird that was going over to H-3 at Ton Son Nhut. My scheduled flight was not until the afternoon, so I thought I would stop into Dad's office at Ton Son Nhut to let the minder there, a Major Kelly, know that I was headed home . . . for good.

When I got to Ton Son Nhut I was told to hustle over to the main PAX terminal ASAP for my flight out. I assumed that this meant that the flight, a scheduled Pan Am 707, was leaving earlier than originally planned. What I discovered was one of the most undignified and repugnant developments I could imagine. I was told to enter a hanger next to the PAX shed where we were told to drop our bags and strip to our underwear, dog tags, and ID cards. Absolutely nothing else was permitted. Someone in the crowd of mostly Army aviators and crewmen then said loudly "I hope they are not taking us to the showers!" This drew some restrained laughter from the group but was obviously not funny for the civilians watching our group. The thought was not lost on most of us. I then thought to myself that this must be some kind of predeparture drug test or medical examination. It was not.

There were about 150 of us, all Army and Air Force personnel, officer and enlisted, but mostly Army from the few remaining aviation units in country. We were then herded out in front of the hangar in our boxer shorts, no T-shirts permitted, and bare feet to a pile of clothing on the ramp. We were then told to pick out whatever fit of these leftover clothes from the now closed PX on the base. There were piles of new shoes in boxes, colorful, tropical-style shirts, and casual pants. No undershirts, no belts, no socks, no hats, just shoes, shirts, and pants. I found a pair of Hush Puppy slip-on shoes, some tan pants, and a Hawaiian shirt. None of it fit exactly right, but at least I had some clothes on. The shoes were size 11.5 and I wear size 10.

There was an Army lieutenant colonel wearing no branch insignia, who was introduced to us as a representative of the Embassy and in charge of our departure. However, I noted that several civilians were lurking about who were clearly giving him instructions on what to do and how to handle us. *What the hell is going on?* I wondered. I asked this lieutenant colonel about our personal bags and the strip search. He looked shocked at my question, hesitated, and then said that we were not permitted to carry out any personal possessions or military gear or uniforms of any kind. I asked about my camera and he said, "No cameras. Especially no cameras."

As a former MP, I knew military law regarding confiscated property, I knew UCMJ, and I knew what was permitted and not permitted under confiscation rules. None of that applied here. This was absolutely illegal and a violation of any number of provisions in UCMJ without signed receipts and provisions for compensation. I protested saying that this was an illegal seizure of personal property. And what about my military personnel file from the unit and my flight logbook, I asked him, which was an FAA requirement for all pilots to record and retain their flight experience history. It was a legal document for us aviators!

He responded with, "Tough shit. You do not need any records;

they will be sent to your next unit for you."

"What about the logbook?" I again protested.

He then said, "Get a new one stateside. Do you want to go home or not" Then he pointed to several heavily armed air police who had now encircled us.

What the fuck was going on here? Who were these guys and where are they taking us?

I never saw my records again nor any of my belongings. To this day that unit level 201 file, which had the key documents about my career up to this point and virtually all my Vietnam service records, has never made it into my official records. I have been told repeatedly that it was burned in a fire in St. Louis in 1973 that involved only WWI records and those of personnel who were in Vietnam in late 1972, just before the cease-fire. Of course, this is bullshit on several counts. First is that I am convinced that these records never made it out of Saigon. Second, all of my active-duty records were reported to have been destroyed, including records for the period before and up to 1975 . . . in a fire in 1973? For the remainder of my career, I had to reconstruct, over and over, my military records for each promotion board and even for my application to the US Army War College in 1992! Every time I would provide copies of those records for most of which I always kept a copy and had mailed home, including the ones from Vietnam, they would once again be "lost."

Shortly after my exchange with this Embassy lieutenant colonel, an Air Force NCO called our attention to a pile of boxes also on the ramp. He told us that it was all the booze left over from the now closed Saigon PX and we could take all we could carry. "Say what?" I said to myself. No cameras, no personal possessions, no military gear of any kind, but all the booze we want. This was not any Army protocol I knew of. I walked over to the pile of boxes and saw that this was all premium, high-dollar liquor that is not what most troops drank. This was stuff from some general's mess. I reached down and picked up a fifth of Pinch. I might as well enjoy the flight, as I doubted there would be much service on board. Little did I know.

Once everyone had at least one bottle of something from the booze pile and all were simply milling about waiting for the next development, one of the civilians asked for our attention. He told us we were about to board our aircraft home. He told us that we would be taken directly to Travis Air Force Base in California. There, he said, we would be told whatever we needed to know about our further travel and reassignment. As I already knew that I was being transferred to Fort Bragg in North Carolina, all I needed was a copy of the transfer order.

Many years later, after Jack Kennedy and I had both retired from military service as full colonels, we spoke about this event. Jack was not physically there but at his office at 1st Aviation Brigade HQ where he was then the operations officer. He said when he found out how we were treated, he was aghast and angry and communicated his anger to Brigadier General Jack Vincent Mackmull, the brigade commander. He told the commander that it was the most insulting, disrespectful, and degrading treatment he had ever heard about before or since. He said he understood our belongings and records all went to the US Embassy. The United States Department of State claims to have no knowledge or records of the event or our belongings and records[24]. Ours was not the only group of departing US servicemen headed home in November and December of 1972.

After this short, mostly uninformative preboarding speech, we were herded down the ramp under a bright, hot Saigon sun to where the 707 jet was waiting to be loaded. For some reason I was again acutely aware of the Vietnam stench in the air. We immediately boarded, with no ticket, no boarding pass, and no paperwork of any kind. What was clear to me at this point was that we were, in effect, sneaking back into the United States. The ultimate insult to American soldiers returning home is to deny him or her the right to wear their uniform proudly upon their return from a combat zone, as they did when they left home. This made me sick and angry. This realization began to dawn on others as well and the displeasure became obvious. As we climbed the stairs of our freedom bird, the conflicting emotions surfaced. Many obscenities and jokes were cast at the civilians watching us and at the place we were leaving.

I moved through the cabin of the plane and sat in an open middle seat in six across, high density seating in the hot and humid cabin. Without uniforms and rank insignia I had no idea who were Army personal or Air Force or who were officers and who were enlisted, though that became clear rather quickly. I did know the other officers from the brigade and several of the NCOs, some of whom were from F/8 Cavalry. The aircraft's crew stood at the door as we entered and said little by way of greeting. They understood what was happening and the sentiment among their new passengers was soon reflected by them. Several of the cabin crew, in fact, were still sitting in their crew seats and did not even get up when we boarded. The loading went quickly, as we had no hand baggage and no bags were being loaded in the baggage compartments of the plane, as far as we could tell. We all just sat down, relieved to be on the plane and looking forward to getting off the ground. While I knew several others on the plane, those immediately around me were unknown to me and were a mix of Army and Air Force.

As the engine started and the door was closed, there was a small cheer that went up among the passengers, though it was brief and did seem not very enthusiastic. As we taxied out to the runway, I heard a distant but all too familiar sound of rounds impacting on the airfield. I looked out the window and saw nothing. Suddenly the aircraft's engine spooled up and the plane seemed to be accelerating rapidly on the taxiway toward the runway threshold. As we began the turn onto the runway, I heard and felt another, louder impact sound that seemed closer. Now everyone was looking out the windows and we knew what we were hearing. That was incoming! The pilot lined up with the runway centerline and poured on the power. I knew that we must be light, so I expected the pilot to rapidly rotate the nose up and climb as fast as he could. Just as we began to rotate, the plane shuddered, and we heard another detonation not too far from the plane. Then we all felt the aircraft being hit by what I assumed was shrapnel. Oh crap! This was not good. Several others around me groaned loudly and we began looking toward the emergency exits, all thinking the same thing . . . how do we get out of here if this goes bad. As we went down the runway, our Pan Am 707 "Freedom Bird" had suffered serious damage as a mortar round impacted near or just below the right wing. So began my personal "Odyssey" home from RVN on Dec 13, 1972.

Soon I realized that although we were in the air, we were not climbing very much. We were gaining speed and I heard the gear come up. Yet we seemed to only be two to three hundred feet in the air! There were radio towers around there higher than that! The cabin crew had a terrified look on their faces and one up forward was on the intercom with, what I assumed, was the flight deck crew. The face of the person I was watching, I soon deduced, was the lead stewardess. Her face quickly turned ashen, and her eyes went wide. This was not good. Someone did not want us leaving Saigon.

Then the aircraft seemed to tremble a bit, but we were climbing, albeit very slowly. It was then that I noticed some very thin gray smoke coming from the right inboard engine. This was not good either. Looking out the window, I could already see the coastline in the distance, so I knew we were headed east, and the pilot was trying to get out of the area. We seemed to level off at about two thousand feet or so. The trembling stopped and all was deathly quiet in the cabin, save for the engine noise and some strange whistling that must have been coming from a new opening or two in the fuselage skin somewhere. That suggested a pressurization problem to me. I do not know what sized ordnance had been used against the airfield, the runway, and our plane, but I assumed it was relatively small based on the sound of the detonations—perhaps Russian 82-mm mortars.

Then the pilot came on the PA system with the bad news. The

runway had taken fire as we rolled on our takeoff. The aircraft was stable and flyable but there were some issues that the crew was sorting out. We had lost some systems (he did not mention the engines at this point, but it was obvious to us that at least one was shut down) but we were clear of danger for now. He told us we could not return to Saigon to land as the runway had been cratered. He then said we were heading to Manila and Clark Air Force base. Because of the problem with a few systems, it would be a low-level flight all the way and, because we would not be at normal cruise altitudes, we needed to prepare for a possibility of a water landing. Just great . . . I get out of Saigon on my DROS flight and I may have to swim part of the way home! The gods were not with us, it seemed. The flight east was tense and unnerving. There were holes in the aircraft. While something we were used to seeing in our combat aircraft, holes were not something we had expected to see on our DROS bird.

At this point, the tension was thick in the cabin; the grumbling had started as we all realized how helpless we were in this situation. As many of us were pilots with lots of combat time, sitting helpless in the back of the plane was both frustrating and unnerving. We were used to being in full control and dealing with the emergency, not being just part of the cargo. We were all very agitated and worried about how this would unfold. The lack of air conditioning became even more apparent as we began to sweat both from the hot, humid air in the cabin and the situation. While it may have been twenty minutes or so, it seemed like just second later that the pilot came back on the PA and told all of us that we needed to stay seated, including the cabin crew, because it may get bumpy flying over the ocean at low altitude. And, almost as a minor additional thought, he informed us that we could not go to Manila because there had been some type of attack on the main civilian terminal there and Clark AFB was now closed to traffic. We were going to fly all the way to Okinawa. There were closer landing options. But it was also clear that this plane was not landing anywhere except on a US military base! To do otherwise, I assumed, given what had transpired on the ramp in Saigon prior to our departure, could be problematic for somebody higher up in authority.

That meant more time over water in a broken plane and a greater chance of a very long swim. Just wonderful! Then someone said, "Well, I am *not* going down sober!" And he lifted his bottle of booze up, waved it around, and proceeded to take a big swallow. That seemed to break the tension a bit and nearly everyone began talking all at once. Liquor bottles were opened, and social drinking began. All the while, the cabin crew sat in their seats, ashen faced, wide-eyed, and not talking or moving. They were clearly scared out of their wits. Most of their passengers, on the other hand, had been so scared so often in the past months that this was just more of the same. Drinking and talking crap about how bad it would be or how long we would have to tread water just seemed natural and a relief.

I did not tap my bottle right away. I was still sizing up the situation in my own head and figuring out what I would do if the plane went into the drink. I figured there was less than a fifty-fifty chance the pilot could put it down in one piece on the water so that we could launch the rafts and actually get out before it sank. The sea below was rough, even though it was a sunny afternoon. The probability was, if we went down in the South China Sea, the plane would touch down wing tip first into a wave and then cartwheel, breaking up as it did. It would not be a fun ride nor survivable for most of us. I was in almost the middle of the plane, so I was near a wing exit, if, by chance, the pilot did a decent, survivable water landing. But if I did get out, I would need to get into a life raft fast, as this area was known for sharks. The picture was not getting any better as I analyzed the situation. The only good news was that the Navy would, no doubt, know about our situation and would be standing by to respond to us and retrieve us. With that thought, I pulled the top off the bottle of Pinch and took a small swallow of its contents. My goodness that was good stuff.

On and on the plane droned. It seemed to me that we were gaining some altitude, but the plane creaked and groaned and was clearly straining to fly at this low attitude without full power from all four engines. Perhaps as we were burning fuel (and possibly leaking it) we were getting lighter. In any case, it was not much of a gain. Every now and then we would encounter turbulence, probably caused by rising warm air from the ocean surface. It was sharp and violent and seemed to stress the cabin crew the most. Soon the liquor was all drunk. Many just urinated on the floor at our seats because it was too dangerous to move around in the cabin. There was no food, though none of us had eaten anything since the night before. The plane soon smelled of urine, salty air, and sweat. And then the stewardess near us started crying loudly.

After a couple of hours, the pilot came on the PA with an update. He informed us that they had a runway prepared for us at Kadena Air Force Base on Okinawa. We would be coming into the field low over the water and would be landing into a barrier net because he was not sure about the status of the brakes or the landing gear. He then told us about the position we would need to assume for the landing and about the need to quickly vacate the aircraft as soon as it stopped on the runway. The pilot instructed us to run directly away from the plane in case it burned. He then told us to put on our life vests in case we did not make it to the runway and had to land on the water. We were clearly leaking fuel and the engine on the inside on the right was not running, though this was probably battle damage not a fuel issue as it had quit not too longer after we took off.

By this time the serious drinking that been going on throughout the cabin was over. Several were nearly dead drunk, with many of the rest pleasantly stewed to some degree. I was probably legally drunk at that point but not seriously drunk. I put the top back on the bottle and put it in its box under the seat in front of me. Then I pulled out the life vest and put it on. All I could do now was wait. I thought about Kelly and Karen and wondered how they would do if

I did not make it out of this situation. I wondered about Mom and what she would do. She would blame Dad for not getting me out of Vietnam sooner on one of the aircraft that he flew back and forth to Vietnam. I wondered about what was going to happen back in Vietnam. I wondered about how the loss of this Pan Am flight and its load of returning soldiers would play out on the evening news, if they were even told about it.

We were soon told to assume the crash position—head down, arms folded over our heads, seat belt tight. Now there was more crying, but I could not see or tell who had joined the tearful chorus. "Well doesn't this just suck!" I said to a seatmate. He just groaned. It was a groan I had heard often in combat as things turned to shit. This trip home had seriously turned to shit. I looked up and around. Several of our fellow passengers were just sitting in their seat, upright and looking out the window. *Fuck it,* I thought, and I sat up and looked out the window at the ocean.

I saw we were descending. Lower and lower we seemed to inch down over about a fifteen-minute period. Pretty soon it seemed that ocean spray was close to getting into the engines. We could not have been more than fifty feet off the surface of the water. Then the pilot gave us a warning of ten minutes to the runway. Then the warning was five minutes. The pilot then shouted, "Prepare for a crash into the runway barrier!" Then he announced, "Brace for impact." The noise suddenly grew very loud in the cabin. The gear must have gone down, or at least the gear doors were now open, but the noise was much louder than normal. The crash bell then sounded (yes, they had a crash bell on the older 707s). The plane groaned even louder as the pilots horsed the wounded airframe into alignment with and down onto the runway.

There was silence inside the plane, as now we all leaned forward with our arms tucked in and head down in the crash position. I glanced out the window and saw rocks passing under the plane close enough, it looked to me, to tear into the bottom of the plane. Then the wheels hit the ground, amazingly softly, and we rolled. I felt no braking action at first. *Oh crap, this is not good,* I thought. Sudden stops from two-hundred-plus knots of speed never end well. Just then I felt us decelerate, followed by more loud noise and the sound of shit breaking and tearing. There was loud crying and shouting as we sped down the first part of the runway. Someone shouted, "Oh shit," which was followed by many more shouts and expletives.

What I heard and felt was, I think, reverse thrust on the three operating engines and, almost at the same time, I felt the plane lurch left and abruptly decelerate, then decelerate suddenly again as we were violently thrown against our seat belts and the seats in front of us. We had hit the barrier, at least the first one. My head hit the seat in front of me rather hard. But the aircraft seemed to tear away from the first barrier, and we were again moving down the runway. I could honestly not tell if we were rolling on the gear or sliding on the struts or other plane parts. The noise was deafening. Then we hit the next barrier and we stopped, violently and the stricken Boeing 707 rocked up on the nose and then fell back very hard, slamming us down in our seats. The noise stopped so suddenly, it was almost a shock in and of itself. For a few moments there seemed to me there was no sound, but I then realized that it was simply the sound of the plane's agony as it slid down the runway that had stopped. I also realized that the stewardess near us was still crying and screaming out for God's help.

"I want the fuck off this plane," I announced. Yes, I do relive this event, along with a few others, in my sleep dreams and daydreams; it is vivid and frightening even today. Then everyone around me started yelling the same thing or something similar. We jumped up into the aisles and a couple of the cabin crew threw open the doors and deployed the escape chutes. Actually, while it seemed chaos prevailed, in truth we all got up in a fairly orderly manner, if a bit unsteady, and walked to the doors and slid down the chutes, a few carrying bottles of liquor, our only possessions, though many were clearly empty. In my memory, I cleared the plane in seconds, but it must have taken several minutes. We got the hell off that dead airliner as fast as we could move. I learned once again how useful adrenalin is. It enabled me, it seemed, to move at seemingly superhuman speed. When I got to the slide, I jumped into it and then followed my shoes down the plastic ramp. They too were in a huge hurry to leave that aircraft. I hit the ground and looked around. There were passengers and crew all giddy and laughing, yet loitering at the end of the ramp. Then someone yelled, "Get the fuck out of here." I looked back at the plane and saw thick black smoke. I grabbed my shoes and I started to run, almost without thinking about it.

There was a hill, actually a modest earthen berm constructed to obstruct view of this runway, to my front and I sprinted up it like a rocket. I wanted to get away from that plane as fast as I could. I have seen fire and wanted none of it. When I got to the top of the hill, I sat down. Suddenly I hurt all over. Everything hurt: my back, my head, and my legs. I looked myself over and bruises were already beginning to appear. Apparently, I had a big one on my forehead. Then it hit—we had cheated death yet again! Well, the gods must have smiled at the end of that flight because we all survived and were all sitting and standing on this small hill. After a few moments, laughter returned and began to spread through the two hundred or so former occupants of that badly fucked up Boeing 707 sitting below us on the runway, with smoke now coming out of every opening. Some openings, with things hanging out, clearly had not existed when we had boarded that beast.

We are on the ground and safe and no one was injured. Amazing for sure. We were laughing and patting each other on the back. As we stood there and laughed the laugh of those just given a reprieve on life, I notice that the plane had little major structural damage to the main fuselage that I could see but I knew, at that point, just how lucky we were to be standing there in one piece.

That plane would clearly never fly again. But it had brought all of us alive back to terra firma. For that we are all, even today, so thankful. Despite serious wounds to its systems and body, it had labored though the skies of the south Pacific to bring us safely to this small rock far out in the vast ocean. As we looked back at the aircraft, we could tell the battle damage from the landing damage. The right wing was a mess. How the hell it stayed on is probably still a mystery at Boeing. I think it was that pilot who had so carefully and tenderly flown that bird at two thousand feet across the ocean that had enabled us to get safely to this speck of land. I never found his name, though I did try. But we all owe him our lives. And I think we owe Boeing our gratitude for creating such a magnificent air machine. It had taken a beating, like its B-17 predecessors in WWII, about whom I had heard so much as a kid from my father's WWII Air Force buddies. There must have been some karma in play here, or the gods just decided to give us all a break after a year of tears, grief, and blood in combat in Vietnam.

This was not the end of our incredible journey. As the two hundred or so Army and Air Force personnel and Pan Am cabin crew were sitting and standing on a small berm to the side of the runway, an Air Force full colonel came running up yelling at all of us to stand up and move off the berm toward the PAX terminal, a good five hundred meters away. No buses, no trucks, and no transport was provided; we had to walk. No big deal at other times, but most of us were now bruised, sore, tired, and in some state of inebriation. At that point, walking in a straight line for some was next to impossible. The colonel yelled at us to face toward the terminal and walk in the direction. *Huh?* I thought. *Who cares where we look.*

Then I heard an earth-shattering roar and half ducked, expecting incoming, and turned toward the noise. Just as I looked back, the doors of a strange-looking hanger snapped open with astonishing speed and out taxied an honest-to-God spaceship. It was big, it was all black, and it was almost scary looking. Then I saw the cockpit and could see the pilot. He was wearing a helmet like astronauts wear.

"What the hell is this?" I said out loud.

A young soldier next to me yelled "Holy shit! What in hell is that?"

The strange craft turned toward a very long runway that paralleled the one on which our badly wounded 707 sat. It then appeared to engage afterburners, or rocket engines of some kind, and screamed down its runway. As it lifted off, it seemed to go nearly vertical and climbed out of sight so fast I was not sure that I saw what I know I saw.

The colonel was still yelling about getting to the PAX terminal but then added, "You did not see that. Remember, you did not see that." After seeing those photos back in October, I now wondered to myself if, just perhaps, we did have a craft that could get into space and return with imagery. Of course, we all know now that what I saw that day was an SR-71 Blackbird. At that time, it was another of our nation's most guarded secrets.

We marched, stumbled, and moseyed over to the PAX terminal on the flight line. There was a cafeteria there and they herded all of us in there for some chow. We were told a replacement Pan Am bird was on the way to Okinawa from Tokyo and would be there in less than two hours to pick us up and continue our journey home. Apparently, Pan Am launched a replacement aircraft as soon as they knew where we were going to land in the battle-damaged airliner. Soon we were back in an aircraft, without any liquor and no food, and on our way to California. It seems the Air Force took a dim view of our intoxicated states and confiscated what was not already drunk as we left the PAX Terminal cafeteria. It was interesting that they let everyone with booze continue to drink in the cafeteria. I suspected they felt having most of us passed out or asleep on the next leg of our travels might be a good thing. There was no service of any kind on that next flight either. No food and nothing to drink except water from a large cooler from which one of the cabin crew might, or might not, bring to you in a small paper cup.

I fell asleep right away on the next leg of the flight. I was awakened by the PA system in the plane announcing that we were landing in five minutes, and everyone had to wake up and be ready to deplane as soon as we landed. I looked outside and saw it was dark, with no stars. Then a wing tip landing light came on and I saw it was snowing!

"What the heck is this?" the guy next to me said.

I then said to him "I wonder where we are."

We soon found out. We were in Anchorage, Alaska for a fueling stop. It was the middle of the night. The plane landed and taxied to the passenger terminal ramp but did not pull up to a gate. Instead, it stopped about two hundred meters away from the terminal. The stewardess then announced that we would have to walk to the terminal through the snow and wait inside until they were ready to go.

Now I was getting aggravated with all of this. Here we were, dressed for a Hawaiian vacation, no socks, no coats, not even undershirts and we had to walk through the snow? Then she told us that it was twenty degrees below zero outside, so we needed to walk very quickly into the terminal. "Yeah, no shit!" someone yelled out. When we got to the ground outside of the aircraft, there was about a foot of snow on the ramp and our feet immediately felt frozen. We had just experienced a 130-degree temperature change in about twelve hours with no time to acclimatize. When we entered the terminal and climbed the stairs up to the passenger level of the building, we were all freezing cold. We began asking about hot coffee and food but were told that nothing was open, as we were not expected, and that there was only ice cream available. Just great!

Two hours later we had to reboard the aircraft for departure. Once again, we walked through the snow to reboard. But once airborne, the cabin crew brought around pots of fresh hot coffee. It was most welcome by everyone. Then they offered drinks but, again, no food. I do not know where the booze came from. I suppose it was on Pan Am, but we all had at least one drink and fell back to sleep. It was midday when we landed at Travis Air Force Base in California. A joyous yell went up in the cabin when we touched down. We clapped and laughed again. It was great to be back in the

United States of America, though it still seemed that we were being treated like criminals being transferred from one prison to another!

The plane taxied up to a hangar and we disembarked directly inside. Then the hangar doors were closed. Once again handlers in uniform and civilian clothes directed us to gather near an elevated engine maintenance ramp. There a gentleman in civilian attire told us we were gathered in this hangar to shield us away from the eyes of any spectators out on the ramps. He told us that he was relieved we made it home in one piece. There were guffaws and jokes about how he might feel, were he one of us. Then we were informed that our return may not be welcome by many Americans. He said that things had changed since we left the States and that soldiers were now very unpopular, and we needed to be prepared for disrespect and even outright abuse. He said it would take some getting used to, but that once at our new assignments or home, we would be fine.

He then informed us that each of would be given three hundred dollars in cash and an airline ticket to our home of record. He told us that we were to wait at our homes for our new orders to arrive in the mail. Then he said that it would be best for us and the country if we did not tell anyone where we had just come from or that we were soldiers until we were home and out of the San Francisco area.

I took the cash and ticket and got into one of the prepaid cabs lined up to take us to SFO to catch flights home. No baggage, no coat, no socks, and a dazed look. Sure, no one will know who we are or where we just came from. Right! In the terminal at SFO airport I found a bar and sat down. I had about two hours to kill until the next flight to Dulles. I had called Karen collect to let her know my arrival flight and time. Now I had to wait, and a cold beer sounded like a good idea. The bartender stepped in front of me. He said, "I know that look. Your money is no good here. What will you have?" I asked for a beer, and he put a twenty-ounce cold one in front of me and reached out to shake my hand. He never said anything else. He just smiled and nodded to me. I drank my beer with some disquiet about the future. I wonder if he ever realized how important that simple gesture was to me.

The flight back to Dulles was long and uncomfortable. The plane was full, and, again, I had a middle seat in coach. It was about three thirty in the morning, Eastern Time, when we landed in a snowstorm at Dulles International Airport. I was cold, tired, hungry, and more than a little irritated to find that Karen had not yet come for me. In fairness, she was dealing with a colicky newborn, the roads were a mess, and traffic was not moving. So, I had to wait about three hours for her to arrive. I was so tired and so hungry, time passed as an out-of-focus blur as I sat in the vast, mainly empty terminal lounge. When my wife finally got there, she also looked worn out, tired, and stressed. No doubt she was. I gather I did not look much better to her. But here she was with my wonderful daughter Kelly, and all was right with the world. We drove back to our apartment in Arlington, Virginia. Once home I held little Kelly in my arms for a short time, but she cried and protested being held by a stranger. No matter. I was home and I wanted nothing more than to be able to help Karen with Kelly and become a real dad myself. So, I gave her up to my wife and I laid down to sleep. I slept the sleep of the near dead until the middle of the night when a siren near the apartment sent me under the bed, where I could not find my helmet or M-16.

Two days later we were in the kitchen of my parent's home at Wright-Patterson Air Force Base in Dayton, Ohio. Just as my mom had breakfast ready, with Kelly in Karen's arms nursing and Dad and I sipping coffee, the phone rang. Dad answered the phone and sat silently listening. Then he said "No, Major Kelly, my son is sitting here having breakfast with the family. He is fine." He hung up and said "My office in Saigon reports that there was a problem with your Pan Am DROS flight. They do not know exactly what happened and they are checking to find out your status." We chuckled, then sat silently for a few moments. It had been a tough year for all of us.

CHAPTER TEN
LIFE GOES ON

WHEN I CAME home, it was without dignity, it was without any customary recognition of a soldier returning home from war, and it was without the simplest welcome. It was also to abuse and, very often, public ridicule. I quickly found that to acknowledge service in Vietnam was to taint you. I even found that to acknowledge I had been a helicopter pilot in Vietnam meant, somehow, that I was crazy or unbalanced. Hollywood and TV have quite frequently fostered this stereotype. When I came home, I was not allowed to wear my uniform on the trip back. We were told that to do so would surely subject us to abuse, possible physical attack by the American population. Imagine, if you can, how that felt. For me it was a smoldering disquiet and hint of resentment for some years afterwards. We were, of course, the easy targets for the blame. We were the crazy ones. We were the cause for this brief intrusion into the peaceful contentment of the evening living room at home, this unwanted disturbance in the unrelenting pursuit of image and money by the shakers and movers of Washington and Hollywood.

I, and many, many others, came home, not only without my uniform, but without respect. This was not the way for a warrior to return home. It did not fit our history and it did not fit me. I packed up Karen and Kelly and we moved to Fort Bragg. There I learned that I had been assigned to duty there since June of the previous year. I, of course, challenged this as both insulting and ridiculous. I was told this this was the way it was, period. I remained there until 1975. Then I set the warrior aside, for a time, as I left active service but not the Army. In 1974 I had submitted a request to resign my commission, under pressure from both my wife and my own resentment. At first, I was on a leave of absence, as my request to resign was initially refused. But in early 1975 I was granted the resignation if I agreed to accept a reserve commission. When I began my out processing at Fort Bragg, I was given a DD 214 that reflected service in the Republic of Vietnam from Dec 1971 to June 1972. I refused to sign it, as it required, because it was incorrect. The personnel NCO was shocked that a captain would refuse to sign his DD 214. The personnel warrant officer at the XVIII Corps headquarters suggested that I speak to the Corps G-1 about the situation. I went up to his office and waited some time to see him. I was not a priority for this busy staff officer. When he did, just at the end of the day, he told me that my assertion that I had been in Vietnam for the period June to December of 1972 was false and I was bringing discredit upon myself and the Army. He called me a liar. I was nearly speechless—for about thirty seconds. Then I told him that not only was I not a liar, but I would be happy to get the deputy chief of Army personnel on the phone to explain to him where I was during that period. I also informed him that I had copies of records for part of my service at that time in Vietnam. He told me that he would check with the Office of the Army Chief of Personnel himself and I was to report to him first thing in the morning with proof of that service in Vietnam.

The next morning, I went to his office and found that he was waiting for me, sitting at his desk. He told me that he had, in fact, checked my claims. He said that he was shocked with what he heard. He asked to see what records I had before he explained further. I gave him copies of several documents, mainly unit orders from F/8 Cavalry and the 48th AHC with my name on them in several places. He looked at them for only a few seconds and then he looked up at me with a most unusual, somewhat confused look on his face.

He then said, "I have heard stories about some units remaining in Vietnam and continuing combat operations after August of 1972, but I was always told this was only false bragging by would-be heroes. I did call a friend at DA yesterday," he continued. "I was told that, contrary to documents in your official personnel file here at Fort Bragg, you were in Vietnam, as you said." He waited a few moments and then said, "I do not know what to say except that you have my apology." He stood up and offered his hand. I shook it as he said, "You will have a correct DD 214 today."

I left active duty and took a break from military duty. Eighteen months later I was offered a position as the operations officer for the 449th Aviation Company, North Carolina National Guard. This unit was manned by pilots who were nearly all Vietnam veterans and I found kindred spirits with like experience. I went on to serve the remainder of my military career in a variety of aviation, infantry, and intelligence assignments, both National Guard and on active duty. In March of 2000, I retired as a colonel after thirty-one years wearing the uniform of my country.

It was not until 2007 that I learned more about the significance of what we had accomplished in October of 1972. In the weeks after our destruction of the Saigon Guns, there was a significant change in the negotiating posture of the North Vietnamese delegation to the Paris Peace Talks. As reported later in the JCS review of the Vietnam War, published in 2007, Secretary of State Henry Kissinger, who was leading the US delegation to the peace talks in Paris, wrote "Hanoi had finally separated the military and political questions . . . .. For nearly four years we had longed for this day. . .."[25] There can be no doubt that the loss of the last North Vietnamese military gambit in Military Region III of South Vietnam and their attempt to directly shell Saigon, played a role in change to the North Vietnamese negotiating position in Paris in October of 1972.

This shift occurred just before October 21, 1972, but the due to the secrecy of the discussions at this time, the exact record is not clear. However, what is clear is that the last major military operation by the North Vietnamese in the Fall of 1972, as a part of their effort to influence the Paris Peace talks, had failed with the discovery and destruction of the guns intended to bring indirect artillery fire on downtown Saigon. With this failed effort, Hanoi, in effect, conceded the overall failure of their Easter Offensive of 1972. Their demands for military concessions as a part of any Paris Peace Accord were now irrelevant and dropped. But what is also important to note is the fact that the United States Joint Chiefs of Staff were just as much in the dark about the negotiations in Paris as we in F/8 Cavalry were in III Corps of RVN about what was happening in the higher US military commands in Washington, DC and in Saigon, who were pulling our strings. We had little idea of the true context of our combat operations during this same period. It was only years later that the facts surrounding these talks became public.

Life after Vietnam was tough for tens of thousands of returning veterans. They were mistreated, abused, and shunned. It was as unfair as it was vile. Worse, it was orchestrated to benefit a political perspective and to protect the reputations of a few, distasteful, and infamous celebrities and politicians. Not only were the media unkind to Vietnam veterans, but even the government, particularly in the late 1970s, was disdainful and negligent toward them. This was manifested in many ways, but the actions of the Veterans Administration toward this new generation of veterans were uncaring and abusive. It began a trend that persisted for decades and prevented thousands of Vietnam-era veterans from getting the care that they needed for both combat wounds and service-related diseases, such as cancer from exposure to chemical defoliants while in Vietnam. It seems that the VA leadership and much of its rank-and-file staff within the benefits offices of the VA had lost their way and focused more on protecting budgets and job security than service to America's veterans. For a period of decades, they clearly lost both the meaning and spirit of President Lincoln's words so elegantly spoken at his second inauguration:

With malice toward none, with charity for all, with firmness in the right as God gives us to see the right, let us strive on to finish the work we are in, to bind up the nation's wounds, to care for him who shall have borne the battle and for his widow, and his orphan, to do all which may achieve and cherish a just and lasting peace among ourselves and with all nations.

It is with more than a little irony, considering the conduct of the VA benefits staff from the 1970s to the new century and even the post 9/11 period, that a portion of those immortal words had become the VA motto in 1959: *To care for him who shall have borne the battle.* But it was not only some in government and many politicians that despised the Vietnam veteran in the aftermath of the war, but it also reached across many segments of American society. Many Americans, to include the local and state court systems, held Vietnam veterans in disdain. And this could and did impact a veteran's ability to get a job, buy a home, or finance a car. In my own case, a banker once cautioned me in 1977 not to reveal I had served in Vietnam because the bank would not finance my new car. Such stories are common among my fellow Vietnam-era veterans. A further insult was the portrayal of Vietnam veterans, particularly helicopter crews, as nut cases or worse by Hollywood, which further supported this prevalent public perception of the Vietnam veteran community in the late 1970s and early 1980s. To this day, my official US Army personnel file retains a document that references the period July to December 1972, and states: "The whereabouts of Captain Hoffman during this period is unknown by this command." The command referenced is XVIII Airborne Corps, Fort Bragg, NC. There are no other documents in my personnel file for that period, save one: a decoration from the government of South Vietnam. I am not alone in this official records situation. All of this is a consequence of former President Nixon's assertion in the summer of 1972 during the run-up to his re-election, that there were no longer any United States Army troops engaged in combat operations in the Republic of South Vietnam.

In 2010 my father died of lung cancer, attributed to exposure to Agent Orange, no doubt occurring during his multiple tours of duty in South Vietnam, operating into and out of Bien Hoa Air Base. He was a veteran of three wars: World War II, Korea, and Vietnam, who served his country for more than thirty-three years on active duty. In April of 2011, a rapidly growing cancer was removed from my own chest by the incredible Dr. Robert Stewart at Walter Reed Army Medical Center. This cancer was quickly assessed as being the result of exposure to Agent Orange in Vietnam. For a year I had flown into and out of two of the now identified twenty-eight Dioxin hot spots in South Vietnam.[26]

I must also note that my initial efforts to engage the support of the VA medical center in my hometown and access its incredible medical care teams was frustrated for several years by the Veterans Administration benefits office that refused to acknowledge my service in Vietnam or that my lung cancer was the result of Agent Orange exposure. The Veterans Administration benefits application process was a true nightmare for me and my family as I dealt with my recovery from the invasive surgery and its aftermath.

The lack of proper records management and preservation at the St. Louis National Personnel Records Center, the utter disrespect I experienced, and the lack of customary attention to detail and due process on the part of the VA staff in Winston-Salem, North Carolina Regional Office of the VA was appalling. To make matters worse for many veterans seeking benefits and medical care, unqualified VA benefits staffers, with little or no actual medical training or background, make life-and-death benefits and medical care access decisions—when they get around to any decision at all. The outcomes are often poor as a result.

After nearly two years of arguing my case with the benefits office in the VA, I was granted access to the top-notch and dedicated

VA medical staff at the Asheville, North Carolina Veterans Administration hospital.

And what of Vietnam itself today? Back during the first week of December 1972 there was a question arising in Saigon. The major offensive effort of the NVA had evaporated. Oh, there were still engagements and the minor rocket or artillery attack here and there, but their operational tempo was way down around Saigon and other areas in South Vietnam. Where did all the NVA offensive action go?

The apparent pull back from these areas in the Republic of Vietnam and the dramatic reduction in engagements in and around its major cities was clear to all as 1972 drew to a close. Obviously the NVA decided that further direct confrontation where American firepower might come into play, was a pointless destruction of their combat power. So, they moved back and shifted their efforts toward making progress at getting the Americans out of Vietnam all together in Paris, depending upon their Soviet mentors to stimulate further discord within the remaining popular support for South Vietnam in the US and in the US media. The objective, clear to all of us at the time, was to get us out so they could come back and conquer South Vietnam after we were gone. They correctly assumed that the US military would not be permitted, given the political climate in the US, to return and help to defend the South Vietnamese. This was the fraud being built in Paris.

The plan worked, at least temporarily. The Russian economy was already on the brink of collapse. They had invested heavily in North Vietnam and their People's Army of Vietnam. The Soviets wanted a warm-water port on the Pacific Rim. They wanted to beat, via proxy, the Americans on the field of battle, which, of course, they never did. They wanted better standing in Central and South America and a win in RVN would give them that.

Yet the world continues to turn and there is a lesson that all must learn: be careful what you wish for. In the case of the Soviet Union, propping up the newly unified Vietnam was much more costly than they expected. The tragic, murderous excesses of their communist minions in the region left a trail of blood and death that is still a scar that Russian army officers, even in the 1990s, would wince at upon being reminded. The strategic value of the port at Cam Ranh Bay fell dramatically once the Soviets occupied it. When we left, we even took up the main runway and removed it along with virtually everything else. Da Nang did not bring them much either. The cost of rebuilding the lost armor and fighter technology from the 1972 Easter Offensive put an enormous burden on Soviet finances. Small wonder it took almost two and a half years from the time we left Vietnam until May of 1975 for the NVA to finally roll into Saigon.

We did leave a few valuable items behind that they exploited rather successfully. For example, the Soviets took the US built M-16 fabrication facility near Saigon and used it to churn out M-16 copies they could distribute worldwide to insurgents and terrorists of all types and not be blamed for their proliferation. A funny thing happened though: few wanted them. The mystique of the AK-47 as the weapon that won the Vietnam War created an extraordinary demand for the AK while the M-16, touted by the Soviets as the weapon that lost the war, found few takers. Yes, the AK is a superb weapon for a less sophisticated military force, such as an insurgency, and yes, it is functional, even in the hands of a ten-year-old. But the fact remains that the two weapons are both very lethal and very effective.

Then there were helicopters, trucks, and some armor that could be used for all types of training and evaluation. The problem for the Soviets was that most of this stuff was already outdated for us and, as the result of lessons learned in Vietnam, we were taking very large technology leaps forward while they invested, through the '70s and early '80s, in the means to counter our Vietnam-era gear. This technology gap widened in the 1980s and ultimately broke the Soviet Union, an indirect result perhaps, but nonetheless a tangible one of the Vietnam War. There is an old military doctrine that states that winning battles, occupying ground, or the appearance of victory is not victory in war. Victory, according to history, is the ultimate outcome of who prevails and who is left standing with one's nation, military, and economy intact.

By the late 1970s the Soviets were failing their Vietnamese protégés. Their support to the country dwindled rapidly. By the 1980s the Vietnamese were reaching out to the west for help through every channel they could open. Today, Vietnam is so integrated and dependent upon the capitalist, developed nations, that without our direct engagement and their participation in global trade, the population would starve, and their economy would collapse. Ho Chi Minh must be spinning in his grave! Of course, he did ask America for help to eject the French first and President Eisenhower refused him. So, he turned to the Soviets.

I grieve for all the blood and sacrifice of our family and that of so many other American families during the Vietnam War. What lessons have we really learned about the nature of warfare, focusing upon strategic objectives, and our role in the international community? What have we learned about how we conserve and protect our national resources, our always limited economic capabilities, and about how we use our power in geo-politics and war? Now that we have extracted our military from much of Southwest Asia, and our war on terrorism, have we really achieved our aims and made America safer? I certainly hope so. But Afghanistan today suggests otherwise.

And what about our citizen soldiers? Vietnam was fought by men and women from every corner and every walk of life in America. There was no military power elite, no foreign legion, no military-industrial force in arms, it was just all of us everyday Americans from every town, every family, and every walk of life. But even though that has changed with our current all-volunteer army, our current policies and perspective have still been shaped by our experience in Vietnam.

Finally, I hope that the current and future generations of

Americans care and respect their military veterans and their families with recognition awards and appreciation of their service and sacrifice. I hope that the media and politicians never again turn on the soldier so that they can ease their own burdens of conscience or for political gain—or to achieve higher TV ratings or to sell more newspapers. Their conduct in the 1970s and 80s was an insult to every American citizen soldier throughout history. It was the height of hypocrisy and remains a stain on the character and legacy of many unworthy Americans. I trust that the lessons learned during and after our engagement in Southeast Asia are well learned and long remembered.

Lastly, as I said at the outset, I am often asked about my experience in Vietnam and what kinds of things remind me of my experiences there. That is easy. While many things can trigger memories, some pleasant other not so, one thing never fails . . . that smell.

ENDNOTES

1 The US Army lost a total of 5607 helicopters lost in the war, with 2165 pilots and 2712 crew members killed. See: heliloss.pdf (vhpa.org)

2 Few today know this term. It was coined, I am informed, during the Civil War as term for the first experience of the horror and fear on the battlefield.

3 A study was initiated in August 1951 at Fort Benning to propose a new Ranger Course. This new Ranger Course would be offered to all combat units of the army, in order to develop leaders in infantry units throughout the Army. This standard, explained by General Mark W. Clark in a letter dated 16 February 1952, must be established in sufficient numbers so that each infantry unit the size of a platoon will have at least one Ranger qualified Soldier. This individual will then act as a seed around which many other similar seeds in the unit will grow. The ultimate goal of this process is to raise the standard of performance of all our infantry units. Today this still remains one of the goals of Ranger School. See: https://www.benning.army.mil/infantry/artb/5th-RTBn/content/PDF/Welcome-Packet.pdf?22NOV2019

For more on the History of the Rangers in the US Army See: https://www.army.mil/ranger/heritage.html

4 The Camp was named for BG Merrill in 1971. For more about General Merrill's exploits in WWII see http://history.army.mil under the search term "Merrill's Marauders: Introduction."

5 The following quotes from Jane Fonda should lay to rest her true views on all of this:

"I would think that if you understood what communism was, you would hope, you would pray on your knees that someday we would someday become communists."—Jane Fonda, 1970, Address to Michigan State University

"I, a Socialist, think we should strive toward a Socialist society, all the way to Communism."

"Bottom line," Fonda continues, "this has gone on far too long, this spreading of lies about me! None of it is true. NONE OF IT! I love my country. I have never done anything to hurt my country or the men and women who have fought and continue to fight for us."—From an article that Fonda wrote for the showbiz website "The Wrap" as a response to QVC refusing to have her appear to promote her book *Prime Time*.

6   The CH-47D, E, and F models, the current-era versions of this venerable Army workhorse, have tandem hooks that can lift up to 26,000 pounds externally and can self-deploy up to 2000 nautical miles. Some versions are even equipped for air-to-air refueling.

7   Most attacks on these bases in 1971 and early 1972 were from small, 60-mm mortars or the occasional 122-mm rocket. The mortars had a relatively small impact area but were deadly if they hit near you. The rockets, on the other hand, were heavy rounds with a large impact area and were very destructive.

8   As air temperature rises and the humidity increases, the density of the air is reduced. This limits the lift that the rotating blades of the helicopter can generate. Therefore, the effective payload is reduced. Flying helicopters in hot and humid environments limits the aircraft to the same reduced performance capabilities that one would find flying the same aircraft at high altitudes, such as in high mountains,

9   Ba Mười Ba was a local Vietnamese beer. The name literally means "thirty-three" in Vietnamese. It was drinkable but not noteworthy. The local joke was that it was called that because the Vietnamese brewers were unsuccessful the first thirty-two attempts to brew beer in Vietnam.

10   AFVN was a radio station operated by the US Army to provide music and entertainment for the US soldiers and airmen serving in Vietnam. We could listen to AFVN on long flights or to lighten the mood when flying by tuning our automatic direction finding (ADF) radio to the AFVN AM frequency. It could be received all over South Vietnam.

11   Captain Casmir (Gary) Garczynski, Field Artillery, flew with F Troop 8th Cav, as an artillery observer, when F/8 was the assigned air recon component of 196th Infantry Brigade from 11/71 to 6/72. At one point in mid-1972 Gary had just returned from ARVN I Corp Forward (Hue) when he found himself functioning as the I Corps artillery commander, directing

the employment of 175-mm guns, four USMC naval gunfire teams, the light cruiser Providence and thirteen destroyers with five-inch 38s and five-inch 54s as deck guns firing in support of ground operations in I Corps. He said, "It was all the tactical artillery support a junior captain could want." This situation was obviously intolerable to higher command in Saigon, so he was supplanted by several field grade officers in a matter of hours.

12   The aircraft were nicknamed "Spads" in RVN. They were late WWII piston-engine fighters that made great ground-attack airplanes and were later replaced by the jet powered A-10.

13   This particular B-52, tail number 60665, was repaired on the runway at Da Nang by a Boeing remote area maintenance team. They removed the damaged wing and replaced it right out on the ramp and returned the aircraft to flyable status so that it could be flown out of Da Nang. The aircraft was fully operational in time to participate in Linebacker II in December 1972. This same aircraft flew four additional missions over North Vietnam before the end of the year. The aircraft was assigned to the 97th Bomb Wing at Blytheville Air Force Base when it was transferred to the United States Air Force Museum in Dayton, Ohio in November 1978. It remains on display at the museum today.

14   See: https://www.jcs.mil/Portals/36/Documents/History/Vietnam/Vietnam_1971-1973.pdf

15   By October 1972 these compromises of classified information reached dangerous levels and the chairman of the Joint Chiefs of Staff initiated a broad investigation. See: https://www.jcs.mil/Portals/36/Documents/History/Vietnam/Vietnam_1971-1973.pdf, page 185

It was many years later that the espionage activities of John Anthony Walker, a member of the US Navy, were found to be at least partly responsible.

16   This was a derogatory term for the NVA soldiers that was popular with the Air Force FACs.

17   When I came into Dad's quarters it was apparent right off that I was interrupting something. Dad was giving General Yeager grief about something, and General Yeager seemed uncharacteristically meek and subdued about whatever they were discussing. Dad was walking out of a side room and very agitated about something and seemed to have stopped midsentence when I came into his living room. Dad and General Yeager recovered very quickly and then became very jovial and happy at my arrival. I did pick up that dad had just flown back into South Vietnam from the States and General Yeager had just arrived from Pakistan. I had not known Dad had been back in the States.

Jump ahead more than ten years and I asked Dad about that meeting and General Yeager. Dad was very quiet for a while and then simply said "I was having a very important counseling session with Chuck." He only said it had to do with the general's flying in Pakistan while there in charge of the US Military Assistance Group amid Pakistan's war with India. I knew they had been friends for decades, yet things were different now. They did not speak very often now, and Chuck Yeager did not come by visit Dad, and vice versa. Years later I saw General Yeager at the 100-year celebration of the Wright Brothers flight at Kitty Hawk, North Carolina. He recognized me as soon as we ran into each other. When I spoke to the general, he was cordial but far more reserved than I remembered him being. He did not ask about dad, which was strange. He wanted to know how my career had gone and was I still flying. We exchanged pleasantries and he walked away. It was the last time I saw him.

About a week later I told Dad about the encounter and that I found it a bit strange, to say the least. I asked Dad, again, what the deal was between he and General Yeager. He then told me more of the story of that meeting in Saigon when we had the five-layer pizza (Dad had always loved to talk about that night . . . except for the Chuck Yeager part).

It turns out that he had been having a serious chat with General Yeager when I had walked in that evening. Dad was the director of international logistics for AFLC at Wright-Patterson AFB. He split his time between there and Saigon because the Vietnam War consumed a great deal of his time in that capacity. In his capacity as the director of international logistics, he was General Yeager's superior, even though he still wore the rank of full Colonel. General Yeager was head of the US Air Force Military Assistance Group in Pakistan. The Air Force was providing first-line fighters to Pakistan in the midst of the India-Pakistan War, then at its height, with serious ground and air combat daily over India and Pakistan.

General Yeager had potentially put Dad, the US Air Force, and the United States of America in serious difficulty. Dad had to bring the issue to General

Yeager and communicate the seriousness of the matter. So, I had walked into the serious conversation between them and interrupted Dad's discussion with General Chuck Yeager. And this was not, I came to understand, the first time.

The Indians, in an air raid on a Pakistani Air Base, had destroyed the Beechcraft airplane General Yeager used for personal transportation around Pakistan. This really angered him. He felt very strongly about the Pakistani cause in this conflict and thought very highly of the Pakistani Air Force pilots. Part of his duty was to help train the Pakistani pilots on the fighter aircraft the United States was supplying Pakistan. Given the circumstances, General Yeager's anger at the Indian Air Force, General Yeager took it upon himself to cause a combat mission to be carried out by the Pakistani Air Force against the Indian fighter group's Russian supplied aircraft that had attacked his airplane (no doubt at the behest of the Indian Air Force's Russian advisors.)

The United States was also providing some routine military material support to India at this time, though the Indians were flying Soviet fighters in this conflict. The United States was not a party to this conflict, was an ally, at some level, of both nations, and had extensive trading relationships with both nations. Having it surface in the media or diplomatic circles that the famous American ACE and test pilot, General Chuck Yeager, might be involved in some manner with missions flown by the Pakistani Air Force against India would not play well in DC and elsewhere.

Dad heard about the mission from his own contacts in the Pakistani Air Force. Dad was fit to be tied over this and had summoned General Yeager to meet him in Saigon that very evening so he could address the issue, admonish General Yeager for his potentially ill-considered actions in the line of duty, and forbid any future involvement in combat sorties by the Pakistani Air Force. Dad wanted to keep the whole thing quiet, out of the media, and out of diplomatic circles. Had this become public back then, the potential consequences might have had both adverse political and strategic implications.

18 This controversy brought considerable discredit to the congress and the president back then. None of the senior officer promotion lists for that period were ever approved by the Senate. General Lavelle was finally exonerated posthumously decades later. See: https://inss.ndu.edu/Media/

News/Article/693816/violating-reality-the-lavelle-affair-nixon-and-the-parsing-of-the-truth/

19 Information on the Corona program and most of its images were declassified in April 1995. Numerous books have been written since that time on Corona and the use of its images. For more information on the Corona Project see: Peebles, Curtis. The Corona Project: America's First Spy Satellites. Annapolis, Md.: Naval Institute Press, 1997

20 I made a trip to the National Archives in College Park, Maryland to see what, if anything, was actually in the official records for this and several other actions in 1972. I confirmed that the day's operational summary, then classified but now declassified, reported the discovery of a large cache of 130-mm artillery rounds by unspecified aircraft and the subsequent engagement of the target by various Navy, Air Force, and Marine aircraft which resulted in its destruction. No mention was made of the actual nature of the mission or the discovery of the artillery itself.

21 This event occurred only a few days before the preliminary agreement between the North Vietnamese and Henry Kissinger in Paris on the text of a cease-fire agreement. The draft agreement language was rejected by President Thieu of South Vietnam on several grounds. There was, we heard after the operation, great indignation in Saigon that in the midst of the negotiation in Paris the North Vietnamese had made one last attempt to destroy Saigon in a final act of the 1972 Easter Invasion by the NVA. It is little wonder that President Thieu was not cooperative at that point. Clearly, in my view, this initial agreement on the part of the North Vietnamese was intended to misdirect the United States and buy time to see if Saigon could be brought under direct long-range fire from smuggled-in Soviet field guns. This nearly Herculean effort to move these guns down the Trail and into the Parrot's Beak area of South Vietnam without detection by conventional reconnaissance had begun shortly after the start of the Easter Offensive in March of 1972. If the NVA had succeeded with this bold plan, the dynamic in Paris would have been very different in the following days. It was only due to the Corona satellite that this Soviet artillery was detected.

22 Courage and Blood: South Vietnam's Repulse of the 1972 Easter Invasion, LEWIS SORLEY

From *Parameters*, Summer 1999, pp. 38-56.

23 A subsequent review from the Joint Chiefs of Staff stated that "In retrospect, the North Vietnamese viewed the 1972 offensive as a time of 'enormous victories' during which 'the nature of the war changed in many important ways.' The enemy claimed to have enlarged his 'liberated area' in South Vietnam. His main force troops held 'secure footholds in the important strategic areas,' and the 'interspersion of areas under our control within areas controlled by the enemy' was 'gradually changing the balance of forces in favor of our side.'

These claims notwithstanding, the enemy's strategic offensive had produced meager gains at best. By the time of the restriction of US air operations in October 1972, the South Vietnamese, with US assistance, had not only stopped the offensive but had pushed the enemy back nearly to positions existing before the campaign began. While the enemy still controlled areas of South Vietnam, it was claimed that only four hundred thousand people of the total population of nineteen million remained under enemy control. Moreover, North Vietnamese casualties during the offensive were estimated at one hundred thousand killed or seriously wounded, and the CIA predicted that it would take eighteen months for North Vietnam to resupply and refit its main forces."

See: https://www.jcs.mil/Portals/36/Documents/History/Vietnam/Vietnam_1971-1973.pdf

24 I have repeatedly tried to find out the disposition of our records from that date. I even requested Senator Richard Burr's office to request the State Department to determine where these records were sent, if anywhere. They responded that they have no records from that period at the US Embassy in Saigon and they have no information on US military records were sent to the embassy, if any actually were. Once again, this was a records dead end for those of us who were serving in combat in RVN in the summer and fall of 1972.

25 See page 272, History of the Joint Chiefs of Staff, The Joint Chiefs of Staff and The War in Vietnam 1971–1973, Willard J. Webb and Walter S. Poole, Office of Joint History, Office of the Chairman of the Joint Chiefs of Staff, Washington, DC. 2007

26 Congressional Research Service Report "US Agent Orange/Dioxin Assistance to Vietnam Updated" February 10, 2021 states:

Bien Hoa airbase was the airport used for the most Agent Orange spraying missions during the war and is where the most herbicide was stored and used by the US military. One study of soil samples from the Bien Hoa airbase found a sample with a TEQ concentration at over 1,000 ppb—higher than typical samples at the Danang airbase, and 1,000 times higher than the international limit. (Page 26)

This same Congressional report lists both Bien Hoa Air Base and Marble Mountain Army Airfield as two of the 28 "Dioxin hotspots" in Vietnam (page 34). See: US Agent Orange/Dioxin Assistance to Vietnam (congress.gov)

ACKNOWLEDGMENTS

I WISH TO acknowledge the help of many former comrades in 1971–72 in filling in gaps and details. I want to thank my brother-in-law, Dan Price, for his help with an initial editing pass through an early draft of this book. I wish to thank CW2 Dwayne Shirley, a fellow pilot from F/8 Cav in 1972, who also assisted me with an early review and edit of a subsequent draft of this manuscript. I also want to thank my early reviewers for their kind words and the team at Koehler Publishing for their expert assistance in getting this book polished and published.

Lastly, I want to thank my wife, Renee, for supporting me over many years as I worked on this manuscript. She provided me the space and time out of our busy lives that I needed writing and editing this effort to document my experience in South Vietnam.

GLOSSARY OF TERMS

A1E   USAF Fighter called a "Spad;" WWII era, rotary engine ground attack aircraft

A-4   Navy fighter bomber; single engine precision ground attack aircraft

A-7   USAF fighter bomber; single engine ground attack aircraft

Air Boss   Navy Air Assets commander; commands Navy air operations on a ship

AC   Aircraft commander; pilot in command

ADF   Automatic direction finder; enabled us to listen to music on AFVN

AFB   Air Force Base

AFLC   Air Force Logistics Command

AFVN   Armed Forces Vietnam; US forces radio and television service in RVN

AGL   Above ground level

AH-1G   Attack helicopter model 1G; the helicopter gunship called a Cobra; also referred to as a Snake in RVN

AHC   Assault helicopter company; typically equipped with UH-1s and AH-1Gs

AK-47   Russian supplied infantry rifle; effective, reliable, automatic infantry rifle

AMC   Air mission commander

ANGLICO Air Naval Gunfire Liaison Company; US Marine fire support forward observers

AO Area of operations

ARVN Army of Vietnam; the Army of South Vietnam

ASHC Assault support helicopter company; equipped with CH-47s

ATC Air traffic control

BDA Bomb damage assessment

B-52 USAF strategic bomber; B-52 bombing missions we called Arc Lights

BOQ Bachelor officer's quarters; temporary housing for transient officers

C-47 An Air Force DC-3; WWII era twin engine transport

C-130 Hercules cargo aircraft; four engine, turbo-prop transport

C-141 Large USAF jet transport

C&C Command and control

CAG Combined aviation group; ad hoc US Army aviation groups in RVN

CH-47 Cargo helicopter model 47; the helicopter called a Chinook three; versions were used in RVN: A, B, and C

CH-53 Medium lift helicopter; rescue helicopter for the USAF, troop transport helicopter for the Navy and Marines

CH-54 Heavy lift helicopter; called a Sky Crane

CO Commanding officer; commander of a unit

CONEX Military shipping container

CP	Command post; HQs of a tactical unit in the field
CORPs	A senior military organization; usually made up of two to five divisions and forty to eighty thousand soldiers
DD-214	Certificate of release or discharge from active duty; lists key aspects of one's service and awards
DC-8	1960s-era four-engine jet airliner; By 1972 mainly used in charter services
DMZ	Demilitarized Zone; between North and South Vietnam 1954–1976
DROS	Date of return from overseas duty; the date you left RVN for home for good
E&E	Escape and evasion
EOD	Explosive ordnance detachment
F-4	USAF fighter bomber; used for ground attack in RVN 1971–72
FAC	Forward air controller; USAF pilots who coordinated air-to-ground ops
FEB	Flight evaluation board; normally assesses violations of procedures
FO	Forward observer; coordinated Artillery fires for ground troops
G-1	Personnel; a primary staff function in the US Army
HAZMAT	Hazardous materials
HQ	Headquarters
Huey	Slang term for UH-1 helicopter
JAG	Judge Advocate General; the US military judicial branch

ICBM   Intercontinental ballistic missile

IFR   Instrument flight rules; applied when weather conditions limit visual flight

IMC   Instrument metrological conditions; requiring operations under IFR rules

LAWs   Light anti-tank weapon system; US weapon widely used in RVN

LI   Ranger School Lane Instructor

LT   Lieutenant; pronounced "El-Tee;" a shorthand reference used in the RVN era

LZ   Landing zone; refers to where troops exit the helicopter

M-1   US infantry rifle in WWII; standard issue from 1942–1958

M-16   Standard US infantry rifle; widely employed in the Vietnam War

M-14   Earlier US infantry rifle; standard issue 1958–1967

M-60   7.62-mm machine gun; mounted in the doors of UH-1

MP   Military police; law enforcement branch of the US Army

NAS   Naval Air Station

NATO   North Atlantic Treaty Organization

NCO   Non-commissioned officer; senior sergeant in the US Army

NVA   North Vietnamese Army; the North Vietnamese Army in the field

OH-6   Observation helicopter model 6; US Army scout helicopter in RVN

OH-58	Observation helicopter model 58; US Army scout helicopter in RVN
OPFOR	Opposing Forces; US Army soldiers who function as the "enemy" during tactical training operations
O-2	Light observation aircraft operated by the USAF
OV-1	US Army reconnaissance airplane; twin turboprop aircraft widely used in RVN
OV-10	Armed observation aircraft operated by USAF and Marine Corps
PAVN	People's Army of Vietnam; usually referred to the overall military leadership of the North Vietnamese military
PAX	USAF term for passengers
Peter pilot	Helicopter co-pilot; US Army term from RVN
PM	Provost marshal; chief police officer on an Army base
PMO	Provost marshal's office; police station on an Army base
PriFly	Control tower on a carrier
PSP	Perforated steel planking; expedient aircraft ramps and runways
PT	Physical training; physical fitness training and testing
PX	Post exchange; retail store on military bases
PZ	Pickup zone; refers to where troops are loaded on board
R&R	Rest and recuperation
RCAF	Royal Canadian Air Force

RI	Ranger instructor
ROTC	Reserve Officers Training Corps; college-level US military officer training program at state and private colleges.
RVN	Republic of Vietnam; refers to South Vietnam
SA-7	Small anti-aircraft missile; copy of US Redeye shoulder-fired missile
SAM	Surface-to-air missile
SEAL	Sea, Air, Land (SEAL) Team; US Navy special operations forces
Slick	Another term for a UH-1
Snuffy	low ranking enlisted soldiers; refers to US Army soldiers who have limited voice and authority in their positions
SPAD	A1E fighter-bomber; WWII-era rotary engine ground attack aircraft
TAC Officer	Tactical training officer; US Army training cadre
TH-55	Training helicopter model 55; primary training helicopter in the US Army
TPT	Tank projectile training; valuable aluminum training rounds
TOE	Table of organization and equipment
TOW	BMG-71 missile; excellent anti-tank missile
UCMJ	Uniform Code of Military Justice
UH-1	Utility helicopter model 1; all transport helicopters are referred to as UH
US EUCOM	US European Command; the senior US forces command in Europe

USO   United Services Organization; provides morale support to deployed troops

VFR   Visual flight rules; when weather conditions do not limit ceiling or visibility when flying

V/R   Visual reconnaissance

VNAF   Vietnam Air Forces; the Air Force of South Vietnam

WOC   Warrant officer candidate; most Army pilots are warrant officers

XO   Executive officer; deputy commander of a unit

Printed in the USA
CPSIA information can be obtained
at www.ICGtesting.com
LVHW040731300823
756538LV00006B/178